A MULTINATIONAL LOOK AT THE TRANSNATIONAL CORPORATION

An international collection of academic and corporate views
on the future of transnational enterprise

Edited by Michael T. Skully

University of New South Wales

DRYDEN PRESS AUSTRALIA

Sydney

1978

Published in Sydney by

Dryden Press Australia
Darlinghurst PO Box 46
Sydney, NSW, 2010
Australia

Australiana Publications
26 Manor Avenue
Caterham
Surrey
England

Australiana Publications
7414 Eldorado Street
Mc Lean, Virginia 22101
USA

National Library of Australia
    Cataloguing — Publication entry

A multinational look at the transnational corporation

    ISBN 0 909162 04 2

    1. Corporations, International — addresses, essays, lectures.
    2. International business enterprises — addresses, essays, lectures.
    I. Skully, Michael Thomas, 1947—, ed.

338.88

First published 1978

Preface

In recent years there has been a great expansion in the number and diversity of international business courses offered by universities in both Australia and overseas. Happily this expansion has been accompanied by an even more rapid growth in the number of international orientated textbooks potentially to support the various lecture programmes. Unfortunately these texts are for the most part published in the USA and perhaps as a result basically tend to reflect an American bias. That in itself is not necessarily a problem — especially in some of the more technical courses, but when one looks to the future of transnational companies, an American viewpoint alone is insufficient. Whereas the home country of transnational firms will remain of importance, the regulation and general attitudes of the host countries — especially the LDC's-are likely to play an increasingly important role in shaping the future. Just as the approaches of individual host countries to the TNC's are likely to differ, so will the responses by the individual companies involved. Thus to obtain some idea of what the future will hold for the transnational firm it would be desirable to examine a variety of national and corporate viewpoints. It has been for that purpose that the articles contained herein have been collected.

The majority of articles appear for the first time in print and were prepared specifically for the publication. Other articles represent papers which have been revised and expanded by contributors from previously presented material, and finally some have been obtained as reprints from existing journal articles. The articles have been organised by subject rather than the residence of the contributor so that in some cases there is a national of one country, residing in another country, and writing about conditions in yet another; perhaps that further emphasises the multinational and even the transnational concept intended by the title.

Regarding the use of the term, transnational corporation, in the title and the term, multinational corporation in all but two articles in the collection, the choice of transnational was done in line with the United Nations' recommended usage of the word. However, for many people interested in the subject, and certainly among members of the business community, the use of multinational seems the most commonplace and has been accepted as submitted.

The book will undoubtedly find its own level of usage within the academic and business community, but it has been intended to provide the reader with a diverse collection of views on the future of the transnational corporation. It should prove a valuable reference for academics preparing any general course in international business, and serve as a most useful textbook or supplementary text in advanced undergraduate or graduate seminars. For the businessman, the book should prove an interesting collection of readings, and for the transnational corporations themselves, useful background material for executive discussion groups and strategic planning seminars.

The task of constructing any such publication is enormous and could not have been accomplished without the assistant of multitude of people. The willingness of the contributors to devote so much of their valuable time in preparing their submissions, the co-operation of the publishers and authors of those previously published articles, and the assistance of the administrative personnel and my colleagues at the University of New South Wales are particularly appreciated.

Sydney, Australia   1978

TABLE OF CONTENTS

THE AMERICAS

THE FINANCIAL ROLE AND FUTURE OF MNCs IN CENTRAL AMERICA

By Vihang R. Errunza*

Introduction

Financing foreign subsidiaries of multinational corporations (MNCs) is complicated by the unique environmental factors not generally encountered in the domestic context. Most common among such factors are the differences in financial norms and practices across countries, the need to cope with the legal and institutional constraints of the host country and the problems of working with a multitude of currencies.

The pioneering work of Stobaugh[1] dealt with a cross-section of 39 U.S. controlled MNCs representing different sizes and industries. In depth interviews were used to study the influence of sizes and industries. In depth interviews were used to study the influence of size, percentage ownership and technology level on financial management strategies. Other important studies on the subject[2] provided an initial conceptual framework for financial decision making. They analyzed the influence of numerous variables on the financial planning function in U.S. based MNCs. Research on MNC subsidiaries operating in a given country/region is generally not available despite its implication for multinational management and host country guidelines on financial behavior of MNCs operating within their jurisdiction.

Hence, the purpose of this study is to analyze the financial mix of a sample of MNC subsidiaries, identify the determinants of their sourcing strategy and provide further evidence on some of the important conclusions reached by previous researchers. MNC subsidiaries operating in three of the Central American Common Market Countries (CACM), Nicaragua, Honduras and Costa Rica were chosen.[3]

Initially, the study reviews MNC activity and financial conditions in the three countries to provide necessary familiarity with the environment. Discussion of the determinants of MNC financial policy in the Central American context follows. We then outline the research methodology and present major findings on historical sources of financing used by MNCs. This is followed by the evaluation of results and comparison of major conclusions with past studies. Finally, the implications of the study for CACM and LDCs in general is examined.

Scope of MNC Activity in the CACM

Historically, external financing has been an important factor in accelerating economic development of Latin America. Given the limitations on external borrowing and access to international capital markets, countries of this region have increasingly depended on private foreign sources such as supplier's credit, private direct investment and commercial bank lending. The official bilateral and multi-lateral components have increased at a much slower pace.

In recent years, the Central American region has accounted for approximately one fifth of the total stock of direct investments in all developing areas — see Table 1. Even though a large portion of these investments has gone to Mexico, the CACM member countries have received substantially higher private overseas direct investments on a per capita basis in comparison to

*Visiting Professor at McGill University, Montreal, Canada. He wishes to acknowledge the research support of Instituto Centroamericano de Administracion de Empresas of Managua, Nicaragua, and in particular the class of MAE 8 for conducting field interviews with multinationals. He would like to thank the various multinationals and officials for their cooperation and Professor Andy Gross for his valuable comments.

similar average figures for all developing countries taken together — Table 2. When compared to declining official and private credit disbursements, the private foreign investor assumes added significance. While total loans declined during the second half of 1960's, the net foreign investment increased substantially during the same period as shown in Table 3.

Thus, the MNCs have increased their investments in CACM substantially over time. Also, the U.S. based MNCs have participated in a broad range of activities.[4]

TABLE 1

Estimated Stock of Direct DAC* Investment in Developing Regions at Year End

Region	$ Billion				Percentage of Total			
	1967	1971	1972	1973	1967	1971	1972	1973
Europe	2.0	3.1	3.5	4.3	6	6	7	7
Africa	6.6	8.4	9.4	10.2	19	18	18	18
Central America*	6.3	9.5	10.3	12.0	18	20	20	21
South America	12.1	14.4	15.5	16.9	34	31	30	29
Middle East	3.1	3.5	3.5	3.9	9	8	8	7
Asia, Oceania	5.0	8.0	8.8	10.5	14	17	17	18
TOTAL	35.1	46.9	51.6	58.2	100	100	100	100

*DAC is the abbreviation for development assistance committee members.
**Includes Mexico, Caribbean and CACM Countries.
Source: *Development Co-operation,* OECD, 1974, 1975 Annual Reviews.

TABLE 2

Private Overseas Direct Investment (PODI) In CACM

Country	Stock at the end of (million $)		PODI CAPITA ($)	
	1972	1973	1972	1973
Costa Rica	185	220	100	122
El Salvador	100	110	27	30
Guatemala	190	225	35	40
Honduras	200	215	77	80
Nicaragua	85	95	40	43
CACM Total	760	865	49	54
All LDCs	52,000	58,000	28	31

Source: *Development Co-operation,* OECD, 1974, 1975 Annual Reviews.

TABLE 3

Comparison Between Total Credit Disbursements and Direct Investment

(In Millions of $)

Country	Total Net Disbursements of Official and Private Loans		Foreign Investment Minus Depreciation	
	1965-67	1968-70	1965-67	1968-70
Costa Rica	128.5	113.7	30.4	54.7
El Salvadore	63.0	44.6	25.5	20.9
Guatemala	81.0	44.8	46.8	69.7
Honduras	38.2	80.8	23.2	31.6
Nicaragua	92.5	103.7	34.9	43.4
TOTAL	403.2	387.6	160.8	220.3

Source:– UNFCLA, *Economic Bulletin for Latin America,* Vol. 17, No. 1, 1st half of 1972, p. 106.

Business Environment

Following is a brief review of the environment within which the MNC financial planning function is undertaken in Central America.

Financial Institutions

The Central American Bank for Economic Integration (CABEI) is a major regional body which undertakes long-term financing of major projects. The stabilization fund of the five CACM central banks deals with balance of payments problems between member countries and their external settlements.

The Nicaraguan financial system is composed of the Central Bank, The National Bank of Nicaragua, the Instituto de Fomento Nacional (INFONAC — government development bank), the national savings and loan system, private financieras (finance companies), insurance companies, bonded warehouses and the National Bank for Popular Credit. The commercial banking system includes many local and foreign banks.

The Honduran institutions include the Central Bank, private (local and foreign) as well as state owned banks, private financieras, Banco Nacional de Fomento (BNF — government development institution), insurance companies and savings banks.

The Costa Rican system consists of the Central Bank, major state owned commercial banks and a few foreign banks, Corporacion Costarricense de Desarrollo (CODESA — state owned development bank), many private financieras and the state owned insurance company.

Securities Markets

In general, the stock and bond markets are in their infancy. Most of the offerings are privately placed by the development banks, financieras, commercial banks and through the connections of various business groups. The secondary markets either don't exist or lack regular trading activity.

In Nicaragua, a few studies have been conducted for the setting up of a securities market.[5] In Honduras, the Corporacion Nacional de Investimento (CONADI) is actively pursuing the formation of a stock exchange. In Costa Rica the Bolsa de Valores (stock exchange) opened in early 1976.

Financial Practices and Norms

The primary source of short-term credit are the commercial banks. Terms are generally determined by the type of business (e.g. agricultural, industrial) and some banks specialize by sectors in their lending operations. Many of the local banks are tied to the various business groups and mainly finance the groups' activities. As a result, the foreign firms rely on foreign banks which provide a full range of services. With the exception of Costa Rica, there are no restrictions on foreign subsidiaries. In Costa Rica, majority foreign-owned subsidiaries need government approval before they can obtain credit from private banks. At times, banks provide medium term financing by roll over of short-term loans.

The major sources for medium and long term funds are the development banks and financieras. With the exception of CONADI and CODESA which do not grant loans to foreign majority owned firms, there are no restrictions on tapping these sources by MNCs. As mentioned earlier, these institutions also provide assistance in raising local equity funds. They underwrite issues, make a market in selected securities and assist in placement. Mortgage banks, savings and loan associations as well as insurance companies provide some medium and long term financing. For the period of this study, there were no real restrictions on obtaining foreign equity or debt. However, some paperwork in the form of registration was necessary in most countries of CACM.

The financial integration within the common market has led to similar industry and overall financial norms (leverage) across CACM countries. On the other hand, statistically significant differences were found in the financial structure of different industries in a given CACM country.[6]

Foreign Exchange

Historically, the CACM countries have maintained stable rates vis-à-vis the U.S. dollar. With the exception of Costa Rica (periods of dual exchange rates) no changes in parities have occured in the recent past. During periods of balance of payments problems, individual countries have required authorization, approval or licensing for imports. However, no significant restrictions existed for payments of interest, dividends or capital repatriation during the period of this study.

Determinants of MNC Subsidiary Financial Policy In CACM

Even though the financial practices of subsidiaries may differ substantially within a given environment, a review of the financial and other variables which influence their decisions would be extremely valuable in understanding the past strategies of MNC subsidiaries in the CACM.

Cost of Alternative Sources

The cost calculations should go beyond a comparison of nominal rates. This is because the cost elements differ across countries and sources. Some alternatives involve risk of exchange whereas others do not. Also, certain expenses may be tax deductible in certain countries. The compensating balance requirements, commitment fees, commissions, securities flotation costs may also be significantly different across countries to make nominal interest rates meaningless.

In Central America, there are no compensating balances for prime customers, however, smaller borrowers pay higher effective interest rates through commissions, discounting etc. Also, the interest rates depend on the usage. Generally, the agricultural credits are cheaper for a given risk class. The development loans are at favourable terms and include technical assistance and other benefits which further reduce their effective costs. The equity and bond financing are more expensive than in the U.S. due to the underdeveloped nature of markets, problems of placement, lack of liquidity (low trading volumes in exchange) and higher underwriting costs.

Foreign Exchange Fluctuations

The changes in exchange rates affect profitability of the subsidiary and the parent company. As Dufey[7] points out, no two firms operating in a country whose currency has devalued will be affected in exactly the same way. Some may gain and some may be worse off as a result of the devaluation. The implications for profits received by the parent company will depend on the combined effect of the loan from currency value change and the changes in expected local currency cash flows. In addition, the devaluation may also give rise to a translation loss on a consolidated basis if the subsidiary has net exposed asset position. It can be minimized in devaluation prone countries by decreasing local currency exposed assets and increasing local currency exposed liabilities. The new exposure in different currencies can be hedged by the headquarters on a worldwide basis if the hedging costs are lower than the expected losses from currency changes. Thus, the expected changes in exchange rates are crucial for the initial investment decision, in allocating funds for further expansion, management of working capital and cash, hedging policies and above all in financing decisions which affect profitability, translation loss and cost of funds.

In Central America, the risk of exchange rate change was minimal during the period of our study. As a result, one would not expect it to play an important role in financing decisions of subsidiaries.

Taxation

Tax treatment varies across countries. In some countries, interest on foreign loans and exchange loss on such interest payments are deductible for tax purposes, whereas others allow only local borrowing costs for income tax deduction. Local taxation of dividends, retained earnings and home country treatment of foreign earnings of parent companies also differ.[8]

In CACM, MNCs are exempt from income tax for up to eight years. The dividends to the parent are taxed at 15% in Costa Rica and Honduras. Nicaragua does not impose this tax. The interest payments for foreign and local sources are treated in the same manner for tax purposes. Thus, one would not expect taxation to be a major consideration in the CACM.

Local Participation

In many less developed countries (LDCs), it is becoming increasingly difficult to operate wholly-owned subsidiaries. At times explicit legislation on maximum foreign ownership confront the MNCs or other devices are used by local governments to increase local participation. The MNC response has been either to use local capital markets or seek joint ventures. In many LDCs, capital markets are underdeveloped and local shareholders demand higher dividend payments than deemed necessary or prudent by the parent. Similarly, the joint venture partners may also demand large payouts. Thus, the local participation may increase equity cost of capital by making it necessary to raise new equity for expansion which is generally more expensive than retained earnings due to issue costs, tax differences etc.

Even then, there are advantages to raising local equity due to its contribution to the development of local markets. The development of local capital markets would boost economic development and provide many future expansion possibilities to the MNC.[9] On the other hand, use of joint ventures would reduce financial demand on the MNC and increase opportunities of local financing.

The CACM capital markets are underdeveloped and the trend towards joint venture is gaining popularity due to local pressures.

Incentives And Disincentives

In many LDCs, special financial benefits accrue to MNCs which establish operations in high development priority sectors and/or economically depressed areas. Normally, soft financing is made available for such ventures. At the same time, controls (disincentives) imposed by home country may significantly affect financial policy of the MNC. Foreign direct investment regulations of the U.S. has had major implications for financial planning.[10] In CACM, MNCs receiving fiscal incentives also qualify for loans from public development institutions.

Thus, a priori, one would except the subsidiary financial policy in CACM to be influenced primarily by:
— Corporate profit motive e.g. effective costs
— Institutional constraints and local norms e.g. credit availability
— Expectations of future changes in the overall environment e.g. currency values.

The Sample

The multinational operations in CACM are rather limited.[11] In addition no centralized data bank on their financial operations exists. Even data on such global categories as value of U.S. direct investment, asset distribution and income earned (by industry classification) are incomplete.[12]

Hence, the sample used reflects availability and willingness on the part of management to provide the necessary information under strict secrecy agreements. All firms in our sample are large and represent important industry groups in their respective countries. The quantitative information was obtained from balance sheets and income statements. Where feasible, cross-checks were made with the central bank and tax authority figures. The data inconsistencies were reconciled and qualitative aspects of financial practices were probed through personal interviews with the management. A few companies were eliminated from the initial sample due to the lack of reliable information, inconsistencies or incompleteness.

The small size and non random character of the sample is a definite limitation for generalizations based on this study. Sophisticated statistical testing across industries and sizes is also not very meaningful due to the sampling procedure which emphasized selection of the largest MNCs from different manufacturing industries. However, one could discern the general determinants of financial policy for large MNCs operating in Costa Rica, Nicaragua and Honduras. Further, the findings may lead to hypothesis which can be statistically tested by future researchers using larger samples.

Evaluation of Results

This section will discuss the findings for the three countries separately. For each country, the analysis of financial mix will be followed by the consensus view from the personal interviews.

Nicaragua

The historical sources of financing are shown in Table 4. The two wholly-owned subsidiaries in our sample were financed with parent's equity and funds from local operations. The subsidiaries' needs for additional working capital and fixed assets were generally obtained from the parent as an addition to the initial capital. Thus, the entire short term and long term financing needs were provided by the parent and its affiliates. When interviewed, the managers expressed desire to use local sources for short term needs, however, the parent has been unwilling to approve such a change because in the past they have secured better terms from external sources than those available in the local market. Since the two subsidiaries primarily act as distributors, the majority of their needs are short term. Hence, the non productive nature of business would restrict them to commercial banks and financieras whose terms would not be favorable in comparison to the external sources tapped by the parent corporation.

The joint venture (A) uses primarily local sources. The short term needs are financed through local branch of a foreign bank, suppliers credit and a development institution. Over the last five years, significant changes have taken place. The foreign investors sold their participation largely to the local investors. Also, increasing use of local sources of financing is being made. The company uses its earnings for debt repayment and expansion. The expensive commercial bank debt is being slowly replaced by larger use of suppliers credits denominated in U.S. $.

The joint venture (B) is mainly financed by parents' equity. It manufactures for the North American export market. The commercial banks have provided long term financing of fixed assets with mortgage and guarantee. The parent provides working capital and all external funds.

TABLE 4

Historical Financial Sources for the Nicaraguan Sample

Average for 1970-1975 in %

Company	A	B	C	D	E
Short Term Sources					
Suppliers	58	–	–	–	–
Commercial Banks	9	–	–	–	100
Other Financial Institutions	33	–	–	–	–
Parent and Affiliates	–	100	100	100	–
TOTAL	100	100	100	100	100
Long Term Sources					
Commercial Banks	7	50	–	–	100
Other Financial Institutions	6	–	–	–	–
Parent and Affiliates	–	50	100	100	–
Other[a]	87	–	–	–	–
TOTAL	100	100	100	100	100
Internal ST[c]	b	–	–	–	100
External ST	b	100	100	100	–
TOTAL		100	100	100	100
Internal LT[d]	b	13	–	–	100
External LT	b	87	100	100	–
TOTAL		100	100	100	100

[a]Local shareholders equity. [b]Internal sources contribute 80% and external 20%. [c]ST means short term. [d]LT means long term.

Note: – Companies A, B and E are joint ventures companies C and D are subsidiaries

8

The joint venture (E) has an explicit policy of using internal sources even-though the external credits are cheaper. The management identifies the needs and sources of funds and obtains approval of board of directors. During interviews, the managers expressed desire to use external credit, however, were constrained by the parents' guidelines.

Thus, in contrast to the wholly-owned subsidiaries, two out of three joint ventures extensively utilize local sources of financing. For our small sample, the parent issues detailed guidelines which the local management uses in preparing financial plans. However, unlike the sample of large firms in the Stobaugh study,[13] the parent approves all plans and makes final decisions. Also, it seems that the special characteristics of the firms in our sample have contributed to their financing decisions. The main criterion for firms A, C and D seems to be cost minimization — firms C and D use exclusively external sources whereas firm A is increasingly moving toward suppliers' credits in U.S.$. On the other hand, parent of firm E appears to be unwilling to use cheaper external credits due to the fear of devaluation.

Honduras

All the firms in our sample are majority-owned by either the parent corporation or foreign nationals. The historical financial sources are shown in Table 5. The major short term sources have been the commercial and development banks. Financieras and the parent have provided between 15-20% of the total short term needs. The major long term source has been the parent and affiliates contribution, with the balance divided among commercial and development banks as well as other institutions. Also, a major part of both short term and long term sources are from the local market.

A large part of the total debt is obtained from local sources. However, on an average, their importance has declined over time — from 89% in 1973 to 61% in 1975. Also, local short term debt is being slowly replaced by long term financing, in particular, the external component. Based on interviews and examination of environment data, this shift can be attributed to tightening of

TABLE 5A

Historical Financial Sources for the Honduran Sample

Average for Eight MNCs in %

Short Term Sources	1973	1974	1975
Commercial Banks	54	67	69
Other Financial Institutions	37	20	31
Parent and Affiliates[a]	9	13	–
TOTAL	100	100	100
Long Term Sources			
Commercial Banks	29	13	19
Other Financial Institutions	21	33	29
Parent and Affiliates	50	54	52
TOTAL	100	100	100

[a]Includes suppliers credits.

Historical Financial Sources for the Honduran Sample

Average for 1973-1975 in %

Company	A	B	C	D	E	F	G	H
Internal ST	59	59	0	86	100	100	76	100
External ST	41	41	0	14	–	–	24	–
TOTAL	100	100		100	100	100	100	100
Internal LT	100	0	100	73	56	73	100	90
External LT	–	0	–	27	44	27	–	10
TOTAL	100		100	100	100	100	100	100

domestic credit, lower external interest rates and reduced uncertainty about the value of local currency.

The sample companies have encountered no major problems in tapping local equity or debt sources, yet MNCs in Honduras have never issued bonds and their stocks are not actively traded due to the less developed nature of the domestic capital market. This is unlike the large firm sample of Stobaugh study which found that 83% of the companies had at least one subsidiary which had issued bonds in the local capital market.[14]

Rapid changes in the debt structure of subsidiaries were observed. Interviews failed to explain these changes. One plausible explanation could be the lack of firm policy at the local level. As regards to the overall decision criteria, interviews with top executives revealed the following process: the sources were chosen on the basis of parent company guidelines, expectations of the economy, cost and other terms of different sources and financial structure considerations.

Costa Rica

Table 6 provides a detailed breakdown for eight large MNCs representing important economic sectors of Costa Rica.

A large part of both short term and long term financing is obtained from external sources. Since the central bank establishes quantitative limits for commercial bank credits, most of the loans are granted by finance companies owned by the commercial banks at 14%-16%. These finance companies do not come under the 9%-12% interest ceilings applicable to banks. Hence, a significant number of loans are obtained from foreign banks (denominated in U.S. $) at the risk of foreign exchange loss. Thus, MNCs have resorted to foreign credits to overcome domestic monetary constraints. This observation was confirmed by interviews.

As in the case of other Central American countries, bonds are not generally issued by private companies due to the intense competition from government bonds which are guaranteed by the state and carry repurchase agreement providing liquidity. The total corporate issues between 1967 and 1974 amounted to $12.5 million whereas the government bonds totaled $39 million during 1972 and 1973. The stock issue market is also very small and underdeveloped with sale or exchange among only certain groups of investors. In some cases, employees and executives have participated as minority holders.

As in the case of Nicaragua, major decisions are made by the headquarters or the regional head office. The local manager generally determines the subsidiary's financial need and potential

TABLE 6

Historical Financial Sources for the Costa Rican Sample

Average for 1969-1974 in %

Company	A	B	C	D	E	F	G	H
Short Term Sources								
Suppliers	13	30	49	56	61	42	56	57
Commercial Banks	87	59	27	44	37	48	9	35
Other Financial Institutions	–	41	–	–	2	10	8	–
Parent and Affiliates	–	–	24	–	–	–	27	8
TOTAL	100	100	100	100	100	100	100	100
Long Term Sources								
Commercial Banks	19	42	–	29	19	37	8	16
Parent and Affiliates	81	53	100	65[a]	81	67	84	57
Other[b]	–	15	–	6	–	–	8	27
TOTAL	100	100	100	100	100	100	100	100
Internal LT	56	61	11	26	16	–	53	27
External LT	44	39	89	74	84	100	47	73
TOTAL	100	100	100	100	100	100	100	100

[a]Includes 45% for preferred stock.   [b]Includes other financial institutions.

Note:– The short term sources could not be divided into internal and external due to unavailability of such a division for commercial bank credits.

sources and reports it to the parent for further action.

Major Implications And Conclusion

To summarize, the major determinants of financing alternatives used by MNC subsidiaries in Central America were the nature of operations, credit terms and exchange risk in Nicaragua; credit terms, financial structure considerations and economic environment including exchange risk in Honduras; and domestic credit constraints (stringent credit terms) in Costa Rica.

The main feature of the decision process are the detailed policy independence from the parent corporation. In Honduras, subsidiaries seem to have independence on implementation within the guidelines. On the other hand, in Nicaragua and Costa Rica, the local management determines the needs and potential sources but parent approval is required before plans can be put into effect.

Also, the MNCs have not contributed to the development of local capital (stock and debt) markets. Being large and most credit worthy, the MNCs along with local government are in the best position to help develop local securities markets by issuing gilt edged securities and restoring confidence of local investors in this form of direct finance.[15] On the other hand, they have had considerable impact on the development of financial institutions, in particular the Honduran commercial banking system. Also, the competition from government bonds and restrictions on issuing bearer stock in Costa Rica have been major obstacles to the development of local market through private initiative.

In addition, MNCs have preferred the use of wholly-owned subsidiaries and branch offices over joint ventures in above countries. They have used cheap long term funds available from development banks by virtue of their activity in the productive sectors. Not much use is made of local suppliers credits which indicates either supply sourcing from abroad or little use of such credits. If further research indicates widespread use of foreign suppliers, then MNCs are not contributing one of the most important development inputs associated with their activity, namely, the training and development of local suppliers.

Transfer of financial resources is generally considered to be one of the important contributions of MNCs towards economic development of LDCs. The evidence based on our study raises some doubts regarding its validity.[16] MNC use of local financing may have pre-empted investments by local entrepreneurs. The question of benefit involves a comparison of investments made by MNCs versus those displaced. If further in-depth research confirms our worst suspicions, then it could have far reaching implications on financial policies of host countries as well as on the future role of MNCs in the developing countries.

To conclude, the understanding of financial policies of MNCs operating in Central America under virtually no official controls, could be valuable not only for determining their activity in CACM but also for future comparison with their financial strategies in other LDCs imposing various restrictions. The insights on MNC behavioral patterns gained from such comparisons would be extremely useful in the formulation of a financial code of conduct.

Future of MNC in Central America

The creation of the CACM enormously increased foreign direct private investments in this rather small region. The broadening of the market, minimal controls on repatriation and high external tariffs attracted foreign investors. Institutionally, the area was more successful in securing international support for its development.[17]

However, in the initial treaty, the foreign investment laws were not harmonized leading to competitive foreign investment incentive schemes by the member countries. Foreign investors favored El Salvador and Guatemala due to better incentives, more attractive home markets, more developed infrastructure, larger pools of skilled labor and economic/political stability.

The new treaty, which is in the advanced stage, proposes common treatment of foreign investment and technology. It encourages standards for registration and approval of foreign investment and technology; common rules for repatriation and acquisition of domestic firms by foreigners; as well as greater domestic control over foreign investments. On the financial front, the treaty calls for monetary co-operation and monetary union of CACM countries. It recommends common monetary policies, joint maintenance of international reserves and setting up of a regional stock exchange. It further calls for promotion and protection of local production and provides for preferential treatment to locally produced goods in official purchasing. The treaty suggests rationalization in formulation and application of fiscal incentives that would benefit industrialization efforts and take advantage of backward and forward linkages to increase local production. The treaty recommends that common minimum wages for the entire region be established along with co-ordination of the social security system. Countries under balance of payments pressure would be allowed to impose capital and import controls which were illegal under the old treaty.[18]

Thus, the new treaty would substantially affect the MNC operations and may in some cases alter their profitability through the closing of certain sectors and capital controls. Nevertheless, this region is expected to continue to welcome new foreign investments warmly, particularly those producing high local content products. The recent energy crisis and inflation have adversely affected CACM. However, generally higher commodity prices and boyant local economies (in comparison to the rest of the world) have largely offset the international factors.

The U.S. Department of Commerce survey of private investment abroad shows that during 1974, U.S. affiliates had higher rate of return in Latin America than in developed countries. Also, the figures are more favorable to Latin America when only manufacturing sector is analysed. With CACM, the book value of all investment increased by 18%, while in manufacturing the increase was 27% and rate of return was 11-12%. Thus, CACM within the Latin American context has been an important region for U.S. MNCs and can be expected to remain so in the foreseeable future.[19]

The biggest influence on future MNC activity in the CACM would undoubtedly come from government actions and the political environment. The intergovernment manoeuvring would decide whether the new treaty will soon be adopted and if so, its final form. At the individual country level, one can expect increased government intervention in the private sector and in particular, the MNC operations.

In Guatemala, the Congress has three new bills that would regulate international firm's activity in oil exploration, banana plantations and banking sector. It provides for added government control in all the above areas and increases the government take from oil and banana operations.

The bribery scandal in Honduras ($1.26 million payment by United Brands which forced the ousting of President Arellano in 1975) will have important repercussions in the relationship between not only the banana industry but the multinational activity as a whole and the new Honduran government.

Historically, Nicaragua has offered the most generous treatment to foreign investments including freedom of exchange and remittances. Up until the present time, MNCs have not been under nationalistic pressures such as those in the neighbouring countries. However, continued political uncertainties resulting from confrontations with the leftists might force some adjustment in the government policy toward foreign investors.

In Costa Rica, the financial problems (budget, balance of payments etc.) forced increased government intervention in capital and foreign exchange markets in 1974-1975 which caused increased friction between the government and private (local and foreign) sector. Thus, the ability of the new government to cope with the economic problems will largely determine the future relationship between the MNCs and Costa Rica.

No major changes in Salvadorean governments attitude towards MNC are forecast. The new CACM treaty and the relationship with Honduras will be important for MNC activity.

The often mentioned expansion of the community to include Panama and/or Caribbean Countries would be of prime importance and benefit to the foreign investor, but such is not expected to happen for some time.

Footnotes

1. Stobaugh, R., "Financing Foreign Subsidiaries of U.S.-Controlled Multinational Enterprises," *Journal of International Business Studies,* Summer 1970, pp. 43-64.
2. Robock, S., "Overseas Financing for U.S. International Business," *Journal of Finance,* XXI, May 1966, 297-307; and Smith, D., "Financial Variables in International Business," *Harvard Business Review,* XLIV, January-February 1966, pp. 93-104.
3. The Common Market was founded in 1960. The member countries are, Costa Rica, El Salvador, Guatemala, Honduras and Nicaragua. The study was limited to three countries due to resource constraint.
4. For further details, see, U.S. Department of Commerce, *U.S. Direct Investment Abroad, 1966,* A Supplement to the Survey of current business, Bureau of Economic Analysis, Washington D.C., 1975.

5. Most important is, Stracham, H., "Caso Projecto Bolsin de Nicaragua (A) and (B)," INCAE, Managua, Nicaragua, 1974.

6. Errunza, V., "Determinants of Financial Structure in Central American Common Market," Working Paper, McGill University, 1976.

7. Dufey, G., "Corporate Finance and Exchange Rate Variations," *Financial Management,* Summer 1972, pp. 51-57.

8. Smith, D., "Financial Variables in International Business."

9. Errunza, V., "Capital Markets in Economic Development," Unpublished Manuscript, McGill University, 1976.

10. Singer, S., "Financial Planning Within the Foreign Direct Investment Regulations," *Financial Executive,* June 1970, pp. 62-68.

11. Following number of (reporting) (U.S. multinationals were active in the manufacturing sectors of: Costa Rica – 36, Honduras – 11, Nicaragua – 22 (Table P-2, *U.S. Direct Investment Abroad, 1966*).

12. See Tables A-3, I-3, and J-3 of *U.S. Direct Investment Abroad, 1966.*

13. Stobaugh, R., "Financing Foreign Subsidiaries of U.S.-Controlled Multinational Enterprises," p. 53.

14. *Ibid*., p. 56.

15. Errunza, V., "Capital Markets in Economic Development." *op. cit.*

16. Similar doubts were raised by the U.S. Senate, Committee on Finance, Investigation No. 332-69, February 1973.

17. R. Hansen, "Times of Trial for the Other Common Market," *Columbia Journal of World Business,* Sept-Oct 1967, p. 97,

18. *Business Latin America*, April 23, 1975, pp. 129-130.

19. *Business Latin America,* Jan, 1976, pp. 30–31.

THE AMERICAN MULTINATIONAL AND ITS FUTURE:

FROM A CORPORATE VIEWPOINT.

By. P. Holmes à Court*

Preface

Perhaps no modern business phenomenon has received so much attention as the multinational corporation. It has been investigated, scrutinized and studied by the press, the academic community, the union movement, governments and a wide variety of supranational agencies. Their goal: to discover what the multinational corporation is, how it works, its benefits and drawbacks.

The study of multinationals is a substantial academic growth business . . . it takes no less than a 70 page pamphlet to list the current research work going on in North America and Europe alone.

During the 60's sales of leading multinationals trebled and capital was expanded 2-1/3 fold. Despite an occasional expropriation by a new nation state, future success seemed inevitable. Academics were forecasting that within this century 300-400 giant corporations would dominate three quarters of the free world's industrial output.

In recent years, the heroes have become villains. It's fashionable to denigrate, criticise and attack them with an emotional intensity which puts the multinational in a no win position. If they keep quiet, they are hiding the facts; when they explain they are said to be over reacting, and so it goes on. Yet no one seriously questions their contribution to world development.

As one United Nations report says "The basic facts still need to be disentangled from the mass of opinion and ideology".

More and more reports are made on the multinationals role in the economy and suggestions made as to how to bring about a better and more balanced relationship between them and governments.

In these reports — including that prepared by the United Nations' Group of Eminent Persons — there is often a tendency to exaggerate the ability of the multinational company to escape national jurisdiction and control.

The practice of comparing gross revenue of a multinational with the gross national product of a country is common, but runs the risk of becoming an overutilized device. Such comparisons can be dramatic but amounts of money cannot automatically be equated with forces of influence.

Economic power is not of the same quality or kind as political power. The smallest nation state has absolute, unquestioned authority over the largest corporation. Ultimately a company has but one real power — to get out. It is hardly surprising that the record shows this is rarely exercised.

The stress on the misdemeanours of multinationals is popular comment and in the literature not adequately balanced by examples of irresponsible behaviour of some nation states. Unilever between 1945 and 1973 had 17 companies taken over or nationalized in 17 countries. It wrote off 140 million dollars investment in developing nations because of government action. Who has the real power!

Multinationals are not only controlled in their host countries but also in their home countries where controls over capital export and rules about taxation of foreign income can be

*Director — IBM Australia, Sydney, Australia

15

major business constraints.

Above all the reports on multinationals tend to take insufficient notice of the wide spectrum of multinational companies. No two industries require the same resources, income and technical capabilities. Their remarkable and significant dissimilarities are usually not pursued.

It would be a serious mistake to ignore the diversity of multinational businesses, their individual characteristics and requirements, the differences in their short-range and longer range contribution to economic development. Rules of conduct formulated with only some types of multinational enterprises in mind, for example, could turn out meaningless or even damaging to other companies with different roles in the fabric of national economics.

IBM: A Multinational

In the belief that a closer understanding of a single multinational corporation would be more advantageous than further deliberation on generalities, I turn now to International Business Machines Corporation, the Australian subsidiary of which I represent.

Known worldwide as IBM, it is ranked about seventh in Fortune magazine's list of the top 500 US industrials with a revenue of around 13 billion US dollars. The revenue earned in the United States approximates that of its subsidiaries in 126 other countries.

IBM's growth, for which it has been noted, has been achieved through expansion of its markets rather than through acquisition. Apart from Science Research Associates, an educational publisher acquired in the 50's, the only other acquisition is that of 1/3 share in a US satellite communications consortium negotiated recently.

IBM has been seeking new markets since its earliest days. Our operations in Germany date back to 1910, France to 1914, Canada and Brazil 1917 and in Japan 1925. In Australia whilst founded in the thirties, the data processing side of our business was not established until the early fifties.

With total employment of over a quarter of a million; a corporate practice of no retrenchment has been maintained for over half a century despite the dramatic impact of new technologies. This proud record along with the acceptance of "respect for the individual" as a basic tenant of the business, accounts for great employee loyalty.

The Computer Industry

The computer industry is situated at the high end of the technology spectrum with special characteristics and requirements of its own. As it happens almost every major computer manufacturer in the world is a multinational.

From a laboratory first during World War II the computer industry has grown into what has been accurately described as a vast knowledge industry. Today in excess of 250,000 computers are installed. As the cost per 100,000 computations has dropped from $1.26 in 1952 to one cent today, the use of computers has expanded dramatically. Currently at least 1,000 firms either produce computers, computer programs or computer parts or are engaged in computer training.

The demand for computer capability is increasing in most nations. What matters is the ability to use computers not simply the ability to manufacture them. The computer can provide developmental leverage for government, science and industry alike. To put it another way: data processing like hydro electric power, transportation and communications, makes other types of advance possible.

The great capital intensiveness of the computer industry imposes three requirements on the way IBM operates. They are —
1.	A worldwide product development effort,
2.	A worldwide product line, and
3.	Decentralised decision making.

Each deserves some explanation.

Worldwide Product Development

IBM has 31 research and development laboratories in 10 countries. Overall there are some 30,000 engineers, scientists and administrators in these laboratories. Each laboratory has a defined set of missions and each is tied in with the other through a computer based communications system.

The laboratories are the pride of our company, and we have special requirements for the location of each.

Our first requirement is an advanced industrial environment, for we need a critical mass of scientific and highly skilled manpower. Second, we must necessarily locate our facilities in areas where there is a market for our products and where we can tap the best talent available — near universities and thriving scientific communities. Finally, our laboratories must be near our manufacturing plants.

There is an historical process involved. More than 50 years ago IBM started in France and Germany with a sales and service operation which marketed, installed and maintained our equipment. The next step was to assemble machines in Europe often from parts purchased locally. As these plants became more sophisticated, engineers were hired and in time development laboratories were established. Today our European laboratories are integrated into the company's worldwide development effort.

What started out as a one-way flow of technology is now decidedly a two-way flow. The United States has no monopoly on high technology today. Much of the development work on IBM's large System/370 Model 158 computer, for example, was done in Europe whilst the Model 125 computer is a product of our German laboratory.

The same process is being repeated today in Mexico and Brazil. In Australia we have purchased land at Wangaratta and are about to launch an assembly operation.

IBM spends around seven hundred million dollars per annum or the equivalent of half the entire corporation's net earnings, on research and development. In addition unusually high education, re-education, training and re-training outlays are required in our rapidly changing high technology industry.

Worldwide Product Line

IBM manufactures the same product for worldwide use. These products must be flexible enough to accommodate national requirements without basic change in design. There are two reasons for this policy.
1.	We find that the problems our products are designed to solve and the solutions themselves are not unique; in some ways, they are universal.
2.	Efficiencies of manufacturing the same product line worldwide are essential to keeping computer costs at reasonable levels.

In addition, manufacturing our products in our largest markets is virtually the only way for IBM to respond to the needs of those markets. About 90% of what we sell in Europe, for example, is produced in our European plants. If major countries had to import all IBM products now sold there, the drain on their payments balances would, in most instances, be burdensome.

IBM is frequently asked, "Why not have more plants in more countries?" The answer is simple. We just can't afford it, and furthermore, technological evolution is permitting existing plants to largely cater for the expanding needs.

On the other hand, hourly labour costs on the production line have less and less to do with our ability to operate in a competitive environment. With progress in technology, labour costs have declined sharply as a percentage of our total costs. In fact, less than one in four IBM employees are employed in manufacturing.

Our plants specialise in producing specific products and parts. An IBM customer in Australia for example, may receive a computer system made up of products produced in half a dozen countries. To make this system work equitably for all IBM subsidiaries, our transfer pricing is uniform. We use a simple cost plus method, that is actual manufacturing cost plus a fixed mark up. This mark up is selected with view to distributing profits in accordance with where the work is performed. The manufacturing of IBM products extends beyond the walls of our own plants. Outside the United States, IBM companies work with in excess of 40,000 vendors; around half of which are in Germany, France and United Kingdom. The value of these purchases is of the order of six hundred million dollars per annum.

By and large each product is manufactured in three locations, with one in each of the United States and Europe. Supplies for Australia are drawn mainly from Japan and Europe. It is a largely unknown fact that a US built IBM product is a rarity in Australia.

The transfer price as well as the selling price in the country of manufacture is declared for each item imported. In IBM's case the Australian Customs Department has access to the records of the exporting company and periodically exercises this right. The existence of such a system in Australia makes one question the sweeping accusation so often made, that multinationals use transfer pricing to unfairly move profits to low tax countries.

With adherence to strict settlement times the exposure to the accusation that one is taking advantage of currency variations is significantly reduced.

Decentralised Decision Making

A common criticism levelled against multinationals is that decisions concerning local operations are often made in a home office thousands of miles away. This is a gross simplification of the complex decision making process, which needs to be better understood.

IBM works hard to make decision making as decentralised as possible. Virtually all IBM employees are nationals of the countries in which they work. In evidence to the Group of Eminent Persons appointed by the United Nations to enquire into multinationals it was pointed out that all US personnel working for IBM abroad could be returned in a single aeroplane. It was conceded that it would have to be a 747.

The appointment of nationals is part of a conscious effort on the part of the corporation to be better attuned to local conditions and aspirations and to have national views genuinely represented in its decision making process.

In Australia all the executives are nationals and there is but one American assignee amongst the 260 managers within IBM Australia.

As a business, IBM is dedicated to planning, with the process starting at the grass roots level. Annually each subsidiary prepares an Operating Plan outlining objectives, anticipated expenses and programs to reach those objectives. This annual planning process serves as a mechanicism for reconciling the interests of each national affiliate with the interests of the entire corporation. In the course of co-ordinating company plans, there is a great deal of give and take and negotiation in which the head of an affiliate is expected to — and does — represent the interests of his country as best he can.

Included amongst the many decisions taken by national management at the country level are such substantive matters as profits and sales. At higher levels decision making mainly consists of reviewing the decisions reached by national managements.

Ownership

The problem of co-ordination is a major reason for IBM's policy of maintaining 100% ownership of its subsidiaries.

For many industries manufacturing is relatively simple but in IBM's case it is a different matter. The key problem here is that IBM is in three different but deeply interrelated businesses within the computer industry. We produce hardware, software and we provide services. These activities require the allocation of our resources on a worldwide basis. We believe that to be the best way to serve both IBM and its customers everywhere.

Various forms of joint ownership have been examined. In fact in the early 1950s IBM UK sold 40,000 shares of its stock. Ultimately, the local company and its shareholders decided that it was not in the best interests of either and in 1959 IBM UK re-purchased the outstanding shares.

The demand for local participation in ownership can often be translated into a demand that a company put the interests of a subsidiary above that of the entire company.

In IBM's opinion, investors should share in the entire worldwide company — not merely in one national subsidiary. Consequently we actively encourage the listing of IBM stock on as many exchanges as possible. Today IBM is listed on more than a dozen major exchanges outside the United States. Tens of thousands of non-US nationals including some 40,000 of our own employees own IBM stock.

In Australia (over the last five years) we have sought permission to list IBM stock on several occasions, however, exchange control regulations do not permit such listing.

Government Relations

A major subject of investigations is the day-to-day relationship of multinationals and the governments which host them.

There are two facets to this relationship for IBM.

The first is that of host and guest. We draw the line at any political activism. But short of that, there is much that multinational companies can do.

In Australia the selection of the site for our plant was influenced by the Australian Government's desire to locate industry inland rather than close to an existing capital city.

We have a senior manager full time investigating ways and means whereby we can assist society in this country. Projects are undertaken ranging from assistance to scholars to study overseas, through scholarships to Papua New Guineas, to special training in management for the leaders of the aboriginal community on Bathurst Island.

IBM encourages its employees to pursue the support of the political party of their choice and grants leave of absence to permit employees to become involved. In support of the belief that the corporation should not be involved in politics there is a worldwide policy prohibiting company donations to political parties. Adherence to this policy is subject to searching international audit.

During the 1969-72 period advances in manufacturing techniques eliminated a substantial number of jobs in our US Plants. To maintain IBM's full employment practice, more than 12,000 people were shifted into new jobs at considerable expense. More than 5,000 of these received major retraining to permit their transfer.

The second aspect of IBM's association with governments is the vendor-customer relationship. We have broad rules of conduct for our day-to-day business that apply to our relations with the outside world. They are set forth in an 80 page booklet entitled "Business Conduct Guidelines" that each person of responsibility in the company is required to read annually, and live up to.

Governments themselves are major IBM customers. Industry statistics indicate government installations amount to 9% of total sales. In many developing countries this figure may reach 90 or even 100%.

Industrial Relations

National labour legislation and prevailing customs and practices determine IBM's industrial relations in each individual country. Hence, they vary a great deal — from no union representation at all in the U.S. for example, to one-third employee representation on the board of IBM Germany.

Within national constraints, the same personnel policies apply to all IBM employees throughout the world, including merit pay, job evaluation and counselling.

Although IBM pays slightly in excess of prevalent local wage levels, this has in no case tended to disrupt national industrial wage structures.

International Controls

There has been growing speculation over the feasibility of establishing international controls over the multinational company. The United Nations, for one, is facing up to this question, as stated in the staff report to the Group of Eminent Persons investigating the role of multinational companies:

"Whether a set of institutions and devices can be worked out which will guide the multinational corporations' exercise of power and introduce some form of accountability to the international community into their activities."

Perhaps such institutions and devices can be created. But it is essential that they be realistic enough and flexible enough to cover the various kinds of multinational companies that exist.

Specifically, IBM's concern is that such "institutions and devices" might encourage guidelines which, while designed to curb or correct what are viewed as excesses, might actually upset the special conditions an industry like data processing needs if it is to continue to play its key role in development.

They might, for example, lead to reduced remittances, requirements for the dispersal of manufacturing and research and development capability, and the demand for divided ownership or local control.

Moves such as these would cripple the effectiveness of many high technology companies, most certainly including IBM. Ultimately, they would seriously limit the contributions multinational companies can make to development.

The U.N. Report states that, as far as multinational companies are concerned, there already is a great deal of information-gathering going on but that there are serious gaps. Many of these could be ascribed to the reluctance of multinational companies to disclose certain types of data.

Some companies may be excessively secretive with data, but there are long-established principles concerning proprietary information in a free-market economy. Competitive considerations alone, for example, may require that a company not release information.

But if a reasonable amount of information can be gathered, as well as model contracts, laws, agreements, tax structures, and so forth, the idea of giving technical help to nations through an international organization is a very positive one. When officials of a lesser developed country negotiate with a multinational company or with a larger country, they often work from different bases of information. Technical co-operation can help equalize those bases.

Next, there is a group of proposals in the U.N. Report which would establish a code of conduct or at least a multinational company register. The report wisely suggests that drafting a code acceptable to all would be extremely difficult and that a rather general and unenforceable document would almost certainly result. Nevertheless, the proposal should be pursued.

There are five points IBM would like to see in any such code, including the U.N.'s:

1. The employment of nationals, totally or predominantly, in affiliates should be strongly encouraged;
2. Similarly, there should be multinational representation in headquarters and on boards of directors;
3. Stock ownership should be on a multinational basis;

4. There should be adequate guidelines on transfer pricing;

5. The performance of a company, particularly in a developing country, should be judged to a degree on its performance in the area of social responsibility.

While IBM recognizes the difficulties involved, it also believes that tax harmonization is a truly worthwhile goal. From a company's viewpoint, such harmonization offers the great advantage of protecting its investment from the inequities of double taxation.

There is much at stake. As a high technology company, one that necessarily invests heavily in people, research and facilities, IBM is very aware of its responsibilities — to its employees, to its customers, to its host governments and to its stockholders. Thus, many of IBM's concerns are unique. In particular, we hope that the special situations that exist in our industry — and others — will be taken into consideration in the establishment of any guidelines.

There is a school of thought that sees the multinational company and the nation state on a collision course. We do not believe that this is so. The two, in our judgment, will work out the differences between them, travel parallel courses and — in the end — complement and enrich each other.

THE MULTINATIONAL CORPORATION AND ITS FUTURE:

FROM THE AMERICAN VIEWPOINT

By Professor Warren J. Keegan *

For the past two decades, manufacturing enterprises in the western market economies have been steadily expanding their global reach. This expression has included the traditional exporting and importing of goods and services, but increasingly it has been based upon investments in marketing, manufacturing, research and development, and engineering which are linked together in the framework of a global strategic plan. By 1971, the estimated production from foreign controlled manufacturing investments in market economies was of 106% of exports of these countries. For mature international investor countries such as the U.S. and Switzerland, foreign production as a percent of exports was 396% and 236% respectively.[1] Since World War II world exports have been growing slightly faster than the gross world product, and international production has been growing faster than world exports.

In 1958, gross world product was $884 billion, world exports were $105 billion and international production was roughly $90 billion. Total international business sales volume, the sum of world exports and international production was $195 billion or 22 percent of gross world product.

In 1973, gross world product was $4,400 billion, world exports were $550 billion, and international production (production controlled by foreign based enterprise) was an estimated $550 billion. In 1973 total international business sales volume was $1,100 billion or 25 percent of that years gross world product (See Table 1)[2]. During the past fifteen years, there has been a slight increase in the export intensity of the world economy, and a 20 percent increase in the intensity of international production. Since large fast growing corporations account for most international production the extrapolation of this international production growth trend has led to forecasts that before the end of this century, world business will be dominated by say 300 supergiant multinational corporations.

Supporting this conclusion are those prophets who feel that emerging technologies have

TABLE 1

International Business As A Percent of Gross World Product

		Billions of U.S. Dollars			
		1958		1973	
			%		%
(1)	Gross World Product	$884		$4,400	
(2)	World Exports	105	11.8	550	12.5
(3)	Estimated International Production	90	10.2	550	12.5
(4)	Total International Business Sales Volume (Col 2 + Col 3)	$195		$1,100	
	International Business as a percent of Gross World Product (Col 4 ÷ Col 1)		22%		25%

Table prepared by author.
Data Sources: GATT, Trade Network Table and United Nations,
Statistical Yearbook, various issues.

*George Washington University, Washington, D.C., U.S.A. The article is a revision of a paper first presented at the Academy of International Business's 1975 Annual meeting.

rendered the nation state obsolete and that the multinational corporation is "a modern concept designed to meet the requirements of a modern age: the nation state is a very old fashioned idea and badly adapted to serve the needs of our present complex world."[3] Sidney Rolfe has expressed the view that the phenomenal progress in communications and transportation technologies has created an interdependence of human activity that has rendered national boundaries obsolete. In his worlds, there[4]

> "is increasing recognition that the nationstate is not the optimum political organization for the international productive scheme and the international company. On the contrary, there is increasing evidence that the conflict of our era is between ethnocentric nationalism and geocentric technology, between the cost of national pride and the benefit of organizing resources optimally in a spatially-expanded purview of the area within which resources can be organized. In the age of jets and telecommunications every fact of the concept of the planet has shrunk; it is, in hindsight, quite natural that economic organization would also thrust into markets and regions, without reference to old national borders. If du Pont can organize its productive facilities, its money flows, its marketing, its managing elite 3,000 miles west of Delaware, why not 3,000 miles east? There is, in fact, no reason. And if du Pont can do it, why not Farbenfabriken Bayer, ICI, or Rhone Poulenc?"

Arnold Toynbee, in similar perspective, sees the multinational corporation as an institution that fills a vacuum in an increasingly interdependent world economy.[5]

> "There is an increasing misfit between the facts of global economic life and the political organization of the world, in say 140 local, so-called sovereign states. They aren't really sovereign because they are dependent upon the rest of the world for raw materials, and sometimes for food itself, in order to live. But they are as sovereign as they can contrive to be. Most of the economic troubles of the world are due to this misfit between the antiquated political setup of local states and the real, global economic setup.

> Multinational corporations precisely bridge this gap. Some of the people say they take unduly big profits for the service they render, but the service has to be done. . . . ."

These prophets who see an expanding future for the MNCs are basing their forecast upon assumed continuation of the technological, social, and political shrinkage of the globe which has been underway for centuries and which has accelerated dramatically during the past three decades. This shrinkage is creating a world of vertical business systems dominated by a handful of giant worldwide companies which find it increasingly easy to manage activities in every corner of the globe. Just as the emerging national oligopolies displaced hundreds of local or regional companies in the U. S. between 1850 and 1950, the emerging international oligopolies are displacing national companies today. For example, in early 1974 Matsushita acquired the color television division of Motorola and was followed a few months later by Philips of the Netherlands which tendered for the shares of Magnavox. This expansion and entry into the U. S. color TV market is threatening even to the largest U. S. color producers, Zenith and RCA whose position is limited to the U. S. market. The continuation of this trend will eventually result in a handful of companies (including Matsushita and Phillips but perhaps not Zenith) operating worldwide instead of a much larger number of companies operating within national boundaries. The same pattern can be observed in dozens of other industries such as automobiles, electrical equipment, optical equipment, computers, drugs, chemicals, and packaged foods.

The MNC expanding future hypothesis is based (1) on the assumption that this vertical system of global oligopolists is more effective than horizontal systems where each country is a framework for small national companies which conduct all business activities, and (2) on the further critical assumption that the technical superiority of the vertical strategy will be recognized and accepted by the nation states of the world.

In the less developed countries, classical trade theory has been viewed as a colonialist plot to extract unfair gains and advantage from poor countries. In a similar vein, MNCs are seen in many less developed countries (LDCs) today as a neo-colonialist replacement for the discredited classical trade doctrine. It is ironic, as this is written that the terms of trade have shifted dramatically against the industrial countries and in favor of the producing countries. Crude oil, for example, has increased from 4 percent of the value of total world exports in 1971 to over 20 percent in 1974. These shifting trade terms will undoubtably affect the view-point of the producing countries who already look to MNCs as possible instruments for converting their vast new wealth into ongoing national productive capabilities. The old concerns about MNC domination and control of host country environments have been overturned by today's concern in MNC home countries about takeovers of MNCs by newly rich producing country interests.

The vertical advantage hypothesis has been challenged on its own terms. The late Stephen Hymer and Robert Rowthorn argue that technology, particularly communications technology, will enable countries to pursue "horizontal" economic strategies.

> "Although it is quite true that modern technology makes it possible to coordinate production and marketing on a global basis, it is also true that modern communications make centralized planning with one country possible. Moreover, high productivity of the new technology allows countries greater scope for national independence, since it becomes far less urgent to concentrate on economizing scarce resources. Most important, improved communications make it easier for small regions and units to obtain the most advanced knowledge quickly and cheaply without formal institutional lines of communication. This provides increased scope for independence and reinforces polycentralism rather than centralism. It is not at all clear that hierarchical authoritarian corporate structures are well suited to this environment."[6]

The Growth Of Multinational Enterprise — Underlying Factors.

The rapid growth of multinational enterprise is undisputed. The costs and benefits of this growth to home and host country are the subject of intense debate, as are the basic underlying advantages and disadvantages of large world scale enterprise as compared to smaller national scale enterprise. To forecast the future of the institution, we must identify the underlying factors which have been responsible for the phenominal growth of multinational enterprise over the past three decades. These factors or forces have been either enabling conditions, that is, environmental circumstances which make it *possible* to successfully establish and manage a worldwide enterprise or they have been driving forces, that is, factors which have pushed and rewarded enterprises for extending their operations geographically. The future prospects of multinational corporations will depend on the development of these underlying factors. Are we approaching a watershed point which will mark the end of an era of multinational development or are we simply at some midpoint in an evolutionary process in the development of this worldwide institution? The answer lies in an examination of the underlying factors.

Worldwide Economic Growth

Since 1945, the world has been in the process of one of the most spectacular periods of economic growth in its history. This sustained worldwide economic growth has created an enabling competitive environment in the various nation states which has allowed foreign companies to enter and expand within the national economic framework without displacing local enterprise. Economic growth has created a non zero sums game environment which has enabled both domestic and international companies to grow and prosper simultaneously. In the absence of this growth, the entry of foreign based companies would frequently have been at the expense of market share and position of local enterprise. If foreign companies had tried to enter markets on this basis, they would have been more frequently challenged and possibly rebuffed by defensive politically enfranchised local interests.

The future of the world economy is cloudy and uncertain at the moment. While it is beyond the scope of this paper to assess the prospects for a revival of worldwide economic growth in the market economies, the absence of growth has removed one of the factors which has facilitated the entry and expansion for multinational corporations.

The Growth Ethic

Another important contributing factor to the emergence of multinational enterprises has been the increasingly wide spread commitment of enterprise all over the world to growth. This commitment has been one of the driving forces that has created national economic growth around the world. Within the enterprise, a growth commitment can be expressed in two broad alternative directions. One is to grow by diversification into new products and technologies. The alternative is to grow by diversification into new markets. This latter diversification can take the form of new customer markets within existing geographical markets or it may take the form of seeking the same customer category within new regions and country markets. A commitment to growth has led most large enterprises to seek diversification on both the horizontal and vertical directions of this matrix.

Strategy And Structure

The strategic commitment of enterprise to growth via geographic diversification has led to evolving structural forms which enable enterprises to achieve their growth objectives. One of the reasons that American companies have been so importantly represented among the sample of large enterprises operating on a global scale has been their willingness to adopt a divisional structure. With a divisional structure, organizational sub-units (divisions) are delegated responsibility for profit and loss within a defined product-market scope of operations. This structure, which is based on the assumption that responsibility can be delegated and that divisional activities can be managed within the framework of planning and control systems, enabled U. S. companies to diversify into new products and technologies and was well suited to facilitate the diversification into new country markets. Today, large European enterprise is imitating this structural approach.[7]

The International Financial Framework

The collapse in 1971 of the Breton Woods agreement should not cloud the fact that this arrangement, created in 1944, was a major factor in enabling companies and individuals to trade and invest on a global scale. Under the Breton Woods system, which restored fixed exchange rates and currency convertibility, businessmen became increasingly comfortable with the risks and complexities of doing business in different currencies. Indeed, mature multinational corporations regard their global investments as a diversified portfolio which reduces risk in the same way that a portfolio manager reduces risk by adding to his portfolio holdings.[8] Convertibility and fixed exchange rates were associated with the emergence of this view.

Since the 1971-72 collapse of the Breton Woods system, only convertibility remains. Today, the value of currencies fluctuates according to market forces and the world financial system is a managed "dirty" floating exchange rate system. (The "dirty" float refers to the fact that governments continue to intervene in exchange markets, but without a commitment to a fixed or pegged rate.) The present system while presenting greater day to day uncertainty, is enormously more sensitive than the old system to market pressures and forces. Indeed, it can be argued that there is less uncertainty today about medium and long term exchange rates than there was under the old fixed rate system. Under the old system, when disequilibrium developed, government control and intervention could distort market forces for years. With floating rates, disequilibrium results in rate adjustments which are small and gradual and which persist until equilibrium is restored.

Apparently, fixed or pegged exchange rates were not a critically important feature of the old system. Today, world trade and investment continue to expand with floating exchange rates. Indeed, it is the view of many, businessmen and bankers that the floating system is better than the fixed system because its sensitivity to currency values insures that adjustment is continuous and therefore precludes the need to interfere with trade and investment to maintain artificially pegged rates.

Communications And Transportation Technology

The modern corporation requires two vital types of information; strategic and operating. Strategic information is needed to make the crucial decisions about resource allocation and corporate direction. Should we invest in product X or Y? Should we expand in France or in Japan? Should we focus upon market segment 1 or segment 100? Operating information is needed to implement operating plans which express overall strategic design. For example, what is current performance against budget in each profit center for the most recent operating period? What is the inventory requirement in location 58 given our policy of order fulfillment within 10 days of order receipt and when must replacement orders be placed to maintain our minimum inventory requirement?

Studies of scanning or information acquisition in large organizations have demonstrated the crucial importance of human or personal sources of strategic information. An extraordinarily high percentage of the important information which guides strategic resource allocation decisions in large corporations is acquired in face to face contact with people in and outside the organization.[9] Operating information, on the other hand, is generated largely within the organization. The management of operations of a large enterprise requires the transmission of vast quantities of data.

The explosion of transportation and telcommunications technologies since 1945 has enormously facilitated both of these crucial forms of communication on a world scale in the modern enterprise. The jet aircraft has literally shrunk the size of the globe. Each company has its own style and system, but all multinationals are held together with the glue of frequent direct face-to-face contact of key executives. ITT's monthly planning and budget review meetings in Brussels which assemble key corporate executives including the Chairman and President and key operating executives from European headquarters and divisional units would be literally impossible without the jet aircraft. The confidence that it takes to make resource allocation decisions for an operating area would simply not exist if it were not possible for key executives to observe directly from time to time the actual physical setting of the operations and to meet directly with the key people responsible for these operations. An executive once expressed this point to me in the following terms.

"If you really want to find out about an area, you must see people personally. There is no comparison between written reports, and actually sitting down with a man and talking. A personal meeting is worth 4,000 written reports."

The availability of telephone and telecommunications services has backed up this pattern of face-to-face contact by allowing instantaneous communication of data by voice, the printed word, or computer data in the world. Satellite and undersea cable communication links have reduced the cost of long distance data communication dramatically.

Even ten years ago, a distance of three or four thousand miles across the ocean was a barrier to communication. Today, particularly in large multinational companies with their own internal communication systems, telephone and teletype contact across oceans is obtained with the same facility as contact with someone in another office in the same building. Indeed, in the emerging global industrial system, a fully developed communications system is an essential element of the infrastructure of any headquarters location. One of the reasons the United States exists as a headquarters location for world business systems is its superb communications system. Not every industrial country in the world can offer comparable communications capabilities. Countries which do not achieve a minimum standard in their telecommunications systems jeopardize their status as a headquarters center for the management of global business. Britain, long a major world center, is today in danger of losing that status for a number of reasons, not the least of which is the country's inadequate telecommunications system:

"Along with all their other troubles, Englishmen are finding it hard to get calls through to Teheran, which is vexing because London is a banking center and Teheran is a good place to find money these days.

Sometimes it takes a day or two to get through. At the Teheran end according to The Financial Times, some 200 to 300 calls have to be cancelled daily for want of an open line.

The Iranians, however, say it isn't their fault. Their phone hook-up with New York works fine. The problem, they claim lies with England's General Post Office, which so they say, doesn't adequately staff its international switchboard and maintain enough trunk channels."[10]

Nationalism

The rise of nationalism today, after 25 years of growing worldwide interdependence, is perhaps an inevitable reaction of broad social forces. Societies move from restriction to freedom and back again as they search for, but never find, the ideal. In the first half of this century, nationalism inflicted upon the world unparalled destruction and misery.

Following World War II, a reaction to the nationalistic horrors of the previous three decades produced three decades of extraordinary international cooperation and increasing economic interdependence. The General Agreement on Tariffs and Trade (GATT) provided a framework for tariff reduction to an average rate on manufactured goods for industrial countries of about 10%, or hardly more than the New York City sales tax. Direct investment by companies and the emergence of the multinational corporation developed at an unprecedented rate. The increasing economic interdependence was questioned, challenged, and even contested, but it was accepted in the essentially liberal post World War II world of 1945—1970.

Today, memories of the 1915—1945 period are dim and the world is more conscious of what is perceived to be exploitation by foreign control. There is a growing feeling in many countries:

"creating a mood in which men prefer to be ordered about, even if this entails ill-treatment, by members of their own faith or nation or class to tutelage, however benevolent, on the part of ultimately patronizing superiors from a foreign land or alien class or milieu."[11]

Developing countries as a group have for many years voiced strong concerns about multinational corporations. Most recently, nationalism appears to be a rising force in the industrialized countries.

Even Canada, historically one of the most open investment environments in the world, has become somewhat hostile toward foreign investment, challenging many traditional practices and raising serious questions about the future of even established foreign owned enterprises.

An important area of national concern about multinationals is where they choose to locate what has been termed "noble" work. To date, most multinational corporation research and development is carried out in the home country. This has led to the complaint that multinational corporation overseas operations are branch plants, not a vital part of the total enterprise, offering little or no opportunity for participation in research and development, advanced engineering, and strategic planning, thus contributing little, if anything, toward the development of national capabilities in these "noble" areas. Moreover, since country operations are merely branch plants, whenever legitimate national or local issues are pressed, the company can ignore these legitimate pressures by closing down the branch plant and substituting production from another identical branch plant somewhere else in the system.

Again, the response of multinational corporations to this area of concern is of critical importance to the future of the institution. If they are prepared to disperse their "noble" work and create worldwide, if not universal opportunities, they can expect a broader base of support. If they refrain from abandoning country operations in disputes, their commitment will be tangibly expressed.

Another area of concern has been the extent to which multinational corporations employ host country nationals in management positions. To the extent that multinational corporations become "equal opportunity" employers on a world scale, they defuse resentment toward foreign control and direction by incorporating nationals into a global decision system. Human resource management is one of the most crucial of all multinational corporation corporate policy decisions because of its impact on the political acceptability of multinational corporations.

An important model is the geocentric company which ignores nationality in human resource management, and picks the best person for the job, regardless of nationality (and race, sex, age, and so on). This is a model. Geocentric purity in human resources management has not yet emerged, yet already leading experts on multinational human resource management are urging companies to take concrete steps in this direction.[12]

The latest source of sustained attack on multinationals has come from their home countries where the concern is predictibly enough not about management's nationality, but about the location of their manufacturing activity, or, if you will, the location of the non-noble work in their global system. In the United States, organized labor argues that multinationals have exported jobs by investing overseas. These objections have been amplified in a growing radical critique of multinational company activity which suggests that multinationals have ended the long term tendency for incomes in the United States to become more evenly distributed and that they are responsible for the apparent slow but persistent trend toward greater income inequality in the United States since 1958. There is no conclusive evidence linking income trends and foreign investment, but the association is suggestive and has led to the hypothesis that the multinationals in building up their overseas empires have neglected the domestic economy which failed to receive the traditional injection of investment and innovation required for productivity gains and rising real income for workers. The only change in the U.S. operations of these companies has been in the kind of jobs they have created on "Park Avenue" in their world headquarters. In pursuing their own goal of profit maximization, it is argued that the companies have shortchanged interests of American workers.[13] This objection, like the objection in the host countries, must be met. If multinationals are to be permitted to create jobs and improve productivity and wages overseas, they must demonstrate that they can maintain employment and improve productivity and wages at home.

Size And Effectiveness

A fundamental factor affecting the future of multinational corporations is the relationship between size or scale and effectiveness. If integrated world scale global business systems are more effective than autonomous national scale systems, then well managed MNCs have an inherent advantage via a vis their local competitors. If vertical systems are at an inherent disadvantage, they will sink under their own weight. One fact if clear: any sample of companies with extensive involvement in world marketing and manufacturing is a list of relatively large companies. In 1967, 80% of the 2,500 foreign manufacturing subsidiaries of the Fortune group of 500 industrials were controlled by 180 enterprises.[14] In 1971, there were 211 manufacturing companies in the market economies of the world with sales of more than one billion dollars.[15] 95% of these companies are significantly involved in international operations. Clearly, there is an overwhelming association between company size and international involvement.

One reason for this association can be traced to the alternatives open to a national company seeking growth. Such a company must choose, as we have demonstrated, between diversification into new product/technology/customer markets at home, or alternatively existing product/technology/customer markets in new national or country markets. Most large national companies either decide that geographic diversification is an opportunity they can effectively pursue, or they conclude that is a path they must pursue to keep up with competitor growth. There is, as we have pointed out, an analogy between the emergence of MNCs and the emergence of the national corporation in the U. S. in the early part of this century. But the association between size and geographic spread still leaves the question of the relationship between size and effectiveness unanswered. Large companies create headquarters organizations and characteristically operate in a management intensive "expensive" mode. There are inherent potential advantages to bigness which I call leverage, which offset these costs.

Leverage

While growth opportunity is clearly a motive for company expansion beyond the home country's boundaries, why have so many companies been able to successfully expand internationally? Obviously, there are and have been many obstacles or restraining forces to this expansion: nationalism; time, distance, and language as communication barriers; ignorance of conditions outside the home market and so on. Offsetting these restraining forces have been major driving forces that have enabled companies to profitably operate on a world scale. I call these driving forces leverage, or the combination of forces that give an effectively managed large firm advantages over smaller competitors.

The traditional micro-economics text assumes that costs of the firm decline with scale and then at some limit of efficient size, rise again. This relationship is shown in Figure I. This average cost curve of the firm from micro-economics is a hypothesis, not a fact.

The evidence, from hundreds of empirical studies suggests that total costs of manufacturing and marketing a product decline at a constant percentage rate, typically 20 to 30 percent, with each doubling of accumulated volume.[16] This empirical relationship of cost and volume which has been called the experience effect, can be represented as a curve on a linear scale or as a straight line on a double logarithmic scale as shown in Figure II. The significant difference between the experience effect and micro-economic theory is the basis for much of the disagreement about the future of the multinational enterprise. Economists such as Hymer, who forsee the corporations demise, point to hierarchical authoritarian structures of large corporations and imply that they will sink under their own weight in competition with smaller, flexible local enterprises. This is a verbal model of the micro-economics cost curve. Those who envisage an unlimited future for MNCs see ever increasing advantages associated with global scale. This is, in effect, a loose verbal model of the experience curve.

There appear to be three sources of the experience effect: learning, specialization, and scale. As experience (volume) grows, given good management and energetic efforts, organizations learn how to "work smarter". Even in industries such as chemicals where there are limits to optimum plant size, when capacity is added it almost always incorporates design improvements that reduce unit costs in constant dollars. Other examples of learning are in program management. In marketing, for example, if markets are at different stages of development a MNC can transfer its marketing experience with products across national boundaries. If done effectively, this gives the MNC an advantage over local companies who face "unique" problems and must generate unique solutions. For the well managed MNC each national market is part of a general world market and represents only an adaptation of the general solution. In each of the key marketing decision areas, for example, product positioning in the market (user targets, etc.), prices, advertising and promotion budgets and appeals, and distribution channels a multinational can transfer experience and thereby raise marketing effectiveness and lower marketing costs.

Specialization and scale are important sources of the experience effect. As enterprises reach market share limits in their home markets, if they wish to continue to grow vertically they must expand internationally to obtain additional gains from vertical specialization and scale. These gains are generated not only in manufacturing, but also and very importantly in areas such as R & D. Today it takes enormous resources to develop new technolgoies — smaller companies, no matter how distinguished, often cannot cope as was recently illustrated in the Rolls Royce effort to develop the RB211 jet engine which led to the company's bankruptcy.

The time lag between investment and payoff in new technologies is growing. It has been estimated that General Electric waited twenty years to achieve a cumulative cash flow break-even position in its Gas Turbine business, which today is a major profit generator for G. E. and an important new source of power for a wide series of applications ranging from off peak electrical power generation to oil and gas pumping. G.E.'s gas turbine business today is fast approaching 60 percent foreign, 40 percent U. S. sales. The foreign sales will contribute enormously to the profitability of this business, and certainly become an important basis for the willingness of companies like G. E. to invest in the development of other new products and technologies.

Specialization and scale advantages can also be developed horizontally at the corporate staff level[17] in strategic planning, forecasting, marketing research, law, human resource management, finance, engineering, manufacturing and marketing. A large, multinational company can, for example, create a corporate strategic planning staff group that upgrades the quality of strategic planning throughout the enterprise. The corporate staff can concentrate on the development and application of strategic planning concepts, tools, and methods and insure that advances in the state of the art, both internally and externally generated, are quickly applied throughout the enterprise.

Conclusion

A review of the underlying factors contributing to MNC growth over the past two and a half decades suggests that leverage will continue to exert a strong driving pressure on MNC expansion. Transportation and communications technology will no doubt continue to improve shrinking even further the size of the globe. The financial framework appears to be responding in an evolutionary way to pressures requiring change and on balance it seems likely that it will continue to facilitate expansion of trade and investment. Companies are becoming increasingly adept at preparing global strategies and at adopting structures which fit their strategies. Two broad areas of question remain: worldwide economic growth and nationalism. Not surprisingly, these two areas, both important to the future of MNCs, are interrelated and are themselves at least partially determined by MNC behavior. MNCs can continue to contribute to world development but today, more than ever, they must respond to legitimate national concerns. The challenge to MNCs will be to respond to these concerns without destroying the leverage they have managed to create as they have developed their global strategy. Nationalism is a rising force in the world today, and it appears to be fundamentally opposed to vertical business systems. However, when countries successfully develop their own vertical business systems or multinational corporations, they develop a greater tolerance for "foreign" MNC activity within their own boundaries. Sweden is an excellent example. It is difficult for Swedes to attack MNCs in their midst, because their own MNCs span the globe. They are an active participating unit in the global industrial system. In general, there is such a degree of cross investment, licensing and exchange between industrial countries today that in the industrial world increasingly each country is a hostage to its own foreign investment and sales. No country with its own assets and market position abroad wants to take action at home which might provoke an attack on its own foreign position. Thus one way to defuse attacks on "foreign" MNCs is to establish home country MNCs and vice versa.

The world faces a choice — a nationalism with economic autarchy or interdependence with global industrial systems. The global industrial system with MNC sub-systems is a world which can share the gains of what I call leverage. It is vital to the continued growth of MNCs that the gains from their leverage be shared equitably, and perhaps even more important that these gains be explained and articulated. Nation States can legislate and regulate the distribution of gains (principally via tax administration, but also in such areas as human resource policy) but MNCs themselves are a major influence on the sharing of gains as they allocate resources and adapt their strategies. Today, as never before, they must broadly define their own corporate interests to include current aspirations of both home and host governments and societies. If they do this, analysis of underlying factors and advantages suggests that further expansion of this important world institution can be expected.

Footnotes

1. United Nations, *Multinational Corporations in World Development* ST/ECA/190, Table 19, p. 159.
2. Data Sources: United Nations *Statistical Yearbook, International Monetary Fund, International Financial Statistics,* GATT, Network of Total International Trade Table, various issues. United Nations, *Multinational Corporations in World Development,* op. cit.
3. G. W. Ball, "The Promise of the Multinational Corporation," *Fortune,* June 1967, p. 80.
4. Sidney Rolf, "Updating Adam Smith", *Interplay,* November 1968, p. 15.
5. Arnold Toynbee, "Are Businessmen Creating Pax Romana?", *Forbes,* April 15, 1974, p. 68.
6. Hymer Stephen and Robert Rowthorn, "Multinational Corporations and International Oligopoly: The Non-American Challenge", Chapter 3 in Kindleberger, Charles P., ed., *The International Corporation: A Synposium,* Cambridge, Mass., The M.I.T. Press, 1970, pp. 87-88.
7. See Franko, Lawrence G., "The Move Toward a Multidivisional Structure in European Organizations", *Administrative Science Quarterly,* December, 1974.
8. It can be demonstrated that international diversification of stock portfolio investment holdings reduces risk. See, for example, Bruno H. Solnik, "Why Not Diversify Internationally Rather Than Domestically?", *Financial Analysts Journal,* July-Aug., 1974, pp. 48-54.
9. See Keegan, Warren J., "Multinational Scanning: A study of the information Sources utilized by Headquarters Executives of Multinational Companies", *Administrative Science Quarterly,* September, 1974.
10. *Wall Street Jornal,* "Alone on the Telephone", November 14, 1974, p. 18.
11. Isaiah Berlin, "The Bent Twig", *Foreign Affairs,* October, 1972, p. 22.
12. Howard V. Perlmutter and David A. Heenan, "How Multinational Should Your Top Managers Be?", *Harvard Business Review,* November — December, 1974.

13   See, for example, Richard J. Barnet and Ronald E. Müller, *Global Reach,* New York, Simon and Schuster, 1975.

14.   Raymond Vernon, *Sovereignty at Bay,* New York, Basic Books 1971, p. 11.

15.   United Nations, *op. cit.,* Table 3, pp. 130-137.

16.   For the major work on this point, see The Boston Consulting Group, Inc. *Perspectives on Experience,* 1972.

17   Corporate staff may be located in an area of regional headquarters as well as at a world headquarters.

Figure I

Traditional micro-economics cost assumption for the firm

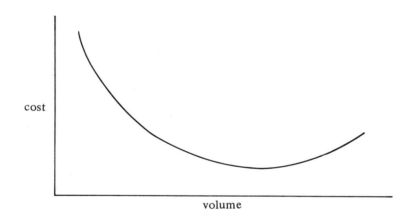

Figure II

Experience Effect — Based on Empirical Observation

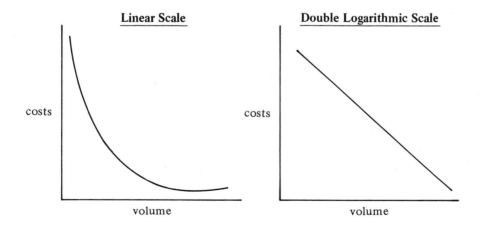

THE MULTINATIONAL RESOURCE COMPANY AND

GOVERNMENT BUSINESS ARRANGEMENTS.

By: Isaiah A. Litvak and Christopher J. Maule*

In the 1960s, the multinational enterprise (MNE) was viewed as a threat to the nation state. Its powers appeared to transcend those of the nation state, because of its ability to exploit the resources of individual nations within its global corporate network, wherein it could play-off the strengths and weaknesses of one state against another. From a corporate decision-making standpoint, the nation state was viewed by some as a sub-system of the MNE, and thus was perceived as a constituent of the corporate system. This perception, however, appears to have changed dramatically in the 1970s as evidenced by the following remarks made by Senator Church to the Senate Foreign Relations Subcommittee on Multinational Corporations::

"It is possible that murder (of multinational enterprises) could occur. . . .For despite their enormous growth and wealth, it is still an unequal contest. Armies march for national governments, whether large or small, and each of these governments possesses, in its sovereign right, the power to tax, to restrict, to discriminate against, or to nationalize foreign-owned businesses, or indeed, to confiscate their properties."[1]

This statement is no exaggeration, for the assault by national governments upon the corporate might wielded by international business is well underway worldwide. Many of its more extreme manifestations emanate from government actions in less developed countries (LDCs), where, in the wake of political independence, many new states sense the persistence of a form of "neo-colonialism" asserted in the guise of foreign direct investment. MNEs have been the principal instruments by which the resources of the LDCs, particularly those in the extractive industries, have been developed. The range of benefits accompanying this capital inflow has been widely extolled, and is desperately needed by most LDCs. Foreign investment, however, has become a mixed blessing, for its effects sometimes thwart an economy's potential or undermine a government's industrial strategy. The last decade witnessed a rash of government interventions into the operations of MNEs, whose adaptabilities are being severely tested as states grope for a more evenly balanced relationship with them.

Government intervention in the operations of MNEs, however, is no longer unique to LDCs. The intervention by the governments of developed countries was precipitated in large measure by the energy crisis of 1973, not only with respect to energy issues, but also over non-fuel minerals.[2] One major manifestation of this intervention is government involvement in the operations of MNEs in mineral exploration and development. This paper explores some of the economic and political implications of the actions taken by the governments of developed and developing countries towards MNEs in mineral resource development.

Reasons for Government Intervention

Many of the mineral producing countries are LDCs which contend that they have been exploited in a process which has controlled the development of their raw materials. In most cases

*Professor and Reader in Economics, Carleton University, Ottawa, Canada
This article is an expanded paper of an earlier article which appeared in *Freedom and Change,* Essays in Honour of Lester B. Pearson (Toronto, McClelland and Stewart Ltd., 1975), pp. 204-216. The authors wish to thank Prof. M. Fry, editor, and the School of International Affairs, Carleton University, for permission to reprint their essay. The authors would also like to acknowledge the financial support provided by the McLean Foundation and Carleton University's Norman Paterson Centre for International Affairs.

their minerals have been developed by foreign investors, and the impact has affected both the economic and political development of their country. A history of colonialism is often involved. The present circumstances are thus entwined with the developing countries' antipathy towards MNEs and colonial linkages.[3]

In the economic sphere, the following arguments are usually put forward by LDCs for government participation: that economic development of the country has been undermined by the failure of foreign companies to expand mineral production, or to generate backward and forward linkages with the rest of the economy; that the minerals are exported to the capital exporting country in a relatively unprocessed state; that there is an under-utilization of local personnel in senior management positions; and that an insufficient share of the rent from mineral development is collected by the developing country. Underlying these complaints are two important concerns: first that the economy of the country is tremendously dependent on one industry, for example, Zambia and Zaire on copper, and Guyana and Jamaica on bauxite; and second, that the type of jobs available to the local work force, because of the stage of mineral production undertaken in the developing country, means that the country is condemned to specialize in unskilled labour tasks which hinder future development.[4]

Politically, the governments of the LDCs view their increasing participation in mineral development as an act of decolonization. Although, in most instances, formal political independence has already been achieved, the presence of foreign investors in mining is viewed as economic colonialism, which has to be modified or terminated if the nation is to enjoy real political independence. The metropole-hinterland analogy is seen to apply to this situation, whereby the large resource companies have their parents located in one country, usually a developed country, and their vertically integrated mining subsidiaries located in developing countries.[5] Government participation is seen as a way of severing this dependency creating linkage.

The view that the actions of governments are illegal or contrary to existing agreements, often made many years earlier, has little force in the developing country, because it is argued that original concession agreements were made in the pre-independence period by individuals who did not represent the country, perhaps under duress, and when the economic significance of the concessions was not known.[6] This point of view is reflected in the UN statement on "Permanent Sovereignty over Natural Resources" to be enjoyed by all countries.[7] Moreover, developing countries are unwilling to submit their investment disputes to international arbitration, on the grounds that it is insulting to infer that their own courts would not handle a dispute objectively, and because it is felt that such action, as proposed by the Centre for the Settlement of Investment Disputes, would detract from the sovereignty which they should exercise over their natural resources.[8]

Recent government actions taken by the developed countries (DACs), which are major mineral consuming nations, have been largely in response to the actions taken by the governments of the LDCs. The sensitivity of governments of DACs to factors affecting the supply of minerals varies by country. In terms of absolute supply, Japan is enormously dependent on a whole range of imported minerals as well as energy; Western Europe imports 90 per cent of its copper, 50 per cent of its bauxite, and 40 per cent of its iron ore; the U.S. imports over 80 per cent of its bauxite/alumina; and Canada imports 100 per cent of its bauxite/alumina.[9] Major areas of industrial development and employment in different countries are thus dependent on imported raw materials. A second area of concern is reflected in the fact that certain materials are considered as strategic materials, for which the government will keep stockpiles, as in the case of aluminum in the United States and in a number of countries in Western Europe.[10]

In the last two years government concern has also arisen because of the inflationary impact of the higher price of energy and raw materials, a situation which poses a threat to the political stability and economic functioning of the developed countries. When faced with these circumstances, governments are forced to react, both to control the activities of MNEs and to respond to the actions of mineral producing countries.

In sum, the counter-strategy of the mineral consuming (developed) countries is part of a sequence of events which can be described approximately as follows. Colonialism and foreign investment in developing countries have evolved to a stage of political independence but continuing economic dependence. In an attempt to eliminate the position of economic dependence, the governments of developing countries have decided, amongst other things, to participate more directly in mineral resource development. This, in turn, has had an impact on mineral consuming countries, causing their governments to reassess their policies and to react accordingly.

Government-MNE Interface: International Implications

In order to increase the benefits flowing to their countries, the governments of mineral producing countries are increasingly altering their contractual relationships with MNEs. From the point of view of the MNEs and the mineral consuming countries, these activities are seen as forms of economic nationalism and wealth deprivation. The forms of government participation include the formation of producer-country cartels, government ownership of companies (either through the creation of companies and marketing boards or the nationalization-expropriation of existing companies), increased taxation and royalty payments, the requirements of local sourcing of inputs (human and non-human), the expansion of export activity, obtaining loans from international organizations for the funding of resource development, and the lobbying of the United Nations and its agencies for assistance in its actions.

While the Organization of Petroleum Exporting Countries (OPEC) is the best known and most successful producer cartel to date, a number of cartels do exist for non-fuel minerals; namely the Inter-governmental Council of Copper Exporting Countries (CIPEC) and the International Bauxite Association (IBA).[11] In addition, inter-governmental consultations have been held by some iron ore developing-exporting countries.[12] The International Tin Council (ITC) is somewhat different, in that both tin-exporting and tin-importing countries are represented on the Council.[13]

Nationalization-expropriation of foreign companies is one of the more explosive acts of developing countries, although the form it takes and the amount of compensation settled on and actually received can defuse the issue to some extent. Partial ownership of foreign firms, say 51 per cent equity participation, is a step towards nationalization and is usually achieved with less disruptive effects, although the experience created by participation tends to lead to later nationalization, as has occurred with the copper industry in Zambia and Chile.

The alteration of concession or other contractual agreements in order to increase tax, or other payments to the host country is a frequently used technique and is well illustrated by the current negotiations between the Jamaican government and the North American aluminium companies.[14] Kaiser Aluminum and Chemical Corporation (U.S.) was the first of the major producers to capitulate to the Jamaican government's demands for equity participation in (and to accepting a substantial increase in tax and other payments connected with) its operations in Jamaica. The new business arrangement is worth noting.

The Jamaican Government – Kaiser Bauxite Joint Venture

Kaiser Bauxite Company in Jamaica is the company's oldest and largest source of bauxite. In 1947 Permanente Metals Corp. (forerunner of Kaiser) began exploring for bauxite in Jamaica and during the same year purchased large tracts of land. In 1950 the Kaiser Bauxite Company was formed and construction of mining facilities began the following year. Shipment of bauxite began in 1952, reached one million tons per year in 1955, two million tons per year in 1957, and four million tons per year in 1962. Kaiser Bauxite's original bauxite mining site was at Port Kaiser on the South Coast of Jamaica. Ore from this deposit was mined, dried and shipped from 1953 until 1967 when operations were transferred to the North Coast. The facilities at Port Kaiser now form part of the bauxite-alumina complex operated by Alumina Partners of Jamaica (Alpart), owned by a consortium comprising Kaiser, Reynolds, and Anaconda. In 1963 Kaiser announced plans to establish bauxite mining, drying and shipping facilities in the Ste. Ann/Trelawny area of the North Coast, and a deep water port was constructed at Port Rhoades on Discovery Bay. The first shipment of bauxite occurred in January 1967. Currently the capacity of the Port Rhoades complex is 4.5 million tons of bauxite per year,[15] with all of the bauxite shipped to Kaiser's U.S. alumina plants at Baton Rouge and Gramercy, Louisiana.

Kaiser Bauxite Company owns the land on which its bauxite reserves are located, but under Jamaican law the bauxite is owned by the government and cannot be mined except under government lease. In 1974, Kaiser's lease still had 25 years to run. In June 1974, the Jamaican government imposed a production levy on bauxite mined in the country equal to 7.5 per cent of the realized price of primary aluminum. The levy was retroactive to January 1, 1974 and was to rise to 8.0 per cent and then to 8.5 per cent of the price of primary aluminum on April 1, 1975 and April 1, 1976 respectively.[16] As a result of the production levy, the tax rose from a level of about $2.50 per long ton to more than $11 per long ton. Kaiser paid a total levy of $54 million for 1974 which included Kaiser Bauxite Company's payment (approximately $43 million) and Kaiser's share of Alpart's payment (approximately $11 million).

In the fall of 1974, preliminary agreement was negotiated by Kaiser Bauxite with the government of Jamaica containing the following points.[17]

(1) Kaiser Bauxite will receive rights to a 40-year supply of bauxite sufficient for the Corporation's Gramercy and Baton Rough facilities' operations at their present production rates. In return for these rights, Kaiser Bauxite will annually pay seven per cent of the government's purchase price for the land under the mining lease.

(2) Kaiser Bauxite will sell to the Government for book value (approximately $12,000,000) all of its bauxite lands, resettlement lands, and other property not required for plant operations. Payment will be received over a 10-year period with a seven per cent annual interest rate.

(3) Kaiser Bauxite will sell 51 per cent of its mining assets to the Government of Jamaica for book value (approximately $16,000,000). This amount would also be paid to Kaiser Bauxite over a 10-year period at 8.5 per cent interest. It was agreed that both Kaiser Bauxite and the Government will form a new partnership, in order to carry out mining activities. The new partnership will have an executive committee with equal voting rights for Kaiser Bauxite and the Government. Kaiser Bauxite will manage the operation under a management agreement which will last for seven years. Kaiser Bauxite will receive bauxite from the partnership at cost including depreciation and will pay the Jamaican Government a return of 12 per cent on its investment. Kaiser Bauxite will continue to sell bauxite to Kaiser Aluminum.

(4) The production levy will remain at 7.5 per cent of the realized price for primary aluminum for 1975, 1976 and 1977. For 1978 and 1979, the production levy will be one per cent less than the percentage provided under Jamaican law at the time.

In one sense, the action is similar to that of expropriation since it involves the issue of "wealth deprivation" of the foreign investor, but in the case of increased taxes, the incidence may fall on the mineral-consumer if the companies can pass on the increased taxes in the form of increased prices, as appears to have been the case with the international oil companies.[18]

Counter-Strategies

The governments of mineral consuming countries have a number of policy approaches in response to the actions of producing countries. The alternatives include the promotion of supply self-sufficiency for the resource, as is the United States objective in terms of energy sources; the promotion of alternative sources of supply in more politically stable areas or in terms of other commodities; the provision of investment insurance for foreign companies; the use of diplomacy including foreign aid and trade levers, and negotiations on behalf of companies, either directly or through international organizations, especially financial institutions; the establishment and use of stockpiles of raw materials for economic as well as strategic reasons; direct ownership of mineral using companies and the promotion of international consortia of companies and governments; and cooperative action with other mineral-consuming countries, i.e., a consuming-country cartel, in order to counter the producer cartels.

Some of these measures are much more effective than others and some are more effective in the long run than the short run. Perhaps the strongest card which the consuming governments have is the substitutability which materials have for each other. This can be promoted by government support for research and development. Incentives can also be given for the discovery of new deposits of raw materials. However, neither action can be implemented at short notice. An important alternative is, therefore, to establish stockpiles of raw materials and to cooperate with other countries that may be able to provide short-term relief from supply shortages.

What are the major international implications of government participation both for the present and the future? The impact of producer cartels has received increasing attention as a result of OPEC's activities. OPEC produced a significant shock to the international economic system and to those countries highly dependent on imported oil. The shock is two-fold: first, the diminished supply, higher price and balance of payments implications for consuming countries; and second, the impact on the international monetary system of the enormous foreign exchange surpluses earned by producing countries. In order to counter these destabilizing forces, the consuming countries are heeding the warning that they should not rely on relatively few sources of oil and of other important minerals. Thus, while the producing countries argue that economic development requires diversification away from single industry economies, the consuming countries argue for diversification of sources of mineral supply in order to reduce dependency on a few countries.

The evasive action by the governments of consuming countries, loosely called government participation in mineral development, can already be seen. For example, the United States Bureau of Mines is financing research into the extraction of aluminum from domestic aluminum bearing clays;[19] support is being given to research undertaken on methods of recycling metals such as copper and aluminum and on developing substitute materials; and exploration is being promoted in less politically risky areas. In the field of energy, the United States has announced its intention of being self-sufficient by 1980. Its ability to achieve self-sufficiency in other minerals is probably much greater because, unlike oil, these minerals tend to be recoverable as scrap. The supply of secondary copper already represents a substantial contribution to total supply, and the price elasticity of supply is sufficiently large to expect increased recovery rates as the price of copper increases.[20]

The evasive action described above may not be as easy to implement for Japan and the countries of Western Europe as it is for the United States, because of the latter's relative self-sufficiency in many minerals. While Japan and Western Europe will move in the same direction as the United States, they may also attempt to negotiate special arrangements with individual mineral supplying countries. Forerunners of this were the deals made by individual countries during the "oil crisis" of 1973. In a sense, this strengthens the possibility for producer cartels and weakens the chances for the formation of consumer cartels. However, once negotiated, such agreements will at the same time tend to drive both the consuming countries from each other and the producing countries from each other. The result could be a form of economic warfare as individual countries attempt to corner particular sources of supply or markets for themselves.

In this scenario, the role of the multinational resource companies will be crucial. If the contractual arrangement is between two governments, with the companies acting as agents, then their role is fairly straightforward. If, however, a government assists one of its companies in making a contractual agreement with another government, the company may then have the option to exercise force majeure in unforeseeable circumstances that may disrupt supplies. The companies may also have flexibility vis-à-vis governments, if they are engaged in shipping a given mineral to several parts of the world. Minerals on the high seas are very mobile and can be switched easily to different destinations.

There have been examples of cooperative action which fall short of a cartel on the part of resource consuming nations. Again the example of oil comes to mind. The actual formation by governments of consumer cartels is difficult to envisage for many minerals, because of the wide disparity of interests on the part of consuming countries. It would certainly involve a high degree of liaison between governments and companies in the consuming countries, something that could be more readily achieved in some countries than in others.

What is more likely to occur is the formation of cartels on the part of multinational resource companies which may receive the tacit approval of the governments of consuming countries. The international oil companies received a formal American antitrust exemption in order to bargain collectively with the oil producing countries. The North American aluminum companies are bargaining collectively with the Jamaican government with no antitrust exemption, but with the knowledge of the United States and Canadian governments.[21] These same companies, together with European aluminum companies, are also involved in a "gentleman's agreement" to protect the price of aluminum in the west from aluminum imported from socialist countries.[22] Collective agreements are also engaged in by iron ore producing companies.[23] While the companies will be forced to change their bargaining strategy, their flexibility will allow them to adjust and probably benefit from changing government policy. The strategy may well be for them to protest measures of economic nationalism in developing countries in order to appease their shareholders and avoid being charged for failure to protect their shareholders' interests, but if they feel they can pass on tax increases or the losses due to expropriation and perhaps increase their profits, they may, in fact, give in to the demands of the mineral producing governments.

Another possibility is that different producer cartels may form alliances to strengthen their bargaining positions, i.e., an alliance of OPEC, CIPEC, and IBA countries. The disparate interests of the member countries would be difficult to reconcile in such an alliance, so that this possibility seems remote. If implemented at all, it would certainly precipitate the governments of mineral consuming countries to take evasive action.

State intervention through whole or partial ownership of mineral producing companies is one definite action taken by producing countries. In a sense they are following the example of many industrialized countries, which have been ready to nationalize some of their domestic companies, to initiate government corporations, and to raise corporate taxes. Another way of looking at this form of intervention is to note that a version of Professor Hirschman's proposal for planned divestment by MNEs in developing countries is already being undertaken.[24]

The extent of state ownership of mineral resources is considerable in the case of copper. In 1960, government participation in copper production amounted to 2½ per cent of free world capacity; by 1971, the figure was 43 per cent mainly due to government participation in and nationalization of copper companies in Zaire, Chile, and Zambia.[25] However, nationalization presents considerable problems for governments and for the countries involved. The case of Kennecott in Chile is illustrative of the problems faced by the Allende government in its attempt in 1970 to nationalize Kennecott without compensation. The company, anticipating this possibility a number of years earlier, had established a web of contractual relationships which meant that the governments of the United States, Japan, and a number of Western European countries would be affected. Kennecott had loans from American institutions, insurance coverage from the United States government, and has sold the collection rights for long term contracts for copper to a number of Asian and European financial institutions.[26] In the end, Allende had to reimburse Kennecott. In Guyana, the government found that in nationalizing Alcan's subsidiary, the Demerara Bauxite Company, it had to take into account the response of the United States as well as the Canadian government, because of United States concern over its aluminum companies in neighbouring Jamaica and Surinam.

The governments of capital exporting countries have particular concern at the time of the foreign nationalization of firms' assets. Their nationals, the owners of the assets, are likely to be subject to wealth deprivation unless "prompt, adequate and effective compensation" is paid.[27] Claims against government investment insurance may have to be paid, and tax revenue may be lost both as a result of income and capital losses. Special circumstances may affect individual countries. Governments may find themselves involved in nationalization situations which they do not really control. The Canadian government was drawn into the Barcelona Traction and International Petroleum Company cases, because the companies were incorporated in Canada although there was almost no Canadian investment in them.[28] Similar situations could reoccur as corporations look for favourable jurisdictions in which to incorporate.

Foreign investment insurance schemes have been used by a number of governments to permit corporations to protect their investments, and in this sense governments participate in the corporations' activities. The future of such schemes subsidized by government is doubtful. In the event that a country nationalizes without fair compensation to an insured company, that country is likely to be struck off the list of countries to which insurance schemes apply. Another problem with investment insurance is that its presence may encourage companies to invite expropriation. Companies may decide to act in this way if they want to withdraw assets from a country, and consider insurance claims as the least costly way of receiving compensation for their assets.

New foreign investment in mineral resource development in developing countries will undoubtedly be on different terms than in the past. The governments of capital exporting countries will have to associate themselves with firms' (the investors') actions, because they are inevitably drawn into disputes that arise at a later date. A number of trends are likely to occur. First, concession agreements will be signed for a much shorter period than previously. One writer suggests "10-15 years rather than the 30-60-99 year pattern, with the expectation that they will be systematically turned over to the host countries in stages according to a definite (or flexible) time-table, with at least the margins of compensation agreed to in advance".[29] The latter part of this quotation refers to a second trend, the use of planned divestment as a technique of withdrawal by companies. This will be associated in many instances with the companies retaining a management contract with the original company, a technique used by Zambia and Zaire with their nationalized copper mines.

A third trend will see the formation of consortia of companies to develop mineral resources. These consortia will include private companies from different countries and the governments of mineral producing countries through their state enterprises. The aluminum industry is illustrative of this technique.[30] Governments of capital exporting countries may also participate directly in such schemes if they have ownership in producing companies, or if certain companies are identified as national champions, e.g., Pechiney in France.

A fourth trend arises out of problems associated with the taxation of vertically integrated companies which are located in different countries. There is a tendency for governments of producing and consuming countries to view tax collection from a company which is partly in their juristiction as a zero-sum game. For example, one reason for the increase in oil taxation in producing countries is the readiness with which governments in consuming countries have raised taxes on gasoline consumption. This kind of outright conflict may be resolved through increasing governmental agreement on the overall profitability of the operation and the share that is due to each government. Obviously this proposal becomes less practical the more governments are involved with any given company. However, the development of tax treaty arrangements may be used both to levy taxes and to control MNEs. Such agreements may also be useful in ensuring that a concession agreement signed by a company is adhered to by the company and the producing country. The government of a consuming country will be more directly involved from the outset of an investment, the terms of the agreement will be public and its tax position specified.

The Metamorphosis of the MNE

In general, the governments of the LDCs hope to harness the affiliates of MNEs as agents of national policy, and to date have been frustrated by their inability to do so, because the policy-making centres of most MNEs are located in the DACs. Despite the fact that the modern MNE is characterized by a separation of ownership and management, host governments argue that, in order to repatriate a subsidiary's decision-making functions, a significant transfer of ownership to the host country is required.

The reason for this is as follows. While ownership and management are typically separated in the parent company, the preference of the parent for wholly- owned subsidiaries, for ease of management, suggests that ownership and management are not separated in the subsidiary. This situation arises because it is the parent's managers not the parent's owners that argue for wholly-owned subsidiaries. In the case of the parent, the managers see their powers increased by separating themselves from the owners; in the case of the subsidiary, the managers see their powers increased by having 100 per cent ownership of the subsidiary so as to reduce outside interference.

Corporate sub-optimization, i.e., the failure to achieve desired profit goals, is the disease that management normally attributes to outside interference. Until recently, the perception of sub-optimization in the MNE tended to result from conflicting pressures emanating from the headquarters company and the pressures brought to bear on its affiliates by the governments of host countries. For example, parent company cost considerations may suggest that a subsidiary company should limit its operations to extraction of minerals, yet this decision may conflict with the host country's desire to promote greater processing as a way of encouraging local industry. This problem becomes more difficult for the MNE if the government of the host country is a shareholder in the operations of its subsidiary.

The current scenario involving the mineral producing and consuming countries has added a new dimension to the problem of corporate suboptimization. More governments with differing objectives are establishing new arrangements with the economic affiliates of the MNEs as a way of achieving their respective national goals. The question of conflict resolution and the role of the MNE in this new configuration involving governmental and corporate actors can only be hypothesized at this time.

The MNE has proven itself to be a highly flexible organization. While these institutions have shown a decided preference for wholly-owned subsidiaries and the greatest resistance to engaging in non-equity contractual arrangements, their perferences in most instances have not prevented them from engaging in hybrid and complex affiliate arrangements. The joint industrial cooperative arrangements entered into by some of the leading MNEs with Soviet and East European state enterprises is but an indication of their flexibility and confidence in maintaining control over their operations, even when outright ownership is absent. Thus, one can expect the MNE to resolve the issue of foreign control in a highly pragmatic fashion. In effect, their tacit acceptance of greater state ownership in hitherto privately held assets suggests that the argument for the "separation of ownership and management" is a valid one, and can be applied even in the extreme case of a subsidiary operation where 100 per cent corporate ownership is replaced by a management contract.

In our view, conflict resolution involving the MNEs and the governments of developing and developed nations can and will be more readily resolved than those which occur between governments with divergent goals and expectations concerning the operations of MNEs. In the former case, the profit motive will be uppermost in determining conflict resolution, and the loyalty and compliance of the MNE will be influenced by the respective economic and political strengths of the governments involved. In the latter, the conflicts will necessitate a higher order of resolution with attendant problems associated with international governmental conflict situations. For example, such a scenario is underway in the formulation and elaboration of a U.N. code of conduct on the activities of "transnational corporations".

In December 1974, following the debate on the United Nations Group of Eminent Persons' report and recommendations, the U.N. decided to establish an Inter-governmental Commission on the Transnational Corporations (TNCs). The U.N. elected to employ the term "TNCs' in order to preserve the term "multinational" for consortiums of government and not private sector investors. The Commission has 48 members and functions as an advisory board to the Economic and Social Council in dealing with the issue of the TNCs. In March of 1976, at the second session of the Commission in Lima, Peru, it was agreed that the U.N. give priority to the preparation of a code of conduct for the TNCs. An inter-governmental Working Group was established and requested to submit an annotated outline of a code to the third session of the Commission in the Spring of 1977, with the objective of presenting a full draft to the Commission's fourth session in the Spring of 1978.

While the members of the Commission agreed that the highest priority should be assigned to the work leading to the formulation of a code of conduct, differences were expressed as to whether the code of conduct should be mandatory in nature, voluntary, or voluntary subject to some form of surveillance. Moreover, some delegations argued that the code of conduct should be applicable to both States and transnational corporations, while other delegations emphasized that the code should apply only to transnational corporations. The differences among the member states with respect to the code of conduct was largely a reflection of their respective stage of economic development and their position of either being a parent or host country to transnational corporations. For example, the "Group of 77" (the Third World) focussed their concern exclusively on "the operations and activities of transnational corporations"; the delegations of France, the Federal Republic of Germany, Italy, the United Kingdom and the U.S. (the major capital exporting countries) drew attention to the "concern which relate to relations between transnational corporations and governments"; while the socialist democracies of Bulgaria, Germany and the Soviet Union, in addition to supporting the concern of the Group of 77, argued for the need to obtain more information about "the negative attitude of TNCs towards the freedom of organization of workers. . . .and the negative impact of TNCs on economic relations between states".[31]

In the context of interstate relations, the multinational enterprise has increased the importance of politico-economic bargaining across multiple issue-areas involving governmental and non-governmental actors. Professor Hoffman noted that, "the competition between states takes place on several chess boards in addition to the traditional military and diplomatic ones; for instance, the chess boards of world trade, of world finance, of aid and technical assistance, of space research and exploration, of military technology, and the chess board of what has been called 'informal procedure,'".[32] In this connection, multinational enterprises have increased the subtle and complex linkages among these chess boards for the players.

While the range of government intervention in the operations of the MNEs in the extractive industry is varied, running the gamut from nationalization to government sponsored insurance schemes, the end result of these actions presents nations with a revised set of payoffs in their interactions with one another.This phenomenon will make the mutated MNE an increasingly important ally or opponent in interstate politics depending on whether the national interests of

41

the governments involved coincide or conflict with those of the corporation. Thus, the MNE may be seen as a constraint on a nation's autonomy, which applies to both parent and host governments. "Murder" of the MNE does not appear to be on the horizon; rather the MNE will probably achieve the legitimization of its corporate existence as an international organization, as more governments become entwined in its global corporate systems.

Footnotes

1. *Multinational Corporations and United States Foreign Policy,* Hearings before the Subcommittee on Multinational Corporations of the Committee on Foreign Relations, U.S. Senate, March 20-22, (Washington, 1973), p. 521.

2. The Spring 1974 Session of the UN General Assembly dealt with this topic, and passed a Draft Resolution on a Programme of Action on the Establishment of a New International Economic Order; also a World Symposium on Energy and Raw Materials was held in Paris in June 1974 (Globe and Mail, Toronto, June 11, 1974). Meetings of producers were held for iron ore (March 24-28, 1974, Geneva), for copper (April 20-May 3, 1974, Vienna), and for mercury (May 16-17, 1974, Algiers) (Financial Times, May 27, 1974). The British-North America Committee discussed this topic at their June 7-9, 1974 meeting at Gleneagles, Scotland. Meetings of the non-aligned countries in Lusaka in 1970 and Georgetown in 1972 dealt with this issue.

3. The Case Studies in R. Mikesell, *Foreign Investment in the Petroleum and Mineral Industries* (Baltimore, 1971) provide excellent examples of this process.

4. A.O. Hirschman, "How to Divest in Latin America and Why", *Essays in International Finance* (Princeton University, International Finance Section, No. 1969), and J.N. Behrman, "International Divestment: Panacea or Pitfall?", *Looking Ahead* (Washington, National Planning Association, 1970).

5. N. Girvan, *The Caribbean Bauxite Industry* (Institute of Social and Economic Research, University of the West Indies, Jamaica, 1967).

6. MLO Faber and J.G. Potter, *Towards economic Independence: Papers on the Nationalization of the Copper Industry in Zambia* (Cambridge, 1971), pp. 28-29.

7. UN Committee on Natural Resources, Report to the Economic and Social Council on the First Session, Feb. 22-March 10, 1971 (New York, U.N., 1972) (Official Records, 50th Session, Supplement No. 6).

8. Statement by Dr. Paul Prebisch, at the Meeting of the Group of Eminent Persons, U.N., Nov. 13, 1973, pp. 9-11. Jamaica withdrew unilaterally from ICSID just prior to its negotiations with the aluminum companies in May 1974.

9. U.S. Department of State Memorandum, "Raw Materials Other than Oil as Economic Weapons Against the U.S. and Other Major Consumers", Jan. 22, 1974; and *Economic Picture of Japan,* 1970-1971, Keidanren, Tokyo, p. 36, *Japan Trade* Bulletin, No. 684, Nov. 1, 1971, p.3.

10. Z. Mikdashi, "Aluminum in West Europe: A Regional Analysis of Business-Government Realtions", Paper presented to Conference on Business-Government Relations in Western Europe, Harvard University, January 1973; and U.S. General Services Administration, *Stockpile Report to the Congress,* July-December, 1973.

11. Member countries of CIPEC are Chile, Peru, Zaire, and Zambia. Participants at the March 1974 meeting establishing the International Bauxite Association were Australia, Guinea, Guyana, Jamaica, Sierra Leone, Surinam, and Yugoslavia.

12. Namely Brazil, Chile, India, Liberia, Peru, and Venezuela which met at Caracas in September 1968 and Geneva in February 1969. With Mauritania, these seven countries in 1967 accounted for 34 per cent of world exports of iron ore and 84 per cent of iron ore exports from developing countries. (*OPEC Bulletin*, No. 3, 1972, p. 7).

13. *Ibid*., p. 10.

14. Government of Jamaica, *Press and Information Kit on the Negotiations,* issued by A.F. Sabo Associates (New York).

15. Kaiser Bauxite Company, Public Affairs Department, "Kaiser Bauxite — In Partnership with Jamaica", company publication, 1970.

16. Securities and Exchange Commission, Form 10-K for Kaiser Aluminum and Chemical Corp., for the period ending Dec. 31, 1975, p. 3.

17. *Ibid.*, p. 3.
18. M. Adelman, "Is the Oil Shortage Real?", *Foreign Policy,* No. 9, Winter 1972-73, pp. 69-107.
19. U.S. Department of Interior, Bureau of Mines, "Methods for Producing Alumina from Clay", Report of Investigations 7758, 1973.
20. K. Takeuchi, "CIPEC and the Copper Export Earnings of Member Countries", *Developing Economies,* X, 1, March 1972, p. 12.
21. Government of Jamaica, *op. cit.,* In order to avoid U.S. antitrust action an independent lawyer is present at all meetings between the companies concerning the negotiations in order to confirm that no antitrust act is violated.
22. *Metal Bulletin,* January 12, 1971, p. 16.
23. *OPEC Bulletin,* op. cit., p. 8.
24. A.O. Hirschman, *op. cit.*
25. Sir R.L. Prain, "State Control in the Free World Copper Industry", A69 (Institution of Mining and Metallurgy, April 1973).
26. For a detailed discussion, see T.H. Moran, "Transnational Strategies of Projection and Defense by Multinational Corporations: Spreading the Risk and Raising the Cost for Nationalization in Natural Resources", *International Organization,* Spring 1973, pp. 273-87.
27. B.H. Weston, "International Law and the Deprivation of Foreign Wealth: A Framework for Future Inquiry – Part II", *Virginia Law Review,* LIV, 7, p. 1330.
28. See *Harvard International Law Journal,* XII, 1, Winter 1971, pp. 91-120, and *International Legal Materials,* XI, 1, Jan. 1972, pp. 97-98.
29. T.H. Moran, "Politics of Economic Nationalism and the Evolution of Concession Agreements", *Proceedings of the American Society of International Law,* LXVU, 4, Sept. 1972.
30. U.S. Department of Mines, *Minerals Yearbook,* 1969, pp. 164-67.
31. Commission on Transnational Corporations, Report to the Economic and Social Council on the Second Session (New York, U.N., 1976), E/C.10/16, p. 26.

THE FUTURE OF THE MULTINATIONAL CORPORATIONS:

THE VIEWS OF AN AMERICAN CONSULTANT.

*By Dr. David Zenoff**

Analysis of the evolutionary patterns of corporate international financial management should not be done in a vacuum. Financial management is responsive to the business environment and how companies are operating therein. Hence, analysis of future patterns of multinational finance must begin with a forecast of: (1) the publics which shape corporate opportunities and operating modes, (2) the basic patterns of multinational activity, and (3) characteristics of management style. This article summarizes my conclusions about these areas.

The single most important trend affecting public response to MNC activities is heightened global sensitivity to their presence. They are in the limelight, and will continue to be. In some cases, this is simply but significantly interpreted as 'you are big and you are bad'. In other cases, we can expect trendsetters, opinion leaders and intellectuals to increase their consideration of the multinational company, and to debate in public forums, in the press, and in the literature the costs and benefits of multinational presence. It is true now, and will be true in the future, that very few people are well-informed about corporate activity. Much misinformation exists. Public opinion is based mostly on a few publicized events involving multinational companies — most of which connote a negative or dubious social value.

Public opinion and sensitivity toward global business operations are closely intertwined with the forces of *nationalism*. Nationalism is a force which can be more emotional and non-rational than rational, more intangible than tangible; for companies it possesses a pronounced *we* and *they* dimension, and affords national leaders wide latitude of interpretation — sometimes allowing differentiation between nationalism and the national interest.

What will continue to fan fires to nationalism as it applies to multinationals and direct its energy toward corporate activities is multinational power: *power* measured correctly or not in comparison with that of nation-states. The data below is making the rounds among opinion leaders in both the private and public sectors who are worried about outsiders' power. While the definition of national economic power as measured by the GNP and corporate economic power as measured by annual sales volume can be attacked on conceptual grounds, the impressions gained by these comparisons are dramatic.

Among this ranking of the 100 largest economic entities in the world, multinational companies account for 43 places.

What are heightened public sensitivity and strong nationalistic forces likely to bring for multinationals? Government clarification of the rules for outsiders' partcipation within their borders? The development and clarification of rules, *per se,* will not indicate disdain towards foreign business. Rather, the rules will represent and be responsive to: (1) pressures on governments to respond to corporate power; and (2) growing knowledge among governments about (a) their goals, (b) the costs and benefits of multinationals presence, and (c) how public

*Formerly a Professor at Columbia University; now President, David B. Zenoff & Associates, New York City, New York, USA. I am grateful to my colleagues, Professors Ashok Kapoor of the New York University Graduate School of Business, and Donald Henley of the Michigan State Business School, who assisted me in the selection and structuring of topics for this presentation.

Reprinted from *Euromoney,* September, 1975, pp. 146-154 with permission of the publishers.

NATIONALISM: SOURCES

Nations and Corporations
(Billions of dollars — 1973)

		$				$
1	United States	1,184·1		51	Thailand	8·0
2	USSR	447·5		52	Standard Oil (California)	7·8
3	Japan	389·6		53	British Pet.	7·7
4	Germany	387·6		54	Peru	7·6
5	France	256·5		55	Nippon Steel	7·6
6	Britain	172·2		56	Chile	7·5
7	Italy	134·3		57	Egypt	7·5
8	China	127·9		58	Nigeria	7·0
9	Canada	119·1		59	Western Electric	7·0
10	Brazil	76·3		60	US Steel	7·0
11	Netherlands	64·2		61	Colombia	6·9
12	India	59·2		62	Bulgaria	6·6
13	Australia	57·0		63	Ireland	6·6
14	Poland	47·6		64	Portugal	6·5
15	Switzerland	44·6		65	Volkswagen	6·4
16	Spain	42·2		66	Pakistan	6·3
17	East Germany	40·6		67	Israel	6·1
18	Mexico	37·5		68	Hitachi	6·0
19	General Motors	35·8		69	Taiwan	5·9
20	Czechosolvakia	33·5		70	Westinghouse	5·7
21	Sweden	33·1		71	Hoechst	5·6
22	Austria	29·9		72	Daimler-Benz	5·6
23	Argentina	29·0		73	Toyota	5·5
24	Exxon	28·0		74	Siemens	5·5
25	Denmark	27·6		75	Standard Oil (Ind)	5·4
26	South Africa	26·9		76	BASF	5·4
27	Ford	23·0		77	ICI	5·3
28	Belgium	22·2		78	Dupont	5·3
29	Turkey	21·0		79	Mitsubishi	5·2
30	Norway	19·6		80	Nestle	5·2
31	Romania	19·5		81	General Telephone	5·1
32	Royal Dutch	18·7		82	North Korea	5·0
33	Venezuela	16·6		83	Shell Oil	4·9
34	Hungary	16·6		84	Nissan	4·9
35	Greece	16·3		85	Puerto Rico	4·8
36	Yugoslavia	13·8		86	Cuba	4·7
37	Iran	11·9		87	Algeria	4·7
38	Chrysler	11·8		88	Goodyear	4·7
39	General Electric	11·6		89	Renault	4·7
40	Texaco	11·4		90	Bayer	4·7
41	Mobil	11·4		91	Malaysia	4·5
42	Unilever	11·0		92	Montedison	4·5
43	IBM	11·0		93	Hong Kong	4·4
44	Korea	10·8		94	Matsushita	4·4
45	Indonesia	10·4		95	British Steel	4·3
46	Philippines	10·3		96	ENI	4·3
47	ITT	10·2		97	Bangladesh	4·2
48	Gulf Oil	8·4		98	RCA	4·2
49	New Zealand	8·1		99	Thyssen-Hutte	4·2
50	Philips	8·1		100	Continental Oil	4·2

policy measures are likely to affect corporate behaviour. The rules of the game will define: the amount of ownership that will be permissible, how control can be exercised, the proper construction of balance of payments-related transactions, the cost and form of technology transfers, personnel policies, the degree of adherence to local regulations and laws which is expected, and the length of foreign tenure within a country.

Government as a participant

We should expect to find government as a more important participant in international business. Government will step in where: the private sector has not fulfilled all required roles, where scarce resources require protection, where the government believes it possesses the special capabilities to fulfil national needs, and for ideological purposes. Hence, we can expect more public sector agencies to be involved in infrastructure development, the exploitation of strategic resources, in heavy industry, and in the services and distribution sectors. In some cases, government agencies will join with private companies as joint venture partners; in other instances, multinationals will find public sector companies as their consumers, or their suppliers, or their competitors.

Government action will also influence the multinational environment through the establishment of new political and economic relationships among nation-states. The emerging relationships will lead to *new commercial flows,* which will present opportunities for some companies and close doors to others; their very nature suggests preferential treatment and emphasis by the participating governments.

Some countries will associate along industry lines following the OPEC model; other countries will associate on geographical bases such as ANCOM, or Southeast Asia and Japan, or China and South Asia. In some cases where special opportunities exist for complimentarity of resource utilization, two or more countries will seek the benefits from close ties. In the latter respect, we might expect Iran and certain Latin American countries to relate more closely, as will Brazil and Japan, and Japan and the Pacific Basin. Multinational companies anxious to exploit these new commercial flows must be able to identify the opportunities before they arise, and be prepared to participate.

As we think of multinational publics, remember that employees around the world are likely to exert increasing influence over top management. The internationalization of unions, although a slowly growing, unsteady and unspectacular movement, is an idea that is well planted and is becoming transformed into a reality. In the United States, the recent struggle for passage of the Burke-Hartke legislation highlights the significant interest which labour has on multinationals. So-called industrial democracy now present in Germany, Norway, Luxembourg, Denmark and Sweden, and expected in France, the UK and Switzerland will tend to formalize employees' involvements on the boards of directors and on supervisory boards of companies. This will affect corporate objectives, strategies, and major economic decisions. Employee pension funds, which we recognize are significant participants in major capital markets, may some day exercise their stockholders' power over corporate directors. And, middle-management unions, now existing in the Netherlands, Germany, Sweden and France can be expected to spread and become more influential in corporate affairs.

Viewed broadly, the multinationals' publics can be expected to produce three sources of pressure on multinationals: more competition for markets and resources, continuous change and more rules of the game.

Patterns of multinational activity

Let's shift our focus to the Board patterns of mutlinational activity, in the years ahead. Who are going to be the players? Where will they play? How will they play?

International business is likely to account for 25% of the world's Gross National Product by the year 1985. The United States will still retain its dominance as the leading investor globally, but Japan and West Germany, the great export competitors, will also be expanding their foreign investment at an astoundingly rapid rate. They will invest internationally to protect market shares developed through exports, to develop new attractive markets, and to obtain resources in response to differentials in inflation rates and currency changes among their major commercial partners.

Japan can be expected to focus much of its foreign direct investment on the development of raw materials sources in South-east Asia, Brazil and the Middle East; on the development of off-shore production sites in South Korea, Taiwan, Singapore, Brazil and the Middle East where labour raw material and energy are available, and regulations pertaining to environmental pollution are relatively lenient. In addition, Japanese companies can be expected to seek foreign market development in the emerging markets of South-east Asia, Brazil, Middle East, United States and Western Europe.

The Japanese, who have competed internationally largely on price, are shifting the basis on which they will compete in the future. They will stress their ability to *initiate* and *package* large technology transfers and the delivery of systems and projects. They will stress high product quality, product variety, their willingness and ability to operate on joint venture bases, and their willingness and ability to make long-term supply contracts with foreign governments and corporations.

By 1985, one-third of the annual capital formation in South Asia and South-east Asia will be financed by some form of Japanese capital. Japanese companies will purchase more than 50% of South-east Asian countries' total exports, and Japanese companies will provide South-east Asia with 50% of its total imports.

Another important pattern of multinational activity in the years ahead will be foreign direct investment in the United States, primarily orientated to the United States market. For many large United States companies, this will be the first real direct invasion of their prime market.

Let us highlight a few specific forms by which multinationals are likely to participate internationally. A growing number of companies will become involved in large-scale international transfers of technology, such as turnkeys, capital goods systems, entire industrial sectors, and urban development. These large-scale technology transfers will reflect the rapidly growing affluency of selected foreign countries, their desire for rapid economic development, their desire for self-sufficiency, and the appeal to them of packages, for they do not want nor are they able to assemble complex systems. For most multinationals, this kind of business opportunity is likely to be attractive because of its gross size; but it will be very complex and difficult to bid, to administer, and to implement. And it will force companies into some new endeavours for which profitability may be elusive and will require rapid corporate learning to compete. Furthermore, large-scale technology transfers frequently involve partnerships with local governments, other mutlinationals, local entrepreneurs, and perhaps with suppliers. These partnerships by themselves will be complex, and very challenging to manage successfully.

Acquisitions, partnerships, and divestitures will characterize much of the multinational's future involvements and plans. Acquisitions will continue to have appeal, for they appear to offer immediate market share, they reduce uncertainty, provide management and marketing know-how, a local franchise, and successful products. More and more, the real challenge for management will be seen in integrating newly acquired foreign companies into the overall corporate family. Hence, most analysis of prospective acquisitions has been of the purchase price; yet the actual value to a purchaser has had to work itself out over time, in the performance of a newly-acquired company, and in the kind of fit or lack of it that is made between the new subsidiary and the rest of the multinational. Not surprisingly, a significant number of foreign acquisitions have not lived up to expectations.

Partnerships or joint ventures will assume increasing importance: often they will be the only means of participating in new attractive large technology transfers, or they will be required by nationalistic host government as the entry price for access to local resources and local markets. Some companies will find partnerships attractive means of obtaining some of the requisites for international success, be they contacts, marketing know-how or management. It is a sobering note that approximately one-third of all United States joint ventures in Western Europe have not succeeded. Hence, we will find considerably more attention paid to the planning and analysis of prospective international partnerships. In this regard, key questions for multinationals that require answers *before* they act are:

Precisely what do we want?

What do our prospective partners want?

What will we be able to contribute to the venture?

What will they have to contribute?

What does the venture require for success?

How should we structure the partnership?

Divestiture will increasingly become a part of international business corporate strategy, as are acquisitions and joint ventures. As corporate objectives and circumstances change and as environmental and commercial conditions evolve, divestiture will become a logical reality for many multinationals. No longer will it be treated as a disgraceful retreat; rather, divestiture will come to be viewed as a resource re-allocation, deserving of the same long-term planning and management care as acquisitions.

Management styles

What management styles can we expect in the years ahead? Of foremost significance, international business will continue to advance out of its second-class status compared to domestic business. There are two reasons for this emergence: (1) increasingly, top corporate management will be comprised of executives who personally have had international business experience and responsibility; (2) international business will account for so significant a portion of income, cash flow and assets that its importance will demand the attention of top management. Hence, there will be a stronger corporate commitment to international business, the multinational concept will become an enunciated priority among corporate objectives, and there will be more top management pressure for international results.

These circumstances and pressures will bring about more global approaches to management. The multinational company model likely to be adopted by a growing number of companies will be: a multinational company links the markets of the world with the resources of the world on a profitable basis. Adoption of this model implies much about top management philosophy, perspective, commitment and resource allocation.

Let us explore some of the possibilities, beginning with the concepts of corporate 'magic' and corporate 'muscle'. Each multinational company has achieved its very large size through an historic blending of unusually successful management talent, product features, marketing knowhow and production capabilities. Today, each company is unique in terms of its place in world commerce and its resources for progressing into the future. I call this corporate magic. Each company also possesses enormous economic power, energies and organizational momentum: corporate muscle. The task in 1975-85 is to apply magic and muscle to international business, to imbue foreign subsidiaries with magic and to harness global power for them so that their success is not limited to or dependent only on what a $10, $20, or $30 million foreign subsidiary can do; but rather on what it, as an extension of an entire global entity, can accomplish in each area.

One approach to blending magic and muscle is by integrating management effort, or by rationalizing it. There are ample opportunities for multinationals to integrate management along functional lines; for example, within the finance function international, cash management; or within the marketing function, global standardization of promotional themes. There are also opportunities to integrate management between functions. For example, to formulate global marketing strategies at the same time as global production strategies are formulated. There are opportunities to integrate management within regions; for example, to co-ordinate and attempt to rationalize plans, facilities, and strategies among European subsidiaries. And, there are opportunities to integrate management between areas of the world, such as between Europe and Latin America.

One further element rounds out our consideration of evolving global approaches to management. In the future, companies will move beyond an exporter's view of world business. Although historically most multinationals have grown internationally by exporting their domestic successes — be they products, technology, people, ideas, or manufacturing processes — opportunities exist to also import foreign ideas, products, technology, and people into the multinational headquarters for use domestically and for redeployment to third-countries. In this manner, headquarters will provide a genuine link between the world's markets and the world's resources.

Management structure

What, then, can we expect of multinational management structure? Headquarters' role will continue to be redefined and clarified, essentially in the direction of transferring magic, flexing and focusing muscle, integrating management, and allocating resources with a global scope. There are at least four functions for which a multinational corporations' headquarters is uniquely well qualified to perform, by virtue of its perspective, its power within the organization, and its special skills.

1. We are likely to see much stronger headquarters leadership in global strategic planning, where headquarters provides more guidance to the field, dictates the rules of the game to the subsidiaries, explicates broad long-term objectives and strategies, and requires line management to become genuinely involved in strategic planning (including contingency planning).

2. Another emerging headquarters' role will be as the corporate student and educator. Headquarters will structure the means to systematically pay attention to what the subsidiaries do, to analyse and observe what their successes and failures are and the reasons for them, and to attempt to figure out where else in the corporate system these experiences and lessons can be usefully applied.

3. Associated with this is headquarters' growing recognition of the need to systematically scan the globe to analyse commercial and economic developments and trends, and the politics relevant to international business. Structuring of a global intelligence system will be designed to reduce the risks associated with being unprepared for change, and to derive the benefits from being able to move rapidly and correctly within a changing environment. Global intelligence systems require top management commitment, a mandate, a structure, a budget, and professional skill.

4. Another headquarters' role will be in manpower. What is required, and therefore what is likely to emerge, is a corporate willingness to make strategic investment in management personnel to ensure a pool of executives at all echelons who possess what it takes to transfer corporate magic. I refer to an executive pool with varied nationalities, professional skills, and language capabilities, with people capable of operating successfully in foreign environments, who know their companies' products, technology, and style of management, and are therefore trusted and respected by headquarters. The right balance of manpower requires planning and anticipation of the long-run needs of the corporation, and top managements

willing to make sizeable investments in manpower recruitment and development.

To conclude with a note on the external affairs function in multinational companies: the earlier discussion emphasized the many publics multinational companies will be facing, and their importance in shaping the environment ranging from regulations, to new commercial flows, to partners, to competitors, to employees, suppliers, and consumers. It is apparent that much of the multinationals' future success is dependent on how well management can anticipate the public's response and how well it can manage relationships with the public. This requires management professionalism. Professionalism in monitoring and anticipating the public's reaction, in understanding the public's viewpoint, in communicating with the public, in formulating strategies and tactics, in negotiating correctly, in determining if and where there exists a commonality of interests and needs between a corporation and its publics; and, very importantly, in better explaining oneself to the world.

AFRICA

MULTINATIONAL ENTERPRISES IN THE

MIDDLE EAST

Lawrence G. Franko*

Any paper on the future of the oil-exporting countries of the Middle East is an exercise in speculation. A paper on the future of industrialization in the Middle East, and on the likely involvement of OECD-based multinational enterprises (MNEs) in that industrialization is probably an exercise in wild speculation. The special development problems of capital-rich, technology-short and (generally) labour-short economies have not been in the mainstream of the literature on economic development, and students of MNE involvement in such countries have not heretofore had much reason to look at MNEs in activities other than oil production. This paper attempts to wrestle with these issues. It cannot pretend to be definitive, or — since we are dealing with a region in flux — complete. It can only hope to help start a discussion concerning problems which may be of importance to policy-makers in both the developed countries and the Middle East during the next ten years.

Industry in the Middle East

Oil production (and some refining) excepted, neither industrialization nor multinational enterpise has heretofore been of much importance to the oil exporting countries of the Middle East. Prior to the 1973-1974 quadrupling of the oil price, industrialization in the oil-exporting countries of the Arab world plus Iran was limited. Table I summarizes the data available on Mid-East industrial activity, including data on the proportion of GDP and employment accounted for by manufacturing in each country. With some 1.4 million people employed in manufacture in 1971, Iran was the exception to the rule. But even relatively populous countries like Iraq were observed to have "few industries of any size!". (Europa Publications, 1975; 373.)

Multinational company activity in wholly or partly MNE-owned industrial enterprises outside the oil sector in the region has also been of exceedingly limited scope. In the Arab oil-exporting countries one found a handful of industrial joint ventures between MNEs and local (usually state) enterprises in natural gas liquification and truck assembly (Algeria), fertilizer (Saudi Arabia, Kuwait, Qatar) and aluminium smelting (Bahrain). In Iran, there were many more industrial companies in which foreign enterprises owned equity shares (including a very few which were 100% foreign owned). The Iranian Ministry of Economy reported that in January 1973 there were a total of 134 concerns, besides banks, operating in Iran with some foreign participation. Out of these, 108 were in manufacturing, 10 in mining, 7 in agriculture, and 9 in services. Nevertheless, before 1973, foreign capital *per se* never accounted for more than 2% of Iran's gross fixed capital formation (Daftary, 1975; World Bank, 1974). Moreover, one suspects that most of the manufacturing operations in Iran were of the assembly and packaging variety, and it is this author's impression that no more than five of the ventures with foreign participation had total sales (much less Iranian produced sales) exceeding $15 million. (These impressions are based on a compilation of published data undertaken by the author, interviews with Iranian businessmen and

*Deputy Assistant Director, International Affairs, Congressional Budget Office, Washington D.C. This article was written while he was on the Faculty of the Center for Education on International Management, Geneva and is based on research undertaken for the OECD Development Center, Paris.

Reprinted from the *World Journal of Trade Law* by permission of the publishers.

TABLE 1

INDICATORS OF INDUSTRIALIZATION AND POTENTIAL FOR INDUSTRIALIZATION
IN OIL PRODUCING COUNTRIES OF THE MIDDLE EAST (YEARS IN PARENTHESES)

Country	GDP $ Billion 1973	GDP % 5 Year growth	Population million 1973	% Male literacy	% GDP from manufacturing (excluding oil)	% Employment in manufacturing (excluding oil)	% Exports manufactured	Active population (Thousands)	University population
Algeria	7·1	?	15·8	25 ('66)	12 ('74)	8 ('66)	10 ('71)	2,281 ('66) (d)	22,568 ('72)
Bahrain	?	?	0·2 ('71)	60 ('71)	5 ('72)	14 ('71) (a)	?	60 ('71)	355 ('73)
Iran	24·3	92·9	31·3	37 ('72)	14 ('72)	17 ('71) (a)	8 ('72)	8,130 ('71)	115,000 ('73)
Iraq	6·1	?	10·4	60 ('72)	9 ('69)	6 ('72)	1 ('72)	2,818 ('72)	48,141
Kuwait	5·3	?	0·9	?	4 ('74)	5 ('74)	2 (c)	239 (e)	CA.2,000 ('73)
Libya	5·6	?	2·2	22 ('71)	2 ('72)	7 ('74)	?	?	800 ('72)
Saudi Arabia	8·9	72·5	CA.4·5 (b)	CA.15 ('72)	2 ('72)	CA.8 ('72)	?	CA.1,500	10,000 ('73)
Qatar	?	?	0·2 ('72)	?	2 ('72)	?	?	CA.100	CA.200
United Arab Emirates	CA.5·0 ('74)	?	–	No official statistics exist		–	?	CA.100	?

Notes: (a) Includes oil sector.
  (b) Based on interviews, not published estimates.
  (c) Manufactured exports from Bahrain include Aluminium ingot; those from Kuwait include fertilizers.
  (d) Some 650,000 Algerians are estimated to be working abroad, principally in France.
  (e) About 50% are non-Kuwaitis.

Sources: *Business International*, "Indicators of Market Size, 1975, Reprint Edition": World Bank Reports; *Economist Intelligence Unit*, "Quarterly Economic Survey and Annual Supplements": Europa Publications, *The Middle East and North Africa, 1974–75.*

officials, and data on subsidiaries of non-US multinational enterprises collected in 1971 by the Comparative Multinational Enterprise Project. See: Vaupei and Curhan, 1974, for sample and methodology. The study in process by Daftary, *et al.*, should throw more light on this issue.)

Beyond Absorptive Capacity?

Adepts of both linear trend extrapolation and of traditional business project evaluation have argued on the basis of such data that prospects for both industrialization and MNE industrial involvement in the region are still quite limited. This conclusion has been defended in spite of the massive industrializaton plans — and massive involvement of MNEs—announced by several countries. Low literacy rates, small populations (excepting Iran, Iraq and Algeria), and a lack of trained industrial workers, managers and technicians have all been cited as proof that countries in the region have low capacities to absorb their vastly increased oil revenues through industrialization efforts. (Business International, 1975, Lelyveld, 1975). And it is, of course, undeniable that all these characteristics plus lack of transport, utilities and public service infrastructure could involve additional (private) costs to MNEs, barring one form or another of subsidy.

One cannot be certain, but this observer, nevertheless, suspects that further analysis will show that limited absorptive capacities and a lack of infrastructure may delay industrial development, but that they are not insuperable bottlenecks. Thoroughly assessing the potential for industrialization in states as diverse as Algeria, Bahrain, Iran, Iraq, Kuwait, Libya, Saudi Arabia, Qatar and the United Arab Emirates is a much broader task than we propose to undertake in this exploratory paper. But it is evident that there would be few prospects for industrial joint ventures in the oil-exporting countries of the Middle East unless there were prospects for feasible paths to some forms of industrial development. A few comments as to why I am not convinced by the trend extrapolation and absorptive-capacity arguments about either industrialization or MNE involvement are therefore in order.

First, the many arguments produced by MNE managers to the effect that they cannot invest in the region because "infrastructure costs are too high" look very much like initial positions for negotiation. OPEC governments can clearly give MNEs a "sufficient" return. OPEC has given the oil-exporting countries the possibility of "reverse dumping" to stimulate industrialization at home. The probable effect of reverse dumping on the oil price in the export market is small, and in any case would not be felt in the short run. Thus, the negotiating range of possibly discriminatory pricing at home ranges to virtually the marginal cost of a barrel of oil ($0.15) or of gas (0+gathering costs). As long as the expected economic return to host countries from any further subsidization of MNEs producing locally (i.e., low interest loans, cash grants for training, etc.) is positive, the host countries will rationally prefer the acquisition of industrial assets (including human skills) to the acquisition of financial assets in developed countries currently earning a negative real rate of interest due to inflation. Subsidization is also in host countries' interest to the extent that the social returns from the social and political insurance policies of economic and export diversification exceed private returns. The limits to which the Middle Eastern countries seem prepared to go in subsidization are suggested by the fact that in the case of each country whose existing, planned, or proposed industrial joint ventures are known to us, the total capital and construction costs to complete all projects appear to be well below one year's oil revenues. This seems to be about the strategy one would expect of a prudent gambler who wants to at least break even if the next turn of the (oil price) wheel is unfavorable.

Secondly, since even only a minor amount of "reverse dumping" of energy appears to have been used successfully in the West to attract MNE production (e.g., Holland's pricing of natural gas and its attraction of chemical works and aluminium smelters), there is reason to suspect that the same tactic will have a similar result in the Middle East. There is irony in the fact that one of the most comprehensive lists of reasons why neither much industrialization nor much MNE involvement in the Middle-East is likely to occur in refining and petrochemicals was drawn up by an executive from a Dutch-based (60%) oil company. (Lelyveld, 1975). It was the same company that, for some reasons apparently having to do with the nature of oligopoly competition among MNEs, was the first to officially agree to build an export refinery and ethylene-based chemical complex in Saudi Arabia (MEES, 21 Feb. 1975). Shell has long wished, but been unable, to match the American majors in across to low cost (or, now, potentially low cost) Saudi crude—for both oil and chemicals.

A third consideration, the lack of skilled manpower, or even of a significant amount of manpower—in some countries in the region—may prove more constraining to both industrialization and MNE activity. But some industrialization strategies available to such "low absorptive capacity" countries, plus MNE involvement could convert this problem into an opportunity. With even Iran experiencing labor shortages down to the level of semi-qualified workers (*Journal de Genève,* 1975) only Iraq and Algeria would seem potential candidates for the type of labor-intensive industrialization usually recommended to less developed countries. (And Algeria, to much criticism, has also opted for a capital-intensive route so far.) MNEs are often accused of bringing "excessively" capital intensive processes to developing countries. From the point of view of many of the labor-poor oil exporters, however, more capital intensity is not only in line with their recently acquired comparative advantage, but may prove to be remarkably adaptable to Islamic, or at least Arab, sociology. The individualism of Islamic values, as well as the strength of family units in the region does not seem to be very much in line with the development of a Western or Japanese (or Soviet) type of industrial proletariat; this impression is quite irresistible when one observes Iranian artisans and Teheran's anarchic traffic, or thinks of the independence of Saudi Ministries or the *laissez faire* competitive (not collectivist) aspects of Algerian state firms. T.E. Lawrence made an observation concerning Arab *mores* which might be as relevant for economic development as it was for warfare. He remarked that the Arab rebellion of 1917—1918 could not be won by traditional Western army discipline "in the sense in which it was restrictive, submergent of individuality, the Lowest Common Denominator of men". He noted rather that the ideal was "to make our battle a series of single combats, our ranks a happy alliance of agile commanders-in-chief" (Lawrence, 1962: 347-8).

The majority of the ventures involving equity ownership participation by OECD-based MNEs in the oil-exporting countries of the Middle East seem nothing but capital intensive. The Shell executive cited above estimated a figure of $160,000 investment for every job likely to be created. The 110 ventures surveyed are skewed both in number and in value toward capital- and energy-intensive petrochemicals and energy-using aluminium and steel projects.[1] All but four of 23 existing and definitely planned ventures in Saudi Arabia, 13 of 37 in Iran, and 10 of 11 in the Gulf States and Libya are in these categories.

Such ventures require a certain amount of skilled technical and maintenance labor which is evidently in short supply in the region. The chemical industry—but not the aluminium or steel industry—uses a great input of technical and scientific personnel on a world-wide basis. But the basic and intermediate petrochemical products (fertilizers, ethylene, etc.) being produced and projected for the Middle East are in the relatively mature, standardized phases of their product life cycles; their production does not require much *scientific* skill (Stobaugh 1971). Moreover, capital-intensive processes, unlike labor-intensive processes, economize on certain types of management skills. It does not seem to be sufficiently recognized in discussions of the choice of production processes in development strategies that labor-intensive methods and industries require either superior management and technical skills in labor relations, work-flow organization, and quality control — or a superior police force. (Certain relgious or ethnic cultures seem to have minimized the problem by equipping workers with their own "internal police force". But it seems to me that the very word Islam, submission, is in conflict with such cultures.)

There is some probability well above zero that the kind of skills necessary to the operation of mature, capital-intensive industries can be mobilized in the oil-exporting countries of the Middle East, particularly if MNEs bring along enough of their own expatriates to begin the job. In a perfect world market for managerial and technical skills of the sort needed for mature, capital-intensive industries, the elasticity of the supply schedule faced by the Middle Eastern countries (which have less than 10 per cent of the population of the OECD nations) would be high indeed. One Iranian development banker opined to the author that his country's problems of management and technical skills would be largely solved if the developed countries could only supply Iran with a large quantity of skilled personnel. He noted, however, that skilled people in developed countries work for firms, and that before getting the skills, one had to interest the firms.

Patterns of MNE Involvement in Middle Eastern Industry

There seems little doubt that some firms are interested in industrial ventures in the Middle East. A proposal recently submitted to one government by an oil and chemicals enterprise seemed to suggest that its level of interest was so high that it desired a mandate to develop the whole of a *country*, not just projects in specific sectors. (It remains to be seen if the government of the state in question will accept promotion to figurehead status − or if it would be happy with that status for very long.)

The MNEs with the most equity involvement in Middle East facilities, existing and proposed, are of course those in the sectors using oil and gas. Some host country and inter-Arab-Agency officials stated their desires for ventures by MNEs in this area in discussions with the author. But outside of the obvious link between agriculture and energy − fertilizer − there is little evidence for likely long-term MNE involvement in agriculture. (And there may not be much in the future. MNEs can easily calculate, and host governments can easily administer the private profits determined by one price, that of energy. But neither MNEs nor governments seem to have a clear idea of the private or social benefits of Middle East business in the sectors of agriculture and energy, or the administrative routes by which sufficient private benefits could be assured.)

American and Japanese MNEs appear also to be disproportionately involved in Middle-East industrialization plans. It has recently become clear that in 1974, the United States and Japan both had the highest total volume of exports to OPEC countries and the highest growth rate in exports to OPEC (after Canada). (OECD Observer, April 1975: 5). The U.S. and Japanese exports in 1974 to OPEC countries totalled perhaps 45 per cent of all OCED exports to OPEC. American and Japanese predominance in production facilities with foreign ownership in the Middle Eastern Oil-Producing Countries appears to be considerably greater, according to the preliminary data summarized in Table 2.

Precisely why American and Japanese companies should be pioneering in the Middle East is not intuitively obvious. Japan as a country is anxious to assure supplies of oil and to continue to supply its established export markets for intermediate and finished goods: "oil for industrialization" is one clear bargaining outcome. But why more so for Japan than European countries? The long American political involvement in the Middle-East and the lengthy experience of U.S. oil companies in the region could help explain U.S. involvement (although some might wonder why historical resentments against U.S. oil companies have not worked in favour of *less* American involvement).

An alternative explanation perhaps lies in the possibility that American and Japanese production processes are more capital intensive (or at least less management and technical-skill

TABLE 2

ESTIMATES OF DISTRIBUTIONS BY MNE HOME COUNTRIES
OF EXISTING AND PLANNED INDUSTRIAL JOINT
VENTURES IN IRAN AND SAUDI ARABIA

Home Countries of MNEs	Number	Estimate of Total Investment (MNE and local)
Existing and Planned Ventures in Saudi Arabia (a)		
U.S.A.	16	$6 to 11 billion
Japan	3	$3.25 billion
Other	4	$0.5 billion
Existing and Planned Ventures in Iran (b)		
U.S.A.	13	$3 to 4 billion (?)
Japan	4	$2 billion
Germany	9 (c)	$1 billion (?)
Other	11	?

Notes: (a) Does not include projects said to be only the subject of "talks" or "negotiation".
 (b) The Iranian Ministry of Economy reported that as of January 1973 there were 108 manufacturing concerns in Iran with some foreign participation. While our survey did not cover all 108 it is believed that it lists the most important foreign ventures.
 (c) Does not include the often postponed, mammoth Boushir refinery-petrochemical proposal.

intensive) than those of potential European competitors. There is considerable historical evidence that American processes have long been less labor intensive than European processes — at least in mature products (Franko 1976: as per chs. II, VII). Some executives assert that in some industries a similar difference now exists between Japanese and European process. The fact that sales-to-employee ratios of many Japanese enterprises substantially exceed those of comparable European (and even American) firms is consistent with the hypothesis that Japanese processes are capital intensive (Keegan, 1975). (Such contrasting ratios could, of course, be the result of factors ranging from employee motivation to quirks in exchange rates.)

Another possible cause of the American and Japanese predominance may have to do with plant and enterprise scale: until the oil-price increase, developing countries sought projects and plants from MNEs. Today, the oil exporters are seeking instant economies. The most likely suppliers of instant economies may be enterprises used to operating on the scale of the continental United States.

Oligopolistic Competition: "Outsider" vs. "Major" MNEs

In addition to being largely American and Japanese, the MNEs involved in the first industrial ventures in the region have tended to be "outsiders" (or "independents") in the industries concerned. Observers of oligopolistically structured industries have presented arguments and evidence suggesting that in such industries, moves by enterprises either to manufacture or extract raw materials in new areas will be led by the firms with the most to gain (or the least to lose) from upsetting a stable division of would market shares in the industry (Vernon, 1974). MNE behavior appears very much to have conformed to this pattern in the Middle East thus far. The first aluminium smelters in the region ("Alba" in Bahrain, and the Arak plant in Iran) were established with minority participations of Kaiser and Reynolds, respectively. Only in 1975 did a "major" like Alcan become involved in negotiations for facilities. General Motors' 1973 assembly of Chevrolets and recently announced massive expansion plans in Iran were preceded by both an abortive American Motors assembly venture and the assembly of Chrysler-Rootes' Hillmans under license by Iran National.

Moves by would-be oligopolists to get a competitive advantage over members of the industry establishment appear to have played a role in the first ventures in chemicals and chemical fertilizers in the Middle-East. Four of the first five chemical ventures in the region (in Saudi Arabia and Kuwait) were undertaken as joint ventures with *oil* companies (see Table 5). And oil companies have been seeking to encroach on chemical company markets for some time (Achilladelis, 1974). All of the first five chemical ventures in Iran, Saudi Arabia, Kuwait and Qatar were undertaken by oil or chemical-based MNEs which, at the time they established these ventures, were smaller in terms of chemical sales volume than any of the first 15 (chemical and oil) companies in chemicals.

Table 4 shows that the world's largest chemical companies still appear to be relatively absent from moves to produce in the Middle East. The largest American chemical companies appear to be (recent) exceptions to this rule, a fact that may be explainable not only in terms of their desire to match rival "chemical" companies,[2] but also by their fear of being held to ransom for feedstock by American "oil" companies, should (1) the currently projected shortage of ethylene actually

TABLE 3

MULTINATIONAL OIL COMPANIES, INDICATORS OF RELATIVE SIZE IN CHEMICAL INDUSTRY, NUMBERS OF EXISTING OR PLANNED VENTURES, COST OF FIXED ASSETS OF VENTURES, AND FIRST OPERATING YEAR OF VENTURES IN MIDDLE EAST

Oil companies with chemical operations	Total sales ($ billion) 1973	Chemical sales ($ billion) 1973	M.E. Ventures		
			No.	($ billion) value	First Year
Shell	18·7	2·0	1	?	1980
Exxon	25·7	1·6	?	?	1980
Occidental	3·1	1·1*	2	0·2	1965
Amoco (Standard Oil of Indiana)	5·4	0·8	1	0.1	1967
Gulf	8·4	0·5	1	?	1966
Philips	3·0	0·8	0	0	0
B.P.	7·2	0·4	1	?	1966
Mobil	11·4	0·6	0	?	0
ENI	4·3	0·4	1	?	1980

Notes: *Includes sales of Hooker Chemical acquired in 1968.

Sources: For total sales: *Fortune.* For chemical sales of chemical companies: *Chemical and Engineering News,* April 16, 1973. For chemical sales of oil companies: Nieuwenhuis, H.K.,' "Petrochemicals in the Changing Energy World Around Us," Chemical Projects Associates, Inc., presentation at C.E.I., Geneva, September 1974.

TABLE 4

MULTINATIONAL CHEMICAL COMPANIES, INDICATORS OF RELATIVE RANKING IN INDUSTRY,
NUMBERS OF EXISTING OR PLANNED VENTURES, COST OF FIXED ASSETS OF VENTURES,
AND FIRST OPERATING YEAR OF VENTURES IN MIDDLE EAST (EXCLUDING PHARMACEUTICAL OPERATIONS)

Chemical companies	1971 C & EN ranking	Total sales ($ billion)		Chemical sales ($ billion) 1971	M.E. ventures established		
		1971	1973		No.	Cost ($ billion)	First operating year
ICI	1	4·0	5·3	3·4	0	–	–
Du Pont	2	3·9	5·3	3·5	2	0·3	1978
Hoechst	3	3·9	5·6	2·4	0	–	–
Montedison	4	3·4	4·4	1·4	0	–	–
BASF	5	3·1	5·4	2·1	0	–	–
Bayer	6	3·1	4·6	2·8	2	0·1	1975
Union Carbide	7	3·0	3·9	1·9	1*	0·7	1980?
Akzo	8	2·5	3·4	2·2	0	–	–
Rhone-Poulenc	9	2·3	4·4	1·1	0	–	–
Monsanto	10	2·0	2·6	1·7	0	–	–
Grace	11	2·1	2·8	0·9	0	–	–
Dow	12	2·0	3·0	1·7	2	1·5	1980?
Courtaulds	13	1·7	2·3	1·5	0	–	–
FMC	14	1·4	1·7	0·6	1	?	?
Allied	15	1·3	1·6	0·8	2	0·2	1969
American Cyanamid	16	1·3	1·5	0·6	0	–	–
Celanese	17	1·2	1·6	1·1	1	?	1980?
Mitsubishi Petrochem	43	0·3	0·5	0·3	2	6·0	1976
Mitsui Petrochem	48	0·2		0·2	1	3·2	1978
Norsk Hydro	50	0·2		0·1	1	0·8	1973

Notes: *Does not include a small battery plant operating in Iran since the 1960s.
Sources: See Table 3.

develop, and (2) should American "oil" companies obtain further control over Middle Eastern feedstock supplies.

Oil MNEs of course have special reasons for interest in the region. Although to the outside world, it appears that their Middle East operations have been "nationalized" in whole or in part, various purchase arrangements assure that they maintain a preferential access to (and marketing and distribution control of) crude oil (Adelman, 1972–1973). Saudi Arabia has publicy stated that it would be quite content to give the oil companies preferential access to crude (and gas) in return for industrial ventures. (Kayhan International, 6 May 1975) Qatar and Libya do not seem to have made equivalent public statements, but their recent arrangements in chemicals with "oil" companies would appear consistent with such a policy. Oil companies therefore see some probability of simultaneously defending (or improving) their market position in crude and refined products, and furthering their two-decade old efforts to encroach on the product and market territory of the "chemical" firms. If such considerations of oligopolistic behavior are in fact underlying company moves in the Middle East, the consequences of this behavior may include the following: first, "outsider" MNEs motivated by the chance of improving world market shares will have few qualms about subsequently exporting to world markets and "disrupting" the positions of "majors"; secondly, MNEs will be "integrating" world markets. Their interest in promoting, say, inter-Arab exports in the manner some exponents of regional integration have desired will be secondary or non-existent, and, to the extent one MNE appears to be gaining an advantage in one country in the region, other oligopolists may be tempted to match in other countries. Such MNE behaviour will not facilitate regional political integration through joint planning and facilities allocation. Countries of the region may also end up competing with one another in giving favorable energy costs and financing to ventures involving MNEs. Oligopolistic thrust and counterthrust may of course facilitate Arab-Iranian-American-Japanese integration by giving many American and Japanese MNEs a vested interest in the industrial success of the Middle East *and* in the maintenance of a high oil export price (and a low local oil price) system.

Host Country Preferences

All of the oil-exporting countries in the Middle East, with the single exception of Iraq, have accepted some equity ownership involvement in industrial ventures by OECD-based MNEs. Iraq is currently the only country of the region legally prohibiting non-Arab (but not all foreign) equity ownership in new ventures. However, according to both Arab and non-Arab observers interviewed in the Middle-East and Europe, there is reason to think that this policy might change. Cited as straws in the wind are the very cordial commercial relationships between Iraqi state companies and some OECD industrial firms, plus the recent signing of a longterm service contract with Boeing by Iraq Air which has taken some 100 American families to Bagdad.[3]

Relative to the importance of industry in its economy Algeria too appears to have accepted relatively few ventures by MNEs.

The small ownership involvement of MNEs in Algeria, and the absence of MNE involvement in Iraq corresponds to these countries' current ideological aversion to foreign enterprise. Algeria, of course, nationalized several foreign-owned firms (mainly French) in the 1960s. An equally plausible economic explanation for low MNE involvement in Iraqi and Algerian industry exists, however. The relatively large populations, low levels of *per capita* income, and limited state of existing industrialization in Algeria and Iraq provide both states with the scope for a considerable amount of important-substituting development, and with an environment favorable to the promotion of relatively unsophisticated basic industry. In such countries, MNEs are not immediately and obviously needed for their knowledge of export markets. And sources of skills appropriate to steel, textiles, electrical apparatus, and building materials other than equity involvement by MNEs exist. (One recalls that there was not very much MNE involvement in Iran, either, when that country was at a comparable level of development.)

Algeria and Iraq continue to seek, and often get alternatives to MNEs, such as turnkey plants. In Iran, Saudi Arabia, and the Gulf States, however, the view is fairly widespread that purchasing turnkey plants is a risky business, especially in the more sophisticated sectors.

One frequently hears the opinion that foreign companies that wish to sell equipment should generally take an equity stake in the venture as a guarantee of good faith and continued interest. Turnkey plants in the Middle East have something of a bad name, and stories of difficult startups are common. Even Algeria appears to be moving toward a similar view of foreign equity participation — although Algeria is presently trying to combine its preference for 100 per cent local ownership with MNE commitment by seeking "product-in-hand", as opposed to "key-in-hand" terms for plant sales (discussions with Algerian state enterprise managers, CEI-INPED seminar, April 1975).

Increasing host country preferences for MNE equity commitments are likely to be met by MNE insistence for participation in (or control of) management decision-making in more tightly oligopolistic industries — especially when ventures are to be export-oriented. Algeria has tried unsuccessfully for several years to obtain a "product-in-hand" accord for the expansion, and conversion from assembly to production of a nationalized facility formerly owned by Renault. Several automobile companies which Algeria has tried to interest have declined to participate without equity participation and control over quality and trademarks, because they do not relish the idea of Algeria eventually exporting to their existing markets. Japanese compaies have declined to sell an aluminium smelter to Iraq, apparently for similar reasons (Metal Bulletin, 1974).

While the laws of several of the Middle East oil exporting countries theoretically permit 100 per cent ownership of production facilities by foreign companies, only a few ventures in Iran dating from the 1960s are in fact wholly owned foreign subsidiaries. Local ownership, and almost invariably majority local ownership participation is being required in new ventures. There seems little reason to expect much change in such host country requirements, even though some Arab governmental officials opined that "now that we've lost our inferiority complex, 100 per cent ownership might be possible for MNEs undertaking particularly useful or challenging ventures, for example, in agrobusiness".

Despite legal niceties, some ventures have been, and others will almost certainly be more joint than others.[4] Few governments in the world are in a position like those of the oil-exporting countries to recognize the distinction between financial ownership participation and management participation, for there have clearly been time lags between the two sorts of participation in the oil sector. In the oil sector, local ownership participation has often functioned primarily as a surrogate for an increase in the level of tax paid by oil companies. Local ownership participation could, of course, serve the same function in manufacturing, and has done so in other parts of the world like Latin America. Indeed, even ownership participation by *private* local partners can function essentially as a fiscal device akin to the ancient practice of tax farming. This is the case when local partners are not involved in management, and when they obtain their shares for a cost of capital lower than the market rate of interest plus monopoly rents derivable from the MNE's contributions (Franko, 1974). Local ownership participation, to be sure, also has symbolic value.

Styles of local partners' participation in management functions (deeper than those of taxation and symbol) vary among types of partners. Impressionistic comments gathered from MNE managers of ventures already operating in Iran and Saudi Arabia suggested that in both countries cooperation was typically smoother with state enterprises and banks than it was with private partners. Such comments were made even by managers of MNEs noted for their commitments to "private" enterprise. These managers stated that bank partners tended to concern themselves with the financial aspects of the venture, and with its following certain broad social and cultural guidelines and allowed the foreign firm to "get on with the show". State enterprises were more interested in learning the business *per se,* but were considered to have adopted the industrial "mentality" of concern with medium to long term objectives and results — even if those objectives and hoped-for results risked future conflict with MNEs. Partnerships with private enterpreneurs and family groups were said to be sometimes more difficult because (so it was asserted by some MNE managers) of partners' desires for immediate, short-term pay-outs from the business, or because of problems of conflict of interest in transfer pricing of goods and services to related local companies.

Problems in Joint Industrial Ventures

While there seem many opportunities for industrial ventures involving MNEs in the oil exporting countries of the Middle East, several of the existing ventures have got underway only with more or less severe difficulty and conflict. And the scope for problems in future ventures is too great to be ignored. Some of the sources of possible problems have little to do with whether or not ventures are joint, or whether MNEs are involved. But since MNEs may be blamed if things go wrong (and since OECD home country governments may be blamed if enough things go wrong in enough ventures involving their MNEs), it is worth noting the variety of possible problems, even at the risk of sounding excessively pessimistic.

One source of problems may be simply the misevaluation of industrialization projects in private or social terms. In theory, this source of problems is separate from foreign enterprise involvement. However, the combination of MNE managers perceiving prospects of large financial returns from Middle Eastern operations, plus the depression in the OECD home countries has led to government and enterprise planners in the Middle East being inundated with proposals. There is rarely time, or personnel available in host government departments to evaluate proposals thoroughly, and diplomatic observers interviewed were convinced that "a lot of cats and dogs were slipping through". Some private Iranian bankers argued that this was a blessing in disguise for their country. Their contention was that in a country with the highest growth rate in the world, rigorous central planning was neither possible nor desirable. They argued that experimentation was necessary, that some failures were useful, and that a country with both reasonably large financial and human resources could dispense with fine (and inevitably erroneous) calculations of opportunity cost. Moreover, they, as well as foreign company and diplomatic officers, were convinced that the Iranian technocracy was of sufficient quality to eliminate the more dubious projects from consideration. Observers of Iraq, including one former Iraqi high-ranking official, argued that the rather large *cadre* of Western (and Eastern) trained government planners, plus the prevailing distrust of foreign enterprise, should help avoid obvious misevaluations in that country. Algerian managers made similar observations about their country.

Observers of Saudi Arabia and some of the Gulf States, including some managers of the long-established oil MNEs, were less sanguine. Some noted with dismay the acceptance of projects for joint vehicle assembly ventures which would have production capacities of some miniscule fraction of minimum economic scale, and would therefore require permanent protection. The use of scarce domestic labor, or the importation of (already socially problematic) foreign labor for such projects was questioned, as were the sales techniques of the foreign enterprises. One firm was said to have used the currently fashionable theme of corporate social responsibility to convince the local government that the firm's principal motivation in establishing vehicle assembly was to make a contribution to the local society. Independent observers were worried that only after such ventures were in operation would both the economic and social impact of them be questioned.

More generally, it was feared that the increases in oil revenues had not only made the concept of financial opportunity cost "go out of the window" but had also led to the neglect of the opportunity cost of scarce local labor and management resources.

Independently of project evaluation, there seems a considerable risk of mistakes in selection of MNEs by hosts — and of local partners by MNEs. On the one hand, MNEs, particularly those new to the region, may be surprised by the results of transferring preferences developed in other areas for private or state or bank partners to the Middle East. On the other hand, hosts appear thus far to have confined their evaluation of projects involving MNEs to financial and engineering project evaluation, and to have not gone very deeply into MNE evaluation. Registration in Iran under the 1955 Law for Attraction and Protection of Foreign Investment is apparently a procedure concerned with financial aspects of ventures only, and the Saudi Arabian Application form for Industrial Licence asks for almost no information concerning parent companies (Kingdom of Saudi Arabia, Industrial Studies and Development Center, 1974).

Perhaps the relative absence of evaluation of foreign firms as potential partners is understandable: even the UN-ECOSOC Committee set up to gather information on MNEs has apparently not yet decided what sort of information to gather for such evaluations. (Discussion with U.N. official, June 1975). And a certain amount of hearsay about foreign firms' performance and conduct in ventures in the region does circulate informally: news of the fact that all had not gone smoothly in the venture between Allied Chemical and Iran's NPC had spread to Saudi Arabia. Nevertheless, one would be reassured of the prospects for successful ventures involving MNEs in the oil exporting countries if national (or regional) organizations took note of MNE characteristics, including (1) the length of experience MNEs have had in foreign operations, especially in other similar developing countries; (2) the state of play in the oligopoly games MNEs might be involved in on a world wide basis; (3) previous MNEs experience in managing export-oriented operations in the presence of local partners; (4) the appropriateness of MNE organization structures to successful export operations (see Franko, 1976, Ch. VIII); (5) the degree to which MNEs have the reputation of being able to teach as well as do; and (6) the degree to which MNEs actually practice "management" as opposed to Western versions of tribal coordination.

Assessment of MNE Partners

Assessment of these characteristics of potential MNE partners may prove important not only for its own sake, but also because this assessment could provide early warning signs of possible divergencies or incompatibilities in objectives between host countries in the region and MNEs.

The host-country objectives for industrialization one hears expressed most frequently in the Middle East are those of export diversification, and the learning of technological and managerial skills. Unfortunately for host country policy making, much of the recent literature on MNEs has given MNEs — any MNE — an image of omnipotence and omniscience that implies that an MNE can of course fulfil host country objectives. One corollary is that if the MNE does not fulfil host objectives, it must be because the MNE is egotistically plotting to keep the host country in its less-developed place.

Whether the very largest MNEs are omnisient or omnipotent is not a matter we can resolve here, but Iranian and Saudi Arabian experience with some of the smaller, outsider MNEs first attracted to the Middle East raises a number of questions. Some companies had, for example, previous international experience, but appeared to be gaining their first experience of manufacturing in *developing* countries in the Middle East. Given the nature of oligopolistic competition in those ventures' industries, Iran and Saudi Arabia might not have been able to attract "insider" companies at any reasonable price: but the fact that foreign enterprises were newcomers led both MNEs and countries to seriously underestimate certain costs of the MNEs learning to operate in these states. And erroneous expectations produced conflict. (One MNE claimed to have expended 1,200,000 (!!) unforeseen man hours in training in one venture. A foreign enterprise from a socialist state caused its local partner great consternation because it was not used to controlling inventories in an environment of uncertain, rapid growth.)

Other MNEs were willing to export from joint ventures in the Middle East, but they possessed few previously existing controlled market outlets in the developed countries where markets existed. Their Middle East ventures had to offer cut prices, and (in the short run) therefore disappointed local partners with poor financial results which had not been forseen.

It should be noted that it is common — if mistaken — to hear that MNEs "never" will export from joint ventures. Export joint ventures pose transfer-pricing problems more severe than local-market ventures. But if the local partner's role is that of a tax collector, the resolution of such problems is in principle no more difficult than that between a wholly-owned subsidiary and a fiscal authority.

Export joint ventures may also pose management problems such as quality control and scheduling synchronization (Franko, 1971, Stopford and Wells, 1972, Franko, 1974). Problems of meeting internationally competitive quality standards and delivery schedules do not arise in import-substituting joint ventures (Franko, 1971, 1975 Ch.V.; Colombo Plan, 1973; 56). However, the severity of such management problems is a function of the novel, non-standardized nature of the products produced. And export ventures, existing and planned, in the Mid-East concern primarily standardized products.

Export joint ventures may also potentially compete with an MNE's existing 100 per cent ventures, but if the MNE can act as a discriminating monopolist and isolate his existing markets from those served by the joint venture, he may choose to enter a joint venture — especially if he foresees no probability of excess capacity in the 100 per cent ventures. Even when markets cannot be isolated, an enterprise which expects the average cost of production in a joint venture to be lower than marginal cost in 100 per cent operations would rationally export from the joint venture at the expense of its 100 per cent operations (Franko, 1971, Ch. II).

In at least two joint ventures entered into by national enterprises that desired to learn management skills, national enterprises (NEs) assumed that their MNE partners had skills to transfer simply because the MNEs were multinational and financially successful. The NE managers learned to their chagrin that the MNEs in question had had many years of relatively leisurely international growth during which to develop a "tribe" of leaders who shared common methods and traditions. However, these MNEs lacked managers who took decisions by explicit, quickly communicable criteria. NE frustrations with those MNEs included the lack of learning much about systematic organization and management control, feelings of annoyance when the tribe of MNE managers ill-concealed their feelings of superiority toward the NE personnel, and NE puzzlement over the personalized nature of relationship between the MNE "sheikhs" sent to the joint venture and the MNE president-emir back at headquarters. (The irony of Middle Eastern encounters with Western tribal management has been piquant indeed to some managers in the area!)

NE difficulties with tribal MNEs as partners were compounded by the fact that these MNEs seemed good at applying technological skills, but not at teaching them. The difference in skills necessary to doing, versus teaching, is more or less widely recognized in the performing arts and in sports, but may be underestimated in business. One observer in the region cited a so-called "cultural conflict" in one relationship similar to a joint venture, a long term contract between a Western firm, and one of the airlines in the area. According to the local personnel, MNE technicians of course do not want the planes to fall down — so they are reluctant to let nationals near so much as a screw-driver. The MNE technicians then notice the locals "doing nothing" and conclude that they are just lazy and backward.

Stability of Joint Ventures and Problems for Home Countries

The foregoing catalogue of current and potential problems in industrial joint ventures in the Middle East does not necessarily imply that most, or even many of these joint ventures will become unstable, in the sense that one or the other partner will buy out, or nationalize, or sell out to the other. The risk that whole projects will fail, due to project misevaluation, or to inadequate MNE screening, seems much higher than the risk that joint ventures *per se* will fail. Historically, joint venture instability has been primarily associated with joint ventures in which one partner no longer needed the other, and especially with ventures where one partner had to be dispensed with to allow the other to carry out a supranationally integrated strategy (Franko, 1971). The few industrial joint ventures in which MNE partners have been bought out in the Middle East appear to have been ventures in which MNEs' contribution of skills and technology or export markets had demonstrably declined.[5] One can imagine MNEs contributions so declining in some of the smaller Iranian ventures. It is more difficult to imagine such a development soon in the less populated states, except perhaps in the more simple and less oligopolistic sectors such as fertilizers.

It is also rather difficult to imagine (many) of the MNEs currently involved in the Middle East attempting to buy out (or, legal or administrative regulations prohibiting this, co-opt) their local partners in order to intimately integrate Middle East export operations into an existing worldwide logistic network. Too many of the MNEs active in the Middle East appear to be "outsiders"; they presumably share their local partners' desire to poach on "insiders'" market shares. (In the case of the oil companies, they may not entirely share such local objectives, but the countries are able to make them offers of access to crude that "they can't refuse".) "Outsiders" in any case have limited world-wide logistical networks into which Middle East operations could be integrated.

The risk of joint venture instability could grow, as the larger MNE "majors" in various industries move to insure against "outsiders" encroachments on market share by matching "outsiders" ventures in the Middle East. Industry majors do have world-wide networks into which Middle East ventures could be fitted. Nevertheless, to the extent that some of the major MNEs are highly diversified, and have strategies of phasing out of old products and moving on to new, stable relationships could result. And in no industry are "majors" as diversified as in chemicals. Even Du Pont, which does not actively seek joint venture partnerships, accepts them as long as they sell under non-Du Pont trademarks. (On the relationship between diversification and joint venture stability, see Franko 1971.)

The risks of MNE involvement in the Middle East, be they of project or firm misevaluation, or risks specific to joint ventures, raise a number of questions for host and home country policy. As suggested above, there is probably room for improvement in the evaluation of the social and economic aspects of the industrial projects being proposed by MNEs to Middle Eastern countries. And the question of assessing MNEs as long term partners appears to have barely been addressed. The simile likening a joint venture to a marriage, while hackneyed, is worth recalling on occasion: the less thought preceeding a marriage the more likely a divorce.

Ordinarily, such questions of evaluation and assessment are the concern of host country governments and national enterprises. In the case of the oil-exporting countries of the Middle East, however, OECD home country governments may not be able to avoid association with their MNEs by reminding hosts of the principle of *caveat emptor*.

Japan and Western Europe's strategic dependence on the passage of the Straits of Hormuz for two thirds of their oil, and Europe's dependence on the Mediterranean for most of the rest, suggests that there will have to be some minimum of fulfilment of the aspirations (industrial and otherwise) of the oil exporting states of the Middle East. (Although European MNEs appear to have thus far avoided, or have been unable to obtain, a significant direct role in the fulfilment of

TABLE 5

GOVERNMENT-TO-GOVERNMENT ACCORDS BETWEEN OECD COUNTRIES AND OIL PRODUCING COUNTRIES OF THE MIDDLE EAST (PRELIMINARY DATA)

Host Country	OECD Country						
	U.S.A.	Japan	France	Germany	Italy	Spain	U.K.
Algeria	—	—	—	Gas-for-30-year DM 100 million loan and DM 85 million LNG terminal	—	—	—
Iran	Joint governmental commission, investment guarantee agreement, $15 billion cash-for-technology accord	—	Joint ministerial commission, oil-for-technology accord	Joint (annual) ministers committee, investment guarantee agreement	—	—	—
Iraq*		Joint commission, $1 billion oil-for-technology-plus-Japanese-loan agreement	Oil-for-technology accord	—	Ten-year oil-for-technology accord (mentions possibility of joint venturing)	Oil-for technology accord	Joint commission
Saudi Arabia	Permanent joint commission, comprehensive economic, industrial * military accord, investment guarantee agreement	Joint committee	—	—	Joint commission for 5 years	—	Joint commission on economic, industrial and technical collaboration

66

those industrial aspirations.)

Moreover, OECD countries have woven a number of intergovernmental agreements with the oil exporting countries of the Middle East, which implicitly or explicitly are open to interpretation as guarantees of industrialization. The agreements of which we are currently aware are summarized in Table 5. The "joint governmental development commission" formula appears to have been particularly favored by the two most important home-countries of MNEs, Japan and the United States, and by Iran, Saudi Arabia and Iraq.

While some governments of MNE home countries, notably that of Japan, may be administratively and legally equipped to monitor the proposals and projects of their MNEs in the Middle East, other home country governments mainly learn about their MNE's activities if and when those activities are reported in the newspapers. And there is some discomfort with this state of affairs in diplomatic circles in the region. When MNE industrial activity in the region was of negligible importance, the irritations caused by a handful of stormy ventures were matters of concern only to firms (all the more so since in a country like Iran, tensions surrounding activities of OECD-based MNEs were just about matched by difficulties with turnkey plants and joint ventures involving Socialist-bloc enterprises). One result of the massive increase in MNE involvement, in terms of project responsibility if not necessarily in terms of MNE financial commitment,[6] may be that firms are no longer the only OECD-based institutions relevant to Middle Eastern industrial success. There is a small, but perhaps real risk that the cumulative problems of firms could become a problem for one or more home-country governments.

Links with the Price of Oil

For home country governments it would be an interesting, if complex, exercise to estimate the sensitivity of the likely commercial success of Middle East ventures involving their MNEs, to changes in oil and gas prices, and to economic growth prospects and policies in the OECD area. Such information, if now known, seems known only to firms. But is there a risk of not only a Catch 23 in the oil-price conundrum, but of a Catch 24? Catch 23, as the reader may recall, is the proposition that if people in consuming countries think the oil price will stay up, it will in fact go down, and that if people think the oil price will go down, it will in fact go up. The argument is that expectations of high oil prices will lead to investment in conservation and substitutes and a decline in demand for oil, while expectations of low oil prices will lead to a lack of such investment and increased demand (and potential market power of OPEC) for oil.

Catch 24 is the proposition that if oil prices go down MNEs will help push them back up. Catch 24 could arise if MNE *equity* involvement is massively attracted to the Middle East by expectations of high oil export prices, and oil prices then threaten to go down. A division of interest would then emerge between MNEs committed to the Middle East and OECD enterprises which stayed out. MNE home-countries could then be tempted to leave MNEs in the Middle East to sink or swim. But MNEs would of course fight back at home. The pressure or the divisiveness of the pressure from MNEs with Middle East operations could lead to political compromises *within* some OECD countries on support for some "medium-high" oil price. Since the MNEs in question are mainly American or Japanese, there could be a similar divergence of interest (and compromise?) *among* OECD countries. And the oil price would not "go down". Or if it did, and the result set Middle East industrialization back greatly, it would "solve" oil-price problem at the expense of creating a new problem of frustrated expectations in the Middle East. Specific MNEs and their specific home governments (not just "the developed countries") might be blamed for such an event.

The author's personal guess is that "Catch 24" is not a highly probable prospect. Growth rates, and industrialization activities were turning sharply upward in the Middle East well before the "oil crisis". Iran and Saudi Arabia were the first and fifth most rapidly growing countries in the world before 1974. Middle East industrialization may not be very sensitive to a decline in oil prices — even of the order of 50 per cent. But we cannot now be sure.

Problems for Western Europe

A different issue concerns the impact of Middle East industrialization on OECD trade policy. The dynamics of technology and of oligopolistic competition in industries such as petrochemicals (and some 90 per cent of chemicals are currently petroleum based) have contributed to a state of affairs in which European MNEs are not very noticeable in Middle East joint ventures. This divergent MNE behavior not only may contribute to a divergence of interest among OECD countries over oil prices, it may also lead to a "new economic order" in certain industries in which Islamo-American and Islamo-Japanese exports seriously menace European market shares in third, and eventually European, markets. Such an eventuality could not occur until Middle East export plants came on stream sometime in the 1980s. But it then could prove contentious indeed. Research is needed on the extent, if any, Middle East production will disrupt existing Western industries. If "too much" production does come flowing out of the Middle East, however, it is already clear who will probably be holding the hose.

To the extent that European firms divest out of the older, more mature products likely to be put into production in the Middle East, there might be a fairly smooth adjustment to such a development. But this author has yet to see any studies which suggest that the ability of industry in most European countries to transform is either very rapid, or increasing. Observers of the industrial democracy (job protection?) movement suggest rather that it may be decreasing (although, to be sure, their observations seem to relate to more labor intensive industries than those discussed here).

Comments made to the author by managers of chemical companies based in several European countries also suggest grounds for concern. Their responses to possible export-oriented development in the Middle East were generally of the variety of "we can't believe it will happen, and if it does we'll get our home-country governments to protect us". (Curiously, the tenor of these comments suggested that the EEC was irrelevant to the matter.)

Expressions of protectionist reflexes by European industrialists and labor movements fortunately do not constitute proof that protectionist reactions to Middle East exports will necessarily be forthcoming. But they do raise questions about intra-OECD relations, and about the impact of MNE commitments on government options. These questions should receive some answers before the answers merely happen.

Questions for Further Research

This exploratory study has focused on the ownership-equity links that OCED-based multinational enterprises have forged with the oil-exporting countries of the Middle East. Moreover, it has dealt exclusively with the activities of manufacturing enterprises. The links between OECD-based firms and the oil-exporting countries of the Middle East are, however, unlikely to be limited to equity ownership, to the territories of the oil-exporting countries themselves, or to bilateral relationships between one manufacturing firm headquartered in one of the OECD countries and its national-enterprise counterpart in the Middle East.

A handful of multi-nation consortia are establishing joint industrial ventures in the oil-exporting countries. Our survey indicates, however, that only five out of some 110 ventures have brought together equity interest from more than two countries. Despite the rarity of these arrangements, such "multinational" ventures might merit a closer examination, since the implications for relationships among OECD countries arising from joint U.S.-European, or Japanese-European projects in the Middle East could be different from those of bilateral MNE-host country ventures.

Another set of links between oil-exporters and MNEs is arising from the small, but growing, number of "triangular" projects in which OPEC money and OECD technology are brought together in the less developed countries. Managers of Arab financial institutions have championed such triangular ventures as one solution to both the problem of the re-cycling of oil revenues and that of the development of the poor countries. (Al-Hamad, 1974). Ventures combining Arab or Iranian funds with MNE equity or technical assistance, have been announced in Egypt, the Sudan, Pakistan, Jordan, Guinea and elsewhere (MEED and EIU, various issues). And OECD technology will probably be linked to Arab finance in less-developed Arab countries by the recently established, intergovernmentally owned regional companies, such as the Arab Company for Mining, or the Arab Petroleum Investment Company (whose mission is to invest in oil-related areas, including industry).

Further research needs to be done to see whether the number and size of triangular ventures will render their importance comparable to that of industrial activity MNEs in the oil-exporting states themselves. Observers in the region feel that the complexities of negotiating such arrangements will cause their realization on a significant scale to lag well behind bilateral ventures in the oil-exporting countries. There are some who argue that an initial enthusiasm for triangular ventures will give way to a much more traditional set of bilateral transactions in which less developed countries would receive loans and aid, and then make their own arrangements with OECD-based suppliers of technology. Financial flows might then be triangular, but the ventures would not. Until a serious survey is undertaken, however, such feelings will be only guesses.

A last set of links between OECD-based enterprises and the oil-exporting countries is that constituted by the licensing, "product-in-hand" and training contracts that imply a long-term relationship between the MNEs and their hosts. Long-term, non-equity cooperation arrangements, whatever they may be called, are clearly an important piece of the mosaic of relationships OECD enterprises are building with the oil-exporting countries. Cooperation agreements, like equity arrangements, may be found in bilateral, consortia, or triangular projects. Despite the move in some oil-exporting countries toward obliging MNEs to demonstrate their good faith by taking equity participation, the arrangements intermediate to simple purchases of plant on the one hand, and MNE ownership on the other, may be the most numerous links of all in terms of host countries' attempts to obtain technological and managerial skills. Unfortunately, both the existence of non-equity, long-term accords and the content of such contracts are subject to much less government and public reporting than are equity arrangements. Why this is so is not clear. Perhaps it is because the disclosure of the very closeness to equity arrangements of some of the longer term cooperation accords might prove discomforting on political grounds for some governments and enterprises. Perhaps it is simply the result of the fact that cooperation accords differ so widely that they cannot be reduced to a simple, observable number of a per cent of equity.

Whether non-equity accords are better or worse than MNE ownership for host countries' development — or for home countries' perceived responsibility for hosts' development — is also a question that should receive investigation in the Middle Eastern context. Our examination of MNE equity links with the region indicates that some host nations have concluded that equity links will be more effective, particularly where exports are desired. Nevertheless, our knowledge of the existing, or desirable relationships between OECD firms and oil-exporting countries will begin to be complete only when the alternatives to multinational enterprise equity are studied.

Sources

I	=	Interviews.
EIU	=	Economist Intelligence Unit.
MEED	=	Middle East Economic Digest.
MEES	=	Middle East Economic Survey.
KAYHAN	=	Kayhan International Newspaper, Teheran.
BUS. PROM.	=	Business Promotion Magazine (Lebanon).
BUS. INTL.	=	Business International, S.A., Geneva.
NPC	=	National Petrochemical Company of Iran, "Petrochemicals in Iran, Past, Present and Future," January 1975.
FT	=	Financial Times.

Refrences

Achilladelis, Basil, "Emerging Changes in the Petrochemical Industry, An Overview", Occasional Paper No. 1, OECD Development Center, November 1974.

Adelman, M. A., "Is the Oil Shortage Real?", *Foreign Policy*, No. 9, Winter 1972-73.

Al-Hamad, Abdlatif, *International Finance, An Arab Point of View*, Kuwait Fund for Arab Economic Development, Kuwait, October 1974.

Arab Economist, The, "Libya Emphasizes Industrial Development", April 1975.

Arab Economist, The, "Saudi Arabia's Five Year Pact with Italy", April 1975.

Business International, "Algeria Re-emerges as Investment Site", 11 May, 1973, p. 151.

Business International, "Research Report: Business Prospects in the Middle East", Business International, S.A., Geneva, April 1975.

Colombo Plan The (Information Bureau), *The Special Topic: Joint Ventures*, Wellington, N.Z., November-December 1973, especially pp. 54–60, "Iran".

Dafter, Ray, "The Chemical Trade Cycle Swings Downward Again", *Financial Times*, 29 November, 1974.

Franko, L. G., *Joint Venture Survival in Multinational Corporations*, Praeger, N.Y., 1971.

Franko, L. G., "International Joint Ventures in Developing Countries, Mystique and Reality", *Law and Policy in International Business*, Spring 1974.

Franko, L. G., "Problems and Prospects of Middle Eastern Entry into Western Industries and Markets", Ms., December 1974.

Franko, L. G., *The European Multinationals*, Harper and Row, London, and Greylock Press, Stamford, Conn., 1976.

Journal de Geneve, "Nouvelle politique d'austérité en Iran", 18 June, 1975.

Keegan, Warren J., "Productivity: Lessons From Japan", *Long Range Planning*, April 1975.

Kingdom of Saudi Arabia, Industrial Studies and Development Center, "Guide to Industrial Investment in Saudi Arabia", 4th Edition, Riyadh, 1974 (1394 A.H.).

Lawrence, T. E., *Seven Pillars of Wisdom*, Penguin edition, London, 1962.

Lelyveld, E., "The Prospects for the Production of Petrochemicals in the Oil Producing Countries of the Middle East: A Discussion Paper", 24 January, 1975.

Metal Bulletin, "Five Japanese Firms Refuse to Participate in Aluminium Smelter Project", 17 December, 1974, p. 23.

Observateur de L'OCDE, L', "La politque de l'énergie et ses incidences sur la situation monetaire internationale", March-April 1975.

Oriental Economist, The, "Japan's Economic Cooperation", January 1975.

Stobaugh, Robert B., "The International Transfer of Technology in the Establishment of the Petrochemical Industry in Developing Countries", UNITAR, N.Y., 1971.

Stopford, John and Wells, Louis T., Jr., *Managing the Multinational Enterprise*, Basic Books, N.Y., 1972.

Vernon, Raymond, "The Location of Economic Activity", in Dunning, John (ed.), *Economic Analysis and the Multinational Enterprise,* George Allen and Unwin, London, 1974.

World Bank, "Current Economic Position and Prospects of Bahrain", 28 December, 1973.

World Bank, "The Economic Development of Iran (Three Volumes)", June 1974.

World Bank, "Current Economic Position and Prospects of Iraq", 9 October, 1974.

Yekom Consultants, "Terms of Reference for the Research Project on Multinational Enterprises and Employment in Iran," *International Labor Office,* Geneva, May 1975.

Footnotes

1. A detailed listing of the 110 ventures surveyed is available in the OECD Development Center, Industry and Technology Occasional Paper No. 8, CD/TI(75)13, prepared by the author.

2. On the dynamics of oligopolistic matching behavior, see Knickerbocker, 1973, Knickerbocker demonstrates that American firms in highly concentrated industries typically matched foreign investment moves by industry rivals as part of a strategy of risk minimization. If one oligopolist established a foreign manufacturing operation, others did the same in order to be at least no worse off than the leader.

3. The recent Iraqi-Italian inter-governmental accord seems to foresee joint ventures. It states that *if* joint ventures are entered, Iraq will have at least 50 per cent ownership (MEED, 26 July '74)..

4. Note: for example, the agreement by the Iranian government to full management control by General Motors in GM's Iranian joint venture (FT, 27 Nov. 1973).

5. MNE contributions had not necessarily ceased, however. In all cases non-equity, licensing agreements existed between the former joint ventures and OECD-based enterprises..

6. Perhaps MNEs will be committed in financial terms. MNEs reported that host countries were indeed trying to get MNEs to finance proportions of projects equal to equity stakes.

The Future of the Multinationals in Africa.

*By Peter Neersø,**

Introduction

It is no easy task to try to predict the future of the multinationals in Africa. It is dependent on a large number of political and economic factors, and these are likely to develop differently in the approx. 50 African countries. Development in African countries with white minority rule will be quite different from that in the rest of Africa and for this reason these countries are not treated here. In the 1960's most African countries pursued very liberal policies on foreign investment. As a result they attracted large investments from foreign firms (mainly multinationals) both for extraction of raw materials and for manufacturing. However, foreign investment did not have the expected favourable impact on the economies of the host countries. Instead it created a number of problems. Therefore, most African governments have revised and tightened their policies on foreign investment. This article attempts to look at the problems created by foreign investment, at recent attempts by African governments to deal with those problems, and to predict the future investment policies of the African countries and their probable impact on the activities of the multinationals in Africa.

The High Cost of Foreign Investment

Like the Latin American and Asian countries, African countries have come to realize that foreign investment has a high cost. The multinationals are not prepared to invest in developing countries if the expected annual after-tax profit is not at least 20—25% of the invested capital. The profit rate demanded is higher, the larger is the perceived risk. In recent years there has been political and economic instability in many African States, and more than half of them have nationalized foreign-owned companies. Therefore the multinationals, especially those based in the U.S.A., have begun to consider investment in Africa to be risky. This implies that the minimum profit required by the multinationals (i.e. the minimum cost of foreign investment to the African countries) is more likely to increase than to decrease in the near future.

However, scattered evidence indicates that in many cases the multinationals get returns far in excess of the above mentioned 20—25% on their investments in Africa. Therefore, the African countries may considerably reduce the profits of the multinationals without precluding themselves from attracting new investments.

One of the reasons for the high profits is that the African subsidiaries of the multinationals borrow money from local banks. Usually these loans carry an interest of only 6—10%, which is considerably less than the expected return to foreign capital and also less than the interest rate prevailing in many developed countries. In most African countries it is easy for the subsidiaries of the multinationals to get local loans, since the banks consider them safer than locally owned companies. In some African countries they can even get loans at concessional interest rates from government financial institutions.

Usually the multinationals are interested in getting as large local loans as possible, not only because they are cheap but also because they reduce the share capital required and thereby reduce the risk. Thus a large part of the high profits earned by the multinationals in Africa does not stem

*Institute for Development Research, Copenhagen, Denmark

from their own capital investment, but from the capital they have borrowed locally at relatively low interest rates. Some of the African countries, e.g. Kenya and Zambia, have realized this and have, therefore, restricted foreign-owned companies' access to local credits.

The main cause for the multinationals having earned large profits in Africa is that they have obtained very liberal concessions including high tariff protection for sales on the local market, duty-free import of inputs, liberal depreciation allowances and tax holidays for 5-10 years. Some African countries have competed with each other in attracting foreign investment by offering liberal concessions. Many of these, i.e. tax holidays, do not affect the most important consideration of the investor, viz. the risk factor, as they only have importance if the investment is profitable. Therefore, they have only a marginal influence on the investment decision and are thus inefficient in attracting foreign investment. But they can increase the profits of the multinationals considerably, and thus raise the cost of foreign investment to the host country.

In the last few years some African countries have realized this and have tightened their system of incentives for foreign investors. However, in most African countries there is still ample scope for foreign investors to negotiate concessions from the host government.

The outcome of the negotiations depends on the bargaining power of the foreign companies, which in turn depends on how sophisticated and monpolized their technological and marketing systems are. The outcome also depends on the ability of the foreign investors to influence government officials including by means of bribery. Bribes are often paid via local middlemen who know which people must be bribed and by how much.

The big, technologically advanced multinational corporations are in the best positions to negotiate large concessions from the African governments. However, even relatively small companies may negotiate large concessions if they are skilful in influencing the proper people.

This is the case with the Danish firm DCK. In 1970 it established a subsidiary in Kenya which produces asparagus fern for consumption in Europe. The concessions given to DCK include an exclusive right to cultivate asparatus fern in Kenya for a period of eight years, along with a 'status quo contract' concerning taxes for 25 years. The latter inplies that possible increases in tax rates or the introduction of new taxes will not apply to DCK. DCK obtained these concessions from the Kenyan Ministry of Agriculture while Bruce McKenzie was Minister of Agriculture. Later McKenzie left the cabinet and became a member of the board of DCK. In 1975 it was reported that he had bought half of the shares of the DCK parent company from its the Danish founder, which would enable him to reap the profits originating from the liberal concessions he himself granted to DCK while he was Minister of Agriculture!

Restrictions on Remittance of Profits.

In many African countries the high profits earned by the multinationals have resulted in a serious drain on their balance of payments. Therefore, many of them have introduced restrictions on remittance of profits from the foreign-owned subsidiaries.

Normally such restrictions do not solve the problems in the long run, as the non-remitted profits are re-invested, in most cases in a lucrative way, thereby adding to the amount of profits which can be remitted later when restrictions are eased. However, the host government may ease the long-term impact on the balance of payments somewhat by compelling the foreign-owned subsidiaries to make investments which are not very profitable. Thus, in 1972 Tanzania introduced an act which enables the Treasury to compel foreign-owned subsidiaries earning large profits to buy government bonds carrying a relatively low interest rate.

The restrictions on remittance of profits may even be inefficient in the short run as multinationals can remit profits in an indirect manner by paying licence fees and by over-invoicing.

This means that the African subsidiary pays artificially high prices for deliveries from the parent company or from one of its subsidiaries in another country. In this way a part of the profits of the African subsidiary is shifted to the parent company or to another subsidiary. An export-oriented subsidiary in African can also shift profits to the parent company by under-invoicing, i.e. by selling products to it at an artificially low price.

Over-invoicing is especially common in the African subsidiaries of the multinationals. Normally, the main purpose of over-invoicing is to circumvent restrictions on remittance of profits, but there may be a number of other reasons for using over-invoicing.

Firstly, the multinationals may reduce their taxes if they shift profits from African countries with high tax rates to countries with low tax rates (e.g. Switzerland).

Secondly, by reducing the profits shown in the accounts of the African subsidiaries, the multinationals are less likely to be criticized for exploiting the host countries. Such criticism might lead either to wage claims on the part of the local workers, or to government introduction of a ceiling on selling prices, or even to outright nationalization. The rise in nationalistic feelings in African countries has made this an important factor.

Thirdly, over-invoicing for machines leads to higher depreciation allowances and thus to lower taxes.

Fourthly, by shifting profits from a joint venture to the parent company, a multinational corporation can cheat local shareholders out of their part of the profits. This factor has become more important in recent years, as the incidence of joint ventures has increased (this is elaborated later).[1]

Some Latin American countries have made systematic studies of the extent of over-invoicing. These show that many multinationals transfer much larger amounts by over-invoicing than by way of declared profits.[2]

Similar systematic studies have not been made for Africa, but there is no reason to believe that the behaviour of the multinationals in Africa should differ significantly from their behaviour in Latin America. As a matter of fact the scope for over-invoicing is greater in Africa than in Latin America, because the African subsidiaries are on the whole more dependent on imported input.

Some African governments try to prevent over-invoicing by comparing world market prices to transfer prices for deliveries from the multinationals to their local subsidiaries. In Tanzania, Kenya and Ghana this task is carried out in collaboration with the General Superintendence Company of Geneva.

Checking of over-invoicing is very cumbersome work. It is almost impossible to perform this task for specialized machines, machine parts and other products which are not traded regularly on the world market, because these products have no world market prices to which transfer prices can be compared. Therefore, the introduction of checking of transfer prices will probably just lead to over-invoicing of regularly traded goods being dropped, while over-invoicing of other goods is increased correspondingly.

Impact on the Local Economy

As described in the preceding chapters, the investments of the multinationals are costly to the African countries, causing a drain on their balance of payments which cannot easily be checked. But the foreign investments may also be costly in an indirect manner, namely by distorting the local economy and blocking its development.

In many cases manufacturing subsidiaries of the multinationals compete with locally owned companies. Usually they are the stronger part in this competition due to their efficient technology, high quality and attractive appearance of products, well-known trade marks and aggressive advertising.

Their main customers are westernized consumers belonging to the upper and higher middle classes, who have a strong preference for products carrying western trade marks. Therefore these products can be sold at higher prices than products carrying local trade marks, even if the real difference in quality is negligible.

The African masses have little money to spend on industrial goods, and therefore they are not natural customers of the multinationals. However, by aggressive advertising some firms have succeeded in making the masses imitate consumption habits of the upper classes, e.g. by buying expensive processed food-stuffs and drinks, which they can scarcely afford. This can lead to a significant change in consumption patterns of the masses, so that e.g. consumption of European-style beer not only diverts demand from local-style beer, but also from vital food-stuffs, textiles, domestic utensils, etc.

A shift in consumption pattern to the benefit of products sold by the multinationals may have a disastrous impact on the nutrition and health of an African family. This can be illustrated by the case of the milk powder sold as baby food by the multinationals. Their aggressive promotion campaigns make many African mothers waste their own milk by giving them the completely wrong impression that the powdered milk is healthier. This change in nutrition of African babies has caused diseases and death to many babies.

There are two reasons for this. Firstly, milk powder is so expensive that poor families buying it cannot afford to give their babies enough food, with the result that these suffer from malnutrition and have little resistance to disease. Secondly, due to lack of clean water, the feeding-bottles are often infected so that the babies catch diseases. Because of the seriousness of this problem, a movement has arisen to stop the aggressive promotion campaigns. The producers acknowledge the problem, but until now they have only made minor modifications in their advertising.[3]

Due to the strong competitive position of the foreign-owned subsidiaries and their impact on the consumption pattern, many locally owned handicraft and small-scale industrial enterprises in Africa have had to close down or have been blocked in their development. This phenomenon has been studied in detail in Kenya. Here the multinationals have, among others, driven local soap producers out of business, not due to superior product quality but due to the consumers' preference for western trade marks[4].

The Kenyan government has introduced a technical and financial assistance programme in order to make the small-scale industries survive and expand, especially in the rural areas. However, for two reasons this programme has not been very successful. Firstly, the programme has only been carried out half-heartedly, because many of the Kenyan politicians and top government officials have close contacts to the mostly foreign-owned large-scale industry and want the government to promote this instead of the small-scale industry. Secondly, even if small-scale industrial and handicraft enterprises receive financial and technical assistance from the government, they find it difficult to compete with large-scale industrial enterprises.

The ousting of locally owned manufacturing enterprises by the multinationals has very negative economic consequences. Firstly, it makes African businessmen prefer to invest in sectors which are not very conducive to development such as commerce, services (restaurants, dry-cleaning shops, etc.) and real estate speculation. Secondly, the locally owned enterprises often use more local inputs than the subsidiaries of the multinationals. For example, for inexpensive footwear the modern shoe factories use imported plastics, whereas the local shoemakers use local wood and locally available scrap rubber from tyres. Thus, the ousting of locally owned companies often has a negative impact on the balance of payments and on the income of the local input producers, i.e. a negative backward linkage effect. Thirdly, the foreign subsidiaries normally use more capital intensive technologies for the production process than the locally owned enterprises with which they compete.

There are three main reasons why the multinationals normally use capital intensive technologies in Africa despite the low wage rates. Firstly, they are accustomed to use these technologies in their home countries and do not find it worthwhile to adapt them to African conditions. Secondly, often capital intensive methods are least costly, even in low-wage countries.[5] Thirdly, in many cases products of a high and stable quality can only be produced by modern capital intensive technologies. Because of the difference in choice of technology the ousting of locally owned enterprises by foreign-owned companies normally has a negative impact on the employment and income possibilities of the masses.

In this way the subsidiaries of the multinationals constitute a link in a vicious circle: the unequal income distribution in Africa gives rise to a large consumption of luxury goods by the upper classes (and to some extent also by the lower classes due to the demonstration effect). These goods are produced by foreign capital intensive technologies providing highly paid jobs to a few technicians, skilled workers etc.; hereby the foreign investments reinforce the unequal income distribution; this promotes the consumption of luxury goods, etc., etc.

Impact on Foreign Exchange Position

The establishment of import-substitution industries in Africa has led to a decrease in use of foreign exchange for imports of consumer goods. But this does not necessarily mean that the African countries are saving foreign exchange. Instead of importing consumer goods they now import capital, technology, machinery, semimanufactured products, and raw materials for the production of these goods. The total bill for all these items may add up to higher than the world market price for the finished consumer goods. The main reason for the often high foreign exchange cost per unit of production is that production in most cases takes place on an uneconomically small-scale due to the limited market in most African states. The high cost of production is reflected in high selling prices which are made possible by tariff protection.

The foreign exchange cost may be reduced by establishment of local production of inputs. Many African governments are promoting this in various ways, e.g. by increasing tariffs on raw materials and semimanufactures. Some progress has been made in this respect, but the subsidiaries of the multinationals still import the bulk of their raw materials and semimanufactures and almost all their machines. The multinationals are often reluctant to use local inputs in their African subsidiaries, because they want to supply these from the parent companies. In this way they can ensure the quality of the inputs (which is essential for the reputation of the trade marks), earn a profit on the sale of the inputs, and transfer profits by over-invoicing if need arises.

If the manufacturing subsidiaries of the multinationals made exports, they would be more likely to have a positive impact on the balance of payments of the African countries. However, most have only negligible exports. One obstacle to exports is the small-scale of production, making prices uncompetitive outside the host country. Many African governments have tried to tackle this by introducing liberal export subsidies.

However, such subsidies have not proved efficient in promoting exports of manufactured goods due to the multinationals' global strategy for covering their markets. According to this strategy subsidiaries in Africa are normally supposed to cover only the market of the host countries. Other markets, including the African ones, are normally covered by the parent company or subsidiaries which are located in "safe countries" (i.e. developed countries) and have an efficient sales organization.

There are, however, a few exceptions as a few of the African subsidiaries of the multinationals export to neighbouring countries which have free trade agreements with the host countries.

A good case can be argued for establishing free trade areas (or common markets) in Africa due to the limited size of most African markets. Among other things, they would promote industrial exports considerably and make investment more attractive to the multinationals, enabling African governments to attract investment on better terms (with less tariff protecting, etc.)

Many free trade associations have been created in Africa, but most of them have never come to function properly in practice as most African countries lack confidence in each other. This is especially true of countries with different political and economic systems. Industrially weak countries also fear that the industrially strong countries will reap the benefits if the provisions for free trade are carried out. For a combination of these reasons, the East African Community encompassing Kenya, Tanzania and Uganda is now on the verge of collapse.

On the basis of this experience one can foresee that an organization like ECOWAS, which encompasses Nigeria along with 14 other, much weaker West African countries has little chance of leading to much freer trade. On the other hand, African countries such as Tanzania and Mocambique which have similar political and economic systems and a similar level of industrial development, have relatively fair chances of making successful free trade arrangements.

Run-away Industries

Besides the subsidiaries which export industrial goods to neighbouring African countries, there are a few which export industrial goods to overseas countries, mainly in Europe. In most cases such exports take place within the structure of a multinational corporation which has shifted its production of labour-intensive goods or components (e.g. electronic and textile products) from a high-wage country to a low-wage African country in order to reduce production costs.

In the 1960's this kind of investment was undertaken mainly by U.S. and Japanese corporations, and was directed towards Central America and East Asia. In about 1970 some European corporations started shifting production to developing countries as a response to rapid wage increases in Europe. A large part of the European "run-away industries" went to North African countries because of their proximity to Europe. Today a large number of black African countries, including Mauritius, Senegal, Ivory Coast and Kenya try to attract export-oriented manufacturing investment. They have difficulties in competing with the East Asian countries, among other things with regard to political stability and availability of cheap skilled labour, but they try to compensate for this by offering lavish government incentives (tax holidays, financing of infrastructure in special "export processing zones", etc.) The Lomé Convention of 1975, which gives most black African countries duty-free access to the countries of the European Communities for all industrial goods, will probably attract run-away industries to black African countries.

The run-away industries are normally foot-loose, i.e. they are not dependent on the raw materials or market of the host country. The investor, therefore, can choose among a large number of host countries and play them off against each other when negotiating for concessions. Thus there is an imminent danger that the African countries will compete with each other in offering incentives for export-oriented investment. The result of this may easily be that foreign investors extract such large profits from the African countries that these get little or no net gain in foreign exchange from export-oriented investments.

Heavy reliance on this kind of investment also increases Africa's dependence on the developed countries especially in the subcontracting components for the overseas parent company. In this case the African country is totally dependent on one specific multinational corporation, since the components normally cannot be sold elsewhere.

By attracting run-away industries, the African states may increase their industrial employment rather rapidly. However, this does not necessarily mean that such policies are beneficial to local workers, as such policies will normally entail an attempt on the part of the government to repress the labour movement in order to keep wages low, thereby maintaining the country's attraction to foreign investors. If the government does not succeed in keeping wages low, run-away industries may run away a second time, viz. to other developing countries where wages are still lower. Thus recent wage increases in Mexico have induced many U.S. corporations to move production from Northern Mexico to Haiti and other low-wage Caribbean countries.

As stated above, the extent of export-oriented industrial investment in Africa is quite dependent on the policies persued by the African countries. But it is perhaps even more dependent on the economic situation in the developed countries.

An economic boom which leads to an expansion of the market and to shortage of labour and wage increases, will increase the inducement to shift production from the developed countries to the developing ones. In many cases the trade unions in the developed countries (especially in USA) try to stop industries (and thereby jobs) from running away, but their resistance is likely to be less stubborn in a period of high employment.

Investments in Extraction of Raw Materials

Despite the endeavours of the African governments to increase industrial exports, these are still rather small and are likely to remain so in the near future for most African countries. Therefore, the African governments know that they will be dependent on their exports of primary commodities for many years, and they are trying to maximize their earnings from them.

This can basically be done in four ways: 1) by expanding the production of primary commodities; 2) by establishing cartels with the aim of increasing the commodity prices; 3) by processing the commodities locally before export; 4) by tightening policies towards foreign-owned companies which exploit the natural resources.

At first sight it would seem that the easiest way of increasing export earnings is by expanding the production of commodities. Almost all African countries have done this since their independence, e.g. by attracting foreign investments in oil fields, mines, plantations, etc. This policy has been very short-sighted. It has increased the dependence of the African countries on foreign markets and foreign corporations and reinforced the lop-sided and disconnected structure of their colonial economy. It has also resulted in the rapid depletion of mineral resources and in the use of much of the most fertile land for export production which may lead to a lack of food-stuffs for local consumption.

The worst aspect about the expansion is that if this policy is pursued at the same time by a number of producers of one specific commodity, it normally does not lead to higher net earnings of foreign exchange. Most African countries have experienced falling terms of trade since the 1950's because they have increased the production of the same commodities and thereby contributed to surpluses on the world market.

This development has been promoted by the developed countries, which are eager to secure stable and cheap sources of raw materials. The European Communities have used their aid for this purpose. The European Development Fund has directed a very large part of its capital to agricultural and infrastructural prospects which aims at increasing the export of commodities from the African countries associated to the EC. The STABEX scheme, introduced in 1975 by the Lomé Convention, offers compensation to the countries associated to the EC, if they experience a serious decline in export earnings from 12 of their most important commodities. The STABEX compensation is only given under certain circumstances, and cannot protect the African countries completely against falling terms of trade, but this "safety net" may induce them to keep up or even expand their production of export commodities.

The developing countries are beginning to realize that the policy of increasing export earnings by expanding the production of export commodities is self-defeating in the long run (except perhaps for a few products like meat which have a high income and price elasticity of demand). Therefore, as an element in a new international economic order they are demanding international arrangements which can regulate the commodity markets and counteract falling terms of trade for commodities. However, up to now little has been achieved in this field due to resistance by the major developed countries. Because of this the developing countries have established producers' associations for a number of commodities, e.g. oil, bauxite, copper, iron ore, coffee and bananas. These associations attempt to increase the export earnings of the member countries, among other things by pushing up commodity prices through cartels. There are many factors which influence the possibility of forming a cartel for a specific commodity.[6] The crucial factor in this is the degree of agreement and loyalty among the member countries. They must agree on a price level and on the extent to which each country must restrict its exports.

If agreement can be reached among all developing producer countries (or at least among the major ones) it will be possible to make cartels for many of Africa's principal export commodities, including coffee, tea, cocoa, tropical timber, copper and bauxite. A number of African countries (Libya, Algeria, Nigeria and Gabon) have gained considerably by OPEC's successful oil cartel, and most other African countries would gain considerably if cartels were established for the above-mentioned products. However, the developed countries fight cartels, and the Lomé Convention may have the effect of splitting the developing countries because it offers most of the African countries better terms for exports than other developing countries. Many of the African countries (mainly the former French colonies) are also extremely dependent on foreign technical and financial assistance and debt moratoria and are thereby open to pressure.

The African countries may not only be impaired by their own weakness but also by that of their partners in producers' associations. This is the case in the copper association CIPEC, which consists of Chile, Peru, Zambia, Zaire and Indonesia. In 1975 the CIPEC countries agreed to cut copper production by 15 per cent and this contributed to raising the copper price in 1975-76. However, CIPEC's cartel is in danger of collapsing as Chile's military government is not following the decision, probably at least partly due to pressure from the U.S. government.

The export earnings of the developing countries can be considerably increased by cartelization, but it is difficult to predict for how many commodity cartels will be established. This question has a direct bearing on the future activities of the multinationals in Africa. If cartels (and thereby restrictions on output) become widespread, the multinationals will have few investment opportunities in the primary sectors in Africa. On the other hand, if cartels fail to materialize, the multinationals will have vast investment opportunities in Africa's hitherto unexploited resources.

Local Processing of Commodities

As has been said above it is still unclear whether the African countries will try to increase their export earnings by expanding the production of export commodities individually or by restricting production of them jointly by way of cartels. But they also have some additional means of gaining more from their natural resources.

One of these possibilities is to establish local processing of commodities. The African governments promote local processing in different ways, e.g. by introducing export taxes or export bans on unprocessed goods. The free-trade provisions of the Lomé Convention facilitate local processing by removing the previous European tariff discrimination against imports of processed goods. However, at the same time the STABEX compensation scheme, introduced by the Lomé Convention, may have a counteracting effect. This scheme only covers unprocessed goods, and if the fall in export earnings from one commodity can be attributed to the establishment of local processing, no compensation is paid. This may weaken the interest of the African countries in processing their own raw materials.

Local processing opens up some new investment opportunities for the multinational corporations. However, often the multinational mining corporations are not interested in establishing local processing of mining products as there are significant economies of scale in the processing. In other cases the reason is that they do not want all production processes, from extraction of raw materials all the way to production of finished goods, taking place in a single developing country. They often want the production process divided between a number of countries. In this way they keep control and make it difficult for the developing countries to nationalize them.

In most cases the multinational aluminium corporations have resisted local processing of bauxite. Outside the communist countries the aluminium industry is dominated by six large multinational corporations, which in 1972 shared between them three quarters of total aluminium production. These corporations are vertically integrated, i.e. they control all links in the aluminium industry from baxuite mining down to production of aluminium and finished aluminium products. A large part of world trade in bauxite and alumina (and to a lesser degree also in aluminium) takes place between subsidiaries of multinational corporations in different countries. Within wide limits, the multinationals can fix the transfer prices for bauxite and alumina arbitrarily, and thus to a great extent decide in which country their profits are to appear.

The smelters in which alumina is transformed into aluminium are traditionally located in developed countries, mainly in places where there is cheap hydro-electric power. The plants in which the bauxite is transformed into alumina are traditionally located close to the smelters.

Developing countries are becoming increasingly dissatisfied with the traditional division of labour by which they export crude bauxite while the entire processing takes place in developed countries. According to an UNCTAD study, a developing country can obtain, approximately, a triplication of its export earnings if it tranforms its bauxite into alumina. If the alumina is further processed into aluminium the export earnings are about eight times greater than the earnings from exports of crude bauxite.[7] The developing countries' dissatisfaction with the present situation is intensified by the fact that the multinational aluminium corporations are using under-invoicing of the bauxite, whereby the host countries are cheated out of both foreign exchange earnings and taxes.

The monopoly of the multinational aluminium corporations is based more on their control over alumina plants and aluminium smelters than on control over bauxite mines. Therefore, it is not easy for developing countries to break the monopoly power of the aluminium multinationals — it is not enough to nationalize the bauxite mines. The Caribbean bauxite countries have begun to tackle the aluminium multinationals, e.g. by increasing taxes and by constructing alumina plants and aluminium smelters. In this way they may get an integrated aluminium industry which is not dominated by the multinationals.

The African bauxite countries are some steps behind the Caribbean countries in this respect and are still very dependent on the multinationals. Africa has ideal natural conditions for an aluminium industry, because the continent possesses about one half of the global reserves of bauxite (mainly in Guinea) and has large quantities of hydraulic power which can produce electricity very cheaply. However, until now the multinationals have succeeded in exploiting these resources without providing the African countries with an integrated aluminium industry. This especially has been the case in Ghana. Here an aluminium company called Valco is jointly owned by two U.S. aluminium corporations, Kaiser (90 per cent of the shares) and Reynolds (10 per cent). In 1960 Valco entered into a contract with the Ghanian government concerning construction of an aluminium smelter. The Ghanians hoped that this would give the country large export earnings and an integrated aluminium production on the basis of Ghana's bauxite deposits.

However, this hope proved to be an illusion because the contract was much more favourable to Valco than to Ghana. Valco was not obliged to establish an alumina plant in Ghana, and Kaiser found it more profitable to make Valco use the alumina produced by Kaiser in Jamaica and elsewhere. Furthermore, the two aluminium corporations succeeded in persuading Ghana to accept an obligation to supply Valco with electricity at a fixed price for 30 years. In view of the cost increases since 1960, this stipulation is extremely beneficial to Valco, which can now buy electricity at less than one fifth of the price of electricity in other countries.

It was very expensive for Ghana to erect the power station because it necessitated the construction of a large dam across the Volta river. An artificial lake was created, and 80,000 people had to be moved from the inundated lands. In order to finance this Ghana had to take out large loans from the U.S. and British governments and from the World Bank (which at that time was completely dominated by the U.S.A.). The lenders backed the aluminium corporations and pressed Ghana to give them a favourable contract.

Today Ghana's aluminium industry is highly disintegrated. Ghana's bauxite is exported to Scotland where the transformation into alumina takes place. The alumina for Valco's smelter is imported from Jamaica and elsewhere. The aluminium produced by the smelter is exported to developed countries where it is manufactured into rolled aluminium, etc. Ultimately, Ghana imports rolled aluminium from developed countries and manufactures it into roofs, etc. Thus, two links in the production process are located outside Ghana. Exports and imports in connection with these two links are carried out by the aluminium multinationals, which thereby have a firm grip on Ghana's aluminium industry. Ghana is now trying to weaken this grip and to get a more integrated aluminium industry. In the first round Ghana wants to establish an alumina plant and later a mill for production of rolled aluminium. In order to achieve this Ghana may try to imitate Guinea which broke its complete dependence on Western firms by entering into co-operation with Arab and communist countries for the establishment of an integrated aluminium industry.

Nationalizations

The African countries can also gain more from their natural resources by tightening their policies towards foreign-owned companies. Most African countries have done this in recent years, e.g. by renegotiating over-generous mining contracts, by increasing taxation, and by nationalizing foreign-owned mining subsidiaries, partly or totally. Because of the complex structure of the aluminium industry, African countries have been more cautious with regard to nationalization of bauxite mines than with regard to nationalization of other mining industries.

The wave of nationalization in Africa began in the more radical countries like Tanzania and Algeria, but has now spread to conservative states like Senegal, Mauritania and Zaire. To a large extent nationalization is a response to growing popular discontent with the neo-colonial economic structure in which the multinationals, especially those engaged in mining, still have a dominant position and earn large profits.

In most cases nationalization has not changed this situation radically, at least not in the short run. In general, the financial gains to the African countries have been modest because they have paid compensation for the nationalizations (although not always up to the full commercial value) and have entered into costly contracts with the former owners for technical and commercial management of the nationalized companies because they lack national managers and easy access to export markets. They want to be on reasonably good terms with the foreign corporations to attract their know-how and capital for future projects. Because of the continued dependence on foreign managers, the African governments have little real control over the exploitation of their own natural resources even if they acquire formal control. Thus, the nationalization of the copper mines in Zaire does not seem to have affected their former owners seriously, neither with regard to profits or real power. The situation may change gradually as the African countries get more experienced national managers.

The multinationals have reacted to nationalization of their mining subsidiaries in various ways. Traditionally they have been hostile to nationalization, but gradually come to realize that it is no longer possible to maintain full ownership and control. Therefore, to an increasing extent they accept partial or total nationalization, provided compensation is paid. Likewise they enter into contracts with African governments or new mining ventures where they have only a minority interest, or perhaps only a management contract.

In many African countries nationalization has not only taken place in the mining sector, but also in the manufacturing, banking, and commercial sectors. Except for the technologically most advanced manufacturing plants, these companies are easier to take over and staff with African personel than large and complex mining enterprises. Therefore, nationalization in these sectors more often implies a loss in real power to the multinationals than nationalization in the mining sector.

Outright nationalization outside the mining sector has mostly taken place in African countries having radical governments, e.g. Algeria, Tanzania, Congo, Somalia and Ethiopia. In countries where private local business is relatively well developed and politically influential, e.g. Nigeria, Ghana, Morocco and Kenya, the take-overs of foreign companies has mainly been confined to strategic sectors such as banking. More importantly, these countries have introduced various kinds of indigenization programmes which aim at increasing private local participation in ownership and management. In a number of countries, e.g. Nigeria and Ghana, some sectors (e.g. commerce and some light industries) are to be completely indigenized.

It has been rather difficult to carry out such indigenization programmes due to lack of local private capital and management experience. But the programmes have been very lucrative to a small group of African capitalists which have been able to buy shares in foreign subsidiaries at a relatively low price.

Normally it is an advantage for the multinational corporations to have their subsidiaries indigenized instead of taken over. Even if local shareholders have a majority, the multinationals have a good chance of maintaining real control, especially if the number of shareholders is large. In subsidiaries where the government has acquired a majority of the shares, multinationals are more (but not absolutely) likely to loss control. However, the degree to which nationalization implies any real change in operations of the subsidiaries is very much dependent on the development strategy of the government in question. It is especially relevant whether the government has a clear will and coherent policies for changing the colonial structure of the economy in order to achieve economic development for the majority of the population (i.e. the poor peasants and the workers), and not just for the upper classes.

Even most of the African governments which claim to be socialist lack such policies, and therefore the emergence of a large state-owned sector has not contributed much to changing the colonial structure.

The state-owned companies are normally run according to private profitability criteria just like the private-owned firms. This implies that the large wage differentials in the nationalized subsidiaries are not significantly reduced, and labour-intensive technologies are not introduced. Therefore, the nationalizations have not contributed much to reduce income inequalities and unemployment. The use of a private profitability criteria also implies that the manufacturing companies continue to produce the goods for which there is an effective demand, i.e. mostly luxury goods for a minority of the population.

The lack of coherent policies for using nationalization as a means of restructuring the economy can, to a large extent, be explained by the ruling elite's lack of real will to carry out such a restructuring. Almost all African quasi-socialist governments (e.g. the ones in Algeria, Libya, Somalia, Ethiopia, Tanzania, Guinea, Congo and Malagasy) are controlled by an educated elite mostly consisting of politicians and top government employees (including the military). They favour an expansion of the state-owned sector, but only to create a strong economic base for their political power.[8]

Although some of the quasi-socialist governments (especially Tanzanian) have taken steps to raise the incomes of the masses (e.g. by increasing the minimum wage in the modern sector), the income distribution is still very unequal with top government employees ranking highest. Generally, the quasi-socialist governments have had more success in coping with the multinationals than the capitalistic governments. They have a clearer view of the problems and more coherent policies, and they are less open to influence by local business interests and outright bribery. Therefore, they have had some success in reducing the cost of foreign investment, but have done little to change the unequal income distribution (which leads to demand for western luxury goods) and have maintained a preference for modern capital intensive technology.

Tanzania probably has done most to restructure the economy with the proclaimed aim of becoming an egalitarian and self-reliant society, but her policies, e.g. with regard to investment criteria and choice of technology, have not been quite clear or consistent.[9]

Because of their failure to restructure the economy, the quasi-socialist countries are still dependent on private foreign capital and technology. They can reduce the cost of these items somewhat by pursuing tight policies and by strengthening their bargaining position, e.g. by negotiating with a number of potential investors for a certain project and playing them off against each other but they cannot escape paying the minimum price for foreign capital. In addition, they cannot guard completely against distortion of the local economy by foreign investment, e.g. ousting of labour intensive enterprises causing increased unemployment.

A Socialist Alternative

Only consequent socialist policies can make it possible for the African countries to break the dependence on the multinationals, but in most African countries socialist revolutions are not very likely in the near future.

In the former Portuguese colonies the masses have gained relatively high ideological consciousness and large political influence due to their participation in the armed struggle against the colonial power. In these countries (especially in Guinea-Bissau) there is a possibility of pursuing socialist policies which may break the dominance of the multinationals. However, these countries are preoccupied now with reconstruction, so it is still too soon to tell which development strategy they will pursue in future. Until now they have pursued pragmatic policies towards the foreign-owned companies, and have carried out few nationalizations.

A similar situation may emerge within a few years in the South African areas which now have white minority rule. Like in the Portuguese colonies, black majority rule will probably only be achieved by a popular armed struggle which opens up the possibility of a transition to socialism.

If an African country opts for a socialist path, can it achieve economic development without relying on the multinational corporations? In order to answer this question we must have a look at the alternatives to private foreign capital and technology. These alternatives are not mere suppositions, but realistic ones, as they have been used (although not consistently) by Tanzania and other quasi-socialist countries.

The most obvious alternative is to rely on local capital and technology. In all African countries more capital can be mobilized, e.g. by taxation of high incomes and by reduction of unemployment. Foreign exchange for imports of machinery can be made available by cuts in imports of non-essential consumer goods.

In all African countries local artisans can produce almost all the consumer goods demanded by the masses (e.g. clothes, furniture and household utensils) by local technology, and this technology can be developed (preferably by co-operation among African countries) to satisfy growing needs.

It is very important for a socialist government to eradicate the political and economic privileges of the former upper class, and to prevent the emergence of a new bureaucratic elite with high salaries and excessive spending habits. This makes it possible to avoid use of foreign exchange for imports of Western luxury goods and establishment of foreign-owned companies for their production.

Conscious technology policies are an important element in a socialist development strategy. In many cases use of relatively simple labour intensive technology (often available locally) is less profitable, but has more favourable effects on the local economy (by creating more employment and by having larger backward linkages) than imported capital intensive technology. Use of labour intensive technology also promotes income equality and thereby directs effective demand towards the simple consumer goods produced by local technology.

A systematic use of labour intensive technology is dependent on use of social cost-benefit criteria instead of private profitability criteria for investment decisions. This means that investment decisions must be taken by the government according to an elaborate planning system (e.g. involving use of "shadow prices" for labour, etc.). Capital intensive and labour intensive enterprises may live in peaceful co-existence (as they do in China), but only where the capital intensive enterprises are not allowed to compete directly with the labour intensive ones and drive them out of business.

Labour intensive technology can be used in more sectors than is commonly believed, especially if the attractive appearance of the product is not given top priority. It can even be used for some kinds of mining where complex capital intensive technology normally is used. Thus in Sierra Leone, extraction of diamonds is not only carried out by a British subsidiary using capital intensive technology, but also by African diggers using simple tools. A few years ago it was calculated that the African diggers made a much larger contribution to Sierra Leone's national income than the British, because almost all the value of their gross output was retained in Sierra Leone, whereas a large part of the turnover in the British company was transferred abroad to pay for capital, equipment and management.[10]

In some sectors (e.g. in parts of the chemical industries) no efficient labour intensive technology exists. If an African socialist country wants to establish an enterprise in one of these sectors it must rely on foreign capital intensive technology. However, there are various possibilities of getting this without becoming dependent on the multinational corporations.

Technological know-how can be provided by a development assistance agency in a developed country. However, there are some limitations as the developed capitalist countries are hesitant to assist public-sector industries in developing countries. In industries using very sophisticated technology there are some additional problems in government-to-government transfer of technology. Firstly, use of such technology is often restricted by patents owned by private firms in the developed countries. Secondly, in industries using sophisticated technology the pertinent know-how is not vested in a single expert, but in a group of experts. Transfer of technology thus requires a team of experts with complemenetary skills. It is very difficult for a development assistance agency to recruit a complete team at one time, and if it is possible, such a team is handicapped by not being able to obtain technical advice from a parent company in a developed country.

United Nations Industrial Development Organization (UNIDO) can assist the African countries in industrial development by recruiting technical experts for them. However, the developed capitalist member countries of UNIDO have not been willing to finance the expansion of this activity to the extent desired, and UNIDO faces the same problems as the bilateral donor agencies with regard to transfer of sophisticated technology.

Countries with a large public industrial sector have the best chances to give government-to-government technical assistance. This also pertains to some of the relatively technologically advanced developing countries. Thus, Egypt gives technical assistance to industrial projects in other Arab countries, and India assists Tanzania in the same way.

The communist countries have even better possibilities of giving this kind of assistance, but have concentrated most of their assistance to a small number of developing countries in which they have a special political interest (e.g. Cuba and some of the Arab countries). Most African countries have benefited little from the assistance programmes of the European communist countries. China has given relatively much assistance to Africa (e.g. to Tanzania and Zambia), but her assistance capacity is limited by her own development needs.

Besides the problems of political interest and assistance capacity, there are some further limitations to the transfer of industrial technology from the communist countries. The African countries are not always interested in receiving this kind of assistance. The communist countries normally offer their assistance as a package deal including supply of machinery, experts, finance, etc., and some components of such packages (e.g. prices of machinery), which may be unacceptable to the African countries. They may also consider technology of communist countries inferior to that of Western countries.

The future economic potential of the communist countries and their political interest in Africa will greatly influence the possibilities of African socialist countries in obtaining industrial technology (including highly sophisticated technology) from the communist countries and thereby escape dependence on the multinationals.

A country's technology policy may influence which communist country it wants to get technical assistance from, since the European communist countries mainly transfer relatively capital intensive technology to developing countries, whereas China transfers primarily labour intensive technology.

Transfers from China therefore seem appropriate to African socialist countries pursuing egalitarian policies. But if China continues her strongly anti-Soviet foreign policies, she is likely to give a large part of her development assistance to only anti-Soviet governments (i.e. mostly highly pro-capitalistic governments), and this will reduce socialist countries' possibilities of getting Chinese assistance.

If an African socialist country cannot use one of the above-mentioned alternatives to private foreign investment and technology, it can try to find a way of co-operating with the multinationals which entails minimal dependence.

In general, licence agreements and management contracts imply less dependence than investments because they only run for an agreed period. However, renewal of the contract may be necessary, because the multinational firm often fails to transfer the core elements of its technology, or fails to train local counterparts to take over the posts of the foreign managers.

The managing agent often does not care to run the African enterprise efficiently if he has no financial interest in it, and he may cheat it deliberately, e.g. by selling it inputs at an inflated price. In general, management contracts entail a more serious dependence than licence agreements, but it is possible for multinational corporations to control vital elements of the activities of African enterprises through licence agreements. By virtue of their technological monopoly the licensers can also compel the African licensees to accept various restrictive clauses, e.g. a ban on exports which may compete with the exports of the licenser.

Thus, licence agreements and management contracts imply dependence on the multinationals and may be very costly to the African countries. If they make use of them, it is very important that they negotiate reasonable terms (e.g. an arrangement by which the remuneration of the managing agent is dependent on efficient management) and control as strictly as possible that the multinationals comply with the provisions of these contracts (e.g. in relation to transfer of core technology and training of local counterparts).

Today management contracts are common in Africa, especially in countries like Tanzania which try to reduce their dependence on foreign capital. In future, when the African countries get more educated technicians, economists etc. the relative importance of management contracts will probably diminish.

On the other hand, the importance of licence agreements (and similar technical cooperation contracts) may increase, at least in the oil exporting countries and in other countries with no need for importing capital. The multinationals prefer to have full control over the use of their technology in foreign countries, but a licence agreement may be acceptable to them because it represents an easy and safe way to earn money. The more nationalization takes place in Africa in future, the more the multinationals will want to transfer their technology to the African countries by way of licence agreements and similar contracts.

Some socialist developing countries consider that licence agreements imply too much dependence on multinationals. Therefore, they have provided for transfer of technology from developed capitalist countries in other ways, e.g. in connection with purchase of sophisticated machinery. Thus, in many cases China makes foreign purveyors of machinery train Chinese technicians and workers (at home or abroad) to master technical problems in the use of the machinery. This way of importing technology can also be used by African socialist countries.

Conclusion

From the preceding analysis of African policies on foreign investment one can try to predict how various factors will influence future activities of the multinationals in Africa.

The African countries are gradually getting more people with technical and managerial skills. This makes it possible for African governments to become less dependent on the multinationals by introducing tight policies on foreign investment and by nationalizing subsidiaries of the multinationals. Whether this will happen depends on the development strategy of the government, which in turn depends on its class composition.

It also depends on the future export earnings of the African countries. If Africa's terms of trade do not change significantly, most African countries will have serious deficits on their balance of payments in coming years. This may lead them to seek desperately for capital and make them liberalize their policies on foreign investment. However, a sudden liberalization is not likely to attract much foreign investment, since these policies can be reversed as soon as the balance of payments crisis is over. Sudden shifts in the investment policies of African countries will interest the multinationals in relatively risk-free engagements in Africa, e.g. licence and management contracts, as well as long-term contracts of sale for African mining products.

Only if liberalization of foreign investment is part of an apparently persistent change in economic policies (as in Egypt after 1970) is it likely to stimulate foreign investment significantly.

The activities of the multinationals will also be dependent on the degree of collaboration between the African states. The more free-trade arrangements among them, the more attractive it will be for the multinationals to invest. On the other hand, if the African countries have a real will to become more independent of the multinationals, regional co-operation will make it easier to undertake the research and investment programmes required for independent development.

A free-trade arrangement may lead to the member countries competing for foreign companies. This can be counteracted by introducing an industry allocation scheme which requires each member country to specialize in certain industries. Such close economic collaboration could strengthen considerably the position of the African countries vis-à-vis the multinationals, but it is not very likely to be carried out to any large degree, due to the difference in economic strength and in ideology among the African states.

There are some special factors which will influence the future of export-oriented investment by the multinationals in Africa. If commodity cartels become widespread, the African countries will restrict exports of commodities rather than expand them, and thereby limit investment opportunities in the primary sectors. Under all circumstances it is likely that there will be many investment opportunities in local processing of commodities. However, it is not certain that the multinationals will want to exploit these opportunities. Among other things, this will depend on the trade policies of the developed countries and on the state of their economy. The more booming it is, the more wages and demand for processed commodities will increase in the developed countries, and this will augment the willingness of the multinationals to install additional processing capacity in the developing countries.

Footnotes

1. Additional reasons for using over-invoicing are given in Sanjaya Lall, "Transfer pricing by Multinational Manufacturing Firms". *Oxford Bulletin of Economics and Statistics,* August 1973.
2. A study of a representative sample of the foreign-owned subsidiaries in the Colombian pharmaceutical industry showed that the amount transferred by over-invoicing was 24 times as high as the amount transferred by way of declared profits. *Policies Relating to Technology of the Countries of the Andean Pact: Their Foundations,* UNCTAD, TD/107/1971, pp. 15-16.
3. The milk powder case is described in Mike Muller, *The Baby Killer,* War on Want: London 1974.
4. Steven Langdon, "Multinational Corporations, Taste Transfer and Underdevelopment: A Case Study from Kenya", *Review of African Political Economy,* Number 2, 1975.
5. An example of this is given in *A Case Study of Choice of Techniques in Two Processes in the Manufacture of Cans in ILO: Employment, Incomes and Equality. A Strategy for Increasing Productive Employment in Kenya,* Geneva 1972.
6. These factors are described in Anthony Edwards, *The Potential for New Commodity Cartels,* QER Special No. 27, The Economist Intelligence Unit, London 1975.
7. *Proportion between Export Prices and Consumer Prices of Selected Commodities Exported by Developing Countries,* UNCTAD TD/184/Supp. 3, 1976, p. 11.
8. For an analysis of the interests of the ruling elite in Tanzania see Issa G. Shivji, *Class Struggles in Tanzania,* London 1976.
9. Tanzania's development strategy and policies on private foreign investment are described in Peter Neersø. "Tanzania's Policies on Private Foreign Investment", in Carl Widstrand (ed.), *Multinational Firms in Africa,* Scandinavian Institute of African Studies 1975.
10. Tony Killick, "The Developmental Impact of Mining Activities in Sierra Leone", in Scott R. Pearson & John Cownie, *Commodity Exports and African Economic Development,* Lexington 1974.

THE MULTINATIONAL CORPORATION IN THE

NIGERIAN ECONOMY

By Dr. W. Okefie Uzoaga*

Introduction:

The activities of multinational corporations in Nigeria may be traced to early 19th century but not until 1912 that twenty-seven foreign companies were legally incorporated in Nigeria. By 1958, 845 companies had been incorporated and of this less than 2 per cent were publicly owned and of their total issued capital less than 25 per cent was held by Nigerians. By 1969, the figure of registered public companies stood at 1320.

During the colonial period and since independence from British rule in 1960 multinational enterprises dominated the private sector of the Nigerian economy. Until the Second National Development Plan 1970—1974 the previous national development programmes seemed to have stuck to the best traditions of laissez faire policy and took little or no account of the scope and influence of the private sector although the sector encompasses vital developmental activities in such sectors as agriculture, mining and quarrying, manufacturing, building and construction, distribution, road transportation and general commercial services. In 1966—67 the sector contributed some 88 per cent of the gross domestic product. Of the total investment programme of N30 billion during the Third National Development Plan period 1975—1980, the private sector is expected to contribute N10 billion. Another index of its significance has been the amount of employment it generates. Some 95 per cent of the labour force are employed in private sector activities with agriculture alone accounting for some 70 per cent of the gainfully employed. But the nation's food import bill has been rising substantially from N62 million in 1970—71 to N131 million 1973—74. Similarly agricultural output has lagged behind the demand for raw materials by the industrial sector with the result that Nigeria has become a net importer of some of her traditionally export products like cotton and palm oil.

Nigeria is essentially an agricultural economy and until recently agriculture was the principal foreign exchange earner for the economy. The substantially increased earnings from crude-oil exports royalty and petroleum profits tax has not only displaced agriculture as a foreign exchange earner but has also placed Nigeria in a strong position to finance her development without reliance on foreign capital. Many economic indicators — the gross domestic product, money supply, exports and imports by 1974 had more than tripled. The rapid growth and spending power have emphasized the country's deficiencies in high-level manpower, handling capacities at the ports, housing, roads, water and electricity supplies. Despite the anti-inflationary measures imposed by the government on such heavily consumed items as bread, beer, fuel and soft-drinks; and other measures such as the wage freeze, dividend restriction and rent control, the annual rate of inflation is over 30 per cent.

The new financial strength based on oil revenue has encouraged Nigeria to launch an ambitious Development Plan 1975—1980 of N30 billion. In per capita terms income is projected to rise from an estimated N205 in 1974—75 at factor cost to about N250 at the end of the Plan period. The projected GDP growth rate as well as the sectoral growth rate over the Plan period is shown in Table I. The projected growth of agricultural sector is expected to make the country more self-reliant on food, regain some of raw material production for domestic industry and its

*Department of Finance, University of Nigeria, Enugu Campus, Nigeria

TABLE I

Annual Sectoral Growth Rates of the Gross Domestic
Product at 1974-75 Factor Cost

Per cent

Sector	1975-76	1976-77	1977-78	1978-79	1979-80	Average Annual Growth Rate 1975-80
1. Agriculture, Forestry and Fishing	3.5	5.0	5.5	5.5	5.5	5.0
2. Mining and Quarrying	5.1	5.2	5.4	5.5	5.6	5.3
3. Manufacturing and Crafts	10.4	15.9	18.7	21.2	23.8	18.0
4. Electricity and Water Supply	15.5	18.0	23.0	24.7	25.5	21.0
5. Building and Construction	14.4	18.6	20.5	23.0	24.0	20.1
6. Distribution	10.0	10.3	11.6	12.0	12.5	11.3
7. Transport and Communication . .	12.5	15.9	17.5	20.0	21.5	17.5
8. General: Government . .	15.0	15.0	20.0	20.0	20.0	18.0
9. Education	19.0	21.0	22.0	23.0	24.0	21.8
10. Health	18.0	19.0	21.0	21.0	21.0	20.0
11. Other Services	8.4	9.0	9.6	10.2	10.8	9.6
12. Aggregate Annual Growth Rate	7.2	8.5	9.8	10.6	11.5	9.5

Source: Culled from *Third National Development Plan* 1975-80 Vol. 1 p. 49

lost share of the export market. However, economic growth is expected to be led by those sectors where the planned public sector investment programme is concentrated such as education, power, health, building and construction, and manufacturing industry with average growth projected around 20 per cent per annum. The steady rise in the Manufacturing and Construction sectors is indicative of the structural changes initiated in 1970 and intended to consolidate and diversify the economy. The emphasis on Manufacturing represents one of the various attempts being made by Nigeria to correct the structural imbalance in her economy.

Colonial Pattern of Investment:

Developing countries like Nigeria were for sometime in their history colonies of a metropolitan country. Their earliest economic contact with the outside world started with trade. They served as producers of raw materials and the metropolitan countries as suppliers of manufactured products. This trade was dominated by subsidiaries of multinational companies based in the metropolitan countries. The pattern of foreign investments that resulted underscored investments in the extractive and distributive trade as against manufacturing industries. This unfortunate pattern of investment designed by transnational firms promoted a specialization based on a static scheme of comparative advantage. As appendages of industrialized economies such a pattern of investment diverted the developing countries into activities that offered less opportunities for technical progress. With independence from colonial tutelage these countries have realized that political independence without a strong prosperous economic base is meaningless in the context of modern power relationships. It would have been contradictory for developing countries to acclaim technological progress in industrialized countries at the same time that in their own countries they preserve oppressive economic structures and relationships tantamount to an aversion to technical knowledge.

Thus in Nigeria economic nationalism does not imply the restriction of international trade but the progressive elimination of foreign dominance in the national economy not only in terms of equity ownership but also in terms of managerial and technological control.

Structure of Ownership of Public Companies in Nigeria:

In 1970 a study of the distribution of ownership and corporate control of 1,320 public companies registered in Nigeria before 1969 was made.[1] The study attempted to show the equity holdings of various groups comprising Nigerian individuals, Nigerian institutions, expatriate individuals, and expatriate institutions. As shown in Table II expatriate individuals alone held almost 40 per cent of the value of total shareholdings as against Nigerian Individuals and Expatriate institutions which held some 32 and 20 per cent respectively. Nigerian institutions held less than 7 per cent of the value of total shareholding. Between them, Nigerian and Expatriate individuals held over 70 per cent of the shares of the value of £10,000 and below. Of all nominal shares Nigerian individuals held 54 per cent as against expatriate holdings of 41 per cent while Nigerian and Expatriate Institutions each accounted for only 2.3 per cent.

TABLE II

DISTRIBUTION OF SHAREHOLDING BY TYPE OF SHAREHOLDER AND VALUE OF SHARES HELD

Type of Shareholder Value of Share Held (£)	No.					percentage				
	NS	NI	ES	EI	Total	NS	NI	ES	EI	Total
1	6	140	6	107	259	2.3	54.1	2.3	41.3	100.0
Over 1- 1,000	18	249	77	341	685	2.6	36.4	11.3	49.8	100.1
1,001- 5,000	24	158	67	126	375	6.4	42.1	17.9	33.6	100.0
5,001- 10,000	4	58	44	80	186	2.2	31.2	23.7	43.0	100.1
10,001- 20,000	10	36	44	38	128	7.8	28.1	34.4	29.7	100.0
20,001- 50,000	26	21	61	67	175	14.9	13.0	34.9	38.3	100.1
50,001-100,000	19	9	49	31	108	17.6	8.3	45.4	28.7	100.0
Above 100,000	37	6	82	38	163	22.7	3.7	50.3	23.3	100.0
Total	144	677	430	828	2,079	6.9	32.6	20.68	39.82	100.0

Source: *The Nigerian Journal of Economic and Social Studies*, March 1972, p. 20.
Notes: NS — Nigerian institutions, i.e., government and government agencies and firms.
NI — Nigerian individuals
ES — Expatriate institutions, largely foreign firms.
EI — Expatriate individuals.

But as the value of shareholding increases above £5,000, Nigerian individual holdings lag behind Expatriate individual holdings. Thus above holdings of the value of £100,000 Expatriate individuals held 23.3 per cent compared to Nigerian individual holdings of some 3.7 per cent.

In all categories of shareholdings below the value of £20,000, Nigerian Institutional holdings accounted for less than 10 per cent. All other categories of shareholding stood between 15 and 23 per cent. Thus almost 60 per cent of the total holdings of Nigerian institutions were concentrated within this range. This is indicative of the important role which Nigerian institutions could play in large-scale business enterprises for which private indigenous capital is inadequate.

In relation to corporate control, as paid up capital increases, the holdings of Nigerian individuals drop more rapidly in contrast to Expatriate individual holdings. Thus Nigerian individuals have majority holdings only in 2.7 per cent of the companies with more than £100,000 paid-up capital as against 27.5 per cent for Expatriate individuals as shown on Table III.

Nigerian Institutions on the other hand accounted for less than 20 per cent of majority shareholdings in all categories of the study firms.

TABLE III

DISTRIBUTION OF MAJORITY SHAREHOLDING BY THE TYPE OF SHAREHOLDER AND SIZE OF FIRM'S PAID-UP CAPITAL

Type of Shareholder	Number					Percentage				
Size of Firm's Paid-Up Capital	NI	NS	EI	ES	Total	NI	NS	EI	ES	Total
Under 1,000	149	8	157	55	369	40.4	2.2	42.5	14.9	100.0
1,000- 5,000	102	8	98	7	215	47.4	3.7	45.6	3.3	100.0
5,001- 10,000	40	2	68	44	154	26.0	1.3	44.2	28.6	100.1
10,001- 20,000	27	4	36	28	95	28.4	4.2	37.9	29.5	100.0
20,001- 50,000	20	7	60	53	140	14.3	5.0	42.9	37.9	100.1
50,001-100,000	4	7	25	34	70	5.7	10.0	35.7	48.6	100.0
Above 100,000	4	27	41	77	149	2.7	18.1	27.5	51.7	100.0
Total	346	63	485	298	1,192	29.0	5.3	40.7	25.0	100.0

Source: Same as for Table II

In firms with paid-up capital of £50,000 or less, majority holdings by Nigerian institutions is generally below 5 per cent compared to Expatriate institutions with more than 48 per cent of majority shareholding on all categories of firms with paid-up capital of more than £50,000. In large scale enterprises Expatriate institutions held almost 52 per cent of all majority shareholdings.

The persistent lopsided ownership and control of the multinational firms, their stubborn rejection of decades of moral suasion by various governments of Nigeria to employ qualified Nigerians in managerial positions coupled with the lip-service they paid to staff training and development and their unreasonable pricing and wage policies, in time, impelled the Federal Government to intervene and "acquire and control on behalf of the Nigerian society, the greater proportion of the productive assets of the country".[2] The strategy has taken various forms. Among them are (i) equity participation in a number of strategic industries (ii) joint partnership with private foreign firms in industrial projects (iii) complete public ownership and control of very strategic industries.

In no case is nationalization contemplated but where it becomes necessary the government will pay compensation "in accordance with internationally accepted norms of equity and fair play".[3] In any form of partnership with private concerns the government would hold the controlling interest. Thus government activities are no longer limited to the public sector but

91

encompasses both sectors in a partnership controlled by the public sector. Only on these terms are existing and future enterprises required to operate.

The Nigerian Enterprises Promotion Decrees 1972 and 1977:

The most significant measure undertaken to dilute the dominance of multinational corporations in the Nigerian economy has been the Nigerian Enterprises Promotion Decree (promulgated in 1972 and re-enacted in 1977). Apart from introducing provisions necessary for the implementation of the second phase of the indigenization programme and enlargement and modifications of the Schedules of affected enterprises, the re-enacted version of the Decree differs from the 1972 Decree largely with respect to the provision for ownership and therefore control of the affected companies.

Under Schedule I of the Decree (1977) forty enterprises are exclusively reserved for Nigerian citizens or associations and no alien enterprises would be permitted to continue operation after December 1978. These are mostly service and light manufacturing enterprises such as advertising, distribution, dry-cleaning, poultry farming, printing, singlet manufacture, and hair-dressing. Under Schedule II of the Decree, unlike the 1972 version which reserved controlling interest to aliens, all enterprises in this category are now required, as a condition of their continuing operation in Nigeria, to sell not less than 60 per cent of their capital stock to Nigerian citizens or associations. Fifty-seven enterprises are affected and include banking, insurance, brewing, construction, mining, and aerial photography. Schedule III of the Decree lists thirty-nine enterprises in which at least 40 per cent equity participation of Nigerians is required. The effective date for compliance with the provisions of the Decree for enterprises in Schedules II & III was June 1977.

The Decree was received with mixed feelings. Nigerian nationals widely acclaimed it as a positive action on the part of the Federal Military Government to re-structure the private sector of the national economy and stimulate active participation of Nigerian citizens in the management and control of the supraterritorial enterprises that dominate it.

There is also the opportunity to foster employment and managerial responsibilities for Nigerians in their own country. With control, the barriers to technical training and staff development would be reduced. More importantly the pattern of investment has a better prospect of being related to national objectives. These expectations were reinforced with the willingness to share in the burdens and profits of these companies as evidenced by the over-subscription to the shares of these companies. For instance the Nigerian Bottling Company's shares were over-subscribed 3.6 times and R. T. Briscoe (Nigeria) Limited 6.5 times.[4] Approximately N103 million[5] was spent by Nigerians in market transactions involving the shares of multinational companies in 1973 and 1974.

On the other hand the multinationals do not appear to have shared the enthusiasm of Nigerians in the emerging relationship due to the assumption that indigenization is nothing other than a creeping nationalization. At least one well-known transational banking firm abhorred the whole idea of participation, closed its banking business and left the country.

Some of the leading transational firms made a run on their retained earnings and paid high dividend rates in 1971 or 1972 as shown on Table IV before they reluctantly complied with the provisions of the 1972 Decree.

Although the 1977 Decree requires that majority ownership stock holdings in Schedule II of enterprises be transferred to Nigerians, multinational firms would not likely pull out their investments from Nigeria because of several reasons. Among them are the heavy commitments of these companies to the firms in Schedule III of the Decree which are largely subsidiaries of the long-established transnational trading firms in Schedule II. Second, indigenization programme has not in anyway detracted from the list of generous investment incentives offered at present to industrial enterprises in Nigeria and embodied in five basic legal instruments.[6] In addition to these there are incentives of non-statutory nature such as the provision of Industrial Estates and the Approved Users Scheme under which manufacturers importing various inputs are charged concessionary rates or exempted from import duty.

TABLE IV

RATE OF DIVIDENDS PAID (1969-72) BY SOME PUBLIC COMPANIES IN NIGERIA

Company	1969 %	1970 %	1971 %	1972 %
Bata Nigeria Limited	20	51.25	66.67	101.54
Nigerian Breweries Limited	50	50	60	110
Lever Brothers Nigeria Limited	30	32	55	76
P.Z. & Co. (Nigeria) Limited	–	12.5	40	60
The Metal Box Co. of Nigeria Ltd	12.5	12.5	28[1]	12.5
R.T. Briscoe (Nigeria) Limited	10	25	40	260
Berger Paints Nigeria Limited	–	25	50	63[1]
Nigerian Bottling Company Ltd	20	75[1]	17.5	30
Vono Products Limited	20	20	60	50
Blackwood Hodge (Nigeria) Ltd	100	128	581	109
Costain (W.A.) Limited	16.5	33	33	130
Daily Times of Nigeria Limited	9	10.8	13.5	20
C.F.A.O. (Nigeria) Limited	7.5	45.8	35	18

Source: Uzoaga and Alozieuwa, *op cit,* Table VI

Thirdly Nigeria is the most populous country in Black Africa with a dynamic and large consumptive market which imports and domestic production have rarely satisfied. The persistent excess demand intensified by oil revenue is not likely to be ignored by existing and prospective foreign investors. Finally even where the multinational firms hold minority interest their influence on pricing, finance, marketing and their long-established world-wide contacts with suppliers may prove to be more crucial than diffused majority holding of outstanding stock.[7] Thus indigenization programme in Nigeria may yet be appreciated as an inducement to accelerate and give direction to true industrial development rather than a snare to entrap and destroy foreign ownership.

Most industrial activities in the country are merely assembly and not manufacturing industries since all the inputs are imported and merely put together behind the tariff wall. The country spent N130 million on beer imports last financial year and yet the beer brewing industry is one of the oldest industry in the country. This implies that this industry has not given much thought to expansion to meet rising local demand and the fact that beer can be profitably brewed in Nigeria from the fermentation of maize, guinea corn, millet and rice.

But unless re-directed this industry would be content with importing its hops, malt and bottles with little or no consideration for the foreign exchange costs to the economy and the possible contribution that could be made to the world at large if suitable local materials are developed and used to increase the world supply of the product.

The Roots of Conflict:

Transnational corporations have frequently drawn attention to the contributions they make to world economy through transmission of technological and managerial skill, acceleration of capital formation and stimulation of economic integration and employment. But in this effort the supraterritorial enterprises have penetrated the strategic sectors of national economies, challenged the sovereignty of host governments, created considerable imbalance in the distribution of economic benefits arising from their investments in the recipient countries, emasculated national industrial developments, encouraged unwholesome international division of labour and frustrated cooperation in the achievement of desirable national economic objectives. Although multinational in their operations they are essentially national in their ownership, control, management structures as well as ideology. They cannot therefore but be seen as colonialists with invisible flags — who strive to infuse their countries' economic philosophy and management theories into the host countries.

Indeed the multinational corporations have been able to breeze their way through the economies and dispositions of host countries largely because of the superiority of their capital resources, managerial and technological skill and collusive control of international markets. But no sooner the host countries are able to acquire some of these resources and apply restraint at least in self-defence, than conflicts and tensions develop and nationalism is made the scapegoat. But we have no evidence to show that under the terms and conditions transnational enterprises had operated any other organizations could not have operated and accumulated larger profits and contributed more considerably and humanely to world peace, capital formation, production, income and employment.

The basis of success of foreign investments by transnational corporations has been primarily due to their ability to secure the control of essential imported raw materials and foods; the markets for their manufactured products and the spheres for the investment of their capital. This has resulted in an interlocking system of control by a few governments and their enterprises over the government and economy of another country. To strengthen their system of control, multinational corporations vertically integrate alternative sources of raw materials or secure them by cartel arrangements.

Their foreign markets are considered necessary because of the profits they generate and because competitors must be prevented from rocking the oligopolistic balance. The profits from this system of control have accrued to the owners of capital and their governments. It would have been embarrassing if a host country failed to take measures such as idigenization of ownership and management of multinationals in Nigeria.

Since the conflicts and tensions that arise are as global as the operations of the multinationals themselves, it would appear that the much-vaunted contributions of the transnational corporations to the world economy could be improved in view of the world-wide concern over their unwholesome activities. Canada and Australia are no less concerned than France with the penetration of strategic sectors of their national economies and the consequences to their economic independence. Argentina, Nigeria and Ghana have attempted to restrict heavy foreign participation in basic sectors to the exclusion of national capital which tended to constrict technological and managerial developments. In Britain mounting fears of dominance in key sectors of the national economy are as real as Europe's fear of pre-emption of her financial and man-power resources to the point of economic and political subservience to the United States of America. The pricing policies of multinational oil-companies has for sometime now pitched the governments of OPEC-member countries against the oil consuming public and their governments.

Finally the struggle by multinationals for raw material concessions, contracts and markets have contributed immensely to the instability of governments in developing countries. It is against these problems that considerations of the future of multinational corporations should be directed.

The Future of Multinationals: Proposals.

State sovereignty is constantly being challenged by transnational enterprises since these enterprises dominate strategic sectors of host economies and their decisions have serious implications for the economy of a state. Where as in Nigeria the activities of subsidiaries of transnational companies are closely regulated by their headquarters in their home-countries it is not infrequent that the interest of the country is relegated to the background. For instance the persistent appeal for cooperation by the Nigerian government to contain inflationary pressures was honoured by multinationals with increased hoarding and sharp increases in prices of their products until stringent price control measures were introduced.

Since supranational firms are channels for transmission of their countries ideology and foreign policies they constitute potential instruments for abrogation of a host country's sovereignty. A host country is therefore rightly afraid — and there are many precedents to substantiate the fear of domination that could arise from the machinations of a multinational company.

However this danger of political interference could be reduced by internationalization of ownership and control; and regulation of the number and quality of expatriate managers assigned to subsidiaries of multinational companies in host countries. This would make multinationals truly international in ownership and control and thus reduce the conflict arising from fear of obstruction of national economic, political and cultural interests. The extent of the conflict between multinationals and host countries is a function of the type of management which in turn is influenced by the extent of mutualization of ownership.

But the desired result would not be achieved if after internationalization of ownership and management the role of the subsidiary is confined to execution of the policies handed down by the headquarters of the multinational. In other words the stringent controls by parent companies over their subsidiaries in respect of decisions on budgets, senior personnel, investments and new product programmes should be modified and entrusted to Boards of Directors and management in the host country. The self-interest of the multinationals demands that they create and sustain decisions and actions that reflect the objectives of the host country than those made by individuals far removed from the environment and perhaps with preconception of what should be good for the host country. The self-interest of the multinationals demands that they create and sustain favourable reputations in host countries desirous of economic development. In virtually all developing economies like Nigeria the colonial pattern of investment which denied the host territory of technical knowledge has been rejected. Hence it is not only a reasonable share of the benefits of industrial development but active participation in the cultivation and advancement of technical knowledge that developing host countries demand from multinationals. This explains the generous incentives in the forms of tax and depreciation concessions accorded industrial enterprises but denied commercial firms in Nigeria. To this may be added the availability of technical schools, institutes and universities.

It is not implied therefore that multinationals should, on sufferance, underwrite the cost of technical education for a host country. But where such basic facilities and other components of technical education exist, multinationals could play an important role in the transference of scientific technologies through overt support to scientific and technical education, and employment of the graduates in challenging positions that are most likely to stimulate their interests in advanced technologies.

Usually a management agreement entered into with multinationals provides for systematic training of nationals in all aspects of an industry. But more often than not such provision is honoured in breach than in observance. In other cases multinationals maintain discriminatory employment policies that favour their own nationals in technical and management positions. Failure of public appeals by labour unions and moral suasion by the government for self-regulation by multinationals finally led to the introduction of the Expatriate Quota Committee to regulate employment of aliens in Nigeria because the government found that it could not "continue to tolerate a situation in which high level Nigeria personnel educated and trained at great cost to the nation, are denied employment in their own country by foreign business establishments".[8]

Related to diffusion of technology by multinationals in host economies is the question of research and development. The role that subsidiaries of multinational companies could play in this regard is severely limited because of rigid centralization of this function at the home country of the parent company. Moreover multinationals are reluctant to use the services or organizations, institutions and individuals in the host country for better understanding of the environmental obstacles faced by the host country, its economic programmes, manufacturing costs and prospects of incorporating local products and adapting manufacturing techniques to local conditions. Policy changes by multinationals in this direction would mitigate the tension caused by imposition of foreign-based objectives on subsidiaries and host countries which rarely coincide with national economic objectives.

The concentration of investments on extractive industries and trading activities by multinationals in developing economies is reminiscent of colonial pattern of investment which attempted to create an international division of labour that subordinated personnel of the host economy to inferior production tasks while complex production functions were reserved to nationals of the metropolitan country. Such technological subordination by inhibiting balanced development is inimical to economic development and has attracted public policy measures in host economies. Multinationals can easily transfer technology and management expertise by extending substantial investment to manufacturing industries either directly or on joint basis with host governments rather than concentration on extractive industries and commerce.

While some level of inflation may be tolerated, the persistently upward inflationary pressure in the last ten years has proved disruptive to the Nigerian economy. Government measures to contain the gnawing inflation through monetary, fiscal, incomes and other measures have proved ineffective. Thus economic development efforts inspite of the oil revenue have suffered reverses as the country struggles to wriggle out of price instability at home coupled with heavy shortages of food and basic infrastructural facilities that must be imported at heavy foreign exchange costs.

One would expect that in situations such as this, multinational corporations would moderate their prices and support economic development efforts in the interest of public welfare and prospects for long-term profit. To exploit the low bargaining leverage of a host country at such times would merely serve to exacerbate tensions between the host government and the multinational companies. Granted that inflation is a world-wide problem, the multinationals are still better placed through their global strategies to restrain its effects but for their position as beneficiaries of inflationary conditions. This hardly enhances the contribution that multinationals could make to public welfare.

Profits repatriation and currency speculation represent another area of concern because of their unsettling effects on the balance of payments position of developing countries. Since multinationals deal in numerous currencies they are in advantageous position to hedge revaluations by forward purchases. The resulting capital flows make fixed parities difficult to maintain. In this way they could increase the weakness of currencies and set off a competitive currency revaluation among countries. But for the oil revenue the rate of profits repatriation from Nigeria during the period preceding the implementation of the Indigenization Decree particularly in 1971 and 1972 would have set off balance of payments crisis as some multinationals especially in the extractive and construction industries depleted their distributable earnings up to 94 per cent to pay large dividends to shareholders most of whom were expatriates. The depletion of retained earnings in this manner and its possible effects on capital resources and on expansion programmes and the balance of payments, attracted public policy measure that has since restricted dividend payments to 30 per cent. This is another example of how multinationals could invite government intervention to control their activities.

Another aspect of the activities of multinationals is the speed and magnitude to which they have carried their much-vaunted marketing capability to corrupt public officials, inspire mutual suspicions and wreck host governments in the process of selling their goods or services.

The alarmingly scandalous deals by multinationals in Japan, Sweden, Zaire and Ghana to name a few — raise questions as to the reliability of multinationals to contribute to the ideals of business ethics fair competition and stability in host countries.

In sum, given the contributions that multinationals have made and can make to the world economy, the constraints they experience in host countries are essentially induced by their own predispositions and indiscretions. The cosmopolitan stance multinationals expect from host countries must be preceded by correction of their own built-in nationalistic ownership and control of their resources, and policy changes on their part to serve not as demonstrators of, but as key instruments for diffusion of technological knowledge and managerial expertise.

The true measure of the efficiency of multinationals would derive from their adaptation of technical knowledge and managerial expertise to diverse environments in which they operate as well as from equitable dispersal of corporate ownership and control.

Thus the restructuring of the monocentric transnationals and adaption of their operations to national objectives of host countries could whittle down most of the tensions and conflicts. The result would be the enlargement of the returns which would rebound to the mutual benefit of both parties and the world economy. Conversely, the propensity of multinationals to dominate a host country's economy would attract more restrictive measures and thus reduce further the potential benefits of mutual cooperation.

References

1. Bailey, R. "International Corporations and Developing Countries", *National Westminister Bank Quarterly Review* August 1970.
2. Baranson, J. "Technology Transfer Through the International Firm", *American Economic Review,* 60, May 1970.
3. Barovick, R. L. "Congress Looks at the Multinational Corporation", *Columbia Journal of World Business,* 5 November, 1970.
4. Bohrman, J. N. *Some Patterns in the Rise of the Multinational Enterprise,* Chapel Hill: University of North Carolina Press, 1969.
5. ————————— "Promoting Free World Economic Development Through Direct Investment", *American Economic Review,* 50, May 1970.
6. Brook, M. C. & Ranmers, H. L. *The Strategy of Multinational Enterprise: Organization and Finance,* London: Longmans, 1970.
7. Dunning, J. H. (Ed) "Capital Movements in the Twentieth Century" *Studies in International Investment,* London: George Allen and Unwin, 1970.
8. Fayerweather, J. (Ed) *International Business Policy and Administration,* New York: The International Executive, 1976.
9. ————————— *International Business Management: A Conceptual Framework,* New York: McGraw-Hill, 1969.
10. Federal Republic of Nigeria: *Second National Development Plan,* 1970–1974, Lagos: Federal Ministry of Information, 1970.

11. Federal Republic of Nigeria: *Third National Development Plan* 1975 – 1980, Lagos; Federal Ministry of Information, 1975.

12. Gordon, W. L. *A Choice for Canada: Independence or Colonial Status,* Toronto: The Canadian Publishers, 1966.

13. Holbik, K. "Canada's Economic Sovereignty and United States Investment", *Quarterly Review of Economics and Business,* 10, 1970.

14. Hoskins, W. R. "The LDC and the MNC: Will They Develop Together", *Columbia Journal of World Business,* 6 September, 1971.

15. Litvak, I. A. *et al* (ed.): "Foreign Investment in Canada", *Foreign Investment: The Experience of Host Countries,* New York: Praeger, 1970.

16. Moyer, R. "British Attitudes Toward U.S. Direct Investments", *MSU Business Topics,* 18, 1970.

17. Mikerell, R. F. (ed.) *Foreign Investments in the Petroleum and Mineral Industries: Case Studies on Investor – Host Country Relations,* Baltimore: The John Hopkins Press, 1971.

18. Mummery, D. *The Protection of International Private Investment: Nigeria and the World Community,* New York: Praeger, 1968.

19. Nehrt, L.C. and Uzoaga, W.O. *Management Policy, Strategy and Planning for Nigeria,* Nigeria: Nwamife Press, 1977.

20. Nigerian Economic Society, *Nigeria's Indigenization Policy,* Ibadan: Caxton Press, 1974.

21. Penrose, E. T. *The Large International Firm in Developing Countries: The International Petroleum Industry,* London: George Allen and Unwin, 1969.

22. Peters, E. W. *A Financial Invasion: The Take-Over of Australia,* Australia: Gobi Press Print, 1968.

23. Robinson, R. D. *International Business Policy,* New York: Holt and Winston, 1964.

24. Safarian, A. E. *Foreign Ownership of Canadian Industry,* Toronto: McGraw Hill, 1966.

25. Shaker, Frank "The Multinational Corporation: The New Imperialism?", *Columbia Journal of World Business,* 5, November, 1970.

26. Teriba, et al "Some Aspects of Ownership and Control of Business Enterprises in a Developing Economy: The Nigerian Case", *The Nigerian Journal of Economic and Social Studies,* March 1972.

27. Vernon, R. *Sovereignty at Bay: The Multinational of U.S. Enterprises,* New York; Basic Books, 1971.

28. ——————— "Foreign Enterprises and Developing Nations in the Raw Materials Industries," *The American Economic Review,* 60, May 1970.

29. ——————— "Multinational Enterprise and National Sovereignty," *Harvard Business Review,* 45, March 1967.

30. Uzoaga, W. O. & Alozieuwa, J.U. "Dividend Policy in an Era of Indigenization", *The Nigerian Journal of Economic and Social Studies,* November 1974.

31. ——————— "Earnings and Dividends of Selected Companies in Nigeria", *The Journal of Management Studies* (Ghana), Vol. 8, No. 1, March 1976.

32. "U.S. Investment in Europe", *Barclays Bank Review,* 44, May 1966.

33. Wolfe, R.D. "Modern Imperialism: The View from the Metropolis", *American Economic Review,* 60, May 1970.

Footnotes

1. Teriba, et al, "Some Aspects of Ownership and Control Structure of Business Enterprises in a Developing Economy: The Nigerian Case", *The Nigerian Journal of Economic and Social Studies,* March 1972, pp. 3-26.

2. Republic of Nigeria, *Second National Development Plan 1970 – 1974,* Federal Ministry of Information (Lagos) 1970, p. 289.

3. *Ibid,* p. 289.

4. Uzoaga, W.O. & Alozieuwa, J.W., "Dividend Policy in an Era of Indigenization," *The Nigerian Journal of Economic and Social Studies,* November 1974, p. 469.

5. The Nigerian Economic Society, *Nigeria's Indigenization Policy,* The Caxton Press (Ibadan), 1974, p. 2.

6. These legal instruments comprise the (i) Industrial Development (Import Tax Relief) Act of 1958; Industrial Development (Import Duties Relief) Act of 1957; Customs Duties (Dumped & Subsidized Goods) Act of 1958; Customs (Draw Back) Regulations of 1958; and Income Tax (Amendment) Act of 1958.

7. Nehrt, L.C. and Uzoaga, W.O., *Managerial Policy, Strategy and Planning for Nigeria,* (un-published manuscript) 1976.

8. Second National Development Plan, *op. cit.,* p. 289.

ASIA

The Role of Multinational Corporations in Taiwan's Future Economy.

By: Dr Tingko Chen

I. Records of Economic Performance

Taiwan is an island with 14,000 square miles, a 16.1 million population and very limited natural resources, and, therefore, the people depend greatly on international trade and investment to become a modern country. During the past twenty-three years, we have devoted our efforts to the industralization and diversification of foreign trade. Perhaps many of you have already known part of the story of Taiwan's successful economic development, however we still would like to brief its growth performance as the preface to discussing the activities of multinational corporations in the Taiwan economy.

A.   GNP Growth

Taiwan's development program implemented by the present Administration in the past twenty-three years has brought about major change in the size and structure of our economy. For the first decade from 1953 to 1962, the average annual growth rate of Gross National Product (GNP) was 7.2 percent in real terms, while in the second decade from 1963 to 1972, it increased to 10.4 percent. The national economy grew by 12.3 percent in 1973, 0.6 percent in 1974, and 2.81 percent in 1975. The low growth in the last two years was affected by the unfavorable international economic situation.

B.   Change of Economic Structure

The general index of agricultural production rose by 153 percent between 1952 and 1975, at an average growth rate of 4.2 percent each year. The industrial growth was much more impressive; its general index rose by 20 times in the 1952-1975 period at an average annual growth rate of 14.3 percent. Last year's rate of industrial growth was 5.8 percent, an upturn from the negative growth of 1.5 percent in 1974. With industrial output increasing at a much faster rate than agricultural output, Taiwan's economic structure has changed. In 1975, industry accounted for more than 35 percent of the total employment and 36.3 percent of the net domestic product compared to only 18 percent in 1952. On the other hand, the contribution of the agricultural sector to the net domestic product dropped to 16.3 percent in 1975 from 36 percent in 1952. The average growth rate in agricultural sector was 4.2% in the 1952-1975 period, much lower than the industrial growth. This proves a simple fact that the past industrialization program really worked.

C.   Growth of International Trade

International trade is another aspect which deserves our attention. Based on the statistics compiled by the Taiwan's Customs Authority, our total foreign trade (import and export) in 1975 amounted to US$11.25 billion, an increase from US$303 million in 1952 or about 37 times growth. The average annual growth rate in the last seven-year period from 1969 to 1975 was more than 30 percent. Although we suffered from the negative trade growth in 1975, which

*Professor of Business Administration, National Taiwan University, Taiwan, ROC

had a minus rate of 5.6% in exports and 14.8% in imports, 1976 has been better. It is estimated that the total trade for 1976 will reach US$13.1 billion, an increase of 16%. We are proud that our international trade in this small island with 16.1 million population is much larger than that in the Chinese mainland with more than 700 million population.

D. Trade Surplus and Deficits

A trade surplus was observed in the 1971-73 period: US$216.5 million for 1971; US$474.6 million for 1972; and US$690.9 million for 1973. Because of the high priced import materials needed by our processing industries in 1974, we incurred a trade deficit of US$1326.7 million in 1974 and of US$642.9 million in 1975. However, the three consecutive monthly surpluses of the first quarter in 1976 has definitely reversed the deficit trend.

As far as the trading areas are concerned, the U.S. is our largest trade partner whereas Taiwan ranks 10th in the US trade statistics. We are confident that this position will be upgraded to the 7th in the next few years. In spite of the fact that we are pursuing growth of international trade as the main outlet of our economic growth, we are trying every effort to balance imports and exports with our trading partners. This effort has brought in positive results as the gaps of Taiwan's surplus against US and deficit against Japan are narrowing year by year.

E. Economic Stability

In the process of economic growth, Taiwan was also able to maintain a large measure of economic stability. Between 1966 and 1972, wholesale prices moved up by only 1.8 percent a year and consumer prices by 3.9 percent, even though this remarkable record was somewhat shattered by 1973's inflations of 22.8 percent in wholesale prices and 11.3 percent in consumer prices. Despite 1973-74's world-wide inflation, Taiwan's Economic Stabilization Program, implemented in January 1974, had immediately achieved its original goal by bringing down wholesale prices 6.3 percent and consumer prices 2.2 percent from March to June 1974. In December 1975, the wholesale prices had dropped 0.6% and consumer prices rose only 0.25%, comparing with those of the same month in 1974. We are optimistic that this expected stability will facilitate further economic growth in the future.[1]

II. Foreign Capital Formation

A. Contributing Factors of Economic Growth

The above mentioned economic performance in Taiwan had been carefully reviewed by a group of world-wide renowned business leaders in a seminar on "Taiwan: A Booming Economy" sponsored by the International Management Association, U.S.A. and China Productivity Center in Taipei, March 1974. They have summarized the following factors as the principal contributing forces to Taiwan's economic growth:

1. successful implementation of the land-to-the-tiller Land Reform Program which laid a strong foundation for agricultural development and benefited the largest sector of the economy;
2. enforcement of an orderly and progressive industrial development policy from light and labor-intensive industries to chemical, heavy, and technology-intensive industries;
3. efficient and effective use of US$1.5 billion American economic aid and US$1 billion Export-Import Bank loans and credit guarantees;
4. encouragement of foreign and domestic private investment;
5. active expansion and diversification of foreign trade;

6.   a stable political and social environment, without the frequent changes in political leadership; and

7.   abundant supply of high quality labor, who are skillful, friendly, intelligent, and eager to make progress.[2]

B.   US Economic Aid

Among these factors we can see the importance of foreign capital formation to the overall progress in Taiwan. The U.S. Aid started in 1949 and terminated in July 1965. The total amount of US$1.5 billion in this period played a very critical role in Taiwan's early economic development; it accounted for as much as 40 percent of Taiwan's total capital formation and sustained an average annual economic growth rate of 7.2 percent. Most of the U.S. Aid was used to upgrade Taiwan's basic industries and infra-structure.

C.   Investment Laws

In the post-aid period, the Government of the Republic of China in Taiwan created a highly favorable climate for private investments. Two most important laws to help create the investment climate, the Statute for the Investment by Foreign Nationals and the Statute for the Encouragement of Investment. The first Act has the following major features:

1.   permission to remit profit and accrued interest as well as repatriate invested capital out of the ROC in the original currency of the foreign investment;

2.   guarantee against expropriation for 20 years on all approved foreign investments, and fair and reasonable compensation for expropriation afterwards, if any;

3.   permission for foreign investors to wholly own the company in which they invested; and

4.   enjoyment of the same treatment as that accorded to similar enterprises established by Chinese nationals.[3]

The second Act extends tax incentives to both domestic and foreign investors, for example, (a) five-year business income tax holiday or accelerated depreciation of equipment; (b) exempted, deferred, or installment payment of import duty on capital equipment; and (c) bonded, written-off, or rebated import duty on raw materials for re-export purposes.[4]

D.   Earlier Inflow of Foreign Direct Investment

Before the Statute for the Encouragement of Investment was promulgated in 1960, five years before the foreseeable termination of U.S. economic aid, the foreign private investment in Taiwan was very minimal. In the year 1952 five Overseas Chinese investment projects of US$1 million landed in Taiwan. The next year, that is 1953, we saw two real foreign nationals' projects of US$1.6 million invested in Taiwan. From 1952 to 1960, the foreign investment, including both Overseas Chinese and foreign national projects, totalled 86 cases and amounted to some US$36.6 million, averaging less than US$4 million per year. In other words, in 1960, the total foreign investment only accounted less than 2 percent of Taiwan's fixed capital formation of US$10.4 billion.

Since 1960, the foreign direct investment reached a higher level than before. From 1961 to 1965, the year of U.S. Aid termination, the total foreign investment projects was 210 cases with US$67 million, averaging US$13.4 million per year, three times the previous period's record.

E.   Pouring of Foreign Capital

After the United States discontinued its economic aid in 1965, the foreign private investment projects attracted by favorable investment climate and economic performance started to pour in in great scale into Taiwan to replace the role played by the U.S. Aid. In December 1975, the cumulative total of foreign investments in Taiwan since 1952 had reached the mark of 2,188 cases with US$1,405 million. Out of this amount, Overseas Chinese capital accounted for 1,231 cases of US$410 million, or roughly one-third of the total, and the remaining US$995 million, or two-third of the total, were from the United States, Japan, and Europe. From 1969 to 1975, the foreign direct investment almost accounted for 10 percent of Taiwan's fixed capital formation, although the cumulative amount since 1952 to 1975 had only represented about 5 percent of the total capital formation. Its role of capital formation was much more important than that in 1950s in terms of relative and absolute senses. It helped Taiwan's economy grow at an average annual rate of 10.4 percent during the post-aid period, much higher than 7.2 percent in the early period.

Despite the monetary turmoil and world-wide inflation tide in 1973-1974, foreign direct investments were still coming to Taiwan. In 1974-1975, 253 new investment cases were approved at the value of US$305 million.

F.   Analysis by Investing Country

During the past twenty-three years from 1952 to 1975, a total of 253 investment projects worth US$470 million originated from the United States while investment projects from Japan, numbering 594, amounted to US$215 million. Investment from Europe did not start coming to Taiwan until 1964. Up to 1975, a total of 42 Europe investment projects worth more than US$161 million had been approved. There was 68 investment projects involving US$140 million from other parts of the world, part of which were made by the overseas subsidiaries of American firms. Therefore, American investments in Taiwan actually constituted more than half of all foreign direct investments combined up to the end of 1975. The new investment projects in 1976 are also mainly shared by the American and European companies.

G.   Analysis by Invested Industry

Up to 1975, foreign investments in the electronics-electrical industry have been most active. About 43.3% of the total foreign investment have been devoted to this particular sector. The other important sectors invested by foreign firms are chemical industry, machinery equipment and instrument industry, and metal products industry. Foreign investments in these three industries accounted 38.2 percent of the total amount. The remaining 18.5% were allocated to other industries, such as textile, services (hotels), finance and insurance, construction transportation, etc.

III.   Operating Experiences of Multinational Corporations

A.   Subsidiaries of Multinational Corporations

Most of the American, European, and some of the Japanese investment projects in Taiwan are the subsidiaries of major multinational corporations, while the Overseas Chinese and most Japanese investments are done by relatively small firms or individuals who do not have big scale foreign operations in many countries. Up to 1974, the survey result indicated that the minority joint-ventures of the foreign investment in Taiwan were 28.4% of the total cases approved, while the majority joint-ventures and wholly-owned investments were 45.2% and 26.4% respectively.[5] The following firms are among the major American multinational companies with direct investment in Taiwan:

·   Admiral Corp. (radios, TV sets, phonograph chassis)
·   American Cyanamid Co. (pharmaceuticals, feeds)

- Atlas Chemical Industries Inc. (dynamite)
- Bendix Corp. (radios)
- Bristol-Myers Co. (nutritional and pharmaceutical products)
- Bulova Watch Co. (watch cases)
- Cornell-Dubilier Electronics Corp. (capacitor)
- Corning Glass Works (electronic TV bulbs)
- Dow Chemical Co. (chemical products)
- Du Pont Co. (chemical products)
- Eli Lily & Company (pharmaceuticals)
- General Instrument Corp. (electronic components)
- Gulf Oil Corp. (lubricants)
- Hewlett-Packard Co. (electronics)
- IBM (memory planes, punched cards)
- Mattel Inc. (toys)
- Minnesota Mining & Manufacturing Co. (industrial & electric tape & ribbon)
- Motorola International Development Corp. (electronic components, TV sets)
- National Distillers & Chemical Corp. (polyethylene)
- Parks David & Co. (pharmaceuticals)
- Pfizer Pharmaceuticals Corp. (pharmaceuticals)
- Philco Corp. (radios, TV sets, phonographs)
- RCA (memory planes, IC, TV sets)
- Singer Manufacturing Co. (sewing machines)
- Sprague Electric Co. (capacitors)
- Texas Instruments Inc. (electronic components, IC)
- TRW Inc. (capacitors, IFT, coils)
- U.S. Time Corp. (watches & components)
- Union Carbide Corp. (petrochemicals)
- World Tableware Corp. (stainless steel tableware)
- Zenith International Inc. (TV sets)
- Ford Motor Co. (vehicle, parts & components)
- Goodyear Tire & Rubber Co. (tires)
- ITT (electronics and communication)
- Eight Major US Banks (Citibank, Bank of America, American Express, Chase Manhatten Bank, Chemical Bank, Continental Bank, Irving Trust, and United California Bank)

The following Japanese multinational firms are also among the firms having direct investments in Taiwan:

- Canon Inc. (camera, electric table calculators)
- Hitachi Ltd. (electronic tubes, TV sets)
- Matsushita Electric Industries Co. (electrical appliances)
- Mitsubishi Electric Corp. (fluorescent lamp, transformers)
- Mitsubishi Rayon Co. (synthetic fiber)
- Nippon Electric Co. (communication equipment)
- Sanyo Electric Co. (electrical appliances)
- Sharp Corp. (TV sets)
- Takeda Chemical Industries Ltd. (pharmaceuticals)
- Teijin Ltd. (synthetic fiber)
- Tokyo Shibaura Electric Co. (transformers, fluorescent lamps)

- Tokyo Bearing Manufacturing Co. (ball bearings)

The representative European multinational firms investing in Taiwan are like the following:

- Bauer & Sun Optical Co. (camera lense, camera parts)
- German Development Corp. (pharmaceutical)
- N.V. Philips (electronics)
- Titan Manufacturing Co. (tungsten carbide tools)

Most of the foreign investors have their own success stories. They have made significant contributions to Taiwan's economy while at the same time become prosperous themselves. It is impossible to report the operating experience and activities of these multinational firms in Taiwan; however, for your reference we would like to cite several cases representing different types of examples.

B. Competition Challenge and Technology Transfer

Case number one is the Singer-Taiwan Company. Singer applied to build a factory in central Taiwan in 1963, when the local sewing machine producers just started to turn out self-made products for domestic consumption. The quality of the locally made products was generally low and some of the vital parts still had to be imported. Understandably, the local firms strongly objected on the grounds that they were too weak to compete with Singer's long reputed image and quality and efficiency. However, the government believed that unless the quality of local products substantially improved, chances to export in large scale would be very limited and therefore development of sewing machine industry in Taiwan would be impossible.

Clearly understanding the problems faced by the local firms, Singer assured that it would assist local producers to improve their products and to help them get access to the world market. The government approved this investment project, Singer-Taiwan really offered technical assistance to local suppliers to make sewing machine parts. Singer's local competitors also obtained similar parts from the aided suppliers and therefore their products were greatly improved. Stimulated by quality improvement, the local firms became friends of Singer and followed suit to improve their management system and production facilities.

Export sales of Taiwan sewing machines rose from about US$40,000 in 1963 to well over US$5 million in 1968, and more than US$40 million in 1975. The major portion of the sales were made by local manufacturers rather than Singer-Taiwan. This is a typical case about a multinational firm's subsidiary catalyzing the development of local industry through technology transfer and challenge of competition.

C. Import Substitution and Management Development

Case number two is the Eli Lily-Taiwan Company. Lily-Taiwan, established in 1967, is one of the non-export oriented firms in Taiwan similar to the subsidiaries of Goodyear, Foremost, Scott Paper, Cargill and Ford. Though Lily-Taiwan's approximately 40 pharmaceutical products are sold in Taiwan, it still exports about 20 percent of products. Prior to 1967, Lily products had been sold in Taiwan more than 15 years through appointed import agent. In 1972, it obtained government approval to expand the scope of business to include several animal husbandry products: A plant was constructed for that purpose and this second operation went on stream in May 1973. In addition to these two manufacturing operations, Lily International sells through two appointed agents products that are not made by Lily-Taiwan. Therefore Lily is not only multinational in manufacturing but also in marketing products manufactured in the U.S.A. Lily-Taiwan is very satisfied with its operations in Taiwan and Taiwan has also benefited from its operations.

Some of the export-oriented American firms that are in labor-intensive industries have faced the pinch of a shortage of workers. However Lily-Taiwan has not experienced this problem since over 75 percent of its employees in Taiwan are college graduates and MBAs. As a matter of fact, Lily-Taiwan helps the economy not only through reducing importation of needed pharmaceutical products but also through training the young qualified people which may be the important candidates for operating local firms when they leave the Lily-Taiwan.

D. Export Creation and Capital-Intensive Investment

Case number three is about Philips-Taiwan Ltd. In order to maintain overall positions in the world, N.V. Philips of Holland selected Taiwan as one of the strong bases to build its multinational kingdom. This is simply because it considered that Taiwan would play a major role in the goods movement from the Far East to the United States, Europe, and other parts of the world. As far back as 1966, Philips-Taiwan built a shop in the Kaohsiung Export Processing Zone starting to manufacture matrices for computer memories, an activity which is still working at top capacity today. Some other items such as capacitors, carbon film resistors, and integrated circuits have been added to the product lines.

In 1969, Philips-Taiwan set up another cathode ray tube facility in the northern part of Taiwan in order to be closer to the prospective customers. There were 170,000 pieces of picture tube produced in 1971. These totals grew to 750,000 pieces in 1972, 2 million in 1973, and 3 million in 1975. Of these quantities Philips-Taiwan export approximately 25% to Europe and 15% to third parties in the Far Eastern and South Asia area. In other words, about 60% of the production remains on this island mainly to be used in television sets manufactured here for export.

Philips-Taiwan also has a third investment project of a glass plant together with the picture tube plant. Obviously, Philips-Taiwan has a lot of reasons to enter into the capital-intensive project, which is contrary to the ordinary electronic assembly plant which needs a lot of inexpensive labor forces. Philips counts quality of the labor and the discipline and flexibility with which they are prepared to work as the key opportunity to use the most up-to-date expensive equipment for more hours during a day than usual in other countries. Right now Philips-Taiwan has more than 3,700 employees.

E. Wholly-Own-Turned Public Company

Case number four is about National Distillers and Chemical Corporation (NDCC) of New York City. NDCC established a wholly-owned subsidiary, the USI Far East Corporation, in 1965 to produce 72 million pounds of low-and-medium density polyethylene (PE) resins per year. At the beginning, USI Far East had to export 70% of its total production to Southeast Asia countries. But due to the rapidly increasing demand and fast expansion of the PE processing industry in Taiwan, a double expansion in 1974 of the production capacity can barely meet the domestic requirement.

USI Far East is the first foreign investment project to become a profitable public company, when in 1972 it sold 6 million new shares, about 50% of the equity, to the Chinese public.

In addition to the double expansion of the USI Far East's original low density PE capacity in 1974, National Petrochemical Corporation of USA, an equally owned subsidiary of NDCC and Owens Illinois, Inc., joined with Chinese and Beligum investors to set up the United Polymers Corporation (UPC) with the purpose to produce high density PE at the annual capacity of 25,000 MT.

F. Multi-Stage Diversified Investment

Case number five is about Gulf Oil Corporation. Gulf has three investment projects in Taiwan. In 1963 it participated in a joint investment with the Chinese Petroleum Corporation, a government owned enterprise, to form the China Gulf Oil Company to manufacture lubricants and related products for the domestic market and for export. The second investment project with local partners was the establishment of China Gulf Plastics Corporation to produce plastics products for domestic and foreign markets. The third venture, Gulf Oil Company of China, in partnership with the Chinese Petroleum Corporation is now conducting exploratory drilling off the coast of Taiwan, where surveys have indicated the possibility of petroleum deposits. One of the four wells drilled has already discovered abundant natural gas. More wells are programmed to be drilled to confirm the discovery.

There are too many successful examples of multinational operations in Taiwan to report in this occasion. The purpose of citing the above five cases is to show a representation of multi-dimensionality of the multinational firms in Taiwan.

IV. Contributions of Multinational Corporations

A. Capital Formation Contribution

The contributions of multinational firms through their direct investments in Taiwan are multifaced. First of all, the capital inflow of more than US$1.4 billion constitutes about 5 to 10 percent of Taiwan's fixed capital formation in recent years. It compensates the gap of needed investment which helps sustain the remarkable economic growth at average rate of 10 percent per year.

B. Employment Opportunity Contribution

Investment projects will create employment opportunities. The 1974 survey on the operations of foreign invested firms indicated that about 250,000 of work force had been employed, which was about 4.61% of the total national employment opportunities of 5.3 million or 16.41% of the manufacturing labor forces of 1.4 million. This means that if there is not any foreign investment, Taiwan's manufacturing industry, the key sector of the economy, will have to face a more than 16.4 percent unemployment rate. Although the figure of 16.4 percent may not be so big as that in other heavily foreign-invested country like Canada or Australia, the importance of this contribution is generally recognized.

C. Gross National Product Contribution

The survey result indicated that the foreign invested firms produced about US$900 million in 1974, which could be counted for 6.24% of Taiwan's GNP, or 15.7% of the manufacturing industry's production value. This contribution is parallel to that in the employment opportunities.

D. Balance-of-Payments Contribution

Since more than half of the US$1.4 billion foreign investment up to 1975 was in export-oriented industries such as electronic-and-electric industry, textile industry, and machinery equipment and instrument industry, the multinational firms have contributed in great extent to Taiwan's trade surplus since 1970. In 1974, the foreign firms exported US$1,611 million of products to foreign markets and imported US$886 million of parts from other countries. Therefore, they contributed about US$725 million to the net balance of payment. In other words, in every dollar the foreign invested firm sold, about 55% was used to buy parts from abroad and 45% was earned for Taiwan. The export of US$1,611 million in 1974 was counted about 29.2% of the total national export in the same year, a relatively high mark to be appreciated. Foreign direct investments contribution in trade surplus together with capital inflows lead Taiwan's Central Bank to enjoy more than US$1.7 billion international reserve, despite trade deficits in 1974 and 1975.

E.   Taxation Contribution

However, there is no surprise that the multinational firms in Taiwan have not contributed much to the local government's public revenue (taxes) so far since most of them have taken the advantage of five-year income tax holiday treatment encouraged by the Statue for the Encouragement of Investment. Nevertheless, when the tax holiday is expired, their obligation of paying taxes will be resumed and the so-called "public revenue effect" will start to work. In 1974, the foreign firms paid more than US$56 million for corporate income taxes, counted about 26.53% of the national income taxes collected by the government.

F.   Technology Transfer and Growth Effect

The most important and durable contribution of the multinational firms to the local society is the transfer of technology. To the local society, the impacts of capital inflow, employment opportunity, import substitution, export creation, and taxation payment accompanying the multinational firms are all temporary contributions in a relative sense. Only the imports of engineering and management technologies can produce an unlimited long-range growth effect. There has been a criticism that most export-oriented multinational firms are interested only in Taiwan's cheap labor, therefore their subsidiaries are essentially the assembly plants, in which not much technology is involved. This argument is telling a partial story and only valid to those electronic firms which usually import all components to assemble into finished goods for re-export.

However, in fact, excluding the investment in the electronic industry, about two-thirds of the US$1.4 billion foreign direct investments in Taiwan are highly technology-oriented, particularly in the chemical, machinery equipment, and metal product industries. Engineering technology transfer usually takes place in the form of licensing or technical cooperation in connection with or without the foreign direct investment, while the management technology transfer mainly goes together with investments. Up to 1975, the approved technical cooperation projects were 897, among which 27 percent, 18 percent, 15 percent, and 13 percent were respectively for the electric-electronic, chemical, machinery equipment, and metal products industries.

The engineering technology transfer can also be taken in the form of establishing the network of satellite plants which supply the parts to the major firms. Usually the manufacturing and quality control techniques have to be transplanted to the sub-contract firms from the major company, in order to assure the zero defect of the final proudct. For example, both RCA-Taiwan and Admiral-Taiwan have more than 150 satellite plants, Zenith-Taiwan has more than 50, and General Instrument Taiwan has more than 100 in the electronic field. The USI-Far East, a subsidiary of the National Distillers and Chemical Corporate, and China Gulf are actively helping the local satellite firms to upgrade the manufacturing skills in the plastics field.

In the management side, the technological contribution is more difficult to be perceived. But when we see many young local talents, who have very few ways to exercise their potentials in the governmental agencies and local enterprises, were effectively utilized and promoted to middle-high managerial positions in the foreign invested firms, we believe that they should have learned some management skills from the parent firm's system transfered to the subsidiary. Furthermore, the overseas training programs of those multinational firms were more active than the local counterpart and thus developed more qualified human resources for the local society. It has been estimated that about 4000 managers and engineers have been sent abroad to study higher skills by those foreign invested firms in Taiwan in the past years.

Our observations on the positive performance of the technology transfer have convinced us that sooner or later the local firms and thus the whole economy will benefit greatly from the technologically advanced multinational firms in Taiwan when the trained managers and engineers move to the local firms or leave the foreign firms to establish their own new ventures. Another important contribution is resulting from the "demonstration" effect of the multinational firms and "imitation" effect by the local firms about the modernization of management practice and quality control. As a matter of fact, the presence of multinational firms, particularly those domestic market oriented ones, have stimulated the whole industry to pay more attention to some important methods of doing business, such as "Research and Development", "Integrated Business Planning", "Combination and Merger", "Cooperated Export Program", etc.

V. Role of the Multinational Corporations in Taiwan's Future Economy

A. Taiwan's Future Economic Development Policy

The advancement toward the petrochemical, heavy, and precision industries is one of the policies of Taiwan's future economic development. This policy is designed to upgrade Taiwan's economic structure on the one hand and improve the economic value of labor skills on the other. The government has a goal of an average 7.5 percent economic growth per year for the next decade.

To facilitate the industries to reach this ambitious goal, the government has energetically implemented six major infrastructure and three manufacturing projects, with total budget of more than US$5 billion, in addition to the nuclear power plant constructed by the Taiwan Power Company. These projects are (a) a modern freeway originating from the Port Keelung in the North and terminating at the Port Kaohsiung in the South; (b) a new railroad connecting the relatively less developed eastern part of Taiwan to the more developed western part; (c) electrification of the existing railway trunk line in the West; (d) building a new international sea port near Taichung in central Taiwan; (e) opening up another new harbor in the north-eastern area; (f) building a new ultra-modern international airport near Taipei (g) establishing an integrated steel mill; (h) setting up an ultra-modern shipbuilding yard; and (i) adding two petrochemical complexes.

It is obvious that upon completion of the six new infrastructure projects, transportation facilities will adequately meet the requirement of the expanding industry and commerce. And when the petro-chemical complexes, steel mill, and the nearly completed nuclear power plants are finished, the textile industry, the present number one foreign exchange earner, will find a much more comfortable raw material source than the present controlled one and the materials needed for the development of shipbuilding, industrial equipment, machinery, transportation facilities and equipment buildings, houses, etc. can be supplied by the local sources.

B. Needs of More Foreign Investment

Since these big government sponsored projects will occupy most part of the government's available budget in the next several years, Taiwan will need a great amount of foreign capital inflow, in the level of US$3.0 to 4.0 billion, both from the direct investment and indirect investment channels, to compensate the gap of capital formation in the other sectors if the economy is expected to be guided in the balanced and growing path. The government has made this need very clearly to the public and identified about 40 potential industries available for private investments. Most of these investment opportunities are in the electronics, electric, chemical, petrochemical, high precision machinery and equipment, and basic metal products industries.

The favorable investment climate, which is continuously improved, and the tax encouraged potential industries are certainly attractive to many profit-and-efficiency-minded investors, particularly the foreign multinational firms. The more the government's budget flows into the infrastructure sector, the more the foreign direct investments are needed in the next few years in Taiwan. Consequently, the role of multinational firms in Taiwan's future economic development will become more important than ever before.

On March 18, 1976, Mr. Y.S. Sun, Minister of the Economic Affairs, made a clear interpretation about the government's future policy on the foreign direct investment in Taiwan before the luncheon of the American Chamber of Commerce in the Republic of China. Minister Sun stated that the following eight categories of industries are definitely welcomed:

(a)   those industries that can upgrade the product quality or reduce the production cost for existing products;

(b)   those industries that can increase the value-added or more effectively utilize the existing production systems;

(c)   the down-stream projects of the petro-chemical and the steel industries;

(d)   those industries that can design and manufacture the whole-plant projects;

(e)   those industries that will manufacture precision machine tools, automotive parts, and mechanical parts;

(f)   those industries that can produce agricultural machineries and transportation tools that can meet the needs in Taiwan and the Southeast Asia area;

(g)   those industries that can make parts and components needed by the color TV, IC, and other electronic products; and

(h)   those industries that can produce heavy electrical machineries, control systems, and basic components.[6]

As we have mentioned in the first part of this report reviewing Taiwan's economic performance, the US Aid in earlier and foreign direct investment in recent years have played an essential role in the past two decades that Taiwan has successfully transformed itself from a predominantly agricultural country to one in which a modern industry has strived. Actually, foreign investment, which although constitutes only a relatively small portion of Taiwan's fixed capital formation, has firmly fitted into our economic structure as a building block, whose importance cannot be lightly overlooked, particularly in the future.

C.   Multidimensional Role of Multinational Corporations

We have believed that the multinational corporations representing the inflow of foreign direct investments will play the following multi-dimensional role in Taiwan:

1.   Capital supplier
2.   Job opportunity creator
3.   Foreign exchange earner
4.   Tax payer
5.   Economic structure change helper
6.   Technology transfer agency
7.   Modern management cultivator
8.   Competition challenger
9.   International friend
10.   Open society contributor

Some people may have the feeling that the Republic of China no longer welcomes labor-intensive industries since the government's future development policy is shifting to capital-and-technology-intensive directions. This is exactly part of the government attitude. As a matter of fact, the government will carefully examine investment applications which involve a great need of labor and energy. The industries with the potentials to contaminate the environment will also be received careful evaluation.

In concluding this report we would like to repeat that it is one of the policies of our government to include foreign direct investment represented by the multinational corporations as one of the key building blocks of Taiwan's future economy. The multinational firms will be welcomed by the Statute for the Encouragement of Investment and the Statute for the Investment by Foreign Nationals on a continuing basis. Taiwan's investment environment will be further improved in order to reinforce the image that Taiwan is one of a few places in the world where good management and modern technology can practically ensure success and profit to both the multinational firms and local society. The role played by the multinational firms in the future Taiwan will be more important than before in the further and well-planned economic development process. It is our willingness to share and exchange our country's experience on the foreign investment with other countries if they so desire.

Footnotes

1.   All the related statistics used in this section can be found from the following sources:
      a.   *Industry of Free China* (Taipei: Economic Planning Council, February 1976).
      b.   *Economic Development in Taiwan, ROC* (Taipei: Ministry of Economic Affairs, March 1976).
2.   *Taiwan: A Booming Economy* (Taipei: China Productivity Center, March 1974), pp. 45-50.
3.   *Statute for Investment by Foreign Nationals,* promulgated on July 1954, and amended on December 14, 1959 (Taipei: Industrial Development and Investment Center, June 1973).
4.   *Statute for Encouragement of Investment,* promulgated in September 1960, and amended January 1, 1974 (Taipei: Industrial Development and Investment Center, June 1973).
5.   *1974's Survey Report on the Operations and Contributions of Foreign Invested Firms in Taiwan* (Taipei: Investment Evaluation Council, MOEA, February 1976) pp. 3-9.
6.   *China Times,* March 19, 1976, p. 2.

MULTINATIONAL CORPORATIONS

BANE OR BOON?

By: Hilarion M. Henares, Jr. *

When the U.S. government and the "paid pipers" of Wall Street and Madison Avenue, tell us that multinational corporations are the bastions of free enterprise and democracy — that multinationals are the most prodigious sources of capital and technology needed for national development — that we must therefore frame the rules of the game so that multinationals can develop our economy to the perfection of the American model — and that we must accept the multinationals as a New World Force transcending the boundaries of all nations with the power to create wealth and allocate resources efficiently on a global scale — we take the attitude that such pious preachments are essentially self-serving and subject to proof.

I would like to present proof that none of what we were told is true — that multinationals are in the aggregate not a source of capital, but a tremendous drain of our resources as a nation — that the rules of the game by which multinationals survive and prosper are a detriment to our national development — that the American model is both an impossible dream and an undesirable one — that multinationals as a New World Force is direct threat to the existence of the nation-state, a threat to free enterprise itself, and a cause of discord in our search for peace.

I Drain on our Resources:

Multinational corporations drain our resources (1) by bringing in a minimal amount of capital and raising an inordinately large portion of their capital needs from local sources; (2) by sending out profits and repatriating capital enormously exceeding their little investment; (3) by using such capital to buy up or displace local firms instead of increasing the productive facilities of the nation; and (4) by overpricing imports and underpricing exports through the practice of "transfer pricing".

1.)   The 1975 financial statement of Ford Philippines filed at the SEC shows that Ford invested only P1.3 million, while borrowing P168.5 million from local sources; as if this is not enough, Ford recently acquired authority to issue short term commercial papers for P232.95 million more.

Ford Philippines is not unique. An NEC report by B.G. Bantegul on 108 American firms doing business in the Philippines, in a period covering 1956 to 1965, shows that out of a total capital expenditure of $489.7 million, only 12% or $58.6 million came from abroad and 88% or $431.1 million was generated from local sources.

The Philippine experience is not unique either. A United Nations study by Fernando Fajnzylber showed that U.S. based multinationals financed 83% of their Latin American investments from reinvested profits and domestic borrowings, so that only 17% therefore represents a real transfer of capital from the United States to the poor countries of Latin America.

It is clear therefore that the entry of multinational corporations does not constitute an appreciable increase in the capital resources of the host country; it means a reduction of capital resources available to domestic producers.

2.)   Having used for the most part the credit resources of the host country the multinationals

*President of the Philippine Pigment & Resin Corporation and former Chairman, National Economic Council of the Philippines.

proceed to remit enormous profits and to repatriate capital out of the host country.

Fajnzylber's U.N. study showed that from 1960 to 1968, American corporations took out an average of 79% of their net profits out of Latin America, even though they contributed only 17% of the total capital expenditure.

In the Philippines, the Bantegui study shows that from 1956 to 1965, 108 American firms remitted $369 million while retaining only $20.8 million as reinvested profits. Thus American companies remit 95% of the profits while contributing only 12% of the capital investment.

The outflow of funds from the Philippines to the United States, by the same 108 American companies was $386.2 million while the inflow was only $58.6 million, or $6.50 sent out for every dollar brought in.

Another report culled from Central Bank cited that in a previous period from 1949 to 1960, only $16.2 million of new foreign investments entered this country while $223 million were sent out, or $14.00 sent out for every dollar brought in.

And if you think this is not happening today, take a look at the statistics compiled by the Foreign Exchange Department of the Central Bank in the invisible Receipts and invisible Payments during the period 1964 to 1972. During that period $580.97 million came in as investments and loans, and $3.29 billion went out as profit, repatriated capital, and loan amortizations, or $5.66 sent out for every dollar brought in.

3.)   Having gotten 88% of their capital requirements from local sources, what did American firms do with the money? Put up new productive facilities? or buy existing local firms, or displaced other local businesses?

A study of the Harvard Business School of the 187 largest U.S. based corporations in Latin America show that out of 717 new manufacturing subsidiaries they established 331 or 46% were established by buying out existing firms. A mere change of ownership does not increase production facilities needed for development.

It does not take more than a passing notice to realize that the same thing is happening here in the Philippines. General Electric bought the Soriano firm, PEMCO for the manufacture of light bulbs, and 30% of Philacor, manufacturers of refrigerators and appliances. General Motors bought out the Yutivo interests and the Francisco Motor interests in the GM assembly plant. Ford Philippines bought out the Mantrade interests in its assembly plant. Boise Cascade took over Bataan Pulp and Paper Mills. And so on ad nauseum.

In 1973, Vicente Valdepeñas reported that foreigners accounted for 60.7% of the output and 59.4% of the input in the wholesale and retail trade; 57.8% of the output and 60.8% of the input in the mining industry; 52.1% of the metal products; 57.6% of the rubber products; 68.9% of the chemicals and chemical products; and 100% of the petroleum products.

By giving multinationals free access to local credit, we handed them our local resources with which they acquire control of our economy at little cost and at considerable profit.

4.)   Statistics on capital outflow due to multinationals, $5.66 sent out for every dollar brought in are appalling enough. But the widespread practice of "transfer pricing" by multinationals suggest that capital outflows are even worse than the statistics suggest.

Company manuals on how to run multinational corporations are filled with detailed instructions on intra-company transfers to maximize the global profits of the parent company.

When multinationals buy from and sell to their own subsidiaries, they establish "transfer prices" that have little connection with the market. In many cases, to save on taxes paid in an underdeveloped country, or merely to effect illegal remittances of profits, exports are undervalued and imports are overvalued in transactions between subsidiaries and their parent companies. A variation often used and even more attractive is to ship underpriced exports and overpriced imports to a tax-free port such as Hong Kong and the Bahamas (known as tax havens), and to re-export the goods at their normal market value or even at an inflated price to another subsidiary in the country where they are to be sold.

This may be the usual practice of the Philippine Packing Corporation which invariably sends its Del Monte canned pineapples to Hong Kong; and from Hong Kong to the rest of the world. Why not export from the Philippines directly to the worldwide market? Why to the tax free port of Hong Kong? How much under pricing of exports has been done all these years, robbing the Filipino people of their rightful dollar income?

Richard Barnet and Ronald E. Müller report that multinational subsidiaries in Latin America trading with their own parent companies, consistently underprice their exports, charging on the average of 40% less than prices charged by local exporting firms. In the Philippines, we have PMC exporting to parent Procter & Gamble, PRC exporting to parent Unilever and so on and so on.

At the same time, when it is to their advantage, multinationals grossly overvalue their imports. Constantine Vaitsos in a detailed study of overpricing in Columbia, reports the following overpricing; drugs, 155%; rubber products, 40%; and electronic products, 16% to 60%. In Columbia, Valium was sold at 82 times the established international market price; Libruim, 62 times; Tetracycline, 10 times; transistors, 11 times. In Chile overpricing ranges from 30% to more than 700%. And according to Pedroleon Diaz, overpricing in Peru ranges from 50% to 300%; in Equador, 75% to 200%.

In the Philippines, a Senate Committee found that Esso Philippines (now Exxon) was buying oil at $1.74 per barrel at the time the price ranged from 99 cents to $1.34 per barrel.

And recently, Esteban Bautista of the U.P. Law Center testified that the local subsidiary of Bristol/Mead Johnson bought from its mother company Ampicillin at prices from $177.98 to $242.99 per kilo, and another subsidiary of Beecham bought the same drug for $251.00 per kilo. On the other hand, a local firm, Doctor's Pharmaceuticals bought from other sources the same drug at prices as low as $91.40 per kilo, almost one-third of the transfer prices of multinational corporations.

According to Robert N. MacVicar in a paper issued by the United Nations Development Programme, the U.N. found that "more than 25% of the value of all international trade appears to be of an intra-group character", i.e. intra-company transfers between multinational companies and their subsidiaries.

Transfer pricing, which is an open secret among multinationals operating in the Philippines, is a cruel act of exploitation of the poor nations of the world who suffer on two counts; 1) they lose needed tax revenues due to understated income and 2) they lose valuable foreign exchange through undervalued exports and overvalued imports.

A global balance of payments table for all third World countries prepared by Angus Madison, shows that for 1963, payments for foreign investments represented the largest individual deficit item amounting to $5.4 billion, one half of the entire Third World deficit. This is a direct result of the intrusion of multinational corporations into the economy of poor nations.

II The Rules of the Game:

Having sold the rest of the so-called "free world" on the necessity and desirability of investments by multinational corporations, the United States and its instrumentalities began to dictate the rules of the game by which multinationals can survive and prosper within the host countries.

The United States has exerted its powerful influence in the IMF, the World Bank, the General Agreement on Tariffs and Trade, and in its own Department of Commerce and the CIA, to serve the ends of multinational corporations — pursuing only one trade policy, free trade, to allow multinationals to penetrate into every market in the globe, and secure their sources of raw materials — pursuing only one monetary policy, free convertability of currency, to allow multinationals to invest in places where they are not even needed and to bring out the profits of their monopoly and to hell with the economies of poor nations.

The United States is not even consistent. While seeking to export into the Philippines any and all kinds of goods without limit, the United States imposed quantitative restrictions on most of our major export products, such as sugar and coconut oil. Even recently the United States forced us to accept "voluntary quotas" on our textile exports to the United States, discriminated against our Philippine mahogany and imposed additional duties on our sugar exports. While trying to convince the rest of the world to accept foreign investment, the United States refused to have Arab interests invest in its airlines, banks and defense industries.

But the most insidious of all are the patents and copyright conventions to which poor nations have been inveigled to be signatories.

It is an accepted principle in our democratic system that "Knowledge is public domain". This is implied in free speech, free press, academic freedom, open covenants and other principles upon which our society is founded. For knowledge is for the betterment of all peoples and all nations.

In one case, does the state limit this domain. By a system of patents and copyrights, a state may limit the use of certain bits of knowledge to those who discovered them, and only for one reason, to encourage the inventiveness and creativity of its own citizens. It is the obligation of the state to reward its own citizens, but certainly not the citizens of other nations.

If a state undertakes to protect the patents and copyrights of other nations within its own borders, it is only for one reason — reciprocity: "I'll protect your patents and copyrights, if you protect mine".

But suppose we in the Third World had no patents for others to protect, why should we protect theirs? That was the rationale behind the demand of the Third World countries during the last UNCTAD conference in Nairobi, that the rich nations free its patents for the immediate use of the poor nations.

Japan before the war recognized no foreign patents; it was derided as a "copy cat" in the international market; but Japan persisted in learning all it could until it achieved a high level of technology and had its own patents for others to protect. Italy, after the war, was also derided as an "industrial pirate," because it made use of foreign patents without due compensation, until the time came when it, too, had patents for others to protect. Taiwan today recognizes no international copyright, so that its citizens can buy books at one-tenth the price they are sold in the international market.

Here in the Philippines, 94% of all patents registered in the Philippine Patent Office are owned by American companies, especially drug firms. Indicated several times in the United States for patent pooling and price fixing, these multinational drug companies pursue their particular avocation in the Philippine with a vengeance. I made a study once on the price of terramycin, a broad spectrum anti-biotic sold in 250 milligram tablets of which one needs 12 tables, taken once 3 times a day for four days to get rid of a serious infection. At the time each tablet was sold for 6 centavos in Italy and 25 centavos in Thailand, the same tablet was sold for P1.20 in the Philippines. 20 times higher here than in Europe. Today, the U.P. Law Center reports that in case of Ampicillin, a 500 milligram tablet it sold by multinationals up to P2.56 per tablet while a lowly local firm sells it for only P1.70 per tablet.

Clearly, the Philippine government by being signatory to the Patent Convention, has undertaken to reward the ingenuity of the Americans at the expense of the health and well-being of the Filipino people.

Many countries realizing the abuse of drug companies, do not provide patent protection for medicinal or pharmaceutical inventions. Among them are Argentina, Austria, Bolivia, Brazil,

Canada, Chile, Columbia, Denmark, Ecuador, Egypt, Iceland, Iraq, Israel, South Korea, Luxemburg, Morocco, New Zealand, Norway, Peru, Portugal, Italy and Switzerland itself which is the biggest exporter of pharmaceutical products. If these countries can do it, I don't see any reason why the Philippines should not cancel all foreign patents in the field of drugs and medicine.

III The Undesirable "American Dream":

Advocates of multinational corporations have sold the rest of the world on the vision of the American dream of unlimited growth and prosperity for all, and pointed to the American Model as the ultimate goal, and to the multinationals as the principal agents of change and progress.

The United States contains only 7% of the population of the world, and uses up 32% of the world's available resources; if the rest of the world were to catch up with the present standard of living of Americans, the world's resources will have to be used up 4½ times as fast — impossible as well as undesirable.

People began to take a closer look at the American Model, a trillion dollar economy beset by unemployment, inflation, crime, pollution, racial violence, terrorism, choked highways, decaying neighborhoods, barely functioning public services, lack of meaningful work and the psychological miseries of affluence — alienation, rootlessness, boredom.

Barry Commoner once calculated that from 1946 to 1970, the pollution levels in the United States rose from 200 to 2000%, while total production rose only by 126%. The average American consumes as much food, clothing and cleaners; occupies the same housing and requires the same freight in 1970 as he did in 1946. But in 1970, the growing of his food requires more chemicals that leach the soil, pollute the rivers and kill the nitrogen fixing bacteria that is the source of natural nitrogen fertilizer. In 1970, he uses detergents instead of soap, but his clothes are no cleaner; detergents has a brightness additive which makes clothes look white without removing the dirt; it takes 3 times more energy to make detergents than to produce soap, and detergents are responsible for the 20 fold increase in polluting phosphates in rivers, lakes and shores. In 1970, he uses synthetic fibers more than natural fibers; and synthetics require more energy to make, are non-biodegradable, which means that to get rid of it, you have to burn it and pollute the atmosphere, or add it to the nation's already staggering rubbish heap. In 1970, he drives as far as he did in 1946, but he uses more power to get there; with an increased compression ratio in his engine, he has to use tetraethyl lead additive in his gasoline, and pollution of the air increased 7 times during the period in question.

Squandering of resources at a geometric rate, and rising ecological damage are the direct consequence of the quest of ever increasing profits by the big corporations. Social costs never show up in the company's annual statement. But the costs of ruined land, depleted resources, filthy water and foul air must be paid by everyone and cannot be paid with cash.

In the Philippines, we are beginning to realize the increasing disparity between what we need and what the multinationals produce, resulting in enormous, unnecessary and criminal waste of our meager resources.

Nowhere is this more apparent than in the food industry. In the Philippines where 58% of our population do not earn enough to provide the minimum requirements of the human body, multinationals persist in creating demand for high cost junk foods with little nutritional value. Pepsi-Cola costs 50 centavos per bottle that contains nothing more nutritional than half a centavo's worth of sugar. A can of Hormel Vienna Sausages costs P3.60. A can of sausages that contains 40% meat and 60% starch filler with a nutritional value of 25 centavos of meat and rice. Packaged food consisting mostly of cornstarch and sugar are being advertised as having "extra-ordinary food value"; and in the poorest regions, it is not uncommon for a family to sell a few eggs and chickens to buy a case of Pepsi, while children waste away for lack of protein. For enormous profits, multinationals spend fortunes in advertising to sell nutritionally marginal food to economically marginal people.

IV Threat to Free Enterprise and World Peace

Today the "hired hacks" and "paid pipers" of Wall Street speak of the multinationals as the champions of free enterprise, and the most powerful agents for the internationalization of human society.

Yet a cursory reading of the capitalist system indicates that truly free competition requires firms to be small relative to the size of the industry. The small firm assures a large number of producers in each field and goes a long way towards creating the competitive independence that is needed.

The rise of large corporations, most of whom are now multinationals, has concentrated corporate power in a few hands and has resulted in an aberration of the capitalist system — monopoly, by a single firm or a few firms in "combination and conspiracy in restraint of trade". The almost hysterical preoccupation of U.S. Federal regulatory agencies to contain corporate monopoly and abuse even came to the point where the Justice Department charged that the mere size of the corporation may be in violation of the Sherman Anti-Trust, that bigness is badness, that the mere ability of a corporation to engage in monopolistic practices may be construed as prima facie evidence of intent.

Yet, while the Sherman Anti-Trust and Clayton Acts tried to curb corporate monopoly within the United States, the Webb Pomerene Act of 1918 exempted associations of American firms operating abroad from prosecution under the Anti-Trust Act.

The United States thus pursues a Janus-faced policy toward its Big Business — behave at home, and do your worst abroad. Multinational corporations are encouraged to engage in monopolistic practices abroad, which if perpetrated in the United States itself would expose them to relentless prosecution.

The abuses of the multinationals have been the subject of many United Nation papers, and the object of concern to many Third World countries. Far from being the champions of private enterprise, multinationals have been a threat to really free competition with their concentration of economic power and monopolistic practices.

Already an interagency committee has recommended to the Monetary Board measures to curb the practice of multinationals of securing unlimited use of domestic funds. Already another committee under Armand Fabella submitted a position paper to the National Economic Development Authority (NEDA) pointing out the restrictive practices of multinationals in the transfer of technology to developing countries, and condemns cartels and their monopolistic practices. Already the Bureau of Internal Revenue is investigating the "transfer pricing" practices of multinational corporations, and the Board of Investments is trying to get fully owned subsidiaries to divest themselves of controlling shares owned by parent companies. Already the NEDA, in its 25-year plan up to the year 2,000 has decided as part of its self-reliance policy to rely less and less on foreign investment to finance the growth of our economy. In India, multinationals are forced to provide their own dollars for their import needs, forcing one chemical firm to be the biggest shrimp exporter in Asia, and tripling the foreign exchange reserves of India. In countries all over Africa and Latin America, multinationals are slowly being expropriated and nationalized.

For indeed, the rise of the multinational corporations is the first direct challenge to the existence of the nation-state. The growth rate of such corporations is 3 times that of the average nation-state. And if we compare their annual sales with the GNP of countries, as Lester Brown has done, we find that General Motors is bigger than Switzerland, bigger than South Africa, and more than 6 times larger than the Philippines. We find that the 32 largest multinationals corporations have sales larger than the GNP of Japan, of any country except that of the United States and the Soviet Union.

Already multinationals have excess funds for use to speculate in gold and world currencies and can cause economic dislocations anywhere. Already they can subvert and corrupt governments, promote revolution and wars, and cause the death of democracy in many countries. Eventually, these Frankenstein monsters will turn against their own master, the United States government, by the corruption of its electoral process through campaign contributions and influence peddling. And eventually they will usher the death of democracy in the land of its birth — a divine retribution so richly deserved by the Americans.

Thus do the intellectuals and policymakers of the rest of the world look upon multinational corporations as the fulfillment of St. John's vision of the Anti-Christ in Chapter 13, Book of Revelations: "A Strange Creature — with seven heads and ten horns, and ten crowns upon its horns. . .requiring everyone to be tatooed with its mark, so that no one could get a job or even buy in a store without the permit of that mark. . . with the Devil's power to fight against God's people and to overcome them, and to rule over all nations and language groups throughout the world".

The Japanese Approach to

"Multinationalism"

By: Professor N. Kobayashi*

This discussion presents in general terms the present status and future prospects of Japanese overseas investments.

As of 31 March 1973, Japanese private investments abroad amounted to the total of 6,730 million dollars. The rate of increase of such investments continued to be rapid for the rest of 1973 and the first few months of 1974. As a result, private investments abroad had reached the level of 10 billion dollars by March 1974. Geographically speaking, 60 per cent of the 6.7 million dollar investments were directed to developing countries, the remaining 40 per cent invested in developed countries. In terms of an industry break-down, 38.7 per cent went to the natural resource developments, 35.5 per cent to commerce, finance and services, and 25.7 per cent to manufacturing industries. Because of the scarcity of domestic resources and of the rapid pace of industrial growth, the weight of Japanese overseas investments in natural resource industries has been much greater than that usually seen among developed countries.

In the field of manufacturing, the scale of investment was comparatively small and directed mainly to the labor-intensive industries in developing countries. In this sector Japanese investors have often chosen to establish a joint venture with a local partner in the host country. In addition to this, because of the lack of experience in overseas operations, a considerable number of Japanese manufacturers joined hands with Japanese trading company partners in entering overseas markets.

Japanese investments in developed countries have been directed to the financial and commercial fields. A small increase was evidenced for investments in manufacturing fields with innovative technologies.

For the future, it is predicted that by 1980, the total amount of Japanese overseas investments will reach 39 to 46 billion dollars (refer to charts 1 and 2 prepared on the basis of a forecast made by the Japan Economic Research Center, Tokyo).

If the Japanese economy continues to grow at 9 per cent in terms of real GNP, the annual rate of increase of overseas investments will be 27 per cent and will reach the total of 46,025 million dollars by the end of 1980. Even if the economic growth rate proceeds at a 5 per cent level, the overseas investments will increase at 24 per cent per annum, reaching a total of 38,500 million dollars in 1980. The more rapid the rate of economic growth, the larger will be the overseas investments in natural resource, chemical, petro-chemical and steel industries. In the case of slower domestic growth case, overseas investments in the machinery, electric appliance and automotive industries will be accelerated. Overall, the Japan Economic Research Center predicts that in the future, investments in overseas productive activities will be stepped up, resulting in a continued progress of multinationalization of Japanese business.

One of the position papers prepared recently by the Ministry of International Trade and Industry (MITI) makes the following projection for the future direction of Japanese overseas investments:

> Confronted with the emergence of nationalism in resource holding countries, more

*Written while Visiting Faculty Member at the Centre d'Etudes Industrielles, Geneva, where this paper was presented to an International Seminar on the Social Responsibilities of the Multinational Corporation, now Professor at Keio University, Tokyo, Japan.

Reprinted from the *Journal of World Trade Law* with permission of the author and publisher.

CHART I
JAPANESE OVERSEAS INVESTMENTS

1960	289 million
1965	956 million
1970	3,595 million
1972	6,773 million
1980*	46,025 million
1980**	38,500 million

* assumes GNP growth at net 9% p.a.

** assumes GNP growth at net 5% p.a.

Source: Figures prepared on the basis of a forecast made by the Japan Economic Research Center, Tokyo, July 1974.

Japanese investments will be made in a joint venture form with host country people and government as partners. In this connection, we feel that the number of Japanese joint ventures with Western enterprises will also increase. In addition to this, we are preparing to invest more in capital-intensive and large-scale refining and processing facilities in resource holding host countries.

Though our investments in the labor intensive industries in developing countries will continue to increase, their weight to total investments may be decreased as the wage scale in such countries is bound to be improved, and as the "localization" program progresses. If we are successful in developing new innovative technologies, our investments in technology-oriented industries in developed countries will expand. We find it necessary to do so in order to meet the requirement for and realize an appropriate division of labor between Japan and the Western countries.

Uniqueness in the Japanese approach to multinationalism

There are a number of characteristics that may distinguish the Japanese approach to

CHART II
JAPANESE OVERSEAS INVESTMENTS

Unit Million Dollars

		1972	1980 (9%)	1980 (5%)
I	NATURAL RESOURCES			
	Agriculture, Forestry and Fishery ..	130	600	520
	Mining	2,270	14,380	10,530
	Pulp and Lumber	300	1,240	1,150
II	MARKET PRESERVATION AND LABOR SAVING			
	Textile	420	1,540	1,420
	Chemical	130	5,060	1,420
	Steel and Non-ferrous	240	3,450	2,780
	Machinery	130	720	750
	Electric	170	1,520	1 700
	Transport Machinery	140	1,070	1,200
	Other Machinery	260	1,200	1,010
III	FINANCE AND COMMERCE			
	Commerce	1,750	3,560	3,230
	Finance and Insurance	540	2,840	2,540
	Others	1,280	8,850	7,930
	––––––––––––––––––––			
	I	39.9%	35.2%	31.7%
	II	20%	31.7%	32.7%
	III	38.1%	33.1%	35.6%
	TOTAL	$6,773m.	$46,025m.	$38,500m.

Source: Same as Chart I.

multinationalism from that exhibited by American or European business firms.

Origins of some European multinationals can be traced to the days of the great colonial empires. They contributed to the expansion of the influence of their nation states on colonizing territories. A great number of American multinationals began their overseas empire building only in the late 1950s and early 1960s. They believed and claimed that they had the sacred mission to spread and use their productive and managerial skills across national borders for the better relocation of limited human resources and thus for the improvement of living standards for everybody on a global scale.

Attitudes of this kind worked rather effectively until the demand for economic independence by the developing nations and criticisms against the misuses of power by big corporations began to overshadow the brilliant image of *laissez faire* rationalism and the validity of the doctrine of efficiency.

Now, however, multinational enterprises are facing a juncture in historical development at which they must re-establish their position in a significant role in the development of human society as well as in the production of physical commodities. It is at this critical moment that the Japanese wish to develop multinational enterprises of their own. It seems clear that Japanese firms need to establish an identity and utility distinguishable from those of the Western multinationals.

American multinational enterprises have recently been under attack from interest groups within their home country for having exported advanced technologies and even job opportunities abroad, thus creating an economic vacuum at home.

In the over-all picture, *the vacuum at home* is the result which Japanese who are living in overcrowded and pollution-bound archipelagos wish to create by making some of their enterprises multinational and thus causing them to move their productive activities abroad. In connection with this, the Japanese strategy is rather simple and straightforward — to export abroad some of the key industries that use a lot of scarce resources, concentrating at home on more knowledge intensive industries with higher value-added. The question that may be crucial to the success of this strategy will be one of ascertaining how easily your plan for the restructuring of the national industry will be accepted by the countries to which the manufacturing facilities would be transplanted.

Another, though not the least important, characteristic in a strategy for developing the so-called Japanese version of multinational enterprises, will be the basis of business-government collaboration. Co-operation between the private and public sector is nothing new in Japan. In fact the major process of our modernization and industrialization was promoted and accomplished in a similar fashion about 100 years ago.

After the political restoration by the *Meiji* emperor in 1868, his government was too impatient to wait for the inevitable but slow process of industrialization. There were a number of entrepreneurs of commercial origin, but they had been too conservative to seize and realize new opportunities quickly. Therefore, the *Meiji* government invited a number of foreign experts to Japan, made such experts into their teachers, and established modern industries. Soon the inefficiency of the government-sponsored industries became apparent. Quick to locate the problem, the *Meiji* government sold these industries to local enterpreneurs including Mitsui, Iwasaki (Mitsubishi) and Sumitomo who by that time had become sufficiently motivated to accelerate the structural change of their business from those of a commercial to those of an industrial nature. The *Meiji* government sold the industries to private entrepreneurs at such a low price that it could expect from the purchasers an appreciation of the special favor extended by the government to them. It is generally believed that in this way, the government succeeded in attaching a string to private businesses, enabling the government to continue to maintain its control and leadership over the private sector of business and industry.

Today, the private businesses are certainly more independent from the government's influence than they were 100 years ago. The government has become rather careful not to intervene directly into the business of private enterprises and, at present, it is safe to say that only in time of crisis and often at the invitation of the businesses themselves does the Japanese government attempt to intervene and participate in the affairs of private enterprise.

Given the above, then what are the reasons that have motivated the Japanese government to go as far as to extend its assistance and co-operation to private enterprises striving to become more multinational?

Reasons for the Japanese motivation to become more multinational

Five major reasons contributing to the high Japanese motivation to become more multinational are stated summarily below:

(i) the Japanese feel a need to invest in the development of new resource deposits and in the development of refining and processing facilities in the resource-holding countries, or fear the crisis of another resource shortage such as oil;

(ii) the need is felt to invest in the so-called import substitution and market export industries in host countries in their early economic development stage, or face the loss of markets;

(iii) the need is felt to invest more in labor intensive industries in developing countries in order to solve labor shortage in domestic industries;

(iv) there is a desire to restructure industry from capital intensive and heavy chemical industry-centered typed to knowledge-intensive industries. Some of the old key industries must be relocated to countries that have more space — although with extra care to prevent the spread of pollution;

(v) finally, the need is felt to invest in technologically-advanced fields in developed countries in order to meet the desire of a better international division of labor.

All these reasons suggest that the Japanese need to go into production activities in their overseas operating units that have in the past been nothing but extended arms of export activity. Therefore, for Japanese businesses, the path to "multinationalism" seems to be an inevitable choice!

Reactions to Japanese overseas investments

There has been criticism voiced both by the developed and developing countries about Japanese managers and their management style. Japanese managers are linguistically weak. They are poor in understanding the cultural environment of host country societies and in adapting themselves to such environment. They have difficulty in establishing their identity in a foreign environment and tend to act in a way seemingly tinted with too much of either a superiority or inferiority complex. They often neglect efforts to integrate into host country societies, and tend to fail in appreciating values inherent in the host countries. They often impose upon local employees preconceived notions of Japanese management, for example, those of permanent employment, seniority system, or the business philosophy of market share rather than profit improvement.

Japanese corporate strategy is often short-sighted and, as a result, activities based on this short-sighted view confuse the economic order of the host country societies. Japanese companies are overly aggressive in their marketing approach and prone to behave in an impolite way.

Japanese management tend to export too many Japanese managers to overseas operating units and consequently neglect efforts to develop and utilize the services of local management talent. Japanese managers in their overseas operating units often lack the confidence and ability to make on-the-spot decisions. In asking the parent company for approval, the speed of decision-making is rather slow.

If Japanese firms continue with the projected level of foreign overseas investment and become increasingly "multinational" and if the basic goal of overseas management is changed from that of extension of export trade to that of overseas production, it will no longer be possible to rely solely on the services of Japanese managers. Full-fledged support and co-operation will be required from people of the countries in which the multinational firms are located. In view of the rising demands for nationalism and localization, such support and co-operation can be gained only if Japanese managers progress in their efforts for integration into their host country societies and in their contribution to such societies.

Responses of Japanese firms: Obstacles inherent in the closed business culture and society in Japan

At the very moment Japanese firms are ready to go more multinational, they are facing increasing criticism of Japanese corporate behavior and are thus faced with a dilemma.

In January 1974, I conducted an opinion poll in Tokyo to ascertain the direction and nature of Japanese business leaders' interest and plans to make their businesses more international. Out of 101 executives, 86 who answered my questionnaire stated that Japanese businesses are capable of being and in fact becoming, more multinational in structure. However, 57 out of these 86 thought that the Japanese version of multinational enterprises would have unique features distinguishable from those of American or European multinational enterprises.

Many agreed that the Japanese multinational enterprises will have a stronger preference in developing multinational management as a joint venture with some integrated trading firms. They would be more willing than the Western multinationals to go into joint venture with local partners. The Japanese multinational enterprises would have an attachment to their parent country stronger than their Western counterparts. They would be more concentrated in natural resources' industries and in developing countries than multinationals of Western origin. By the nature of the unique Japanese style of management, parent companies of Japanese multinationals would have a control over their overseas operating units stronger than that of their Western counterparts.

Some executives pointed out that overseas operating units of Japanese multinational enterprises will be smaller than those of Western multinationals. The Japanese multinationals will be easily satisfied with minority control over their overseas operating units. Employees in host country societies will find a smaller opportunity to be promoted to managerial positions. Seniority-oriented, permanent employment will be maintained even in overseas operating units. The Japanese multinationals will emphasize the contribution to the economic development of host country societies more than their Western counterparts.

Why is there such an unwillingness to change on the part of the executives polled? One of the reasons can be found in the smallness of the contribution made by overseas activities to the total corporate output in Japan. In terms of sales it is only 1.3 per cent, of fixed assets 1.65 per cent, and of the number of employees 4.94 per cent. If this is the only reason for reticence, change will soon come as the percentage of contribution of the overseas activities increases. However, in the author's opinion, their problem is not so simple but more fundamental; they are suffering from obstacles inherent in the Japanese closed business culture.

Fortunately, there seems to be an increasingly strong indication that the current changes in environmental factors are too large and serious to be ignored by even a most conservative businessman in Japan. Once the critical nature of the matter is realized, it should be thought that they will manifest the will and ability to solve their problems by use of the most effective combination of management styles available to them regardless of the traditional ones on which their predecessors had relied. In the author's opinion, the most important prerequisite for Japanese executive is to take the courage to see new problems beyond obstacles inherent in the closed Japanese business culture and to take actions to overcome the obstacles.

Before ending this note, some positive prospects for the future of Japanese efforts along this line of development as manifested by its efforts in South East Asia will be commented upon.

In spite of the existence of unpopular features attributed to the Japanese way of conducting business abroad, my 1973 study of South east Asian countries revealed that all of the host country people visited looked towards the future with desire for expanded co-operation from Japan. Some asked for Japanese assistance in their regional development programs. Others sought co-operation from Japan in undertaking feasibility studies of new projects that they believed would contribute to their country's economic development. Still others asked for practical co-operation in the supply of money and in personal development programs both on technical and managerial levels.

In a white paper published in August 1974, the Japanese Ministry of International Trade and Industry (MITI) evaluated the positive effects of Japanese investments in Thailand and South Korea. A simple examination of the trade balance between Thailand and Japan shows Thailand with a deficit of 28.3 billion yen. However, it is a mistake to take this figure as an absolute indication of an imbalance in international payments. The Japanese co-operation with Thailand began with a number of "import subsitution industries" in that country. In 1972-3, new industries begun with Japanese capital created a big domestic supply of hitherto imported commodities. If the amount of the value of such new supply of commodities is added to the receipt from exports, while subtracting from the added amount the payments for imported materials and equipments, then there remains a positive balance of 38.9 billion yen.

In the case of South Korea, the trade balance with Japan is in Korea's favor in the amount of 3.5 billion yen. If the balance is rewritten by integrating in it the contribution made by import substitution industries by integrating in it the contribution made by import substitution industries begun with Japanese capital, the balance will improve to the amount of 38.6 billion yen.

Taking Asia as a whole, MITI emphasizes some other fall-out effects of Japanese investments in the form of creation of some 161,300 jobs and in the diffusion of Japanese technologies.

If Japanese businesses wish to survive and grow in the world market, they must learn how to harmonize differences of opinion and interests between the offeree and the offerer of foreign direct investment. To live through this age of discontinuity requiring new adjustments, Japanese businesses desirous of becoming more multinational should learn how to build a bridge over the communication and credibility gap now often developing against "big international business" all over the world and thus reap the benefits of expanded international production.

The Multinationals and the Philippines:

since Martial Law.

By: Dr. Robyn Lim*

September 21 1977 marked the fifth anniversary of the declaration of martial law in the Philippines. The 'New Society' has based its development strategy on removing impediments to foreign investment, and on promoting exports. In this strategy, the role of multinational corporations (MNC's) is crucial. Investment by MNC's is said to provide much-needed capital; to transfer advanced technology and skills; and to generate employment. These claims have been effectively rebuted by, among others, Magdoff[1] and Barnet and Müller[2]. This chapter argues that the Philippines, like Brazil, is a classic case of 'growth' without 'development', and that MNC's are important actors in that process. The first part of the chapter examines the pre-martial law situation with emphasis on the nationalist movement's opposition to unrestricted foreign investment. In the second section, the relationship between the MNC's and the 'New Society' is discussed. Finally, some of the consequences for Philippine 'development' are outlined.

Philippine 'independence' in 1946 was largely a myth. The U.S. retained important military bases, which despite the rhetoric of the present regime in the Philippines, remain crucial for U.S. strategy in the Pacific. Political power was handed over to a comprador elite whose members had a vested interest in the maintenance of the *status quo* and which controlled most of the wealth. Massive amounts of American military assistance helped defeat the Huk revolt in the early 1950's. Economically, the mechanisms of control were the Bell Trade Act and the Laurel-Langley Agreement. The Bell Trade Act was forced on the newly 'independent' Philippine government in 1946, despite considerable domestic opposition.[3] The U.S. government in fact threatened to withhold much-needed rehabilitation funds unless the act was passed. The Bell Act provided for eight years of free trade between the U.S. and the Philippines from July 1946 and for gradually increasing tariffs for the following twenty years. In effect this provision continued the pre-war colonial relationship based on free trade. The Bell Act also enshrined the "parity" provision, which gave U.S. citizens equal rights with Filipinos in the exploitation of natural resources. 'Parity' actually necessitated an amendment of the Philippine constitution. The Bell Act also prevented the Philippine government from controlling its own currency, since it could not impose exchange controls or restrict capital movements without the approval of the U.S. President. In 1954 American economic control was made somewhat more subtle when the Bell Act was replaced by the Laurel-Langley Agreement. This finally gave the Philippines control over its currency and ended free trade by scheduling the gradual elimination of mutual preferences in trade between the Philippines and the U.S., The agreement was to expire on 4 July 1974 when 'parity' was to end.

Mainly because of the 'conspicuous consumption' of the elite, an exchange crisis occurred in 1949, and with the consent of the U.S. President, exchange controls were imposed. During the period 1946-1962, industrial development was characterized by import substitution and 'Filipinization' of some sections of the economy. The import substitution strategy, however, encouraged American MNC's to move in behind tariff barriers to produce locally the goods they had previously imported. Many of these goods were consumer and luxury items catering for the taste of the elite and had little relevance for the needs of an under developed economy. The import substitution strategy did not alleviate the balance of payments problem, since heavy imports of equipment and materials were required. Exchange controls also contributed to widespread and high

*Lecturer in Political Science, Department of General Studies, University of New South Wales, Sydney, Australia

126

level corruption. MNC's controlled vital areas of the economy, such as the production and distribution of oil. Some of the world's largest MNC's were also entrenched in the agricultural sector. In particular, the fruit processing industry was dominated by Philippine Packing Corporation (Philpak) and Dole Philippines (Dolfil), respectively subsidiaries of Del Monte and Castle and Cook.

By the late 1950's, the limits to the import substitution strategy were beginning to be reached, and there were also strong pressures for the abolition of exchange controls. When Macapagal defeated Garcia in the 1961 Presidential elections, he promised to end controls and welcome additional foreign investment. One of the conditions imposed by the I.M.F. in return for a $300 million stabilization loan was a credit squeeze which led to the bankruptcy of many Filipino companies and their takeover by American MNC's. Lichauco[4] points out, for example, that during the decontrol programme, the Filipino majority shareholders in Filoil capitulated and sold out to Gulf Oil. Decontrol also produced a *de facto* devaluation of the currency which was made official in 1965 at the rate of 3.9 pesos to the dollar (in 1962 the rate had been 2:1). Apart from the MNC's, the group which benefited most from decontrol were the wealthy landowners and exporters, especially the sugar lobby. Devaluation also contributed substantially to inflation which worsened the plight of the poor. Structural changes were produced in the economy, as manufacturing declined in importance while the traditional export industries such as a plantation agriculture and mining benefited most.[5] A sharp rise in spending on luxury goods contributed to an increase in national indebtedness.

The first Marcos administration (1966-1970) was heavily indebted to the sugar lobby. Despite nationalist protestations, Marcos was as much a promoter of US interests as his predecessors had been. In his determination to become the first president to be re-elected, Marcos virtually bankrupted the country in the 1969 elections. By 1970, the internal debt reached $1.7 billion[6] and was rising. The World Bank and the I.M.F. pressed for a devaluation, and the lifting of remaining exchange controls. In February 1970 the peso was devalued by allowing it to float. The inflationary consequences were immediately felt, especially by the poor. By mid-October, the peso had been devalued by 54%, and was "stabilized" at p.6.70 to the dollar. National indebtedness had reached the point where $770 million in repayments was due in 1970 alone, and the World Bank convened an 'Aid Philippines' group similar to the aid consortium to Indonesia.

In foreign policy, Marcos proved himself a useful promoter of U.S. interests, and took some of the credit for the formation of ASEAN in 1967. His development strategy for the Philippines was similarly designed to protect and promote U.S. interests. To attract investment in underdeveloped sectors of the economy, the Investments Incentives Act of 1967 offered "generous tax advantages" to both domestic and foreign companies. There were two categories of investment which the Act sough to encourage. The first was joint ventures involving primarily Filipino capital and meeting certain special criteria. Equity had to be 60% Filipino and the endeavour had to satisfy criteria such as whether additional export earnings or import savings would be generated and whether the industry would use more Philippine employees and domestic raw materials. If these requirements were met, the venture was labelled a preferred industry and qualified for a number of benefits. The Act also stated that in the preferred areas where investments were desirable there would be a three year waiting period to allow Filipino companies to make the investments. After three years up to 100% foreign ownership was to be allowed. The second category of investment were those engaged in new and risky undertakings. Firms had to either produce goods not already being locally manufactured on a commercial scale or to introduce some new or untried process or formula with a strong preference for utilization of local materials. Wholly-owned foreign firms could qualify if they followed a prescribed Filipinization schedule within 20 years and would be allowed as many incentives as Philippine-controlled firms. Ventures which qualified under these criteria were named 'Pioneer industries' and received all but one of the benefits of the preferred industries plus exemption from all taxes except income tax, at a declining rate, and tariff protection up to 50% of the dutiable value of other competing imports. To overcome the chronic balance of payments problems, export industries were stimulated. The Export Incentives Act of 1970 provided a wide range of incentives to producers and exporters of products and services. The execution of these Acts controlling foreign investment was placed in the hands of the Board of Investments (BOI), which was given the task of delineating the sectors of the economy where investment was welcome and prohibiting it in which there was already heavy investment. The BOI was also to regulate foreign investment where the foreign participation was over 30%.

These Acts marked the shift from the import substitution industrialization of the 50's to export oriented industrialization. Many of the architects of this investment strategy were the technocrats produced by American universities Gregorio Licaros, Sixto Roxas, Vincente Paterno and Gerardo Sicat. The technocrats espoused 'de-politicalization' of economic matters when charged by their critics with working against Philippine interests by promoting foreign, especially American, investment. As the C.I.C. Report puts it, "the depoliticization espoused by the technocrats is not that at all but rather a deeper politicization toward the interests and needs of foreign investors."[7]

By 1970, approximately 80% of foreign investment was American.[8] American holdings comprised 19.5% of all Philippine assets in manufacturing, commerce, services, utilities, mining and agriculture. Total worth was an estimated $2 billion. These investments were heavily concentrated in the oil industry, which was 80% American owned, and accounted for more than half of all American investment in manufacturing. American corporate wealth was concentrated in the largest companies. Of the top 190 firms listed by *Business Day* by 1970, 50 were American.[9] Many of these companies had done very well out of the 1970 devaluation. The return per peso on invested capital to Philpak was reputedly 13.94 pesos in 1971.[10] American firms also raised significant amounts of their capital and credit from *within* the Philippines, particularly in the form of short-term loans.[11]

The 1950's and 1960's saw a growing nationalist movement directed against U.S. "neocolonialism" in the Philippines. The bases were an obvious target, but control of the Philippine economy was also condemned. The sections of the local business elite which had not been seduced into 'arrangements' with the MNC's joined the outcry against decontrol in 1962. In particular, the oil MNC's were the focus of criticism by Senator Diokno and his Senate Committee on Economic Affairs. From 1970 onwards, when the oil companies raised their prices, there were large scale demonstrations of students and jeepney drivers. The Marcos regime responded with increasing levels of repression, the infrastructure of which was funded by American agencies.

Nationalist pressures were also strong in the Constitutional Convention, elected in 1970 to write a new constitution. By massive bribery, Macos tried to head off the pressure from this quarter, but on the eve of martial law, the Convention was concluding the drafting of a new constitution which would have drastically curtailed the entry and operations of MNC's. Nor was Marcos able to muzzle the Supreme Court. In the important "Quasha Case" in August 1972, the Court declared that all property purchased by American citizens since Philippine independence had been acquired illegally, and that all parity rights would expire on 3 July 1974. This ruling caused considerable consternation to American investors. A second decision in August 1972 (Luzon Stevedoring Case) declared that companies in sectors reserved to Filipinos could not have foreign directors or top management personnel. After July 1974, this ban would apply to U.S. citizens. The declaration of martial law only one month after these two decisions was hardly coincidental, and the Supreme Court was one of the first institutions emasculated by the new martial law regime.

The details of the declaration of martial law in September 1972 lie outside the scope of this paper.[12] Exactly how far U.S. business interests in the Philippines were involved in its planning is hard to quantify. Before martial law, the American Chamber of Commerce had lobbied the Constitutional Convention on the 'parity' issue (under the Laurel-Langley Agreement 'parity' was due to expire in July 1974), and had openly attacked 'ultra-nationalistic' and 'socialist' tendencies in the Convention. American business publications hammered the theme that instability in the Philippines was making the country less attractive for foreign investment in the face of strong competition from countries such as Singapore and Taiwan.

The immediate effect of the declaration of martial law were encouraging for business: strikes and demonstrations were banned; nationalists such as Senator Diokno were jailed; 'law and order' was imposed; and the bureaucracy allegedly made more efficient and less corrupt. Marcos immediately made it clear that foreign capital would be protected. The response of the American Chamber of Commerce was predictably enthusiastic. On 27 September 1972, five days after the declaration of martial law, it sent the following cable to Marcos:

> The American Chamber of Commerce wishes you every success in your endeavors to restore peace and order, business confidence, economic growth, and the well-being of the Filipino people and nation. We assure you of our confidence in achieving these objectives. We are communicating these feelings to our associates and affiliates in the United States.[13]

The main incentives to foreign investments are the Investments Incentives Act (1967) and the Export Incentives Act (1970) as already outlined. Martial law amendments to the Export Incentives Act substantially liberalized incentives for foreign investment in export-oriented manufacturing and labor-intensive industry. These amendments allowed tax incentives for majority owned foreign firms which exported 70% of their manufactured goods. The Board of Investments (BOI) set up an Assistance Team for Foreign Investors in Labor-Intensive Export Projects, in order to aid and inform potential investors. Other new incentives were announced by Presidential decree. These included liberalization of visa requirements for potential foreign investors and reduction of taxes on interest on foreign loans. On 14th March 1973 Marcos announced that foreign investments were guaranteed complete freedom of repatriation, covering both invested principal and profits. (There had previously been a limit of 25% on repatriation of profits and dividends.) An overt attempt was made to compete with Singapore and Hong Kong in the incentives offered to MNC's. In June 1973 it was announced that corporations which made Manila the headquarters of their Asian operations would be exempted from all forms of local licenses, fees, dues, imports, or any other municipal or provincial taxes or burdens. American corporations which had been worried by the impending termination of 'parity' when the Laurel-Langely Agreement expired in July 1974 were reassured by decrees which allowed them to donate or sell their holdings to companies with 60% Filipino equity, and then lease back their holdings. Caltex Philippines, for example, decided to sell its land to the government-owned National Development Corporation, then lease back the land for 25 years, renewable for another 25 years.[14] Other American corporations followed this lead.

Impediments to some types of foreign investment were removed. The Rice and Corn Nationalization Law, which had been part of the 'Filipinization' legislation of the 1950's, was amended to allow foreign enterprises in the production of cereals. The Treaty of Amity, Commerce and Navigation with Japan, which the Philippine Senate had refused to approve, was ratified soon after the declaration of martial law.[15] Incentives were also aimed at specific industries. The Philippines is heavily dependent on foreign oil imports, and soon after the declaration of martial law, incentives were offered for foreign corporations to invest in oil exploration. As previously noted, the oil industry in the Philippines is dominated by American MNC's.

Overall, it should be emphasized that martial law did not make a *qualitative* change in Marcos's development strategy. The incentives to foreign investment had already been enacted in 1967 and 1970. As has been indicated, this represented a shift from the import-substitution strategy of the 1950's to an export-oriented strategy. It was tailor-made to suit the changing objectives of MNC's which were establishing 'export platforms' around the globe and were particularly attracted by the resources and cheap labor of the Pacific Basin. What martial law meant was that the threat of legislation to restrict MNC's in the Philippines had been removed. Critics such as Diokno were silenced, and the Supreme Court rendered powerless. Labor leaders were imprisoned, and strikes banned. With the 'old oligarchs' dispossessed, the technocrats were able to implement changes which had been impossible in the Old Society. 'Stabilization' measures to curb inflation, largely at the expense of the urban and rural working class, could be taken without fear of strikes and demonstrations. In effect, the 'old oligarchs' who had controlled the Philippines during the 'democratic' period, were succeeded by a new elite, consisting of the families of Marcos and Imelda, the mainly Ilocano leaders of the armed forces, and the technocrats. All of them had a close identity of interest with MNC.s.

From February 1970, when the Central Bank began to monitor capital inflow, until June 1977, total foreign investments reached $724 million.[16] About 37% was invested in BOI-approved projects. Of total foreign investment, $377 million went into manufacturing; $166 million into banks and other financial institutions; $61 million into mining; $43 million into commerce; and $29 million into services. American investment comprised the bulk of total foreign investment — $323 million or 45%, followed by Japanese investment of $172 million or 24%.[17] U.S. MNC's remain firmly entrenched in the economy. A 1974 study by the Securities and Exchange Commission indicated that of the top 100 corporations (which accounted for more than 32.7% of G.N.P. in 1974), 33 were controlled by U.S. corporations, either alone or together with Japanese, European or overseas Chinese capital; 6 were owned by European interests; 7 had significant Japanese investment, and 6 were controlled by overseas Chinese.[18] With its new-found 'stability' under martial law, the Philippines became attractive for MNC's. One of the most important attractions was low wages. For example, while Ford's hourly labor cost in the US reached nearly $7.50 in 1971, the average hourly rate for skilled labour in the Philippines was under $0.30. Similarly, Dolfil has found that labour costs were much cheaper in the Philippines than in Hawaii.[19] Advertisements in the foreign press emphasised that 'labor costs for the foreign company setting up plant in Manila could work out from 35 to 50 per cent lower than they would in either Hong Kong or Singapore".[20] The 'minimum' wage is presently (1977) P.10 per day for non-agricultural workers in Metropolitan Manila, and P.9 per day in the rest of the country. Under martial law, strikes are illegal and only tame unions allowed to operate. Marcos's lifting of all restrictions on the remittance of profits from January 1973 was designed to make the country more attractive to foreign investors. The Philippines has also set up the Bataan Export Processing Zone (BEPZ).

The legislation to establish the BEPZ was passed in 1969, but the Zone did not start operations until after martial law. In late 1972, the Progressive Car Manufacturing Program (PCMP) was announced as part of the plans to make ASEAN a kind of common market. The plan called for the complementary production of principal automotives parts in various countries of Southeast and Northeast Asia. Ford opened its body stamping plant in the BEPZ in February 1976. The plant has very little to do with Philippine development, since the majority of the body parts are exported to other overseas plants in Australia, Britain, New Zealand, Taiwan and Singapore. The advantages to Ford of this scheme are obvious. The company can utilize the double advantage of modern technology combined with cheap, educated, non-union labour. As Barnet and Müller have pointed out, this is a strategy which is widely being adopted by multinational companies. The BEPZ is in fact a classic 'export platform'. The PCMP programme also has the advantage that since only part of the manufacturing cycle is produced in one country, there is no transfer of technology. The risk of nationalist pressures is also reduced. The enterprise, orchestrated from headquarters in Melbourne, has undoubtedly been profitable for Ford. Constantino states that Ford Philippines, established in 1967, is now 37th on the list of the 1,000 largest corporations in the Philippines.[21] By July 1976, there were twenty-nine companies in operation in the Zone, nine in various stages of implementation of their projects, seven whose projects had been approved in principle, and eight service firms. Exports from the Zone grew from $119,807 in 1973 to $30 million in 1976.[22] Foreign firms operating in the Zone are offered a wide range of concessions and tax relief as part of the Philippines export-oriented industrialization strategy. The country's first nuclear reactor, which is being built by Westinghouse and financed by the US Export-Import Bank, is to be completed in 1982 and will supply power to the BEPZ. This project will reduce dependence on foreign oil supplies, which are still predominantly controlled by American MNC's, but will not reduce dependence on technology supplied by other MNC's.

Japanese MNC's are also involved in investments which have few benefits for the Philippine economy. The most controversial project is the Philippine Sintering Corporation set up by Kawasaki Steel in Mindanao. The plant is closely related to the Tubarao project in Brazil, and is an example of the Japanese success in relocating highly pollutive industries outside Japan itself. For some time the Philippine government has been pressing the Japanese government to finance an integrated steel mill near the Kawasaki plant. At the ASEAN Kuala Lumpur summit in August 1977, Marcos pressed Fukuda on this issue; the negative response of the Japanese was predictable at a time when Japan's steel mills, which supply 60% of Philippine steel imports, are producing below capacity. Kawasaki's main purpose in locating the sintering plant in Mindanao is to escape pressures from the Japanese environmentalist lobby which prevented Kawasaki from establishing another sintering plant in Chiba.[23] The operation is already very profitable. From mid-April 1977, when the plant started operation, to mid-Setpember 1977, the plant earned over $16 million.[24]

A further example of the role of the Philippines in the strategy of American and Japanese MNC's is the massive intervention in the Philippine economy of the global banks and investment houses. Before martial law, banking laws had allowed only two U.S. banks, Bank of America and Citibank to have branches in Manila. There was considerable criticism of these banks for raising funds from local savings and then making them available for the promotion of U.S. business interests. Although other American banks such as Chase Manhattan had representative offices in Manila, they could not accept deposits. Until the declaration of martial law, the local banking community resisted the encroachment of foreign banks. Just before martial law, Senate Bill 340 which called for the nationalization of banking, was brought before Congress. The bill required foreign banks to physically bring in capital instead of operating on local deposits. A 60% Filipino equity in the existing foreign banks was also required after a transition period of ten years. Led by Citibank and Bank of America, the foreign banks actively lobbied against the bill, and an official of the U.S. Embassy reportedly warned the Senate committee that if the nationalization bill were passed, the Philippines might not get additional U.S. loans.[25] Immediately after the declaration of martial law, a presidential decree opened up the Philippine banking system to foreign interests by allowing up to 40% foreign equity in Philippine banks and allowing the existing foreign banks to continue their 100% foreign equity. After adopting the recommendations of an IMF survey, the government also encouraged banking mergers, so that the smaller banks were forced out of business or to merge with foreign banks. As former Senator Salonga, a long-time critic of MNC's has put it, "what we have now is the spectacle of banking multinationals from the United States, Japan, and Europe getting into the strategic banking sector of our economy in one fell swoop."[26] Global banks have also penetrated investment houses. All but two of the twelve investment houses in operation have foreign shareholders, since the law permits up to 49% of voting stock to be foreign controlled.[27] As in other areas of Southeast Asia, the global banks are also heavily represented in the new field of merchant banking. To give a few examples: the U.S. owned Philippine-American Insurance Co. joined with the Chase Manhattan Overseas Banking Corporation to form the merchant bank Philippine American Investment Corporation; the First National City Bank Overseas Investment Corporation has a 49% stake in Citicorp Investment Philippines; the Fuji Bank has a 22.5% investment in Investment and Underwriting Corporation of the Philippines. Nearly all of these merchant banks are located in Makati, the 'modern' enclave outside Manila.

Mention should also be made of Bancom, which is an essential part of Marcos's strategy to make the Philippines the centre of an ASEAN financial network. Bancom Development Corporation (BDC) was established in Manila as an investment house in 1964. Bankers International (a subsidiary of Bankers Trust Co. of N.Y.) and Lincoln National Life Insurance Co. held a combined interest of nearly 30%. In 1973, American Express International Development Corporation acquired Bankers Trust's interest in BDC. It now holds 29.17% of BDC's shares and has a representative on the Board.[28] By 1975, the Bancom Group consisted of eight domestic subsidiaries; BIDTECH, a corporation in development technology; and offshore investment house in Hong Kong, and BDC itself.[29] In 1977, the Bancom Group joined with American Express to form a new regional merchant banking company, Amex Bancom Ltd. The Philippine government's attempts to compete with Singapore and Hong Kong in banking and finance has also manifested itself in the Philippines' joining the Asia Dollar Market. In late 1976, the government approved operations of Offshore Banking Units (OBU's) and Foreign Currency Deposit Units (FCDU's). Profits from offshore operations are to be taxed at a lower rate than that which applies in Singapore. Domestic banks are reportedly concerned that OBU's and FCDU's will result in even greater competition from the global banks. By August 1977, fifteen foreign banks had acquired OBU's and four had acquired licenses to operate FCDU's.[30] The global banks had also been heavily involved in lending programmes in the Philippines.

In the agricultural sector, MNC's have also benefited from martial law. The Quasha case (see above) had threatened to put an end to American hopes of extending parity beyond July 1974. After the imposition of martial law, foreign investors in agricultural land were assured that their interests would be protected. The MNC's engaged in 'agrobusiness' have also benefited from the imprisonment of outspoken peasant leaders and the emasculation of rural unions. The much vaunted land reform programme, partly funded by USAID, has been mostly window-dressing. It has not adversely affected the interests of MNC's, or of the Marcos family, which is one of the biggest landowners.[31] Despite land reform, MNC's such as United Fruit and Sumitomo have actually been expanding their holdings, often displacing indigenous land holders. Some sources estimate that in the banana industry, which is dominanted by MNC's, foreign corporations in 1974 were earning approximately $1,785 per hectare per year while the labourer cultivating a hectare would earn only $240 p.a.[32] A presidential decree requiring all companies with 500 or more employees to provide rice for their employees has enabled American corporations to buy up rice lands far in excess of their needs. Stanfilco (Castle & Cook) has bought a large rice farm in Mindanao which it is cultivating by fully mechanized methods. Dolfil, another subsidiary of Castle and Cook, also has large semi-mechanized rice ranches in Central Luzon. Such agrobusiness is very lucrative, but hardly related to the needs of a country with high unemployment and underemployment.

One of the supposed reasons for the imposition of martial law was to end the corruption of the 'old society'. Certainly corruption in the bureaucracy, as far as it inhibited would-be foreign investors and tourists, appears to have been reduced to some extent. The new elite, however, has made spectacular gains from martial law. In 1976, Marcos's former press secretary 'Tibo' Mijares, wrote a book entitled *The Conjugal Dictatorship* which detailed the corruption of the First Family.[33] The export-oriented industrialization strategy provides a multitude of linkages between the elite and MNC's. Mrs. Marcos, for example, has cultivated the Ford (i.e. Henry Ford II) family, as indeed she has attempted to ingratiate herself with royalty and quasi-royalty everywhere. Critics claim that the regime chose Westinghouse's bid for the construction of the Bataan nuclear plant despite lower bids by French and West German firms. The reason was allegedly the involvement in the project of Herdis Management and Investment Corporation, headed by Herminio Disini. Disini is a cousin of Imelda Marcos. The Herdis organisation in late 1975 acquired ownership of Asia Industries, which holds the franchise for Westinghouse products and is heavily involved in the nuclear plant project through various subsidiaries including an insurance company, Summa Insurance Co.[34] Many Philippine ambassadors, including Mrs. Marcos's brother, are relatives or personal friends of the First Family. The BEPZ is rumoured to be controlled by Marcos's relatives. The division of the spoils, in fact, is apparently a source of friction between members of the extended families of the President and his wife. The feud is exacerbated by the fact that his family are Ilocanos from the north, while hers are Visayans from the central Philippines; regional loyalties are still very strong in the Philippines. There are also many linkages between MNC's and U.S. officials and agencies in the Philippines. Former U.S. Ambassador Blair, for instance, is said to represent Reynolds Philippine Corporation, a subsidiary of Reynolds Aluminium Export Co. of the U.S. At least one Philippine company, San Miguel, has become a multinational company, and Philippine Foreign Secretary Carlos P. Romulo has recently been elected to its board. Many universities are also linked to MNC's. Philpak, for example, supports the College of Agriculture at Xavier University, and also grants scholarships in engineering and business administration at the Ateneo de Manila.[35] Academics in the most influential posts in economics and politics since martial law are almost invariably advocates of foreign investment, and are often recipients of largesses from MNC's in the form of research grants, scholarships etc. Political scientists who support the regime concern themselves with 'crisis management' and the maintenance of 'stability'. The writings of the New Society technocrats on development frequently reflect the views of S.P. Huntington, the political scientist most identified with advocacy of authoritarianism for achieving development.[36] A leading exponent of this view is O.D. Corpuz, whom Marcos has installed as President of the University of the Philippines to replace the less pliant S.P. Lopez. As in other countries, the MNC's also provide a recruiting ground for Philippine graduates. The education system in the Philippines has always been one of the most important mechanisms of neo-colonial control.

MNC's are also connected with the repressive nature of the martial law regime. The institutional use of torture has been well documented by the Association of Major Religious Superiors, Amnesty International and the International Commission of Jurists. The imprisonment of Marcos's political opponents such as Senator Aquino, also continues despite the Carter Administration's emphasis on 'human rights'. The fact that there is a direct relationship between the export-oriented industrialization strategy and repression is not as well known. The most important linkage is the regime's role in preventing strikes and keeping wages low. When a strike occurred in July 1976 at the Mead Johnson plant in Manila, the army moved in to arrest many of the strikers. Some were sacked by the American management.[37] The Philippine Constabulary were also called in when industrial trouble occurred in March 1974 at the Gelmart factory in Manila. In the BEPZ, barrio dwellers have been removed from their homes without adequate compensation. Similar events have occurred in Cagayan de Oro at the site of the Kawasaki sintering plant. In other cases, squatters living in areas need by the regime as a site for export-oriented industries have been forcibly removed. The case which had received most international publicity is the Tondo foreshore project. With World Bank approval, the government wants to develop the Tondo Foreshore Area in Manila Bay into an industrial and commercial area which would attract MNC's. Despite army repression, the Tondo slumdwellers formed organizations such as ZOTO (Zone One Tondo Organization). When the World Bank sent a mission to discuss the Tondo Foreshore Development scheme in 1975, one of the ZOTO leaders, Ms Trinidad Herrera, was locked up until the W.B. group had left. She was invited to attend a U.N. Human Settlements design competition in Canada in February 1976, but had to go into hiding when her arrest was ordered. In April 1977 she was arrested and tortured. An outcry from the Catholic hierarchy and religious orders, many of whom are now outspoken critics of the regime, helped to secure her release. The torturers, however have been acquitted and Ms. Herrera has been charged with 'subversion'. Although some individual U.S. corporate managers in the Philippines might express distaste at such events, the U.S. business community in general remains enthusiastic about the New Society. Officials of the World Bank, the I.M.F., the A.D.B. and the eleven member Consultative Group for the Philippines (formed in 1971) also approve of the Philippine 'development' model. Despite Carter's 'human rights' policy, the U.S. government continues to fund the plethora of 'security' agencies which the Philippine government needs to assist foreign investors by keeping wages low, preventing strikes and demonstrations, and subduing unions and political opponents.

The Marcos regime claims that its 'modernization' programme is succeeding, citing growing of G.N.P. as 10% in 1973, 5.9% in 1974, 5.9% in 1975 and 6.3% in 1976.[38] Although this does not match the 'economic miracle' of Brazil, it is an impressive record. What many of Marcos's critics have failed to appreciate is that in many less developed countries (LDC's) there is a clear relationship between political authoritarianism and economic dynamism. Martial law in the Philippines has meant that Marcos has been able to push through many measures which would have been impossible during the 'democratic' period. As in Brazil, however, the 'reforms' have largely been made at the expense of the urban and rural workers. Real wages for both skilled and unskilled workers have declined in the last five years. Using 1972 as a base line with 100 index points, real wages for skilled workers dropped to 95.4 in 1973, 77.4 in 1974, 74.4 in 1975 and 71.2 in 1976; for unskilled workers the decline was from 92.9 points to 72.2[39] In 1975, the government considered the idea of raising the daily minimum wage from P. 8, but abandoned it for fear of raising the cost of exports and frightening off foreign investors.[40] The threat of strikes in mid 1976 forced the regime to raise the minimum urban wage to P. 10, but it then allowed the price of rice and other controlled basic commodities to rise, in effect wiping out the gains of the workers. On a poverty line drawn at U.S. $1,081-1,351 p.a. for a family of six (the average family size) 75% of the nation's families are poor.[41] Despite the regime's verbal commitment to 'equality', a number of recent studies by Philippine scholars indicates that there has not been any improvement in the maldistribution of income, and that the Philippines remains in the top 20% of countries with the worst distribution of income. A recent study from the National Census and Statistics Office confirms this view. According to this study, 8.6 million Filipinos, or 20% of the population, control 53% of the wealth, 17.2 million Filipinos, or the poorest 40%, earn only 15% of the income, and these trends are continuing.[42] Like many other less developed countries (LDC's), the Philippines has high levels of unemployed and under-employed which are often disguised in official statistics. The drift to the cities has resulted in more than one million squatters living in Metropolitan Manila. The regime's response is often to demolish squatter shanties, or to construct hoardings to hide them from tourists and convention delegates. One of the reasons for increasing radicalism in the Church is that the priests and nuns are in a position to observe the 'marginalization' which the New Society has imposed on the weakest sections of society.

Another indication of the failure of the New Society to meet the basic needs of Filipinos was a survey by the Department of Agriculture in 1975. The survey indicated that there was a slight increase in the total amount of cereals consumed between 1970 and 1974, with the increase largely accounted for by an increased consumption of cheaper corn products. Consumption of meat fell drastically. Consumption of poultry, meat and eggs dropped by approximately one-third, dairy products by half, sea food by a third, fresh fruit by nearly a third, fresh vegetables by a third except for a sharp increase in the use of cheap roots and tubers.[43] The recent World Bank study on the Philippines concluded that "inadequate nutrition appears to be commonplace among low income groups in the Philippines".[44] At the same time, MNC's such as Castle and Cook, Del Monte, United Brands and Sumitomo are exporting vast quantities of bananas, pineapples and other fruit to the developed countries.

The Philippines also faces problems of indebtedness, both to multilateral agencies and the global banks. Since 1972, external debt has jumped from $2 billion to $3.8 billion in 1975 and $5.5 billion in 1976 (the Bataan nuclear plant is a heavy contributor to the 1976 figure).[45] The debt service ratio is estimated to be 15% for 1976 and 1977. Despite the regime's claim that a ratio under 20% is 'safe', it has received warnings from the I.M.F. The recently retired U.S. Ambassador Sullivan has also warned that the Philippines and other developing countries will find it increasingly difficult to borrow from international financial institutions and private banks abroad. He reportedly pointed out that the Philippines was nearing its foreign borrowing limits.[46]

Criticism of the Marcos regime is increasing both in the U.S. and in the Philippines, and Marcos occasionally promises to end martial law. But it is clear that the current 'development' strategy cannot be pursued without repression. On the other hand, the consequences of falling real wages and the suppression of dissent are potentially explosive in a country as highly politicized as the Philippines, even if the Maoist New People's Army cannot be regarded as a real threat to the regime. At times Marcos has found it necessary to make some concessions to 'nationalist' pressures within the Philippines. Similar pressures apply externally. Harbouring as it does the only remaining U.S. bases in Southeast Asia, the Philippine government is anxious to present itself as a respectable member of the Third World. The so-called 'reorientation' of Philippine foreign policy can be interpreted in this light. The Philippines is also a member of the Association of Southeast Asian Nations (ASEAN) which supports the demands of other LDC's for a New International Economic Order (NIEO). Criticism of MNC's for transfer pricing, excessive profit making, refusal to transfer technology, and raising capital within the LDC's has been an important part of the demand for a NIEO. The leaders of the ASEAN countries are also very aware that the socialist states of Indochina now offer an alternative 'self-sufficiency' model of development which is very different from their own foreign investment-oriented 'trickle-down' model.

As has been indicated, for about two years after the declaration of martial law, the Philippine government removed previous impediments to capital inflow and decreed additional incentives to foreign investment. Since about 1975, however, some criticism of MNC's has been allowed to appear in Manila controlled press. Hilarion Henares, former chief government economic planner, has accused Ford of draining resources from the Philippines by generating its capital locally. Vicente Jayme, President of the Private Development Corporation of the Philippines, has accused MNC's of excessive pricing for licensing agreements which allow manufacture of their products in the Philippines.[47] Claims of excessive profit making have also been levelled at MNC's. G.P. Sicat, Director General of the National Economic Development Authority and one of the chief architects of the Philippine development strategy, claimed in 1976 that in the tyre industry, returns on equity for Goodyear Philippines, Goodrich Philippines and Firestone Philippines were respectively 28.5%, 21.3% and 13.6%. These three subsidiaries of MNC's accounted for 73% of total sales, 86% of total equity, and 91% of total net profits in the tyre industry.[48] Even Vicente Paterno, also a notable supporter of foreign investment, has complained that MNC's prevent any real transfer of technology. It is a frequently heard complaint that 90 out of every 100 patent holders in the Philippines are foreigners. Criticisms of Japanese MNC's have also been made openly. The Philippine government's disappointment with Japan's refusal to fund an integrated steel mill at the site of the Kawasaki sintering plant in Mindanao prompted an apparent press leak by the Department of Public Information which stated that "Filipinos are already beginning to complain that the only technology which the Japanese are exporting is in those industries that the Japanese government has prohibited at home as pollution-exporting".[49] Since 1975 there has also apparently been increasing awareness that heavy reliance on an export-oriented industrialization strategy means that the Philippines is very vulnerable to fluctuations in world trade, especially at a time when there is concern over protectionism in the metropolitan countries.

Some concrete action has followed the complaints about MNC's. A patent law proposed in 1976 included approval and registration of all licensing agreements; a limit on royalty payments to 5% of nett wholesale price; and provisions to force patent holders to manufacture their products locally. Also in 1976, Presidential decrease 270, 396 and 402 placed a ceiling on the amount private corporations, whether local or foreign, could pay as dividends to stockholders; this was designed to ensure that a certain portion of profits will be reinvested.[50] Marcos has also decreed that foreign technicians are now required to train Filipinos and then leave within five years. In July 1977, it was further announced that new 'debt-equity' rules would be applied to limit borrowings of pesos to a proportion of equity. Companies at least 40% foreign-owned would be subject to requirements that to borrow pesos in the Philippines, they would need the certificate of a government committee that such borrowings met specified ratios of debt-to-equity.[51] These new guidelines were designed to ensure that foreign companies did not raise most of their capital within the Philippines and then remit excess profits to the metropolitan countries.

Despite such measures, the regime has limited room to manouvre, even if the criticism of MNC's is more than rhetoric. The export-oriented development strategy is based on attracting foreign investment As a latecomer to the establishment of 'export platforms', the Philippines must compete with Hong Kong, Singapore and South Korea in attracting foreign investors. In addition, there are strong links between the elite and many MNC's. The country is also indebted to the global banks and the multilateral agencies which insist on the economy being open to foreign capital. But euphoria with which MNC's greeted the declaration of martial law in 1972 is rapidly disappearing. By late 1976, at least five foreign banks involved in Philippine finance companies had pulled out.[52] A small number of MNC's such as ESSO have sold their subsidiaries to the government. There have been persistent reports of disenchantment with the Philippines on the part of some corporations, on the grounds of corruption and inefficiency. Mrs. Marcos in particular has created resentment because of the 'squeeze' she exerts on both foreign and domestic corporations to finance her pet projects such as the new convention center. There has in fact been a decline in new U.S. investment over the past two years.[53] Former U.S. Ambassador Sullivan told a gathering of local and foreign bankers in Manila in May 1977 that new capital inflow was 'slow'. He reportedly attributed this to a combination of negative factors: the restraining impact of the recent world recession of the availability of investible funds; a wait-and-see attitude on the part of certain foreign investors *re* the stability of the political structure of the country; adverse reactions by certain foreign investors to Third World rhetoric with which the Philippines was said to have identified itself; and uncertainly arising from sudden or abrupt changes in policies affecting foreign investments [54]

The Ambassador particularly mentioned the new debt-to-equity rules which were supposed to come into effect on 1st October 1977. Marcos's retreat on this issue clearly demonstrates the limits on the regime's ability to restrict the activities of MNC's. In response to complaints by the U.S. Embassy and the American Chamber of Commerce, by the end of October, three MNC's (Ford Philippines, Caltex Philippines and General Motors Philippines) were given exemptions from the new requirements. Marcos himself has recently been at pains to emphasise that the Philippines is still safe and profitable for foreign investment. In a satellite telecast to an American business seminar on the fifth anniversary of martial law, he said that the government was 'very flexible' in its requirements relating to the training of Filipino technicians by foreigners. He also said that agrobusiness companies shouldn't be worried by the new land reform measures since they don't apply to plantations.[55] Predictions about the Philippines are always difficult. Despite criticism of martial law in the U.S., it is hard to foresee any fundamental change in the *status quo* in the immediate future. Marcos's position, however, will remain delicately balanced. He will need to make some concessions to 'nationalist' pressures both internal and external, but at the same time will need to try to keep the Philippines attractive for foreign investors. One of the most important questions for the future also centres on the relationships between Japanese and American MNC's in the Philippines. There are a myriad of 'arrangements' between them, but also increasing evidence of competition. Whether this competition will allow Marcos to play them off against each other remains to be seen.

This examination of the relationship between MNC's and martial law in the Philippines clearly indicates the need for more research, even though independent research is difficult under martial law conditions. It is also obvious that the theoretical basis of this research requires careful examination. Many observers of 'dependency' have assumed a traditional view of economic imperialism which holds that the basic relationship between a developed capitalist economy such as the U.S. and an underdeveloped economy such as the Philippines is one of exploitation and stagnation. Clearly that assumption is no longer valid. As Cardoso has pointed out, in many underdeveloped countries "the massive investment of foreign capital aimed at manufacturing and selling consumer goods to the growing urban middle and upper classes is consistent with, and indeed dependent on, fairly rapid economic growth in at least some crucial sectors of the dependent country."[5][6] Economic 'growth' in this situation also depends on the technological, financial and market connections that only MNC's can provide. It is pointless to argue that MNC's have not contributed to economic 'growth' in the Philippines. The major argument, as this chapter has tried to point out, is that there remains a clear distinction between 'growth' and 'development' if 'development' is thought of in the sense of satisfying mass needs. 'Growth' in terms of the Brazilian model apparently being followed by the Philippines presupposes political authoritarianism, an emphasis on luxury and consumer items for the elite and middle class, increasing foreign indebtedness, and a regressive pattern of income distribution. The model seemed to work well (in its own terms) for the first three years of martial law, but the indications now of a slow-down in foreign investment and increasing political opposition do not augur well for the long-term 'stability' so beloved by the global corporations.

Footnotes

1. H. Magdoff, "Multinational Corporations and Undeveloped Countries" in W. Sichel (ed.), *The Economic Effects of Multinational Corporations.* (Michigan Business Papers, Graduate School of Business Administration, University of Michigan, 1975).
2. R. Barnet and R. Müller, *Global Reach: The Power of the Multinational Corporations* (Cape, London, 1974).
3. The elected representatives of the Huk supported Democratic Alliance were removed from their seats so the Bill could be forced through Congress.
4. Alejandro Lichauco, "The Lichauco Paper; Imperialism in the Philippines", *Monthly Review,* July-August 1973. pp. 35, Lichauco was formerly president of the Philippine Petroleum Association and executive vice-president of the Anglo-Philippine Oil and Mining Corporation. He was elected as delegate to the Constitutional Convention in 1970, where he led the struggle to have clauses written in to the new constitution which would control foreign investment. He was arrested when martial law was delcared. Lichauco's paper represents the viewpoint of the Philippine industrial elite *vis-a-vis* the American multinationals.
5. Payer, *op. cit.,* p. 70.
6. IDOC, *The Philippines: American Corporations, Martial Law and Undevelopment.* A Report Prepared by the Corporate Information Center of the National Council of Churches of Christ in the U.S.A., 1973- p. 16 (hereafter cited as CIC Report).
7. C.I.C. Report, p. 17.
8. Robert B. Stauffer, "The Political Economy of a Coup: Transnational Linkages and Philippine Political Response", *Journal of Peace Research,* vol. II, No. 3, 1974, p. 166.
9. *Ibid*
10. Lichauco, *op. cit.,* p. 32

11. C.I.C. Report, *op. cit.,* p.18.
12. See Stauffer, *op. cit.,* Gabriel Kolko, "The U.S. and the Philippines", *AICD Occasional Paper No. 4,* May 1973.
13. C.I.C. Report, p. 32.
14. *Far Eastern Economic Review,* 23 May, 1975.
15. The Philippine government has belatedly realized, as the Senate had predicted, that the Treaty gives 'unfair' advantages to Japan. It also blocks Philippine plans to extend special trading preferences to other ASEAN countries. The Philippines is trying to renegotiate the Treaty, so far without success.
16. *Business Day,* 28 September, 1977.
17. *Business Day,* 28 September, 1977.
18. *People Toiling Under Pharoah,* Report of the Action-Research Process on Economic Justice in Asia. Urban-Rural Mission and Christian Conference on Asia, 1976, p. 43, Hereafter cited as URM/CCA Report.
19. C.I.C. Report, p. 55.
20. Advertisement, *Insight,* August, 1975.
21. R. Constantino, "Global Enterprises and the Transfer of Technology", *Journal of Contemporary Asia,* Vol. 7, No. 1, 1977, pp. 47-48.
22. T.Q. Pena, "The Bataan Export Processing Zone Comes of Age". *Fookien Times Philippine Yearbook.* 1976, p. 177.
23. See Kido Junko, "Philippines: Kawasaki Steel Corporations Sinter Plant in Mindanao", Free Trade Zones and Industrialization of Asia, Special Issue of *AMPO,* 1977.
24. *Business Day.* 30 September, 1977.
25. C.I.C. Report, p. 46.
26. J. Salonga, "Multinationals in the Philippines: A Brief Analysis and a Proposed Approach", Lecturer delivered in Manila, 28 August 1975. Quoted in CCA/URM Report, p. 50.
27. M. Skully, *Merchant Banking in the Far East,* (Banker Research Unit, 1976), p. 80.
28. *Ibid.,* p. 96.
29. BDC Report, 1975.
30. *Asian Wall Street Journal,* 25 August, 1977.
31. Benedict J. Kerkvliet, "Land Reform in the Philippines since the Marcos Coup", *Pacific Affairs,* Vol. 47, No. 3, Fall 1974, p. 291.
32. B. Wildman, "Banana Boom: Fruits for Only a Few", *Far Eastern Economic Review,* 21 January, 1974.
33. Despite alleged attempts to intimidate and bribe him, Mijares testified against the Marcos regime in human rights hearings before the U.S. Congress in 1975. He has now disappeared, and it appears he may have been murdered.
34. *Philippine Liberation Courier,* 7 October, 1977.
35. C.I.C. Report, p. 39.
36. See R. Stauffer, "Philippine Authoritarianism: Framework for Peripheral 'Development'," University of Hawaii, 1976.
37. W. Bello, "Marcos and the World Bank", *Pacific Research,* Vol. VII, No. 6, Sept.-Oct. 1976, p. 9-10.
38. Gerado P. Sicat, "The Climate for Foreign Investment" in *Asia Corporate Profile and National Finance,* 1977.
39. R. Tasker, "The Five Year Itch", *Far Eastern Economic Review,* 30 September, 1977.
40. *Far Eastern Economic Review's Asia 1976 Yearbook,* p. 264.
41. *Asian Wall Street Journal,* 31 August, 1977.
42. *Asian Wall Street Journal,* 31 August, 1977.
43. Stauffer, "Philippine Authoritarianism", p. 20.
44. *The Philippines: Priorities and Prospects for Development,* A World Bank Country Economic Report, 1976, p. 268.
45. *Far Eastern Economic Review,* 3 January, 1977.
46. *Amcham Journal* (The American Chamber of Commerce in the Philippines), May 1977, p.4.
47. Leo Gonzaga, "Letter from Manila", *Far Eastern Economic Review,* 3 October, 1977.
48. Leo Gonzaga, "Philippines Eyes Tariff Cuts", *Far Eastern Economic Review,* 24 September, 1976.
49. *Asian Wall Street Journal,* 18 August, 1977.
50. Leo Gonzaga, "Foreign Investors Confused", *Far Eastern Economic Review,* 24 September, 1976.
51. *Asian Wall Street Journal,* 22 October, 1977.
52. *Ibid.,* 3 November, 1976.
53. Of a total inflow of $252 million in the past two years, $82 million has come from the U.S. in comparison with $102 million from Japan. Norberto K. Katigbak, "Philippines: Clearing the Decks for a

Breakthrough", *Asian Corporate Profile and National Finance,* 1977.
54.   *Amcham Journal,* May 1977, p. 4.
55.   *Asian Wall Street Journal,* 22 October, 1977.
56.   F.H. Cardoso, "Associated Dependent Development: Theoretical and Practical Implications" in A. Stepan, *Authoritarian Brazil* (Yale, 1973), p. 149.

The Future of the Multinational Corporation:

from the Japanese viewpoint.

By E. Mekata*

Among the so-called multinational corporations, I think the Japanese trading firms such as Mitsui, Mitsubishi, etc. is most spectacular in its world-wide extensive activities in various fields, having so many overseas offices throughout the world with excellent communications and expertise that cover a multitude of skills unsurpassed in the world today.

The trading firm, actually, is not only involved in export and import and domestic business but it actively participates in investment throughout the world in various fields such as the development of minerals and energy, primary products, shipping, insurance, warehousing, banking and many manufacturing industries.

Many people seem to have the idea that a multinational corporation is one that operates in many countries with one object to maximise profits from those countries. Let us be factual as happenings such as above have occurred but seem less likely to occur in future, because of the many restrictions being made in many countries on foreign investment. Some of these restrictions were overdue but we should remember that many countries owe their present position in the world to the help given by foreign investment.

Nevertheless, the activities of a multinational in Australia are always subject to the will of the Australian people through their government and the company can only do what that government permits.

The reason why such a giant trading activity was created in Japan may require some explanation and I would say the following may have been the main motive.

Japan was practically secluded from the rest of the world until about 100 years ago and its way of living and the language are totally different from any other place, even from the Chinese. Japan having once decided to open its doors, needed some specialist company which had many specially trained people in international trade. As you know, Japan is almost 80% mountains and only 20% arable and therefore requires practically all kinds of major materials namely oil, coal, iron ore, bauxite and many other minerals as well as wool, cotton, wheat, barley, soya-beans, maize, sorghum, meat, dairy products, etc.

In order to pay for these commodities to be imported, Japan must obtain foreign exchange by processing them and exporting to the other parts of the world. Consequently, import and export business has a tremendous significance for the Japanese — perhaps much more important than for any other country in the world, if you consider the population at present is more than 100 million in a small country.

In other words, Japan must trade actively and internationally for its survival which requires expertise, foresight, experience and more importantly, well timed courageous actions with a proper follow-through in the ever-changing and risky business of international trade and ventures.

Such a multinational Japanese trading company is also heavily involved in introducing new technical developments from overseas or from Japan to other countries, thus it is called "a think tank".

Let me tell you something about my company. The present total number of employees is about 14,000. It has 136 overseas offices where some 1,000 Japanese are stationed around the world and employs about 2,400 local overseas staff. These people are busily engaged in trading,

*Managing Director, Mitsui (Australia) & Co., Sydney, Australia.

financing, planning and exchanging economical, political and technical information throughout the world.

Mitsui's global communications network is one of the most modern of its kind in the world. The system is controlled by 3 key computer stations — Tokyo, London, New York. Each station has a computer for switching messages between the private leased telegraph channels within its area, for example, Tokyo handles Japan and Asia. The above 3 key computer stations also have an optical character reader. The OCR scans a type written message and produces punched tape at the rate of 2,000 characters per second.

In training Japanese personnel for such international activities, Mitsui so far has sent about 400 young employees to various overseas universities, mainly for the purpose of learning foreign languages and to become assimilated into such foreign countries. During this period they do not have to work at all for Mitsui's business but after one year's stay in the university, another one year or so must be spent in the local Mitsui office for the purpose of on-job training.

Mitsui has a number of overseas joint venture companies in 47 different countries and there are about 274 overseas joint venture projects presently in operation. Mitsui's investment amounts to some US$370 million including some non-profit making projects to assist underdeveloped countries with their economical development.

Out of the total of Mitsui & Co's annual turnover of about US$30,000 million, approximately 50% is Japanese domestic business, 40% is export and import business with Japan and 10% is what we call off-shore Japan business, such as grain from Australia to Taiwan or coal from Australia to South America or steel products from Australia to the Middle East or oil from the Middle East to Brazil etc.

In Australia, Mitsui is a partner in the Mt. Newman Iron Ore Project, Robe River Iron Ore Project, Thiess Dampier Mitsui Coal Company, Australian Tube Mill Project and some others.

Perhaps I have taken too much time in the explanation of Mitsui & Co's activity but the most important question is how such a multinational company should behave or is behaving in a foreign country. Obviously any private enterprise is seeking profit but in the case of the Japanese multinationals the supply assurance of major essential materials and a stable market for its manufactured products are even more important than a mere profit. In Australia, Japanese interest in any major ventures is satisfied with a minority equity and to leave the management to some Australian or other company involved in the joint venture. So far as Mitsui is concerned, it is fully aware of the importance to take into consideration the local welfare and the local sentiment when it tries to invest in any overseas country. The local equity participation of more than 50% is its basic principle.

Any government must carefully plan its own economic development program but over-suspicion against foreign multinational investment is sometimes damaging. Do not over-simplify that multinationals are getting very advantageous concessions from a foreign country.

In the case of Australia, any development requires a huge amount of finance which is sometimes very risky for Australian companies and more particularly, for the overseas investors. The production scale of any major development will have to be large enough to make it economically viable and must be internationally competitive as the Australian local demand is very limited and demand is usually localised due to Australia being a huge country and internal transportation costs are very expensive and sometimes inefficient. In this respect, I suggest that the Australian Government should take a more positive attitude to improve local transportation systems — land, sea and air.

I also feel that the Australian Government should forget about the "buying back the farm" sentiment but rather should take an attitude to consult with the Australian venturers as well as with the overseas venturers on how to achieve a systematic development of its natural resources and its manufacturing industry.

Right after the war, Japan was under American occupation for some period and it was under strong pressure, I understand, by American giant automotive industries to come into Japan but the Japanese Government resisted and as I remember, it took a firm policy of creating the Japanese automotive industry without much overseas participation.

There were some other major basic industries where the Japanese Government avoided overseas interest participation such as in the public utility companies and steel industry. I think this policy proved to be a success as Japan, with its 100 million population, could provide a sufficiently large market within Japan. However, whether such a principle could be advantageously adopted in the case of Australia is questionable.

It is my opinion that in the case of Australia, where local demand is limited and localised, you need more active participation of overseas interests and, for example, if the North-West Shelf gas is to be developed, it would perhaps be more advantageous to invite active overseas participation and plan to export its product after satisfying West Australia's demand and this would require a long term stable overseas market.

However clever a lawyer you may be, you can hardly draft up an agreement with a long-term pricing formula satisfactory to the seller and the buyer, taking into account all the future unknown factors such as inflation, cost up, labour situation, fluctuation of international currency, government intervention etc. One good solution for this difficulty would be to invite the buyer to become one of the joint venturers of the project.

Money is basically a very timid thing so you should take a more open-minded attitude towards overseas investors and plan a steady systematic development which would perhaps be the most practical way whether your government will be Liberal or Labor.

During the last few years in Japan there has been a social phenomena whereby "bigness" was blamed, multinationals were blamed, profit-making was considered a sin.

I do not know whether this is somewhat of a universal sentiment including Australia but profit is a great motive for mankind to think hard and to work hard which will improve the economy and public welfare. A good businessman is well aware that a selfish and egoistic action will not bring a profit. Any first class so-called multinational company is usually very keen in the sense of "give and take" and its obligation to contribute to the society to which it belongs which ultimately works in favour of the company.

142

Indonesia: The Multinationals and the Future.

By Kate Short*

Since the military coup of 1965, the Indonesian economy has experienced a massive and unprecedented inflow of foreign capital in the form of both aid funds and private foreign investment. These funds are, in the eyes of the Indonesian planners and their foreign advisers, necessary prerequisites for the sustained growth of the economy; aid funds are forthcoming from both bilateral and multilateral sources whilst private capital inflows originate in the main from the multinational corporations of the advanced capitalist economies.

The rapid and extensive volume of capital that has penetrated the Indonesian economy, particularly after the stabilisation period of 1966 to 1969, stands in marked contrast to that experienced by the economy in the turbulent years prior to the military coup. During that period the economy was marked by hyperinflation, loss of confidence by foreign investors in the economic policies pursued by Sukarno, a marked underutilisation of existing capital resources, a severe balance of payments problem, a huge international debt of US$2,400 million,[1] and widespread corruption and inefficiency within the bureaucracy.

By 1964 all foreign enterprises had been nationalised and the state banking sector weakened and abused by excessive government spending and malpractice. Moreover, the Indonesian businessmen, the pribumi,[2] were not overkeen to invest in industrial projects, hampered as they were by the existence of excessive government controls.[3] Furthermore, the foreign exchange licensing system, adopted during the "Guided Economy" period, coupled as it was with a massive inflation rate, distorted the pattern of investment by creating a poor climate for productive investment[4] conducive to speculative and commercial economic activity. During the "Guided Economy" period then, the efforts by the government to develop the economy by strengthening the public sector at the expense of the private, lead to a decline in productivity, output and employment.

Sukarno's government was unable to successfully ensure the allocation of capital into productive rather than non-productive sectors; thus attempts to foster the growth of a healthy and indigenous capital accumulation and at the same time encourage a lively process of accumulation did not meet with success.[5] However, since the advent of the "New Order government" there has been some noticeable changes and at present Indonesia is experiencing a considerable increase in capital formation. The main stimulus for this has been from both public and private foreign capital and to a much lesser extent, private domestic investment. The causes for the change are many and it is fitting to preface the main theme of the text with some brief mention of public policy.

With the advice and often heavy handed guidance of the IMF, the World Bank, and the Intergovernmental Group on Indonesia,[6] the recently installed military government of Indonesia has set about to create an investment climate conducive to the rapid and voluminous inflow of private foreign capital.[7] Following the military coup of 1965, the government embarked upon a program of economic stabilisation, the thrust of which was strictly within the parameters of IMF policy.[8] Consisting of tough fiscal and monetary measures, the stabilisation program was designed to reduce the rate of inflation, secure a moratorium on Indonesia's foreign debt and obtain emergency aid to cover the balance of payments deficit.[9] These measures were paralleled by moves to decontrol the economy and to encourage private foreign capital investment in resource extractive and manufacturing projects. Overall, the essence of these and other measures taken after the coup was to promote economic growth by heavy reliance on private sector market forces. The large inflows of foreign capital and technology were expected to facilitate the industrialisation of

*University of Adelaide, Adelaide, Australia.

the country, and assist the government in its aim of increasing employment and capital accumulation. The role of the government in the economy is essentially supportive rather than initiatory. Although state planning is institutionalised through numerous boards, the provision of the infrastructure necessary for industrialisation remains its most important function. As one text observed:

"On the face of it, the planners are being asked to formulate a plan which will provide adequate opportunities for the expansion of the private sector."[10]

One of the major problems that face Indonesia's policy markers is that of increasing the capacity of the economy to absorb capital as well as ensuring that the process is continual. Without attention to the financial, legal and physical conditions within the country, forthcoming foreign investment will be insufficient to play its alloted role in the economy. As a consequence, the Indonesian government, with the advice and assistance of the World Bank and the IMF, has been attempting to develop an infrastructure capable of absorbing large inflows of foreign capital. As one official expressed it:

"The government is to concentrate on providing the infrastructure and to leave the key capital-intensive areas to foreign capital and to local industry. . . . So you will see that there is a division of labour with the government providing the infrastructure . . . the stage for private investors."[11]

With respect to the development of the financial infrastructure (the banks, other financial institutions, etc.) the result of government activity has been to create a system that assists the growth of the modern and predominantly foreign owned sectors. Reforms to the banking system centred on the need to regulate the state and foreign banking networks, and to stimulate their competition and specialisation.[12] These resulted in the strengthening of the foreign banks and the continual protection of the state owned institutions. The former have been able to secure for themselves a large, if not the largest share of the market for foreign exchange transactions, as well as short and long term credits. The fact that nearly all internationally known banks have established representative offices or branches in Jakarta, attests to the profitability of the foreign owned banking sector.[13] Whilst these institutions well serve the needs of the foreign businessman in Indonesia and supply the much needed credit to finance investment projects, they do not adequately serve the needs of the indigenous firms. Historically, the allocation of credit to the pribumi has been poor, and the establishment of a modern banking sector does not appear to have significantly altered the situation. Thus, despite some effort by the government to equalise the cost of credit to the indigenous investor, his credit availability remains poor.[14] One such move by the government has been the establishment of eight merchant banks and a stock exchange; though the move to develop the money and capital market was to assist the growth of indigenous investment, it will in fact increase the mobilisation of domestic capital for use by the foreign investor, leaving the majority of the indigenous enterprises in the same, if not a worse position. In short, the present direction of growth of the financial infrastructure is one that assists foreign firms in their almost unhindered access *to the new growth industries,* whilst the majority of pribumi owned firms continue without significant assistance from the state.[15]

The increasingly unequal relationship between foreign and indigenous firms is also assisted by the development of the legal infrastructure within which both operate. An examination of the Indonesian legal framework especially as it relates to the regulation and control of capital investment, reveals not only its weakness, but also its tendency to assist the foreigner at the expense of the pribumi firm. Law no. 1. 1967 (the Foreign Investment Law) was enacted hastily to create a favourable impression with the international financiers and facilitate the quick and easy entry of foreign capital into the economy. In addition, it offered a wide variety of fiscal incentives to the foreign investor, particularly taxation concessions and tax holidays.[16] Further incentives include exemption from stamp duties, import duties and sales tax, and subsequent amendments to the law have shown an even more generous attitude to foreign capital.

To complement these developments in the legal and financial areas, it is necessary to briefly examine the creation of the physical infrastructure. In harmony with the thrust of these policies, an examination of the growth of the physical infrastructure shows it to be one most easily exploitable by foreign capital. Serious problems, however, remain;[17] communications and transport facilities are run down and often uncoordinated. Electricity and water supplies are sporadic and suitable industrial land, difficult to find. Moreover, the colonial orientation of the existing infrastructure for land transport and communications is concentrated in the island of Java.[18]

The task of upgrading the physical infrastructure of Indonesia, an archipelago which extends thousands of miles, is not an easy one. The Indonesian government, through its development budget and the provision of international aid funds, is actively engaged in the provision of improved and modern infrastructure. While such development is vital to the growth of the modern industrial and agricultural sectors, it has tended to accelerate the accumulation of capital by foreign rather than pribumi firms. The provision of industrial sites which are suitable for use by large predominantly foreign owned firms, in Jakarta and eventually in Surabaya, are good examples.[19] As one observer noted, the development of physically separate facilities for the foreigner bypasses bureaucratic problems, as well as providing modern facilities unavailable to most pribumi firms.[20] The development of the industrial estates has been paralleled by bonded warehouses and duty free processing zones. To induce export oriented labour intensive light manufacturing and assembly plants, the government has offered cheap rents and a high degree of efficiency.

These and other developments demonstrate again that infrastructural improvements generally assist the foreign and wealthier pribumi firms, and offer little to small and medium sized indigenous producers. In sum, the attempt to foster a lively and sustained process of capital accumulation has resulted in the most rapid growth of the foreign owned sectors of the economy; it is within this context that the gains made by the present government of Indonesia must be viewed. Economic development is occurring but it is a process which is uneven and which favours foreign over pribumi capital. The infrastructural backup necessary to increase investments involves the development of a western, capital intensive and highly sophisticated infrastructure which is both initially expensive and requires constant overseas support.

It is within this context that the assessment of motives, activities and prospects of multinational firms operating in Indonesia must be made. For to a large extent their present profitability, position of privilege within the domestic market, and dominance in leading areas of production are all conditional upon certain infrastructural developments being undertaken by the government. These infrastructural improvements have clearly assisted the increase in capital inflow, and facilitated investment in resource extractive, manufacturing and service sectors. The following sections offer some detail as to the source and volume of direct private foreign investment in the Indonesian economy.

The volume of foreign investment approved by the government since the coup and subsequent stabilisation period has been large and directed in the main toward "enclave" type investment in resource extraction, particularly in oil, timber and minerals. Such projects are capital intensive and employ complex technological processes completely reliant on imported know-how. In the manufacturing and service industries, too, there has been significant investments approved, which are also heavily reliant on imported technology and human resources. The official amount of approved foreign investment 1967 to 1975, excluding oil, is in the order of US$3.879 billion,[21] but only a proportion of this has actually been implemented.[22]

In the early period of the "New Order government," foreign investments were concentrated · in the resource extractive sectors, mainly in mining and oil exploration and extraction. Initially, American firms dominated this area but subsequently, Japanese firms have made substantial investments in forestry and fisheries. Huge areas of the resource-rich outer islands, particularly Kalimantan (formerly Borneo), were made available to the multinationals through leasing arrangements, and the oil bearing seabeds surrounding much of the archipelago were divided between the foreign oil companies.[23] In no important area, save that of the oil industry, did the Indonesian government itself partake in actual production or exploration. Similarly, private Indonesian firms could not participate in these developments as the huge capital costs effectively exclude competition with foreign firms. Thus, in a most important sector of the economy (especially with regard to the generation of valuable foreign exchange), the controlling interest remains foreign. Furthermore, the present nature of the resource extractive industry itself restricts the possibility of a substantial reinvestment of profits within Indonesia, and limits the generation of linkages to the rest of the economy.[24] Its capital intensive nature creates very few employment opportunities in relation to the money invested, and has meant the mass importation of professional and skilled workers from abroad. Thus in all ways, the resource extractive sector of the Indonesian economy remains an enclave of foreign investment, operating within an infrastructural framework that advantages it with respect to other sectors.

However, since 1970-71 there has also been significant foreign investments in import substitution manufacturing from Japanese and American sources as well as Chinese capital from Hong Kong, Singapore and the Philippines. Smaller, but still significant amounts, have also come from Europe and Australia.[25] The project list of such investments is impressive with 12 approved projects worth US$34.1 million by the end of 1967 and by December 1972, 314 investments worth US$654.2 million or 28.9 per cent of the total intended investment.[26] Within the manufacturing sector, there has been concentration on the production of certain types of commodities. In the consumer goods sector, for example — especially in clothing, textiles, footwear, food processing, chemicals (mainly pharmaceuticals) and transport equipment — there has been overdevelopment with a large numbers of firms competing for a share of the small market. In contrast, virtually all intermediate and capital goods industries are poorly developed. Moreover the foreign manufacturing firms tend to import not only the production machinery, but also most raw materials and component parts. Thus there is little stimulus for the domestic economy to supply the inputs necessary for production. The imbalances within the manufacturing sector are further increased by the regional concentration of investments in urban centres — particularly Jakarta.[27] Finally, the dominance of foreign and also non-indigenous local capital (Chinese Indonesians) within the capital intensive, highly productive modern sub-sectors of the manufacturing industry, stands in contrast to the position of the private Indonesian entrepreneur, whose production is on the whole characterised by labour intensive technology and low levels of output per worker.[28]

Thus since the installation of the "New Order government," there have been significant additions to capital formation in Indonesia not only in the resource extractive sectors, but also within the import substitution manufacturing sector. But it is an industrialisation process that is imbalanced, heavily reliant on foreign inputs, and thus extremely demanding on foreign exchange.[29] Furthermore the type of products manufactured and the nature of the market served are such that they too reinforce the imbalanced nature of the foreign dominated modern manufacturing sector. The examples of the textile, automobile assembly and pharmaceutical industries serve well to illustrate the point.

These three industries have been stimulated by large inflows of Japanese and American capital as well as significant investments from Australian based multinationals and European firms. The growth of the textile industry, for example, has been largely the result of Japanese investment.[30] Their highly capital intensive technology and modern methods of production have

146

raised productivity but at the same time caused the decline of the local textile industry and increased unemployment.[31] Thus although textile production has quickly increased, it has occurred at the expense of locally owned industries and of hundreds of thousands of textile workers. In the pharmaceutical industry too, there has been a large number of foreign investments by America, European and Australian multinationals.[32] Indeed, so much so, that the large number of firms operating within the same area have caused an oversupply of some commodities. Furthermore, the costs of the products they manufacture make them accessible to only a small minority of middle and lower middle class urban dwellers in Jakarta and other major urban centres. Similarly, the assembly of a large number of different types of automobiles in the factories of Jakarta and Surabaya has helped the development of the transport industry, but only very few people can afford to purchase private transport. Despite this fact and the pressing need to upgrade the public transport system, some 14 automobile assembly plants have now been set up in Indonesia.[33]

In all three areas of manufacturing then, the fact of increased production and capital accumulation must be considered along with other factors relating to their social and economic effects. Increases to production have been achieved at the expense of local industry and employment and rely heavily, if not exclusively, on imported technology and production inputs. Furthermore, the foreign firms in general enjoy high degrees of protection, adequate supplies of credit and often operate under the patronage of one or more high ranking military officers (or their wives). In terms of the demands these investments make on the economy, apart from the high foreign exchange costs, their need for skilled and professional workers draw such labour away from the locally owned sectors of the economy. Furthermore, although it is true that these industries have created employment opportunities that did not exist before, it is also true that they are highly capital intensive, and result in few jobs relative to the capital invested. Also as the jobs that are created in the main require little skill,[34] little transfer of skills can be expected from these investments. Finally, the growth of an import substitution based manufacturing sector will eventually be restricted through the saturation of the domestic market and the unlikelihood of significant exports. As one economist observed:

"if .... the shelter of import restriction is permitted to create industries within the economy producing goods whose import is restricted, then the objective of growth is frustrated; the economy surrenders through the back door what it secures by the front door.... It is one thing to conserve foreign exchange for the import of plant and machinery designed to help economic growth; it is an entirely different thing to use import restrictions as a device for stimulating domestic manufacture of 'protected' goods. Industrialisation is not synonomous with economic growth."[35]

The Indonesian government is aware of problems related to an import substitution based manufacturing sector as well as those generated by the enclave nature of the resource extractive sector. Although it appears that the majority of investments continue to be of this type, plans are afoot to alter the pattern of investment towards one more capable of generating continuous and more diversified industrial growth. The need for change in development strategy is also recognised by the international institutions of the capitalist world, and the economic conditions within the rich industrialised nations have prompted many multinational firms to seek increased investment opportunities in the poor countries. In important respects these are investments which correspond closely to those recommended by the IMF, the World Bank and the Asian Development Bank. With this in mind, it is now appropriate to discuss in some detail the proposals made by the international institutions for the restructuring of poor country economies, away from the import substitution and "enclave" investments to ones more capable of stimulating diversified and continuous economic growth. Such plans have been formulated, and to some extent implemented, by the Indonesian government and once an evaluation of these recent developments has been made, it will be possible to make some comment on the future role of the multinational firm in Indonesia.

Institutional Reports

It has long been the concern of the various international institutions to propose solutions to the poverty and underdevelopment in poor countries. Their most recent strategy seeks to increase and diversify the industrial capacity of poor nations through the capacities of multinational firms.[36] Various institutions have made policy recommendations to poor country governments, aimed at facilitating an increased inflow of private foreign capital capable of stimulating industrial growth in both the manufacturing and the resource extractive sectors. For example, the Asian Development Bank report was concerned to emphasise "the domestic economic policies which South East Asian countries can pursue on their own to improve their 'absorptive capacity' for the available aid and trade opportunities."[37] The objective is to redirect development priorities away from import substitution to a more outward looking strategy based on expanded trade and stimulated by private foreign capital, in the form of the multinational firm. The new strategy is adjudged to more effectively utilise the factor endowments of the country concerned, namely cheap and abundant labour and huge and untapped natural resources. It is a strategy of export substitution which involves a shift from the export of unprocessed raw materials (both agricultural and mineral) to the export of processed and semi-processed materials.[38] Trade assumes a most important role in this proposed restructuring, because it is argued that the foreign exchange earnings will increase, that there will be economies of scale created through industrial complementarity,[39] and that the abundant labour will be utilised at low cost. The type of exports recommended fall into three broad categories. Firstly, the processed and semi-processed agricultural and mineral products; edible oils, processed food, fodder processing, timber milling and veneer and plywood manufacture. These industries involve relatively simple technology and are labour intensive. Secondly, manufacture involving complex technology coupled with a skilled labour force for assembling intermediate or component goods for final assembly overseas. The third and final category recommended by the ADB is the manufacture of consumer goods like toiletries, simple electrical equipment, matches, textiles and clothing. Of course the dynamic for this proposed industrial growth is the large, integrated multinational firm, whose access to both technology and world markets make them well suited to the task.

A similar concern for a new industrialisation strategy is evident in a number of reports published by Ecosen.[40] These studies are interested in the South East Asian region, especially with respect to its capacity for increased and diversified trade. Their prerequisite is not surprisingly a shift from import to export substitution,[41] coupled with increased export of unprocessed raw materials.[42] A shift in the restructuring of production to serve the export market similar to that practiced by Taiwan and South Korea is recommended "so that . . . exports could become the main engine of growth."[43] The role of investment by multinational firms is vital to this process; they are

> "expected to serve developing countries through finding promised export markets and furnishing them with their output as well as through the transplanting of technology, managerial skills and capital, which are the most scarce factors of production in developing countries."[44]

Thus their recommendations for a more suitable policy of industrialisation are very similar to the Asian Development Bank report. They include the achievement of regional cooperation between the nations of South East Asia in order to achieve complementary production and economies of scale; government promoted export drives; foreign investment in export oriented production and its cooperation with indigenous capital through the joint-venture arrangement; and finally, the removal of the infrastructural and legal difficulties that hamper the growth of industry.

The final report considered in this brief overview of industrialisation strategies is that put forward by the United Nations.[45] A UN conference on industrialisation examined the problems and policies of the "first development decade" (1961-1970), identified the root causes of the difficulties encountered, and went on to suggest a range of policies that could stimulate greater and more rapid economic growth. The report found that under the import substitution method of industrialisation, foreign exchange shortages, high degrees of protection for often inefficient industries, and inadequate employment generation were common. The conference recommended a development pattern that reduced the import content of industrialisation and made greater use of local resources. In short it recommended a more balanced growth between industry and agriculture, a far greater mobilisation of domestic and foreign capital, the efficient manning of industries, increased management and technical training, and greater trade both globally and within the region.

A major concern of the report was the need to increase production through the application of improved management techniques and the use of modern equipment. Thus it recommended that serious attention to modern techniques and adequate scale of industry be given high priority. Yet this concern to increase the competitiveness of products from the poor countries on world markets conflicts greatly with the need for increased employment opportunities. To overcome this problem, the report suggested that whilst large scale industries should concentrate in a few favourable areas, the establishment of satellite industries would create the volume of employment necessary. For a report that is apparently concerned with the problem of unemployment in the region, this position seems surprisingly trite. It stresses the adoption of an industrialisation strategy that favours modern techniques, the role of the multinational firm and the need for production for the world market; considerations of employment remain secondary.[46]

The UN report also argued that the principle of industrial complementarity be applied to the region. Because of the smallness of domestic markets and the relative lack of capital within each country, the production in key areas could not be confined to the national scale, but must instead be based on regional cooperation. The technological sophistication embodied in large scale industries makes production for just the local market inefficient, thus each country of the region is advised to follow a policy of selective industrialisation and regional cooperation; the long term objective being the eventual establishment of an Asian common market.[47] Such cooperation is viewed not merely as desirable "but would be imperative if the accelerated pace of industrialisation . . . was to take place."[48] Increased trade within the region depends " . . . to a large extent on the differences in degree of industrialisation and stages of growth within the region."[49] The factor endowments of Indonesia may well mean that the country will be generally maintained at a relatively low technological level. In short, the rate and content of Indonesia's economic growth under this proposed scheme, will be dependent upon external forces for both its stimulus and continuation.

To sum up, the recommendations of the planning bodies involve the development of an industrial base which is more mature than at present, which will be owned by the multinational firms and directed toward the development of external markets. It excludes the possibility for a genuinely national base industrialisation. Labour intensive processes may be fostered in Indonesia, with more complex production introduced elsewhere — probably in Singapore.[50] For Indonesia one report recommends resource based industrial growth with the take off to demand oriented manufacture taking place later than elsewhere in South East Asia.

149

United Nations Recommendations and New Order Policy; a limited convergence.

It is of course much easier to see the problems faced by a country like Indonesia than it is to devise and implement policies for their solution. The recommendations of the UN report require that governments of poor countries encourage investment by multinational firms which will assist the redirection of industrial growth. To a limited degree the "New Order government" is achieving this. More importantly, it is implementing a number of infrastructural changes which will encourage investment capital in the recommended industries. The following pages offer a brief outline of the economic policies of the Indonesian government in the light of some of the recommendations of the UN report.[51]

The first of these is the need to plan the direction of investment without stifling the initiative of the private sector. In this respect the function of the government is to promote an investment climate without excessive controls. Under the first five year plan, the government's desire for foreign capital resulted in the almost uncontrolled inflow into the resource extractive and manufacturing sectors. Overall the volume of employment created was low for the volume of capital invested, and little training of indigenies was undertaken. The early willingness of the government to accommodate the foreign investor at all costs, has been tempered to a degree with a discernible shift toward an increased emphasis on the training and employment of Indonesians, and on the necessity of encouraging labour intensive and foreign exchange saving (or earning) industries. Control of foreign capital and the direction of investment funds was also attempted by the closure of certain industries to further foreign investment, and the issuance of a list of priority industries.[52] These included agricultural estates, cattle breeding, the manufacture of commodities for use in the agricultural sector, the development of fisheries and forestry, textiles and export oriented manufacture, including the processing of raw materials. According to the Department of Light Industry, industrial activity is to be directed at the promotion of raw material processing and of industries that saved or earned foreign exchange.[53] The planned development of Batam Island (off Singapore) was to have facilitated "offshore" export oriented labour intensive manufacturing; an indepth survey of the islands potential proposed the establishment of a free trade zone with industrial estates involving one to three large refineries, a port, agricultural projects and tourist facilities.[54] Further plans include Batam as the major collection centre for Indonesia's imports and exports, and the establishment of bonded warehouses within the proposed complex was to give teeth to plans to increase the islands export role in the processing of raw materials. However, it now appears that due to the crisis of the state owned oil company, Pertamina, this comprehensive project has been indefinitely shelved. Nevertheless, the existence of this type of long term industrial project does indicate an awareness among Indonesia's policy markers of the necessity of developing a broader and more diversified industrial base.

The second of the UN recommendations pertains to the development of agricultural and mineral based industries as they both would increase employment opportunities and foreign exchange. Pelita two, Indonesia's second five year plan, focussed on the need to increase the processing of raw materials into basic and intermediate products and to diversify exports to include non-traditional as well as traditional products. As one government official put it;

> "... in regard to the export of commodities, Indonesia will be exporting more and more processed materials and manufactured goods."[55]

At the present time, investment in resource based agri-industries is mainly concentrated in fisheries and forestry. Yet there is a definite trend towards more broadly based agricultural investment.[56] A similar concern to promote an increased and diversified industrial base is reflected in the government's policy on mineral exports. By 1973 the aim was to maximise the processing of mineral exports and priority was officially given to investments that included integrated operations through processing and refining; tax differentials have been introduced to encourage this. Besides this type of export promotion, the government is also keen to increase and diversify the exports of manufactured and semi-manufactured goods, and export taxes on over sixty finished goods have been lifted.[57] Low technology and labour intensive assembly line operations are dominant in these areas of production, and it is hoped that the export of manufactured goods will have a high growth rate. Although the exports of light manufactured goods is small in comparison to other commodities, its growth has been rapid and expected to increase in the future. Current items exported include glass pipes and electric bulbs, by the Philips-Ralin company, and air conditioners and radios by several Japanese joint-venture firms.

The third UN recommendation considered here relates to the structure of multilateral and bilateral aid. The proposed industrialisation requires that aid be redirected more in favour of recipient countries and to help raise living standards, accelerate technology transfer, and develop the infrastructure and research within the host country. Since previously the flow of aid to the poor countries has emphasised prevailing trade discrimination, it is reasonable to expect that aid priorities must also change. Indeed, this is the view of the Asian Development Bank report which states:

> "Aid and investment should be more heavily concentrated in directly productive export oriented industries. Aid for agricultural investment and the provision of agricultural inputs . . . deserve attention in view of the promise of the green revolution."[59]

Within Indonesia there has been quiet but growing criticism of the nature of the various aid sponsored projects, and moves to liberalise aid contracts will undoubtedly be welcome by military leaders who are very much aware of the social and political tensions generated by these economic policies. Pressure is being exerted by the Indonesian government and the international bodies to effect the restructuring of ". . . financial aid to the development of export opportunity in developing countries."[60] Thus whilst much of the multilateral aid received by Indonesia does remain tied to the donor countries, its relative importance appears to be falling. Purchases can thus be made in the cheaper markets of neighbouring countries. In addition, with respect to increased technical training, World Bank and UN sponsored aid has recently been directed to the building of technical schools to help produce the much needed middle order management and technicians. US AID[61] technical assistance is being offered in the case of fertilisers and high yielding varieties of rice, and a recent report by this institution indicates a re-orientation of American aid in the direction recommended by the planners.[62] Other multilateral aid groups are also implementing similar policies.[63] These and other shifts in aid priorities reflect that the proposed new direction of industrialisation requires agriculture to be modernised through green revolution technology and its output directed towards the world market; furthermore, the industrial sectors must be assisted in their diversification and modernisation through new aid priorities.

To a limited degree the thrust of the recommendations of the UN have found expression in the policies of the Indonesian government. Yet the choice in favour of either import substitution or export substitution cannot be taken exclusively in favour of either. For Indonesia especially, the decision cannot be clearcut. Although in the long run, formal policy decisions already favour the growth of export oriented investment (through the multinational firms), significant problems remain and the government plans a continuation of import substitution manufacturing in some fields. Official criterion for its continuation are stated in terms of employment generation and technology transfer. Yet the capacity of the government to control the activities of foreign capital is limited, and it is probable that a large amount of import substitution manufacturing will continue for some time. The problem for the Indonesian government to decide is which industries shall be continued and which discouraged; the strength of the multinational lobby within Indonesia will ensure that such decisions will not be taken on a purely "rational" economic basis. The dilemma was well expressed by an official of the government when he stated that import substitution policies "in the longer run . . . will face severe problems when the domestic market becomes saturated. This may not come until ten or fifteen years later, but once we have set up high cost industries behind protective walls, it will be extremely difficult to change the orientation of those industries from the domestic market towards markets abroad."[64]

Whilst this important question remains a problem for the economic planners in Indonesia, for the large, integrated multinational firms operating in that country and the Southeast Asian region, the prospects for the future do not appear to be wrought with the same kind of hazards or uncertainties. If firms choose to operate within the bounds of the import substitution system, with its high degree of protection and considerable incentives, then they will no doubt continue to experience the adequate profit margins that they have taken for granted in the past. Certainly, they may be obliged to increase the training of the local workforce and pay more taxes to the state, but due to the nature of their production process and the weakness of government institutions enforcing the new guidelines, it is unlikely that significant training or increases in taxation will result. Furthermore, the type of future import substituting industries to be established in Indonesia are not likely to generate supportive industrial activities within the locally owned sectors of the economy. Remaining as they will, heavily reliant on imported capital goods and component parts, and serving the limited urban market, there will be little "spread" effect to the rest of the economy. They will remain as manufacturing enclaves, grafted onto but not integrated within the remainder of the Indonesian economy.

For the multinational firm investing in the export oriented manufacturing and raw material processing industries, the prospects in Indonesia do not appear to offer great promise. Although the government has begun an infrastructural development program to encourage this type of investment and some has been made, there are a number of factors which militate against this occurrence. For in addition to the thrust of economic planning and future needs of the multinational firm, there exist wider political and economic issues that must also be taken into account. Of particular importance to Indonesia is the growing competition from the industrial growth in other nations of the region, especially in Singaproe, Malaysia (most important is Penang) and the Philippines. In terms of infrastructural development, the quality of the labour force, and a better developed industrial base, the other areas appear more attractive. In the processing of raw materials Indonesia may have the greatest abundance of natural resources in the region. However the capital cost of setting up a plant to process say, bauxite or timber, may preclude its implementation for a number of years. Already in West Papua (West Irian) million of dollars worth of copper have been sabotaged by freedom fighters.[65] Such political instability is a deterrent to the establishment of processing facilities and of a more general long range commitment to develop the industrial capacity of Indonesia.

Further obstacles to the significant growth of export oriented industries and a more mature and diversified economic base is the nature of the Indonesian state itself. Whilst sections of this military bureaucratic apparatus clearly aim to improve the absorptive capacity of the economy and to improve the investment climate for the foreigner, the political question of local participation in economic growth may force greater restrictions on the activities of foreign investors in future years. Furthermore, the widespread incidence of "corruption," the inconsistencies between and within government departments, and the fact that they still remain outside the effective control of the central planning and decision making bodies, all contribute to an investment climate which is unfavourably compared with other nations in the region. Recent disclosures of bribery at high levels, and the continuous complaints of the foreign businessman in Jakarta concerning the highly "irregular" activities of the bureaucracy (particularly the powerful departments of Customs and Taxation) contribute to the instability of the investment climate.

There remains one further point to be discussed, that of achieving regional cooperation and complementary production between nations of the region. Such a development will be extremely difficult, not only because of political factors and rivalry between different nations, but also because the economies of the region are competitive rather than complementary.[66] Furthermore, Indonesia, the nation with the largest market and the least developed industrial base, has understandably been the most reticent on the question of an integrated regional market[67] as it is probable that Singapore would achieve most from this proposed development and Indonesia the least. Given the rivalry between the two nations, and Indonesia's not unwarranted apprehension of domination by Chinese capital, it is unlikely that the development of regional markets and complementary industrial bases will be easy to achieve. When or if it does occur, those who stand to gain the most will be the multinational firms and the more affluent countries or areas of the region.

In conclusion, it appears that future prospects for the multinational firm in Indonesia remain good in terms of profitability; but the prospects for increased industrial growth, as a result of new waves of export oriented foreign investments, are not substantial. Within the region there is good reason to anticipate increased and diversified industrial growth, but Indonesia is not in a position to be a prime beneficiary. No doubt export oriented, labour intensive manufacturing industries will be established there, but the quantities will not be sufficient to significantly correct the employment problem, nor be the prime stimulus for more diversified economic activity. There are too many domestic and external factors which militate against this possibility.

Footnotes

1. Legge, J.D., *Sukarno, A Political Biography,* Penguin, 1972, p. 285.
2. Pribumi means literally "son of the soil," and refers in the text to the indigenous Indonesian businessman, as distinct from those Indonesians of (predominantly) Chinese descent.
3. Douglas Paauw describes well the psychological effect that government policy toward the private sector had engendered. "From Colonial to Guided Economy" in McVey, R.T. (ed.) *Indonesia,* HRAF Press, 1967.
4. See Corden, W.A. and Mackie, J.A.C., "The Development of the Indonesian Exchange Rate System," *The Malayan Economic Review,* April, 1962.
5. It is not the author's intention to imply that the problems of the Indonesian economy were the result of Sukarno's policies alone. On the contrary, his task was made incredibly difficult by circumstances quite beyond his control. As Glassburner points out, the economic power of the post independence governments were severely circumscribed by the colonial pattern of ownership and control of key sectors of the economy. For details see Glassburner, B., *The Economy of Indonesia,* Cornell University Press, 1971.
6. The Intergovernmental Group on Indonesia (IGGI) was formed in Paris from the creditor nations who were owed money by Indonesia. The creditor nations were the USA, Japan, Australia, France, West Germany, Italy, and the Netherlands. For further detail see Posthumus, G.A., "The Intergovernmental Group on Indonesia," *Bulletin of Indonesian Economic Studies* (BIES), July, 1972.
7. The ideological essence of the government program may be found in the decision of the Parliament (MPRS), of 23 July, 1966. Panglaykim, Y., and Thomas, K.D., *The New Order and the Economy,* Research School of Pacific Studies, 1966.
8. For detail on IMF policy toward Indonesia see Payer, C., *The Debt Trap,* Penguin, 1974.
9. For details on these measures see Tomasson, G., "Indonesia: Economic Stabilisation 1966-69," *Development Digest,* January, 1975.
10. Panglaykim, Y., and Thomas, K.D., "Indonesia – The Effect of Past Policies and President Suharto's Plans for the Future", *CEDA P Series II* (Melbourne), November 1973, p. 19.
11. *Indonesian Newsletter,* 29/11/74, Statement by Salim.
12. *Annual Report of the Bank Indonesia,* Various issues.
13. For a list of all foreign banks operating in Jakarta see *Indonesia; Guide to the Market,* Australian

Department of Overseas Trade, 1975, p. 36.

14. Present credit facilities available to the pribumi have been upgraded by the government. Efforts to equalise the cost of capital to the indigenous investor have taken several paths, one of which has been the establishment of the state development banks and the Investasi Program. See Panglaykim, Y. "Financial Institutions in Indonesia," *The Indonesia Quarterly,* vol. 3, no. 1, October, 1974.

15. It is true of course that a number of indigenous Indonesians, by virtue of their special relationship to foreign capital, are benefiting economically from the growth of the industrial base. In their capacity as joint venture partners (sections of the military particularly) are participants in the growth of the most modern and dynamic sectors of the economy. See Crouch, H., "The Generals and Business in Indonesia", *Pacific Affairs,* vol. 48, no. 4, Winter, 1975-76. Also Utrecht, E., "The Military Elite," in Caldwell, M. (ed.), *Ten Years Military Terror in Indonesia,* Spokesman Books, 1975.

16. As one report observed, "The law, is in effect, an enabling act leaving wide discretionary powers to the administration on many important issues. It is purposely vague and even ambiguous to permit increasingly liberal attitudes to be given full administrative effect. . . ." Stanford Research Institute, *Indonesia,* 1967.

17. For a precise and comprehensive outline of these infrastructural problems see Australian Senate Standing Committee on Industry and Trades report, *Prospects for Trade between Indonesia and Australia,* Australian Government Publishing Service, 1975.

18. Central Bank of Indonesia, *Economic Data for Investors,* Jakarta, 1968.

19. For detail on industrial estate development see *The Indonesia Letter,* no. 30, March, 1972.

20. Hughes, H., *South East Asia's Economy in the 1970s, the Manufacturing Industry Sector,* International Bank for Reconstruction and Development, Economics Department Working Paper, no. 178, May 1970, p. 74.

21. *Bulletin of Indonesian Economic Studies,* "Survey of Recent Developments," July, 1975.

22. Only a small amount of approved investment is actually implemented. The time lag factor plus the many procedural difficulties, and a number of false applications designed to allow access to state bank credits, resulted in a large proportion of delayed implementation of investment. Mining shows a 25 per cent implementation rate, and forestry 27 per cent. *Far Eastern Economic Review,* 28/8/71.

23. For some detail on this division of Indonesia's natural wealth see "Foreign Participation in Mining in Indonesia, 1967-70," Ministry of Mines (RI) Jakarta. All the major mining companies of the capitalist world are represented. Con Zinz Rio Tinto, Bethlehem Steel, Kennecott, Billiton, Freeport, Alcoa and Inco, were some of the first multinationals to obtain leases for exploration and extraction in Indonesia.

24. At present there is negligible processing of minerals and most are exported in their raw state to the industrialised nations. However plans are being made to redress this situation and to encourage the processing of raw materials in Indonesia itself. This point will be discussed later.

25. See *Bulletin of Indonesian Economic Studies,* "Survey of Recent Developments," July, 1975, pp. 24-25.

26. Dönges, J.B., Stecher, B., and Wolter, F., "Industrialisation in Indonesia: Recent Developments and Prospective Policies," a paper drawn on a monograph "Industrial Development Policies for Indonesia," Institute fur Welwirtschaft,, Kiel, 1973.

27. *Economic Intelligence Unit,* no. 3, 1972. Jakarta's share of total investment seems to be increasing, and despite government incentives for producers to manufacture outside the Jakarta and West Java region. It appears that the serious lack of infrastructural facilities and the vagaries of regional government attitudes to foreign investment, makes the possibility of regionally diversified investment unattractive to the majority of investors. As early as 1972 nearly half of all implemented foreign investments were concentrated in Jakarta. See *Harian Kami,* 30/9/71.

28. Hughes, H., *op. cit.,* p. 40.

29. For a comprehensive outline of the problems associated with industrialisation through the method of import substitution in poor countries see the report of the Asian Development Bank, *South East Asia's Economy in the 1970s,* Longman, 1971. Also the United Nations Report, *Report of the Second Asian Conference on Industrialisation* (held in Tokyo, 8-21 September 1970), United Nations, 1971.

30. As of January 1971 some eight large Japanese firms and six American and Hong Kong firms had made direct investments in the Indonesian textile and synthetic fibre industries. From a table filed in the Indonesian Project Collection at the Research School of Pacific Studies (ANU, Canberra).

31. See Palmer, I., and Castles, L., "The Textile Industry" in Glassburner, B., *op. cit.*

32. The following pharmaceutical companies have made direct investments in the industry: Richardson-Merril (US), the East Asiatic Company (Hong Kong), Abbott (USA), Squib and Sons (USA), Glaxo (UK), Cheeseborough Ponds (UK), Max Factor (USA), Tancho Co. Ltd. (West Germany), Hoetsch (Germany), Bayer (Germany), Pfizer (USA), Ciba (Switzerland), Scanphan (UK), Lloyds (UK), The Chemical Corporation of Singapore Ltd. (Singapore), Schering (Germany), and Nicholas (Australia).

33. The following firms have automobile assembly plants in Indonesia: GMH, Chrysler, Mercedes Benz, Fiat, Volkswagon, Bedford, Volvo, Suzuki, Honda, Citroen, BMW, Mazda, Toyota and International Harvester.

34. For detailed survey of findings on these and other problems related to import substitution manufacture and "enclave" type resource extractive foreign investments, see the United Nations report on Industrialisation, *op. cit.,* and the various reports by the ECOSEN group (The Economic Cooperation Centre of the Asian Pacific Council, Bangkok), particularly; Allen, T.W., *Direct Investments of United States Enterprises in South East Asia,* February, 1973; Allen, T.W., *Direct Investment of Japanese Enterprises in South East Asia,* February, 1973; Brewster, M., *The expansion of exports from developing Pacific Asian countries,* October, 1973.

35. Das Gupta, A.K. *Planning and Economic Growth,* George Allen and Unwin, 1965, p. 140.

36. UN Report, *op. cit.,* Ecosen Reports, *op. cit.,* ADB Report, *op. cit.*

37. ADB Report, *op. cit.,* p. 4.

38. *Ibid.,* pp. 18-22.

39. The question of potential regional complementarity within the region is an important one. Because of the smallness of domestic markets within each individual country, production in key areas must not be confined to the national scale, but must be based on regional cooperation. Each country is recommended to follow a policy of selective industrialisation so that goods produced in one country are done so with a view to supplying the whole region. In this way economies of scale can be achieved and efficiency therefore increased.

40. Ecosen, Draper, and Brewster, M., *op. cit.*

41. "A reorientation of the economic structures of these countries will enable them to move away from the often self defeating "import substituting" era into an export substitution era — the substitution of exports of processed primary goods or manufactures for raw material production" Ecosen (1), Draper, *op. cit.,* p. 15.

42. This is similar to the ADB recommendation of "export substitution which is hitched on to a policy of expanding primary exports." ADB Report, *op. cit.,* p. 21.

43. Ecosen (Brewster) *op. cit.,* p. 3.

44. Ecosen (Draper) *op. cit.,* p. 3.

45. UN Report *op. cit.*

46. Australian economist D.W. Arndt, well known for his work on the Indonesian economy, has this to say on the problem of capital and labour in Indonesia ". . . it is increasingly recognised that many of the big manufacturing investments, particularly by foreign companies, do not create all that many jobs." To satisfy the need for efficiency and profitability, and at the same time create employment, Professor Arndt concludes that whilst you cannot change the actual manufacturing process, it is possible to create ancilliary activities, "packing and that sort of thing" to establish employment. Paper to the Australian Indonesian Business Cooperation Committee (AIBCC) Seminar, "Investment in Indonesia — 1973 and beyond," September 13-14, Sydney, 1973.

47. "Neither self sufficiency within countries nor within the region as a whole is an appropriate end in itself. The overall aim is to promote an efficient and growing industrial sector." UN Report, *op. cit.,s, p. 7.*

48. *Ibid.,* p. 21.

49. *Ibid.,* p. 22.

50. Singapore has already put restrictions on the entry of the more labour intensive industries to the country, and officially seeks investments requiring more skills and sophistication.

51. In all, there were six recommendations made. The three most relevant to the subject under discussion have been chosen.

52. Although the Indonesian government has made a number of policy moves and introduced regulations to implement them, it must be recognised that the "corrupt" nature of the bureaucracy means that more often than not, businessmen can (for a sum of money) be immune. The author's own research in Indonesia also found this to be the case.

53. From an address prepared by the Department of Light Industry, "The Prospects of Industrial Development in the Second Five Year Development Plan," the AIBCC Seminar, Jakarta, 1974, p. 5.

54. The survey was conducted for Pertamina, the state owned oil company, by two Japanese and American firms. See also "The Island of Batam. A Blueprint for Development" in *EIU,* no. 1, 1973.

55. AIBCC, *op. cit.,* Department of Light Industry Report, p. 1.

56. By 1970, the value of fish exports had risen significantly to three times the value of the previous year. By mid 1972, prawning rights were given to four Japanese-Indonesian joint-ventures, one wholly owned Japanese enterprise and several domestically owned firms. The large scale modern sector was reportedly doing well, whilst the small scale peasant sector was in an increasingly depressed condition. *BIES.* March 1973. Pertamina had made extensive plans to develop a new capital intensive rice estate in Lampung

155

province in Sumatra in collaboration with Japanese capital. *BIES,* July, 1972, *BIES* March, 1973, *BIES,* July 1973, and *EIU,* no. 1, 1974.

57.   Overseas Business Reports (US Department of Commerce), January, 1973.

58.   *BIES,* "Survey of recent developments," July, 1972.

59.   ADB Report, *op. cit.,* p. 332.

60.   Ecosen (Draper), *op. cit.,* p. 7.

61.   USAID stands for United States Agency for International Development.

62.   USAID/Indonesia and US assistance."

63.   See for example *FAO/UNDP Country Program Digest,* 1/2/74; and *FAO/UNDP Country Program Management Plan Digest,* August 1974. See also *EIU,* "Quarterly Economic Survey-Indonesia," no. 1, 1974.

64.   Mangkusuwondo, S., "Dilemma of Indonesian Economic Development," *BIES* July, 1973, pp. 34-35.

65.   The freedom fighters, calling themselves Organisasi Papua Merdeka (OPM) have as their objective independence from all foreign domination, including that of the Indonesian government who currently occupy the country that the OPM calls West Papua.

66.   *EIU,* no. 3, 1973, p. 4.

67.   *Ibid.*

The Future of Transnational Corporations in

the Developing World.

By: Ernst Utrecht*

World-wide economic recession: in the centers of metropolitan capitalism

Any assessment of the future of transnational corporations (TNCs) in the developing world has to be made against the background of economic development in both the developed capitalist and developing (or underdeveloped) worlds. In both worlds there is still a continuing economic recession. Despite the post-war rise of the two "economic miracles", West Germany and Japan, and the recent formation of economic power within the European Economic Community (EEC),[1] which is more and more becoming a counter-balance to American economic penetration in many parts of the world, economic development in the US still remains an important influence in world economic development.

In spite of the slight post-Vietnam war recovery in the American economy, which encouraged quite a number of big West European companies to establish subsidiaries across the Atlantic,[2] investment in the US is now barely keeping up with growth.[3] Traditional monetary and fiscal tools have so far done little to stimulate investment in the face of the high costs of capital and capital goods. Moreover, there is much uncertainty over President Carter's energy and tax programs.[4] Among those who make spending decisions there is a deep fear that the world capitalist system may soon plunge back into the morass of inflation and recession that held it fast in the first half of the 1970s.

> "The distressing fact, is that the level of capital investing in the US is still lower than it was in 1974, with the increase in investing coming more slowly than in any previous postwar recovery. Further, this is for all industry. In such industries as computers, steel, textiles, tires and rubber, and the airlines, there is hardly any investment growth even now.
>
> Nor does that tell the whole story. A disproportionate share of total investment dollars is going into such comparatively small and young industries as food and lodging, oil service and supply, and electonics rather than into the giant basic industries around which the nation's economy has been built — suggesting that the US may be in the throes of a more fundamental shift than economists have anticipated. What money is going into the basic industries today tends to be for replacement, pollution control, and adaptation to alternative energy forms; little of it is going to build whole new facilities that would provide additional capacity."[5]

Chase Econometric Associates' president, Michael Evans, even predicts that the US economy will go into recession in 1978-79, and unemployment will "skyrocket" to 8.5% from the present 7.1%.[6]

In 1975-76, that is, in the first year of the post-Vietnam war era, US TNCs drastically cut back on overseas capital spending. This caused a considerable slowdown in new investment.[7] But in the course of 1976-77 US companies raised the direct investment in their foreign operations by 10.5%.

> "Direct investment in developed countries grew 11.2% to $101.15 billion in 1976, while direct investment in developing countries climbed 10.8% to $29.05 billion. Adjusted earnings, the return on the direct investment position, increased 13.4% to $18.84 billion in 1976. Receipts of income (adjusted earnings minus reinvested income) climbed 29.9% to

*Research Consultant, Transnational Corporation Research Project, University of Sydney, Sydney, Australia.

$11.13 billion. More than half the increase in receipts came from petroleum affiliates in developing countries."[8]

But this new flare up of US investment overseas is far below the levels of about 10-15 years ago, when the annual increase often exceeded 40-50%. The bulk of the recent US overseas capital investment went to West Europe. Some US firms started activities in East Europe. It seems that for many US TNCs Europe still offers the best guarantees for overseas investment.

"One thing seems certain about the American TNCs in Europe. Maybe they will never engulf it, but certainly they will not go away. Those who foresee the early death of TNCs are heroically applying the sound and fury of the developing world to the developed world, where it does not apply — and where most transnational business is done. Many developing-world governments indeed want to squeeze the TNCs mercilessly. In the rich world, only Australia, Canada, and occasionally Britain and France, squeeze even gently — not least because every country has TNCs of its own."[9]

It is in particular the North Sea oil exploration and exploitation which now attract US TNCs to again invade West Europe. During the last two years the rigs of American offshore oil drilling companies have engulfed literally the North Sea. The oil has not only been a lifesaver for the British economy and a bonanza for a few parts of Scotland, it has also proved a healthy boost to profits for a number of small and medium-sized American oil companies. In all, 43% of the oil planned for development, British and Norwegian, will flow through American hands.[10]

TABLE I

Ownership of Proven North Sea Oil Reserves by Nationality of Oil Company

Nationality	Percentage of Total Reserves (15,645 million barrels)
United States	43
Britain	26
Norway	13
Holland	7
Belgium	5
France	2
Italy	2
West Germany	1.5
Canada	0.5

Source: *The Economist*, September 24, 1977

Also, in the economies of the members of the EEC and Japan there is still a considerable slowdown. For instance, West Germany's real economic growth for 1977 will be under 3% whereas the previous year it could reach the government's target of 5%.[11] Because West Germany's economic expansion forms the "locomotive" for West European growth, the present slowdown is a worry. Foreign investment dropped to DM (German Mark) 2.5 billion from DM4.5 billion in 1974. West German industrial production fell at an annual rate of 17.1% in April 1977 (and 21.7% in May 1977), mainly reflecting weakness in domestic demand.[12] (Like Japan, West Germany has a strong export sector.) There will possibly be a slight upturn in capital spending over 1978, but the Germans expect to live off plant and equipment installed during the capital-goods spree of 1970-71. Most of the money will be absorbed by "replacement and rationalization", only 20-30% of additional investment will be going into new capacity.[13]

Some German commentaries on the present economic slowdown resent the German companies who, during the past seven or eight years, have transferred production or branches of

TABLE II

North American Companies' Reserves in Present Commercial Fields

Company	Million barrels
Exxon	1,679
Phillips	974
Mobil	711
Conoco	682
Occidental	442
Getty	326
Gulf	320
Texaco	256
Allied Chemical	242
Socal	187
Amerada Hess	171
Texas Eastern	157
Amoco	105
Santa Fe	81
Murphy	77
Odeco	77
Ranger	66
Tenneco	46
Ashland	27
Hamilton	9
Total	2,636

Source: The Economist, September 24, 1977

production to the cheap-labor havens in the developing world.[14] However, one may doubt whether the outflow of production, which in many cases also was the result of environmentalist obstacles at home, have caused a significant outflow of capital. Usually the overseas subsidiaries generate about 80% of their operative capital locally. The biggest impact of such type of capital outflow on the home economy is the often considerable increase of unemployment. In 1975-76 unemployment in West Germany rose to above one million.[15]

In another important member of the EEC, France, investment by foreign concerns is declining, while at the same time, the growth of capital spending abroad by French companies other than oil firms is slowing.

"A recently released study by the Finance Ministry in Paris, which covers the years 1971-75, remarks, that although foreign investment in France rose the four years up to 1975, a marked drop of 14% to Fr. 6.065 billion was observed in 1975 and this seems "to have continued into 1976".

Direct foreign investment in France tumbled by 48% in 1976 from 1975, according to latest provisional estimates. The decline was essentially due to a drop in investment by EEC members to Fr.3.117 billion from a Fr.4.536 billion a year earlier. Capital spending by US interests remained steady at Fr.1.399 billion against Fr.1.408 billion, while that by non-industrialized nations more than tripled to Fr.978 million from 295 million."[16]

The overseas spending by the French oil companies gives much better prospects. It has been rising rapidly. In 1975 the oil companies invested a total of Fr.3.266 billion compared with Fr.1.75 billion in 1973 and Fr.1.125 billion in 1969.

French direct investment in the US is tending to increase. Over 1974-75 French investment in the US accounted for 17% of all overseas French investment compared with 12% over 1971-72 and 4% over 1968-69.

After the "Chrysler crisis" in November-December 1975,[17] the investment climate in Britain improved. A number of British firms stepped up their investment activity at home and abroad. In Britain, 29 new projects were initiated, some of them with the participation of American capital.[18] Ford Motor Company of the US, for instance, decided to establish a major new engine plant in South Wales in one of the largest single foreign investments to be made in Britain over the last ten years.

> "Ford said it would be investing about £180 million on the plant, which is expected to go into operation in the early 1980s. The Ford engine plant will be built at Bridgend in South Wales and employ about 2,500 people. Under regional grant programs, the British government will contribute 20% of the capital investment cost. Ford will also receive interest relief grants."[19]

In the foregoing, I already mentioned the US investment in the North Sea oil industry. Britain still retains its first place in America's European interests, even after so many years of slow growth and of a slipping pound.[20]

It is one of the priorities of the British Labor Party's political program to attract as many foreign investments as possible. One of Britain's foremost labor unionists, Australian-born Huge Scanlon, told Australian colleagues at a seminar organized by the Australian Confederation of Trade Unions (ACTU) in Melbourne, November 22-23, 1976, that the only way for Britain to become an equal partner in the EEC would be to improve her investment climate and, through more foreign investments, build up an industrial apparatus that could compete with that of, in particular, West Germany, France and Italy. The British government now subsidizes new industrial undertakings and favors them with special tax facilities.[21]

Another contribution to the improvement of Britain's investment climate, in particular for British investors, is the surging strength of the Pound, which is now floating free above the US$1.85 level.[22] Providing that for the moment the wages do not rise, the rising Pound will almost certainly act to curb inflation by lowering import costs and interest rates. This, consequently, should increase real consumer income and demand for goods. Many companies that have been holding back on capital investment will then consider some expansion in their operations. If wages do rise, a price stop — a measure which has rarely been taken even by Western social-democrat governments — should be considered.

But on the other hand, a higher Pound might result in a cut in Britain's international export competitiveness. If this occurs, the demand for capital investment coming from the export sector will not come on stream. In a capitalist economy, this will form an impediment to "development" and deteriorate the investment climate.

Among the biggest centers of metropolitan capitalism, Japan at the moment perhaps has the strongest potential of overseas capital spending. However, the outlook for capital spending in the country itself is even gloomier than in West Germany.[23] (Again, like West Germany, Japan's strongest economic sector has been the export). The Japanese giant Nomura Securities Company forecasts a real internal investment growth of only 3% for fiscal 1977 (ending March 31, 1978) compared with an average annual growth in internal capital investment of 13.5% in the 1960s. Kanju Sugimoto, one of Nomura's managers, has said that the 1977 government stimulation plan is not likely to boost internal capital investment, and stronger measures such as tax credits are needed if Japan is to avoid "a future gap in productivity". Also many Japanese bankers and businessmen fear that the trend toward low internal capital investment may become the main feature of the Japanese economy for years to come. The Japanese economy continues to adjust to higher oil prices, a slower rate of economic growth and a gradual reduction of excess capacity. To protect the national industry and save employment, the Japanese government has increased the import tariffs on foreign-made consumer goods.[24]

Because of the slowdown in the internal capital market, Japan's huge capital surplus has to find a new outlet at the international capital market. Japanese bankers and businessmen are expecting a sharp rise in Japanese overseas investment soon, perhaps as early as during the first half of 1978.

"Japanese investment, after a dramatic climb in 1972 and 1973, has been languishing for the past four years along with the domestic and world economy. From a fiscal 1973 peak of nearly (US)$3.5 billion in licensed overseas investments, including shares, loans and direct investment, Japanese overseas investment dropped to about $2.4 billion in fiscal 1974, mostly due to the oil crisis.

But investment began climbing again the next year, up 37% to nearly $3.3 billion in fiscal 1975, and up again to almost $3.5 billion in fiscal 1976.

The improvement was attributed to the large-scale development projects that finally got off the ground, relaxation of money in Japan and the business recovery in Western developed countries in the second half of 1975.

The fiscal 1977 figure is expected to again be somewhat higher than last year. However, despite the improvement, many Japanese companies have adopted a "wait and see" attitude for the past several years — hoping for further improvement in the world economy and more activity at home."[25]

In the face of the strong anti-Japanese import movement in the US and West Europe and the many complaints in these parts of the world about increased Japanese production of cars, steel, radio-transistors, television sets, cameras, watches, and many other consumer goods, most Japanese companies have shown increasing interest in moving production to the US and other buying countries. This investment strategy is based on the assumption that by establishing plants in the centers and sub-centers of metropolitan capitalism (like Australia, Canada, New Zealand, Singapore, South Africa) the opposition to Japanese goods might be abated and at the same time high tariff walls and special tax regulations avoided. This policy was successfully implemented in Australia when a joint-venture of Toyota and General Motors' Australian subsidiary, Holden, produced the first small-sized Australian-Japanese car, the Gemini. Japanese entrepreneurs are admired as well as despised world-wide for their "flexibility" in doing business.

World-wide economic recession: in the peripheries of metropolitan capitalism
Since 1974 there has also been a slowdown in capital investment in many a developing country,[26] which is to a large extent the result of the slowdown in the economies of the US and the members of the EEC, while Japanese corporate investors are more interested in establishing subsidiaries in the countries with populations that have retained reasonable purchasing power. It also seems that the present stage in the internationalization of capital, that is, the use of cheap labor, particularly in the developing countries, in order to maximize the internationalization of the production of surplus value, has come to an end.

The imperialist exploitation of the peoples of the developing countries through Western capital investment (which usually introduced the capitalist modes of production) has developed through different stages.[27] In the traditional pattern of imperialist exploitation which developed in the 19th century, capital invested in the developing countries (most of which were colonies at that time) was concentrated in the production of foodstuffs, minerals and industrial raw materials for export to the imperialist centers (of metropolitan capital) on terms highly advantageous to the latter. Earnings from these exports (along with further capital inflows) would then finance imports of manufactured goods from the imperialist centers, providing entrepreneurs there with additional markets as well as raw materials. The developing countries have reached their present condition after undergoing, over many decades and in a fashion that served the needs of the main capitalist countries rather than those of their own populations — a process that has been termed "growth without development" or "development of underdevelopment".[28]

In the second half of the 1950s and the 1960s, the international division of labor developed new dimensions. There was a tremendous exodus of labor-intensive manufacturing industries from the developed capitalist nations into the developing world — an exodus largely promoted by the TNCs based in the developed countries themselves. This occurred for a number of fundamental reasons.

In the first place, there was the problem of "too high wages" in many industrialized countries. In their home countries, where they had their basic plants providing employment for their own national labor force, the companies constantly had to comply with the demands from their workers for higher wages and better social conditions. Since they did not wish to cut down on their profits and feared any restriction of the expansion of their investments and the modernization of their plants (destined to facilitate competition with other companies), they had no alternative but to raise the prices of their products. Excessive production costs became for many a corporation an inevitable threat of the loss of both profits and markets in the affluent consumer societies of the home countries. There developed a new impetus for establishing overseas subsidiaries in order to continue the accumulation of capital: to make use of cheap labor in less developed, populous countries where a huge agrarian crisis is uprooting millions of peasant farmers and driving them into shanty towns and city slums. Comparative costs (of production) proved that there was much more profit to gain by relocating production overseas, in cheap-labor countries, and by then importing consumer goods fabricated by one's own overseas subsidiaries. That the export of employment might damage the interests of their own national work force did not cause too serious considerations for the corporations which relocated production internationally.[29]

Secondly, the *comprador* bourgeoisie of the developing countries[30] which could offer the foreign companies the wanted cheap labor, did all they could to attract foreign capital investment. They removed all usual restrictions on the transfer of profits, granted a so-called "grace period" for the initial investment, and forced local workers to accept the lowest possible wages. They hoped that in this way they could prevent social upheavals by creating new jobs for the vast numbers of unemployed and under-employed in these countries.

Since the early 1960s, *comprador* elites (in the developing world) have been seeking ways to attract foreign investment by establishing production and trade enclaves called "industrial zones", "industrial estates", or "free trade (or production) zones", where international companies can cheaply produce for the world market, paying the lowest possible wages, totally protected against unionism or any form of labor "unrest". Such enclaves can be found in many parts of the developing world.[31] In these zones, workers are subjected to particularly poor working conditions, intense exploitation, and strong political repression. It is in these cheap-labor havens that the internationalization of the production of surplus value can be maximized perfectly. In these cheap-labor havens one encounters the highest stage of human exploitation by internationalized capital.

The third factor promoting the transfer of labor-intensive manufacturing industry to developing countries was the fact that the traditional division of labor was considerably weakened when the former colonies gained political independence. Companies engaged in taking minerals and other raw materials out of these countries now face host governments which increasingly seek to control this process and to maximize the benefits they can obtain from it through so-called "resources diplomacy". Where these governments can succeed in establishing monopolistic control over the utilization of their own natural resources through international cartels such as the Organization of Petroleum Exporting Countries (OPEC), they will be able to restrict export and raise world prices, so that the benefits flow to the producer nations rather than the consumer nations of the developed world. Even a world power such as the US was not able to do much against the resources diplomacy of OPEC but to attempt to reduce its own use of petroleum.

162

Since 1974, however, in many cheap-labor havens the investment boom of the 1960s and early 1970s is over. TNCs, already in the havens, stopped or slowed down the expansion of their operations. The number of new projects has dropped drastically. The *comprador* elites, in a desperate effort to promote a new influx of foreign investments, have stepped up the oppression of the local labor force — no increase in wages, a ban on strikes and demonstrations, a prohibition for workers in the "free production zones" to join labor unions while the unions have been banned from the zones, arrest of militant union leaders, the Singapore government even arrested the unions' lawyers (among others, Gopalan Raman, while another lawyer sought by the Singapore Police's Special Branch managed to escape by leaving the city-state in time).

At the moment the gravest deterioration in investment occurs in Indonesia, a country with the highest number of political prisoners in the world.[32] The *Far Eastern Economic Review's* correspondent in Indonesia, David Jenkins, gives the following account:

"On January 10, 1967, the Indonesian government enacted a landmark foreign investment law which opened the door wide to foreign capital and paved the way for a resurgence in the national economy after the decline and stagnation of the Sukarno years. Today, 10 years later, the momentum created by that decree has been lost. The rate of new foreign investment, sluggish for the past two years, is slipping back month by month.

In 1976, the value of applications approved by the Capital Investment Co-ordinating Board (BKPM) totalled only US\$423 million, as against \$1,944 million the previous year, \$1,392 million in 1974 and a 10-year average of \$681 million a year. (The 1975 figure is misleadingly high due to the signing that year of the huge \$850 million contract for the Asahan hydro-electric project.)

Approval was sought in 1976 for only 34 new projects, in contrast to the average since 1967 of 85 a year. This was the lowest number of new projects in 10 years.

More disturbing still, barely half the \$423 million was for new investment; a total of \$189 million was for increased capitalization of existing investment, only \$234 million for totally new investment. Over the past 10 years, 75% of the \$6,800 million in foreign investment approvals has been for new investment, as opposed to expansion of existing plant. The situation so far this year (1977) is even worse."[33]

In the oil industry, which is dominated by Japanese and American companies, it is expected that a number of Japanese firms will gradually move their operations to China in order to restore the balance in the trade between Japan and Indonesia.

Even in South Korea, where cheap-labor havens Masan and Iri are most popular among foreign investors, the reception of direct foreign investment during 1976-77 slowed down sharply from the peak years of 1973-75.

"Official statistics show that the inflow of foreign equity investment into South Korea during last year (1976) totalled US\$65 million involving 44 projects. The figure during the first five months this year (1977) indicated that its pace did not pick up. The 1976 figure compared with \$199 million in 1975, \$121 million in 1974 and \$262 million in 1973."[34]

In Malaysia, where since 1970 a number of cheap-labor havens have been established in the vicinity of the capital of Kuala Lumpur and the island of Penang, in 1976 a total of 425 new projects were approved compared to 461 in 1975 and 525 in 1974, a numerical decrease which reflected a sharp drop in total authorized capital to M\$1,021 million (US\$411.69 million) from M\$1,366 million the previous year.[35]

The slump in capital investment in the cheap-labor countries has also been caused by factors other than the slowdown in capital spending in the centers of metropolitan capitalism. For instance, according to a report by *Far Eastern Economic Review's* correspondent in Seoul, Kim Sam-o, one of the reasons for the growing reluctance to invest in South Korea seems to be the fear for deteriorating political conditions in the aftermath of the planned withdrawal of American troops from the Korean peninsular.[36] There are more countries in the peripheral world where political conditions are not favorable for capital accumulation. Moreover, the managements of many a TNC are generally less inclined to invest capital in countries which are ruled by, often unpredictable, military regimes.

Another, more general, reason for less capital spending in the developing countries are the policies of quite a number of developed countries to surround their territories by high tariff walls against the imports of goods manufactured in countries with cheap labor. In mid-1977, for instance, a tariff war broke out between the five members of the Association of Southeast Asian Nations (ASEAN) — Thailand, Malaysia, Singapore, Indonesia and the Philippines — and Australia..

> "The five ASEAN members called today (August 6, 1977) on developed countries to drop immediately protectionist measures which they said affected the livelihood of their 200 million people. The demand came in a 20-page communiqué issued after two days of summit talks here (Kuala Lumpur) between ASEAN leaders.
>
> They called for policies in the richer countries which would promote trade with ASEAN nations and increase investment, which has fallen in recent years in Thailand, Singapore and Malaysia. The five leaders said they wanted better access to markets outside Southeast Asia for their new materials — primarily rice, as well as manufactured and semi-processed goods."[37]

Also the Australian companies in the ASEAN countries[38] are hit by Australia's protectionist policies. But so far Australia has refused to lower the tariffs on grounds that she has to save employment for her workers.[39] Therefore, the Australian workers support the policy of high tariff walls, whereas the Australian companies support the ASEAN governments' efforts to get the walls down. The companies also accuse the Australian workers of having claimed "too high wages", which was the main reason why they went to the cheap-labor countries in Asia. In August 1977, the Australian government even took further steps. It posed sharp cutbacks on the imports of Asian textiles.[40]

Also the EEC members have imposed curbs on imports of goods manufactured in the cheap-labor countries. For instance, on the same day when the Australian government announced its new import curbs the British government sharply restricted the import of shoes and other leather products from Taiwan.

It will nowadays become difficult to maximize the production of surplus value in the cheap-labor havens of the developing countries. In the near future, a reversed trend might develop: the return of TNCs, that in the past went to the peripherical world, to the centers of metroplitan capital because the conditions for capital accumulation have become more favorable in the centers than in the peripheries. We may not forget that so far the peripheries can only offer cheap labor as the most valuable asset in the reproduction of capital, while the markets are mainly kept in the centers.

Footnotes

1. The EEC activities are not confined to economic co-operation only. People are beginning to speak about the "European Community" (EC) because integration has gradually been expanded beyond the inter-economic sector of the West European community.
2. During 1976 foreign companies announced 250 new investments in the US. The majority of the companies were West European firms. See, for instance, *The Australian Financial Review,* January 25, 1977; *De Volkskrant,* April 14, 1977 (reporting that Holland's giant transnational electronics industry Philips has moved branches of its production plants to the US); *International Herald Tribune,* September 3, 1977 (increase of French investment in the US).

3. Special Report, "The Slow-investment Economy", *Business Week,* October 17, 1977, pp. 60-3.

4. *The New York Times,* September 13, 1977.

5. Special Report, p. 60.

6. For the present slowdown in the US economy see *International Herald Tribune,* September *9, 1977,* (Chase Econometric Associates is a subsidiary of Chase Manhattan Bank.) See also *International Herald Tribune,* September 21, 1977. However, there are still other American leaders who have confidence in considerable future economic expansion in the US: Generally, the business leaders say the economy's condition is not nearly as precarious as some people think. "There is a gap between reality and perception. The economy is in good shape. The growth is slowing because of the maturity of the expansion, which is 30 months old", says William Miller, chairman of Tectron Inc. "The question is whether a glass of water is half full or half empty. I think we are looking at the economy as if it were half empty".
    The corporate officials cite several factors that should bolster the economy in the short run, the most important being an anticipated upturn in capital spending. "A lot of our people say that for the first time in a year or two business people are dusting off their plans for plant expansion", Mr David Rockefeller says. "That is an encouraging indication of renewed interest in capital spending" ("Confidence on Expansion in US", *International Herald Tribune,* September 17, 1977).

7. See, for instance, *The Australian Financial Review,* April 9, 1976.

8. *The Wall Street Journal,* August 30, 1977.

9. "Over here. A survey of American companies in Europe", *The Economist,* September 10, 1977.

10. "Who does best out of America's 43% of North Sea oil", *The Economist,* September 24, 1977.

11. See, for instance, *International Herald Tribune,* September 21, 1977.

12. *International Herald Tribune,* August 29, 1977.

13. Special Report, p. 63.
    The only bright spot in the West German investment picture is the automobile industry, which is operating at peak capacity and plans to expand heavily. Both General Motors Corporation's Opel subsidiary and Daimler-Benz have announced multi-billion Dollar-programs for long-term investment. Other German companies are planning to invest — but they are going overseas to buy foreign companies, such as Bayer's bid to buy Miles Laboratories Inc.

14. *International Herald Tribune,* March 14, 1977.

15. There are cases in which the amount of profit derived from the operations of overseas subsidiaries is much higher than the amount of unemployment benefits that have to be paid to the workers laid off by the parent company. In other words, the government should force the parent company to pay the benefits to its former, unemployed, workers as long as they cannot find other employment.

16. *International Herald Tribune,* September 3, 1977.

17. In 1975 the Chrysler Motor Company decided to move its autombile plant in Britain to France where it had already taken over the French-Italian Simca plant. The plant in Britain was obsolete. Its productivity was low whereas the production costs were too high because of the many industrial relations problems. France was a much better place to renovate production. The British government, however, managed to keep the Chrysler plant in Britain and save some employment for the British automobile workers. For the Chrysler case see "The Chrysler retreat", *The Economist,* December 13, 1975; "The political economy of cars", *The Economist,* December 20, 1975.

18. *International Herald Tribune,* August 23, 1977.

19. *International Herald Tribune,* September 10, 1977.
    Considering Ford officials' complaints of low productivity and serious industrial relations problems in Britain, the decision to build the plant in Britain came as somewhat of a surprise.

20. "Over here".

21. *NRC/Handelsblad,* October 21, 1977.

22. *International Herald Tribune,* November 1, 1977; *The Guardian,* November 1, 1977. Till November 1, 1977, the Bank of England had been keeping the Pound artificially low by its support for the US Dollar. But on November 1 the British government allowed its currency to float upwards. Within a couple of hours the Pound raced ahead 6.5 Dollar cents to US$1.8420, the best level since May 1976. The "disconnection" of the Pound from the Dollar was welcomed by the other EEC members, it reflected a "positive improvement" in Britain's economic conditions. Also many US companies welcomed the measure.

23. Special Report p. 63.

24. A source of mounting irritation to both governments and people in North America, West Europe, Australia and the developing countries as well — and more particularly to their leaders — is the massive annual

export surplus of Japan which is also a result of protectionist trade policies. It is highly likely that fiscal 1977 will see Japan boasting a trade surplus of approximately $15-16 billion.

Far Eastern Economic Review, June 24, 1977:

Combined with Japan's huge trade surpluses with the EEC and the US for fiscal 1976 of $3.882 billion and $4.043 billion respectively, Fukuda's promises to reduce Tokyo's international payments imbalances are unlikely to carry much weight with Western critics. Europeans remain particularly sceptical. EEC trade with Japan has fallen into increasingly large deficits since the early 1970s. Watching substantially cheaper Japanese imports erode their market shares, producers of cars, consumer electronics, steel, ball-bearings and ships have blamed Japanese dumping — selling exports at prices below Japanese domestic level and other unsavory trade tactics — for poor performance and rising unemployment.

So far, EEC leaders have managed to keep such widespread sentiments from boiling over into outright protectionism. But recent statements, most notably by British Secretary of State for Foreign Trade Edmund Dell in Tokyo in April, and by British Prime Minister James Callaghan during the London meeting, have made Europe's message to Tokyo abundantly clear: faced with high levels of unemployment, governments will be politically unable to maintain free trade principles unless Japan moves to open its closely guarded domestic sales network to imports.

25. *International Herald Tribune,* Special Report on Japan, September 1977, p. 1.

26. For the Asian countries see *Far Eastern Economic Review,* July 29, 1977, Investment in Asia '77.

27. I have mentioned these stages in an earlier study, "Imperialism in Singapore", *Intervention,* No. 8 (March 1977), pp. 21 ff.

28. For the Baran-Frank thesis see E.L. Wheelwright, "Under-Development or Revolution? The Baran-Frank Thesis", in Wheelright, *Radical Political Economy,* Sydney 1974, pp. 249-58.

29. According to Barnet and Müller, labor union hostility to TNCs is based not only on objections to the exploitation of cheap labor, but also because their own bargaining positions are undercut by this development. Companies now deliberately duplicate production facilities so that they can shift operations smoothly from one plant to another in the event of trouble (Richard J. Barnet and Ronald E. Müller, *Global Reach — The Power of the Multinational,* New York 1974, p. 22).

30. Ernst Utrecht, "Corporate Compradors in Southeast Asia", *Arena,* Nos 47-48 (August 1977), pp. 107-19.

31. Cheap-labor havens in East and Southeast Asia: in South Korea, Masan Free Export Zone (MAFEZ) and Iri Free Export Zone (IFEZ), and more than ten others; Hong Kong; in Taiwan, Kaohsiung Export Processing Zone (KEPZ) and Nantz Export Processing Zone (NEPZ); in Thailand, Chon Buri and Chieng Mai; in Malaysia, Penang Island and Kuala Lumpur; in Singapore, Jurong Industrial Estates and a number of similar areas; in Indonesia, Tanjung Priok near Jakarta; in the Philippines, Bataan Export Processing Zone (Mariveles). See Special Issue of *Ampo,* Free Trade Zones and Industrialization of Asia, Tokyo 1977. For Singapore see Ernst Utrecht, *Industrial Estates and Australian Companies in Singapore,* Monograph University of Sydney, Sydney 1976.

32. Amnesty International, *Indonesia, An Amnesty International Report,* London 1977.

33. Investment in Asia '77, p. 59.

34. Investment in Asia '77, pp. 56-7.

35. Investment in Asia '77, p. 62.

36. Investment in Asia '77, p. 57.

37. *The Sydney Morning Herald,* August 6, 1977.

38. For Australian companies which have moved to Southeast Asia and the Pacific see the five articles by Michael Southern in *The Australian Financial Review,* November 23-25, 1976, and January 11-12, 1977.

39. *The Sydney Morning Herald,* August 8, 1977.

40. *The Asian Wall Street Journal,* August 19, 1977.

AUSTRALIA

Australian Multinationals:

Growth or Survival?

*W. D. BREIT**

Discussion about "multinationals" is bound to draw reaction, both hostile and defensive from many Australians today. Thirty per cent of Australia's manufacturing industry and 62 per cent of the mineral industry is foreign owned.[1] Economic nationalism aimed against multinational companies has been simmering for some time and has led to the aphorism that "Australia was selling off a bit of the farm". Spurred on by such slogans as "buy back Australia", multinational "bashing" became a popular political pastime in the early 1970s.

Few Australians realize, however, that there is another kind of multinational — the Australian company — which has expanded overseas and which will in the future play an increasingly important role in Australia's economy and industrial development.

Australian direct investment overseas has always been small, almost trivial by comparison with the flow of investment into Australia. In the late 1960s, however, it grew from A $13 million in 1964 to A $161 million in 1973/4. Recently, Australia's largest company, Broken Hill Proprietary Co., Ltd. was investigating the feasibility of a joint venture with Iran in a major steel rolling complex,[2] one of many indications that Australian industry is now looking beyond its own shores, not only for exports but for investment.

The forces behind the expansion of Australian manufacturing industry abroad will be examined in the body of this paper.

Recent Economic and Political Background to Australian Overseas Investment

The most important economic event that has occurred in Australia in the past decade has been the break-through in its balance of trade. With Australia's new-found mineral wealth it now has the potential to maintain a permanent trade surplus. Since 1968/69 Australia has had surpluses reaching a record high in 1972/3 of A $2 billion. Surpluses were achieved during the post-war years before 1968, but these were always heavily dependent on the fluctuations in world food and wool prices.

Australia's economic policies were protective and characteristic of a trade deficit country: balancing payments through encouraging foreign investment, restricting imports through high tariffs, encouraging exports through subsidization. A benign public and laissez-faire attitude of the Government encouraged the development of a broadly-based import substituting manufacturing industry and the exploitation of Australia's mineral resources with the aid of foreign technology, capital, and entrepreneurship. This policy paid off and exports of mineral products, processed and unprocessed, increased from 9.1 per cent of total Australian exports in 1964 to 24.8 per cent in 1970. Exports of manufactures increased from 12.5 per cent to 20.5 per cent over the same period. By the late sixties, minerals and manufactures had pushed Australia into a new era as a net exporter of goods and services.

What is the impact of such a change on economic policy? With the prospect of a permanent

*This article was written while the author was a participant in a course in international management at the Centre for Education in International Management, Geneva, spring 1975.

Reprinted from the *Journal of World Trade Law* by permission of the publishers.

trade surplus, economic policy should be directed towards achieving outflow of capital by discouraging short-term and long-term capital inflow (including direct foreign investment) and releasing restrictions on capital outflow, to balance the excessive build-up of foreign exchange reserves. The amount of capital that the country should export would depend upon the magnitude of the surplus, which can be minimised by removing export subsidies and reducing import tariffs, i.e. a move towards free trade.

A surplus country would therefore seem to foster the economic forces favouring the investment of capital abroad and therefore the expansion of companies to overseas locations.

Australia's Painful Transition to a Position of Balance of Trade Surplus

How did actual Australian economic policy adjust to this inflexion in its trade account? And how did Australian manufacturing industry respond to this fundamental economic change?

A dramatic increase in net capital inflow over the years 1969 to 1972 accompanied the surplus in the balance of trade. This was caused by a strong upsurge in direct foreign investment, foreign portfolio investment and speculative short-term capital movements in anticipation of a revaluation of the Australian dollar. The effect was a A $3.4 billion increase in domestic money supply from 1971 to 1972 and a build-up of international reserves from A $1.2 billion in 1967 to A $6 billion in 1972. It was not until mid-1972 that the Government made any significant move to curb capital inflow and to release the valve on capital outflow. Overseas portfolio investment became permissible for Australian citizens for the first time since 1939. Also in 1972, Mr. D. Anthony, then Minister for Trade and Industry, suggested that capital could be released by issuing trade credits to poorer countries for otherwise unsaleable agricultural and manufactured products.[3]

But too little and too late! The laissez-faire deficit-oriented policies of the Liberal Government, which had so successfully nurtured economic growth in post-war Australia, had in fact sown the seeds for its own destruction. The trade surplus provided the basis for a growing nationalistic movement that was to carry Mr. Whitlam and his Australian Labor Party into office for the first time in 23 years.

The Liberal Party had ostensibly not taken account of the economic significance of the inflexion in the trade balance and had not adjusted its economic policies accordingly. Mr. Whitlam, who inherited a difficult liquidity situation with an extraordinarily high domestic money supply fueling a domestic boom, along with shortages and inflation, took immediate and rather precipitative action aimed at (i) curbing speculative capital inflow through two devaluations, raising the minimum deposit requirement to two years, and introducing the variable deposit scheme (25 per cent and later 33 per cent of borrowed foreign capital deposited interest free with the Reserve Bank); (ii) dissuading direct foreign investment by adopting an anti-industry, anti-multinational position; (iii) increasing imports by lowering tariffs an *ad hoc* 25 per cent across the board; (iv) reducing exports by removing tax rebate incentives; (v) and more significantly to the theme of this paper, encouraging direct overseas investment by Australian companies by offering new incentives.[4]

For Mr. Whitlam this economic policy also coincided with his political objectives of achieving greater economic nationalism, loosening of ties with the United Kingdom and the United States and increasing orientation towards South East Asia for economic and political cooperation.

The effect that these measures had on the economy and on Australian investment overseas should also be examined. Mr. Whitlam's measures were certainly aimed in the right direction but executed with too much rigidity. Foreign investors, direct and portfolio, were frightened off and an import boom was followed by a severe liquidity crisis. This, coupled with rampant inflation,

169

wage hikes, labour unrest and an impending world-wide recession was to leave a shell-shocked and confused business community fighting in 1974 for survival against cash-flow problems and inflation.

Towards the end of 1974, these events resulted in unemployment of around 5 per cent and a trade deficit. Mr. Whitlam, along with other world leaders, introduced reflationary policies which in fact represented a complete economic volte-face for the Labor Government. Such policies included: a 12 per cent devaluation, a return to liberalization of capital inflow, protective trade measures with import quotas and selective application of tariffs. Hence, a return to deficit economic policies but with a shift in degree to more guidance and more centralized control than those which characterized the Liberal Government's economic management prior to 1972. These policies have resulted in successive trade surpluses in the first half of 1975.

The transition period from 1969/70 to 1975 represented a painful readjustment by Australia to changed economic circumstances. A sleepy Government followed by an inexperienced one, a world monetary crisis, inflation, the oil crisis, a world-wide economic boom followed by recession all contributed towards this protracted transition.

For Australian industry, this period was a disturbing one, resulting in postponed and cancelled domestic and foreign investment plans. Against this background, Australian industrialists must now take stock and carefully assess the advantages and disadvantages of expanding their operations overseas.

Australian industry and direct investment overseas

Exchange control applied to direct investment overseas by Australian companies has for 20 years been very liberal. Although requiring approval by the Reserve Bank, this approval is generally granted if the investment meets certain requirements: (i) involves a significant measure of Australian managerial participation in the overseas enterprise and the export of managerial and technical skills; (ii) promotes development of markets for Australian exports; or (iii) protects an existing investment abroad.[5] Against the political and economic background reviewed above, we shall now discuss in what ways Australian industry has expanded overseas.

Statistics available on Australian investment overseas are published by the Australian Bureau of Statistics[6] but are rather general as companies are not required by law to publish details of their overseas interests. The Bureau of Statistics defines a direct Australian shareholder as a company in Australia whose shareholding is 25 per cent or more of the ordinary shares or voting stock of a company overseas.

In this paper, the author refers to an Australian Company as one in which the equity is either majority Australian-owned (51 per cent or more) or is essentially Australian "in character", i.e. a company registered in Australia that is not constrained domestically or internationally by the regional policy of a majority foreign equity holder.

Australian direct overseas investment has increased from $13 million in 1963/4 to $161 million in 1973/4, with Papua-New Guinea accounting for over 50 per cent of the total since 1967/68. There has been an easing of investment in Papua-New Guinea since 1972 with increases directed towards the United Kingdom, New Zealand, U.S.A. and Canada as evidenced in Table I.

As a proportion of incoming direct investment, Australia's direct overseas investment ran in the range of 8 to 10 per cent between 1965 and 1970 and rose sharply to 42 per cent in 1972/3 as the Labour Government's restrictive policies began to reverse the flow of capital in 1973/4. Excluding Government transactions and undistributed income (which do not represent an actual movement of funds), Australia actually became a net exporter of capital in 1973 with an outflow of $1053 million compared with a net inflow of $1620 million in 1972.[7]

TABLE I

OUTFLOW OF AUSTRALIAN INVESTMENT OVERSEAS BY COUNTRY*
($ A MILLION)

Year	United Kingdom	New Zealand	U.S.A. and Canada	Papua-New Guinea	Other countries	Total (a)	(b)
1963/4	−14	18	−1		4	8	13
1964/5	−15	14	−1		17	15	32
1965/6	−6	17	7	11	4	33	38
1966/7	−1	12	4	18	6	39	37
1967/8	5	9	−1	21	8	42	47
1968/9	13	13	−2	24	5	52	59
1969/70	32	9	2	83	7	132	125
1970/1	−4	17	1	55	14	82	65
1971/2	−9	24	11	84	29	139	119
1972/3	1	21	−4	68	42	128	115
1973/4	39	31	35	42	35	182	161

(a) Includes portfolio investment and institutional loans.
(b) Direct investment.
*Source: Overseas Investment 1972-3 and 1973-4. Reference No. 5.20.
Australian Bureau of Statistics, Canberra.

The total income from Australian investments overseas reached A $166 million in 1973/74 which is approximately 0.33 per cent of the Australian Gross Domestic Product of A $50,434 million during the corresponding period. Although not entirely comparable, it is of interest to note that the overseas earnings as a percentage of Gross National Product in 1966 for Norway were recorded at 0.24 per cent, Sweden, 0.22 per cent, Italy, 0.16 per cent, and France, 0.15 per cent. The respective percentages for U.S.A., United Kingdom and Switzerland were 0.76 per cent, 1.10 per cent and 2.54 per cent.[8]

The characteristics of Australian direct investment overseas are treated in the following with reference to the three periods of Australia's recent economic development as defined:
(i) The deficit, protective period (mid 1960s to mid 1972).
(ii) The transitional period (mid 1972 to late 1974).
(iii) Present and future period (1975+).

(1) The Deficit Period (prior to mid 1972)

Although not actively promoted during this period, foreign direct investment was not restricted and was granted exchange control approval provided it met the criteria previously listed.

Exports were promoted by an Overseas Trade Commission network and export incentives in the form of payroll tax rebates of 2½ per cent. Double tax deduction of expenses involved in overseas market development were applied. The main sources of imports were, in order of magnitude, U.K., U.S.A., Japan, Germany, which were also the main sources of foreign investment into Australia. This is a well-established correlation between trade and foreign investment.[9]

Australia's main customers for manufactures were, in order of importance: New Zealand, U.S.A., Papua-New Guinea, Japan, South Africa, Singapore, United Kingdom, Hong Kong, Indonesia, Canada and Malaysia. 1970 figures[10] show that of a total of A $292 million of overseas proprietorship and liabilities directly held by Australian companies Papua-New Guinea accounted for 40 per cent; New Zealand 25 per cent; United Kingdom 11 per cent; U.S.A. 4 per cent; South Africa 3 per cent; and South East Asia 4 per cent. Again a loose correlation is observed between trading partners and the recipient countries of Australian investment. Apart from the special case of Papua-New Guinea, there was a bias in Australian investment towards Western developed countries. South East Asia (Hong Kong, Malaysia, Philippines, Thailand, Indonesia, Singapore), who had accounted for 31 per cent of Australia's exports of manufactures, received only 4 per cent of its investments. No doubt the political unrest in South East Asia during the 1960s had an important bearing on investment decisions.

A summary extracted from the Annual Reports of twelve Australian companies with overseas interests is tabulated in Appendix I. Each of these companies were either established overseas or had initiated substantial investments abroad prior to the "transition period" (mid 1972-4). The following observations may be made about these companies' overseas activities:

(i)   The mining and metals companies expanded vertically in an oligopolistic manner into either exploration (Broken Hill Proprietary Co. Ltd.) or downstream operations of metal processing and manufacturing (BHP, Comalco Ltd., Australian Mining and Smelting Ltd.).

(ii) The manufacturing companies expanded horizontally, either following exports or opening new markets. Repco Ltd. set up operations in South Africa and India to meet local content requirements for the automotive industry. Australian Consolidated Industries Ltd., Rheem Australia Ltd., and the manufacturing operations of BHP went to New Zealand and the various countries of South East Asia to capture markets for products that do not, owing to their bulky nature, lend themselves to efficient transport: steel drums, containers, glass and plastic packaging. Concrete Industries (Monier) Ltd., likewise opened up new markets with roof tile manufacturing units in the U.S.A., New Zealand, Japan, Indonesia, and Germany.
      Wormald International Ltd., a company manufacturing fire protection and security equipment with operations in Fiji, Hong Kong, New Zealand, Papua-New Guinea and Singapore, announced in 1972 that they had devised "a global investment strategy and laid the groundwork for further expansion overseas. . . . In catering to Australia's limited market (the company) has been forced to establish a broad product range. In larger markets such as the U.K. and the U.S.A., firms tend to specialize in certain areas of fire protection and security and W.I.L. is convinced that this fact gives them a competitive edge. Having a tenable package to market world-wide, the company hopes to boost total overseas earnings, now amounting to 15 per cent of the company's revenue to at least 50 per cent within five years. To reach this goal Wormald International Ltd. intends to start up manufacturing units in Canada, Latin America, South Africa, the United Kingdom and the United States. . . ."[11]
      In the author's opinion, this statement characterizes the attitude of the more aggressive Australian manufacturers during this period who had reached market saturation in Australia. In order to sustain the growth of their companies, such firms took entrepreneurial opportunities overseas based on one form of differentiation or another — product, service or managerial expertise.

(iii) The more dynamic service companies opened up new markets in North America, Europe, and Latin America. For Thomas Nationwide Transport Ltd., expansion by acquisition was a fundamental policy to achieve an international transport network. Travelodge Ltd. hotels followed the Australian Tourist across the Pacific to North America and Africa.

It is apparent from this summary that, although small, there was an increasing trend among Australian companies to expand abroad in the late 1960s and early 1970s. The forces behind this expansion were relatively simple. The decision to invest overseas was generally an "aggressive" one aimed at gaining new markets, gaining new resources and/or supporting export markets.

(2) The transition period (mid 1972 to late 1974)

Following the days of laissez-faire, protectionist economics, the centralist Labor Government came into power on a nationalistic platform of reform and took immediate steps to correct the bloated reserves and excess money supply it had inherited. The confusion and uncertainty caused by the adoption of a series of monetary measures and the lack of coordinated, long-term Government policy hit at the root of business confidence. Instead of investing for growth, companies were combatting inflation, wage demands, and price controls. Not surprisingly, foreign direct investment declined sharply. Although the statistics show an increase from A $119 million of foreign direct investment in 1971/2 to A $161 million in 1973/74, this actually disguises the fact that the drop in direct capital outflow was offset by large increases in undistributed profits by overseas subsidiaries. This means that the volume of new projects and new expansion overseas actually fell during the 1972-3 period.

Industrialists were frustrated and irate. At the 1974 Annual General Meeting of Broken Hill Proprietary Co. Ltd., the chairman, Sir Ian McLennan, said that there are great problems and uncertainties ahead for both Australia and B.H.P. and added "there are so many uncertainties facing us that I hesitate to make any firm forecasts".[12] A senior executive from one of the twelve companies considered earlier wrote the following comments to the author. "Unfortunately, the current economic climate in Australia is totally unsuitable for capital expenditure and therefore expansion either domestically or overseas. This has been caused by a series of "anti-industrialist" policies by the Government. Naturally the result of all this has been a rapid disintegration of all Australian labour intensive industries, especially the white goods, electronics, textiles, shoes, and the automotive industries . . . yes, there was a growing trend among Australian manufacturing companies to invest in manufacturing facilities abroad. . . . For instance Australian National Industries Ltd. were planning an extensive forging facility in the Philippines whilst Repco Ltd., were far advanced, with a plan to manufacture certain engine parts in Indonesia, as well as a rubber manufacturing facility in Malaysia. . . ."

The economic and political environment in which Australian companies were operating had clearly changed. Some protection was stripped from Australia's manufacturing industry to expose less productive companies and companies using labour-intensive techniques to strong competition from lower-cost foreign producers. In its 1974 report "The Development of Industries in Australia", the Industries Assistance Commission (I.A.C.) recommended those industries that should be fostered by the Government for the sake of their long-term contribution to economic growth. It proposed that a reduction in tariff protection be directed to those high-cost industries that were overprotected and recorded below average output per worker.

Mr. Whitlam actively promoted expansion of industry overseas during this period. He stressed that "the Australian Government was anxious to encourage private Australian investment in developing countries on a joint venture basis in accordance with those countries' social and economic development plans and their investment policies and procedures. . . . ." Such encouragement was provided through improved incentives in the Government foreign investment policy. The Export Payments Insurance Corporation Act was amended to broaden its scope in providing insurance cover not only for investments that give export benefits to Australia but also for "new worthwhile direct investments which can assist in the economic and social development of an overseas country". An overseas investment feasibility fund of $250,000 was set up to assist Australian companies to meet the costs of pre-investment feasibility studies in developing countries. A proposal was forwarded to negotiate, where appropriate, bilateral investment guarantee agreements with overseas countries. The intention was stated to give early consideration to acceding to the International Convention for the Settlement of Investment Disputes. And finally, a provision of $100,000 was included in the 1973/74 Budget to strengthen the service provided by the Department of Overseas Trade to potential Australian investors.

These changes have created the stimulus for a new set of forces which have pushed the lesser efficient industries towards locations of lower-cost production, particularly to Australia's neighbours in South East Asia. Government policy directed towards achieving greater economic and political cooperation with South East Asian Pacific countries went as far as favouring regional integration with ASEAN countries in schemes of complementary production like automobile manufacture.[13]

Some companies responded quickly to these changes and opportunities. Australian Motor Industries Ltd. announced in 1974 their intention to build an auto-components plant in the Philippines.[14] Nicholas International Ltd. has planned production plants in Malaysia and Kenya and will cease to supply the South East Asian and African markets through exports from Australia as soon as these operations come on stream. In its 1974 Annual Report, the Chairman of Nicholas International claimed that its Australian operations were those of the highest cost world-wide.[15] Hanimex Corporation Limited reached agreement with the Government of Ireland to locate an operation there "under very favourable terms" that will supply the EEC and U.S. markets. Its 1974 Annual Report states that recent developments have "drastically affected Australian manufacturers' ability to compete on export markets and even to compete successfully on their own domestic market". Hanimex planned to "rely more on the importation of completed products into Australia than local manufacture".

Definitions of "defensive" and "aggressive" expansion in foreign direct investment leave much scope for debate. But it would seem that the Government switch in 1972 to policies characteristic of a trade surplus country generated a set of forces that led to expansion primarily for "defensive" reasons. Both the efficient and less-efficient producers were subjected to increased competition from imports and found it more difficult to compete in export markets. Overseas expansion after 1973 could be seen therefore as a necessary expedient for retention of market share, earnings, or even for pure survival. It could on the other hand, also be seen as a healthy evolutionary step in the growth of a firm located in a country with a small domestic market and limited potential for domestic expansion.

To expand on this, it is useful to refer to Vernon's Product Life Cycle hypothesis[16] that describes the migration of a product from a high technology country like the United States where it is manufactured as an "innovation" to a developed country like Australia where it is adopted as a "maturing" product and finally, to a lesser-developed country where it must be exploited as a "standardized" product requiring new markets and low production costs. As a generalization, Australian manufacturing industry fits into this cycle at the "mature" and "standardized" end. Australian protectionist policies prior to 1973 have allowed standardized production to survive in Australia. In other words, maturing and standardized products have become bottled up behind Australia's tariff wall which has frustrated the process of restructuring and upgrading of Australian manufacturing industry. Some standardized products have recently been passed on to developing countries and these characterize the investments made by Australian firms in South East Asia in such activities as corrugated fibre and glass containers, plaster board, paper, batteries, flour milling, materials handling equipment, aluminium extrusions, adhesive, carpets, leather products, polish, etc. Australia became the fourth or fifth most important investing country in Indonesia, Hong Kong and the Philippines accounting in 1973 and 1974 for roughly 4 to 5 per cent of the total foreign investments placed in these countries.[17]

(3) Present and Future Period (1975+)

The present regression to protectionist policies gives Australian industrialists a chance to recover their breath as well as an important opportunity to re-appraise the future of their companies and industries in light of the past and formulate medium to long-range corporate strategies adapted to the new economic environment.

Projecting a situation of surplus in the balance of trade in the future it was said earlier that policies in such a case should be directed towards the promotion of free trade. The U.S. Trade Reform Act of 1974 urges the phasing out of tariffs world-wide and it is winning the support of a growing number of nations — Sweden, Switzerland, Japan, Holland and Germany — which like Australia, tend to produce trade surpluses. Australia should therefore in the future revert to policies appropriate to a surplus trading nation and create conditions to stimulate the restructuring of Australian manufacturing industry.

If Australian companies are going to shed their more labour-intensive, standardized production and set up operations in developing countries, they are certain to encounter strong labour union opposition in Australia unless jobs can be replaced with alternative production. The I.A.C. states that Australia should encourage what it terms "low cost" industries, or those that can survive with little or no tariff or other state aid. It lists in this category "most service industries; manufacturing industries which are agro or mineral-based (e.g. processing foodstuffs or minerals); manufacturing industries based on new skills, innovations and designs; most rural industries; and ventures based on iron ore, bauxite, nickel, coal and natural gas which can sell their output overseas".[18]

To move in this direction, Australian companies must follow one or a combination of the following alternatives: (i) actively promote Research and Development, or more appropriately "imitation and development" in the U.S. sense (this has been supported since 1967 by generous Government subsidies for research and development); (ii) actively import technology through licenses and adapt this technology to Australian market conditions; or (iii) form joint ventures with foreign partners who have access to more advanced technology. As an example, Century Battery Limited diversified their product range in 1974 through a joint venture with E.S.B. Incorporated of the U.S.A. but preceded this joint venture by expansion to Malaysia and Indonesia. The Malayan operation has proved very profitable.[19] Such an example demonstrates the various steps of the Product Life Cycle theory, with the initial innovation and later the maturing product being exploited in Australia and the less-competitive, standardized product being exploited in lower-cost locations.

Owing to Australia's small domestic market, overseas expansion and/or product diversification is essential for company and national growth. This has been seen in the "aggressive" expansion of Australian foreign direct investment prior to 1973 in order to sustain company growth and seize entrepreneurial opportunities, and in the "defensive" nature of overseas expansion following 1973 when domestic tariff protection was lowered and export subsidies eliminated. No matter what the stimulus, growth will continue to be necessary to generate the increased earnings required to support the upgrading of product and technology to meet the changing demands of the Australian market. Expansion and replacement are therefore the key elements for a dynamic model of Australia's manufacturing industry which will hopefully evolve under more liberal trade conditions than the present.

Twelve Australian Companies
(Source: The following information has been extracted from recent company Annual Reports).

Company	Operations/type of Business	Nature of Overseas Expansion

1. *Broken Hill Proprietary Co. Ltd.*
Revenue A $1,296 m (1974)
Total Assets A $2,356 m (1974)
Australian ownership 84 per cent.
Australia's largest company.

Mining (iron ore, manganese) Steelmaking, oil and natural gas, manufacturing in most part related to steel end use, mining exploration.

Vertical expansion downstream into manufacture of steel products. Upstream into mining and petroleum. Some diversification in minerals and manufacturing through acquisition of textile interests.
a. *Operations*
1. Manufacturing outlets for steel—*Malaysia* wire drawing and steel ropery: *New Guinea* — wire and steel drawing: *Taiwan* — tungsten carbide manufacture: *New Zealand* — steel drums: *Indonesia* — metal containers.
2. Exploration for minerals and petroleum in Malaysia, Indonesia and New Guinea.
b. *Exports.* Account for approximately 10 per cent of sales.

2. *Comalco Ltd*
Revenue A $192 m (1973)
Total Assets A $358 m (1973)
Australian ownership about 20 per cent through C.R.A.'s 50 per cent interest. Australia's ninth largest company based on 1974 market capitalization.

Bauxite and alumina, primary aluminium, semi-fabricated and fabricated products, salt mining.

Vertical expansion to secure market outlets for aluminium fabricated and semi-fabricated products. Preference for joint-ventures in South East Asian expansion. Products are very standardized.
a. *Operations*
N.Z. aluminium smelting, aluminium semi-fabricated and fabricated products;
New Guinea—Semi-fabricated and fabricated aluminium products:
Hong Kong—Joint venture fabricated products, containers and cans:
Indonesia—Extrusions, roll-forming.
b. *Exports*—34 per cent of revenue.

3. *Australian Mining and Smelting Ltd.*
Revenue A $166 m (1973)

Lead and zinc mining and smelting sulphuric acid, silver, cadmium, zinc processing, coal and coke, timber. Exploration and development in nickel, coal and bauxite.

Vertical expansion downstream into processing and smelting of zinc. Have 50 per cent joint venture in Netherlands and a U.K. processing firm.
a. *Operations. U.K.*—zinc smelting: *Holland*—zinc smelting; *U.K.*—zinc processing (die casting, anodes).
b. *Exports*—Overseas subsidiary accounts for 52 per cent of total sales. Exports are directed towards S.E. Asia and U.S.A. and represent 15 per cent of total sales.

4. *Concrete Industries (Monier) Ltd.*
Revenue A $116m (1974)
48 per cent increase over 1973.
Total Assets A $41 m (1974)
Australian ownership about 100 per cent. Australia's 49th largest company (1974).

Manufacture and distribution of concrete pipes, roofing tiles, masonary, clay bricks and other building materials. Quarrying of sand and stone; Manufacture of consumer durable products; Manufacture and distribution of caravans and caravan components. Cement lining of water mains and construction of concrete reservoirs.

Horizontal expansion for increased market and growth. Tile product is sufficiently differentiated for profitable overseas expansion. Expansion began in late 1960s. Expansion to U.S., Japan, Indonesia, Malaysia, are 1970s developments.
Operations
U.S.A.—roofing the manufacture. California (100 per cent); *N.Z.* roofing tiles (100 per cent); *Japan*—roofing tiles; *Indonesia*—roofing tiles (100 per cent); *Malaysia*—roofing tiles (100 per cent); *Germany*—roofing tiles; *Thailand*—roofing tiles.

5. *Pioneer Concrete Services Ltd.*
Revenue A $170 m (1972)
Total Assets A $41 m (1972)
Australian ownership about 100 per cent.
Australia's 38th largest company (1974)

Quarrying, masonry, asphalt, plastics, tea plantations.

Horizontal expansion to increase market and sustain growth. One product with standardized process. Australia and U.S. lead in ready-mixed concrete technology. Major growth in sales and profitability achieved by overseas expansion in face of increased competition and market downturn in Australia.
Operations
Hong Kong—quarrying and concrete mixing. *U.K.*—concrete mixing; *Italy*—concrete mixing; *Spain*—concrete mixing; *South Africa*—concrete mixing; *Germany*—concrete mixing; *Portugal*—concrete mixing; *New Guinea*—tea plantations.

6. *Repco Ltd.*
Revenue A $212 m (1974)
Total Assets A $184 m (1974)
Australian ownership approximately 100 per cent.
Australia's 28th largest company (1974).

Research, manufacture and distribution of parts and systems for automotive maintenance and new vehicle production, garage equipment, machine tools, textile machinery, cycles, other products and services for automotive, agricultural, general industrial and commercial use.

Horizontal expansion to secure market outlets where Government stipulates minimum content Standardized products. Plans for manufacture in *Indonesia*—engine parts; *Malaysia*—rubber manufacture; *Holland*—have been postponed pending improved economic conditions in Australia.
a. *Operations*
1. *N.Z.* 2. *South Africa*—to meet local content requirement of Governments. All automotive parts.
b. *Exports*—10 per cent of sales with distribution outlets and warehousing in Switzerland, U.S.A., New Zealand, Canada, India, U.K., S.E. Asia, Hong Kong.

7. *Australian Consolidated Industries Ltd.*
Revenue A $375 m (1974).
Australian ownership 90–100 per cent. Australia's 21st largest company (1974).

Packaging (63 per cent) – glass, plastic, metal fibre, paper, canning.
Building products: fibreglass, hardboard, casting, etc., aluminium.

With exception of N.Z. expansion into S.E. Asia has been with a limited range of products. Glass bottles and corrugated fibre manufacturing essentially; Thus, horizontal expansion with very standardized products to

177

Specialized scientific, electronic, testing equipment

capture foreign markets. Expansion very active in mid 1970s.
a. *Operations*
21 per cent of total assets are in New Zealand 5 per cent in other areas. *N.Z.*—entire range of products; *P.N.G.*—glass bottles, corrugated fibre containers. Blow moulded plastic containers; *Singapore*—glass bottles, fibre containers, textile tubes; *Malaysia*—bottles, fibre containers, tableware; *Thailand*—bottles, tableware, corrugated fibre containers; *Indonesia*—bottles and tableware; *Fiji*—metal containers, kitchenware.

8. *Nicholas International Ltd.*
Revenue A $84m (1974).
Total Assets A $68 m (1974).
100 per cent Australian owned.
Australia's 97th largest company (1974).

Home medication products. Prescription medicines (18 per cent) Toiletries (22 per cent). Scientific equipment (18 per cent)

Prewar overseas expansion with original product "ASPRO". Production operations followed export markets. Cost of manufacture in Australia led to decision to build plant in Malaysia and Kenya.
a. *Operations*
Manufacturing in *U.K.*—for U.K. region; *France*—for European region: *N.Z.; Indonesia*—50:50. Joint venture with Parke Davies Planned Manufacture in *Keyna* and *Malaysia*.
b. 34 per cent of total sales are in Australia.

9. *Rheem Australia Ltd.*
Revenue A $91 m (1972).
Total Assets A $76 m (1973)
Approximately 100 per cent Australian owned.
Australia's 77th largest company—a subsidiary of Broken Hill Proprietary Co. Ltd.

Manufacture and sale of hot water systems. Manufacture of steel containers, gas pressure vessels, liquid storage tanks and general fabrications; Manufacture of rigid and flexible packages in plastic and paper.
Fabric printers, timber, cattle, property.

Horizontal expansion with standardized unsophisticated products.
Operations
New Guinea—steel fabricating, cattle, timber, soft drinks; *N.Z.*—steel and plastic containers; *Indonesia*—steel drums and pails, stainless steel and aluminium special purpose containers.

10. *Hanimex Corporation Ltd.*
Revenue A $40 m (1974).
Total Assets A $36 m (1974).
100 per cent Australian owned

Merchandizing and manufacture of consumer products; electrical—radios, cassette recorders, clocks, etc., sporting goods—squash raquets, outboard motors, bicycles, bicycles, educational products. Industrial—import and distribution of film.

Horizontal expansion with differentiated products to low labour cost locations—Hong Kong and Ireland. World-wide distribution network for own manufactured and branded products. Rapidly expanding, very responsive to Government policy and changing industrial environment. Planning to import more from overseas manufacturing operations.
a. *Operations*
Distribution outlets in U.K., W. Germany, France, Canada, U.S., N.Z., Hong Kong, Rep. of Ireland (planned)

		for supply of slide projectors and photographic equipment to EEC and N. America. 45 per cent of sales outside Australia/N.Z. b. *Exports*—have been severely affected by Government policy.
11. *Travelodge Australia Ltd.* Revenue A \$25 m (1974). Total Assets A \$53 m (1974).	Accommodation and food and beverage.	Travelodge has followed the Australian tourist. As a result of Government monetary policies—more tourists have been leaving Australia. Business slack in Australia—expansion only abroad. Hotels in Fiji, N.Z., P.N.G., Tahiti, Indonesia, New Caledonia, U.S.A., Canada, Mexico, Japan.
12. *Thomas Nationwide Transport Ltd.* Revenue A \$249 m (1974). Total Assets A \$134 m (1974). Australian ownership 100 per cent. Australia's 49th largest company (1974)	International transport—rail, road, sea and air. TNT Kwikasair Alltrans Acme Fast Freight	Expansion by acquisition in U.S.A., Brazil, Canada, etc. Expansion in fundamental policy in developing TNT into an international transport group. The group has significant operations in Australia, Canada, U.S.A., N.Z., and Brazil. Lesser operations in U.K., Europe and Singapore. Largest market in U.S.A. 50 per cent of Group revenue outside Australia.

Footnotes

1. Treasury Press Release No. 97, *Foreign Investment and the Balance of Payments,* Address by Hon. Frank Crean, Treasurer to C.E.D.A., 22 November 1974.
2. *Financial Times,* September 24, 1974.
3. "A Cool Look at Capital Outflow", *Australian Financial Review,* 17 March 1972.
4. Press Statement No. 175, 22 January 1974, by the Prime Minister, Hon. Mr. G. Whitlam.
5. Reserve Bank of Australia.
6. *Overseas Investment 1972-73,* Australian Bureau of Statistics, Canberra Bulletin, Reference No. 5120.
7. *National Bank Monthly Summary,* February 1974.
8. John G. Dunning (Ed.), *International Investment,* Penguin, 1972.
9. Donald T. Brash, *American Investment in Australian Industry,* Harvard University Press, Cambridge, Mass. 1966.
10. *Annual Bulletin of Overseas Investment,* Commonwealth Bureau of Census and Statistics, Canberra, Australia.
11. "Solving Asia/Pacific Business Problems", *Business Asia,* Report 1974, Volume 1: Investment, Acquisition, Expansion.
12. Broken Hill Proprietary Ltd., Annual Report, 1974.
13. "Australia considers Restructuring Car Industry, favouring Imports", *Business Asia,* 2 August 1974.
14. "Australia in Asia, Bigger role in trade and investment", *Business Asia,* March 15, 1974.
15. Nicholas International Ltd., Annual Report, 1974.
16. Raymond Vernon. "International Investment and International Trade in the Product Cycle", *The Quarterly Journal of Economics,* Volume LXXX, No. 1, May 1966.
17. *Business Asia,* March, August and December issues, 1974, and *Financial Times,* 24 March 1975.
18. "How Australia beckons investment while tightening controls on it", *Business Asia,* December 27, 1974.
19. "Australian Dry Cell Venture with 60% U.S. Equity approved." *Business Asia,* 17 May 1974.

The Future of Multinational Corporations:

from the Australian Viewpoint

By Mr. M.J. Hayes*

Before we can attempt to make some forecasts on the likely future of multinational corporations it is essential that we have the historical and contemporary context of multinational corporations clearly in our minds. The first question to try to decide is how have multinational corporations developed? I would like to suggest that multinational corporations are inheritors of a very long historical tradition. Inter-country trade has been a feature of the world for the whole of recorded time. Countries produce various commodities, early ones were gold, diamonds, spices, frankincense, myrrh and there were always people anxious to go and obtain, buy if you like, these products from the originating country and take them to some other country where they had a greater value. Thus I suggest that the habit of exporting/importing of various commodities, transfer of international trade, is in fact the origin of multi-national corporations and will go on in some form or other as long as civilised man inhabits this planet.

Many successful companies operating in their own markets have sought alternative markets in other countries, usually in countries adjacent to them, and into which they can sell some of their product. At first the product is made as marginal production in their existing factories so that there can often be very considerable benefits to the company. Basically this is how most of the multi-nationals have started. They started by seeking export markets for their products.

In most cases companies would prefer to still produce from a single centralised source located in their home country to supply other markets because they would then have only the one known set of problems such as availability of raw materials, machinery, finance and banking facilities, laws and customs, availability of personnel with the right skills and general business practices with which they are familiar.

The extractive industries don't fall into this category naturally, they have to operate in the country from which they are extracting the various minerals. But most manufacturing companies would far prefer to manufacture from a central point and export to other countries. This applies to a whole range of products whether they be machinery, pharmaceuticals, other consumer goods, because in that situation the company is operating under known terms and conditions and therefore feels secure in the way it is operating. Many companies never develop beyond that point of exporting their product from the one single manufacturing source in their home country.

The multi-national corporations that we generally regard in this context are those with manufacturing plants in other countries, as well as those having multi-national/international marketing operations. Corporations that have manufacturing facilities in more than one country are to a very large extent the product of economic nationalism. In numerous cases the host country has made it a condition of continuing to operate in that country that a local plant was set up. So that the spread of multi-nationals in the full sense of the word has, to a degree, not been at the volition of the multi-nationals themselves. It has been initiated by economic nationalism for various reasons, mainly the desire to have sources of manufacture in their own country. Clearly these companies are invited into the host countries because it is felt by the host countries themselves that the company has a significant contribution to make to the local economy. They provide jobs, introduce new technology, stimulate training of skilled workers as obvious benefits.

However the fact that they make a significant contribution to the raising of standards of living and other standards in the host countries does not by itself make multi-national corporations

*Vice-President, Nicholas International Limited, Melbourne, Australia

popular. In this regard they are of course in a great tradition. The old romantic traders of days gone by, were not popular. They were often attacked by the natives as well as by pirates from other countries and they were never sure if they were going to get away from their host country with their precious cargoes. They were in fact highly hazardous operations.

What I'm saying is that people who engage in international trade may be providing benefits to the country with whom they are trading but that historically they have never been popular with the people with whom they are conducting their trade. They are after all foreigners and foreigners are always viewed with suspicion. They are foreigners seen to be making money out of the efforts of the host country and it is relatively easy for anyone to fuel attitudes of suspicion and antagonism in such a situation.

Let us look again at the benefits which the typical less developed country's LDC's receive from the presence of say a manufacturing unit of one of the multi-nationals.

First new ideas are generated, there are new inputs of technology, new products are available on the market, marketing organisations are established and local people develop business experience, utilising the techniques that the corporation have developed, very often in other places and other situations, adapting them to the local situation.

Secondly, people are trained locally, both local managers and technicians and skilled workers are developed which helps to create a stable middle class and also helps to speed the economic development of the host country.

Thirdly, a new venture supplies goods otherwise unavailable or available at greater expense and/or smaller quantities. The venture also tends to develop local resources.

Fourthly, the obvious savings in the cost of imports where the local manufactured goods displace imported goods and foreign exchange losses otherwise incurred in bringing in finished goods is very beneficial for the host country.

Exports contribute to the countries' foreign exchange earnings and sometimes even provide world-wide marketing networks. This is the case when the multinational corporation uses the plant as a source of supply for other countries. It also pays taxes, it pays wages and salaries to employees, it provides employment opportunities, it helps to raise living standards, creates purchasing power as well as the tax revenue we just mentioned.

Next there are purchases from ancillary industries which act as a spur to local industry, developing diversified local suppliers and in turn raising incomes, tax revenue and development carrying on the process we mentioned earlier.

Then of course this and other local expenditure stimulates all types of service industries from insurance and banking to shipping and advertising, raising incomes and tax revenues, raising the whole level of sophistication of the local environment. Sometimes local dividends are paid strengthening purchasing power and stimulating a savings industry.

Various attempts have been made to quantify the multiplier effect of investment by MNC's. Clearly the figures given in the studies depend on whether we only consider the purchases from ancillary industries or whether on attempt is made to quantify the employment created in the ancillary industries. For example, Siemens believe that for every person they have employed in their Brazilian operation that they have created 1.5 jobs outside the company. Philips on the other hand have figured that its Indian operations have generated seven jobs outside the plant for each one inside. Philips has also estimated that its investments in the U.K. have indirectly created between 40,000 and 45,000 other jobs in the U.K.

The existence of companies operating in a country acts as a stimulus to other foreign investors which in turn leads to further capital inflow into the country and also it acts as a stimulus to local investors. The multinational corporations also make contributions to local charities, help education, boost social welfare programmes, and MNC's are pacesetters in improving working conditions and rewards and consequently will continue to be the subject of attack from local business leaders as well as politicians who will use nationalistic arguments which may inhibit the increased standards of living of the people. Naturally raising wages and conditions of work is resented by some local employers who have to try to compete with the multinational corporations. Thus it is easy to see how some of the resentments arise and are fostered.

There are of course some negative factors and the ones that weigh heaviest with host governments are usually the remittances of dividends, royalties, fees, interest and other payments which tend to damage their balance of payments. Certain materials and components are often imported. There is also the fear that huge foreign investors sometimes create a situation which acts as a damper on local investors and of course the biggest negative factor is a lack of local understanding. Foreign subsidiares, generally are managed in world-wide terms rather than in the interests of the one country and so that the local host country has relatively low level of understanding of the nature of the operations and the management of it. Thus, the guidelines and factors that really count inside that organisation are not necessarily the same as those of the host country.

I have suggested that multi-national corporations, as well as being in the great historical tradition of the traders of the past, are also inheritors of the suspicion and distrust which the traders of the past have experienced and this bring us very much to the present day situation.

Multinational corporations must not expect to be loved purely because of the benefits that they confer on the host country. It would be running in the face of tradition and all history if that were the situation. So where do we stand at the present time? We stand at the point where there are several very large multinational corporations and there are some small multinational corporations around the world. They have been subject over the last two to three years to suspicion, mistrust and general antagonism which has not only been restricted to the host countries. A considerable proportion of the antagonism to the multinational corporations has been expressed in the home based countries in which these companies operate in the U.S.A., the European countries and countries like Australia which have their share of multinationals.

It is interesting, just for a moment to wonder why this should be so because quite clearly the multinational corporations are providing fairly substantial economic benefits to their home country in earning foreign exchange and raising the standards and so on. I suggest that this arises as a response not particularly to their multinational characters but just to their sheer bigness. It is somehow felt that they are beyond control, that by their sheer size they have a disproportionate influence on the way that political decisions and other important decisions are made; that they somehow have a power to flout political decisions if that is their wish and this vague unease that exists in the minds of a high proportion of the population is part of the reason why the multinationals have been identified as a popular whipping boy in the last few years. Things like the bribery and illegal payments scandals just serve to fuel these kind of feelings. Today many multinational corporations exist and contribute very substantially to the standards of life, to the emerging economies of many countries but for a variety of reasons they appear to be unpopular.

So what of the future — One thing is certain, international trade will continue. Also, the existence and continuance of multinational corporations is inextricably tied up with the free enterprise system. In fact it is really the international expression of that system. In other words we can think of the multinational corporations as being the expression of the capitalist system in countries other than the originating one and consequently they are a popular target for countries of communist regimes and of similar political persuasion. This explains to some extent why the votes at the United Nations or the investigations by the United Nations usually produce results which are antagonistic to the multinational corporations. The fact remains that most under-developed countries are anxious to improve their own standards and to develop, and the multi-national corporations are the most effective means whereby developing countries can acquire advanced technology in both the material sense and in the managerial sense which they are so anxious to acquire.

During the next few years we are also likely to see a couple of interesting developments in the nature of the multinational corporations, for example, we are likely to see far more of the State owned multinationals operating in many countries of the world. We easily think of companies like the Italian Oil Company, Agip, the French motor car company, Renault, and there are several others. It seems likely that as the countries of Europe nationalise various industries which are anxious to expand their business horizons, motivated in a very similar manner to the ordinary corporations, that we will see a very substantial increase in the activities of State owned multinational corporations.

A second feature likely to develop is that the communist regimes are likely to extend their multinational activities from the selling of arms into much wider and more proliferated kinds of activities. They have already developed considerable sophistication in selling arms to other countries and it seems likely that at the trading level they will be anxious to sell other commodities on a much wider scale. We have seen in certain countries in Africa they have taken a part in assisting in building certain operations — The Tanzanian railway built by the Chinese is an example. It seems likely that in the future we will have some State owned multinationals originating from the communist regimes of Eastern Europe and Asia.

One consequence of the difficulties and criticisms that have taken place over the multinational corporations in the past few years is likely to be that companies are going to be more cautious in establishing plants and activities in host countries and likewise the host countries are going to be more careful and possibly more suspicious of the kinds of agreements that they are likely to make with the companies. It seems that the standards of behaviour, the guidelines within which the companies will operate will be examined in a much more formal manner than previously. The "Elements of Global Business Conduct" developed by the Chamber of Commerce of the United States which are public statements on principles of global business behaviour will be useful expressions of existing practices and act as guides to companies deciding to engage in establishing plants in other countries. Similarly the Business International Summary of Guidelines for International Investment will also act as a useful check-list for deciding on investments and I think it is worth going through some of the important points of these two documents at this stage.

In relation to the corporate commitment it is essential that the multinational corporations realise that they must obey the laws and regulations of all the countries in which the corporation operates. It must also respect the policies of the host country. It should refrain from any involvement in party political activity. They may, however, communicate their public position through appropriate channels on issues relating to their business operations. Clearly the multinational corporations do have relationships with host governments and it will be and must be completely proper for them to be able to make those opinions clearly available to the host government.

The company should also contribute to the economic development process of the host country for example, by choosing local sources of goods and services over those from foreign sources when price and quality are competitive. It should also make sure that the project fits into the local development plans and priorities. It needs also to contribute to the health, safety, environmental and development objectives of the host countries. It is essential in order that the multinational corporations can do these things that the host government should make its priorities well known to prospective investors and if possible consult with the private sector in its own country when drawing up such plans. The host governments should also refrain from discriminating against a company because it is foreign owned. It should naturally provide legal protection for minority shareholders, it should grant fair and non-discriminatory treatment to foreign property and make effective and prompt payment of just compensation in the event of expropriation or nationalisation. Also, very importantly, it must agree to settle investment disputes by international arbitration.

On the question of ownership the company should be responsive to the host country's investors desires for an opportunity to participate in the ownership of the affiliate with the corporation itself and should consider forming joint ventures with local partners and offering stock of the foreign subsidiary to local investors. In return the host government should recognise that it is possible that 100% foreign ownership may be the only way to make certain investments. It should make any laws requiring local participation as flexible as possible and non-retroactive. The company should also make maximum use of qualified local personnel and contribute to the training of local manpower by hiring trainees and promoting qualified national personnel at all levels of the operation to the maximum possible extent and by providing wages and benefits in line with competitive practices and national norms. If it is necessary to make shifts in production or employment it should be done in such a way as to minimise any adverse impact on employees and they should also confer and consult with organisations representing employees. In turn the host government should develop technical and managerial training and should permit employment of foreign personnel for efficient operations or for training purposes. On technology the company should also improve productivity by keeping up to date as required all technology used by affiliates and to charge reasonable fees for such technology transferred. It should make technological changes with due regard to increasing employment opportunities and training of the labour forces in the host country and should establish local research and development facilities in accordance with the principles of efficient operation while taking into consideration the needs and capabilities of the host country. It should also minimise damage to the environment and co-operate with the host country in examining the effect of the plant on the environment.

In return the host government should recognise that the companies will only share technology if they are adequately compensated. They should also encourage international companies to perform research locally and they should grant effective legal protection to industrial property rights including freedom of licencing. They should refrain also from imposing too onerous withholding taxes on fees and royalties. Transfer pricing and trade policy generally are another sensitive area and the company should aim to price goods and services, traded within the corporation but between countries where affiliates are located, on a uniform basis reflecting the cost of the goods or services transferred and to follow responsible financial practices whenever the corporation is represented and to conduct all transactions between the corporation and affiliates according to arms length principles. It should not seek undue protection from the competition of imported manufactured products and it should help its local affiliate to develop exports and place no obstacles to exports except for economic reasons of existing obligations to third parties and when possible should also give preference to local supplies of components and raw materials. In return the host government should refrain from imposing export obligations on the investor beyond those contractually entered into and it should also permit the foreign investor to import equipment and materials without undue interference.

On financial matters the investor should take the host countries balance of payments situation and availability of funds to local enterprises into consideration when making its financial plans. By pursuing a policy of conducting foreign exchange operations in accordance with normal business requirements and to utilise currency holdings to cover normal business transactions, a firm can protect its financial position in those currencies. It should hold no exchange balances for speculative purposes and follow responsible monetary and credit practices in all countries in which it is located. It should also consider re-investing profits in the host country and pursue a policy that affiliates will re-invest a reasonable proportion of their earnings in the countries from which they are derived. It should also allow its affiliates to disclose profits and other financial information if such disclosure is generally required by the host country. In return the host government should place no restrictions on remittances of interest, fees and royalties except where the contract calling for such transfers has not been approved, and it should not impose restrictions on profit remittances and capital repatriation after an investment has already been made. If it is going to apply restriction on borrowing it should make them apply to local as well as to foreign investors. On taxation matters the investor should observe the tax laws of the host country and be able to justify transfer prices. In return the host government should not impose taxes greater than from the net profits arising in the host country and should not impose higher taxes on foreign owned companies than on locally owned firms.

In summary, therefore, it seems that the negotiations between multinational corporations and the host countries are likely to be tougher and also likely to be more cautious before allowing plants to be established than they were through the 50's and 60's. In addition multinational corporations are likely to insist at the outset that investment disputes be settled by international arbitration. This will be particularly important because developing countries are currently criticising MNC's for their negative attitudes towards renegotiation of original concessions.

Finally it seems likely that relationships between multinational corporations and host governments will be constantly evolving and at any moment in time there will be countries at various stages of this evolution. These range from countries of the developed nations which accept MNC's originating from other countries just as ordinary members of the business community. At the opposite extreme are the under-developed countries who are anxious to establish industry in their countries and are anxious to attract multinational corporations and are willing to go along with the necessary conditions which these corporations require. As the country develops there will be political demands for greater local control of the business such as we see today in countries like Nigeria and India where greater and greater local participation is being demanded. It seems likely that in the efflux of time as these countries improve their economies and build their own operations that they will ease off from this position and will come to accept MNC's on the basis of fully developed countries accepting each other organisations.

Arising from the recognised benefits which MNC's provide to host countries combined with the MNC's reluctance to expose themselves to the kind of attacks which have characterised the mid 1970's, they will be criticised and vilified for not doing enough to help the LDC's in the late 1970's and early 1980's.

A recent report has been published by the ILO, which is the oldest of the UN organisations and actually pre-dates the UN itself. Whilst studies by other UN agencies have reached conclusions which are critical of MNC's the ILO has arrived at the opposite verdict. This research for this report started in 1973 and is based on replies to questionaires sent to:—
(1)   Management of international companies and their subsidiaries.
(2)   Worker organisations
(3)   Employer organisations
(4)   Host country governments
(5)   Home country governments.

Because of the thoroughness and objectivity of this report it can fairly claim to be the most authoritative study on this subject to date. Nevertheless MNC's will be very cautious for the next few years.

Thus in summary it seems likely that multinational corporations will continue to exist and operate. There will be more formality in the preparation of agreements and greater care given to the choice of both the host country and the company to be invited to operate in the country. The character of some of the multi-nationals will change by the intervention of state multinationals from both the East and West blocks. Hopefully a universal code of practice will be developed preferably by the United Nations or one of its agencies such as U.N.C.T.A.D. which will form the basis against which all multinationals will be judged but in spite of all this it seems most unlikely that the multinationals will be loved.

The Australian Multinational and Its Future:

a case study of the TNT Group

By Sir Peter Abeles*

There is a tendency when discussing multinational corporations to concentrate on American, European, and, more recently, Japanese based companies. While these areas are undoubtedly the most important in terms of numbers and sales volumes, there are nevertheless a number of firms which have grown from completely different national bases. Indeed it can be expected that as world economic development continues that many other countries — especially within the third world — will be the birthplace of new multinational enterprises. Australia as a developed country has not surprisingly already produced a number of multinational firms and companies such as Broken Hill Proprietary Co., Comalco, Pioneer Concrete, A.C.I., Nicholas International, Repco, and Hanimex have all added their names to a multitude of overseas operations. Though the experience of these companies overseas might seem the same as their European or American counterparts, it must be remembered that the Australian multinational operates from a similar but nevertheless different socio-economic base, and differences in tax laws, business practices and even in the culture itself are likely to make the Australian based firm respond somewhat differently than his counterparts overseas. As these differences will undoubtedly affect the future of Australian based multinational companies, they are certainly worthy of discussion but perhaps can be expressed best through an examination of the experiences of one such company, Thomas Nationwide Transport Ltd. Its business is perhaps one of the more internationalised of Australian firms with operations in the U.S.A., Brazil, Canada, New Zealand, Singapore, and Europe. This article will first look briefly at the history of the T.N.T. Group and its philosophy behind international expansion, then examine its progress and restraints in international operations, and finally discuss some of the factors which will be of importance in determining the future of both it and other Australian based multinationals.

Brief History of the TNT Group

The business originated as a sole venture in 1946 when Mr. K.W. Thomas commenced a one truck operation. Following steady expansion of activities it was formed into a private company during 1951. The public company, Thomas Nationwide Transport Limited, was incorporated in November 1961 under the laws of the Australian Capital Territory and official listing on the Sydney Stock Exchange was granted the following year.

At that stage in TNT's corporate development its principal activities were road and rail forwarding of interstate freight within Australia. Subsequently these two modes of transport were integrated by the introduction of a flexivan rail trailer service (a loaded pantechnicon unit is transferred from a road vehicle to a rail car for linehaul and then transferred back to a road vehicle for final delivery). To support this service TNT concentrated on the development of its own efficient railhead distribution centres throughout Australia.

From 1962 TNT embarked upon a programme of expansion by development of its own operations and by the acquisition of companies already operating in the transport industry. In 1967 TNT acquired a substantial proportion of the Australian business of the U.K. based

*Managing Director, Thomas Nationwide Transport Limited, Sydney, Australia.

Transport Development Group which provided a substantial increase in the volume of goods handled and expanded TNT's activities into car carrying, customs clearance and bond and free stores as well as local and wharf cartage. In the same year, TNT merged with Alltrans Pty. Limited, the largest privately owned unlisted company then operating in the Australian freight transport industry, giving TNT a wider coverage of services in Australia, expansion into New Zealand and making TNT the largest non-Government freight transport group in Australia. Prior to the merger, Alltrans Pty. Limited had pioneered the development of freight forwarding methods throughout New Zealand and, with the advent of roll-on roll-off ships, TNT was able to offer door-to-door service throughout Australia and New Zealand. During this period TNT also expanded into overnight interstate express delivery service (Comet and Kwikasair) and intracity courier operations.

In 1969, TNT entered the North American market with the acquisition of a Californian transport company, Walkup's Merchants Express Inc. (since renamed Alltrans Express U.S.A. Inc.). This was followed in 1970, by the acquisition of GILL Interprovincial Lines Limited (since re-established as Alltrans Express Limited), a major Canadian interprovincial on-forwarder.

TNT became involved in Australian coastal sea transport by the acquisition initially of a 33 1/3% interest, since increased to 62½% interest, in Bulkships Limited; TNT gained an interest in the air transport industry in 1972, when it acquired 23.4% of Ansett Transport Industries Limited, one of Australia's two major domestic airlines.

These ventures were followed by further expansion into Brazil, Singapore, the United Kingdom and Europe. Since 1971 Kwikasair Divisions have been established in most of TNT's countries of operation to handle TNT's express freight business.

The most recent major acquisitions were those of Overland Western Limited in 1973, a trucking company operating in Ontario, New York and Michigan, and, in the same year, Acme Fast Freight Inc., a rail forwarder with operations extending across the U.S.A. Following the acquisition of Acme Fast Freight Inc., TNT now owns and operates a widespread system of transport licences in the U.S.A.

The Philosophy Behind International Expansion

As transport operators, TNT developed unique operating systems and pioneered major developments in transport in a newly emerging post-war economy. Advanced management and control systems were developed and proven in a rapidly growing environment. The success of these new skills and systems ensured adequate returns to shareholders and provided employees with an environment of success.

The Australian economy represents only a small market by international standards and, although growth was rapid in the 50's and 60's, TNT believed that its future growth would be dictated by the rate of growth of the domestic economy and this growth rate was lower than the overall corporate objective. To achieve a lower growth was not acceptable to management and would have been depressing to shareholders and to employees, so alternative growth strategies were considered. Two broad strategies were formulated. The first strategy involved diversification of TNT's group activities within Australia into other industries where benefits may arise through, for example, distribution economies, management controls and finance. A second strategy was to agressively develop in the area our management had pioneered and in the area our systems were proven, but in a larger market place — the global market. The risks of developing internationally, compared with risks associated with diversification of activities, appeared less, and the rewards, in the longer run, were likely to be greater. Also the momentum from such geographic diversification would generate benefits in the form of economies and higher returns.

Adoption of a strategy involving international expansion was considered in the light of experience already gained from previous overseas investments. The Alltrans Group, prior to merging with TNT had, commenced operations in New Zealand. This venture had placed heavy demands on management time and was just commencing to generate profit after almost five years of development.

TNT's Progress as an International Company

Some 13 years after the initial overseas investment TNT's progress has been significant. In 1975/76 over half of Group revenue came from overseas and over 34% of profit came from these overseas activities. In 1976/77 59% of revenue came from overseas activities and shipping.

REVENUE AND PROFIT BY COUNTRY

COUNTRY	REVENUE AS'000			NET PROFIT AS' 000		
	1975	1976	%	1975	1976	%
AUSTRALIA	142,881	158,490	46.4	7,658	7,877	61.4
NEW ZEALAND	21,903	21,993	6.5	537	890	6.9
U.S.A.	51,127	61,672	18.0	(729)	673	5.3
CANADA	61,154	78,725	23.0	1,147	2,870	22.3
BRAZIL	10,983	12,174	3.6	123	121	0.9
OTHER (INCL. ASSOC. COMPANIES)	4,214	8,604	2.5	271	408	3.2
TOTAL	292,262	341,658	100.0	9,007	12,839	100.0

Historically the first overseas investment was in New Zealand where Alltrans Group (N.Z.) Limited was established in 1964 and a small bulk freighting and forwarding business, Transport and Storage Limited, was acquired. Losses were incurred in the formative years. Management introduced new transport techniques, including container operations using flat top wagons, and the company achieved profitability in 1969.

The successful development in New Zealand was followed by the acquisition of Walkup's Merchants Express Inc. in 1969, a loss-making Californian road trucking business. Major updating of facilities and equipment was undertaken but the business continued to incur substantial losses. Steps were taken to rationalize the Californian operations and, in 1974-75 the rights to carry freight between San Francisco and Los Angeles, together with the assets used in connection with these rights, were sold. The remaining activities are now concentrated on profitable local cartage in Los Angeles and San Francisco and benefits from the rationalization are emerging.

The acquisition of Acme Fast Freight Inc. in 1973 provided TNT with operating rights in all States of the U.S.A. and extending into Canada and Mexico. For some years prior to acquisition, the Acme Group had incurred substantial losses. Losses were expected to continue while extensive reorganisation and rationalization took place. Nevertheless small trading profits were achieved soon after reorganisation commenced. Considerable development work is being undertaken to bring this subsidiary to a level of profitability and control in line with Group standards. The extensive network of licences held by Acme throughout the U.S.A. has substantially extended the base for further development in that country.

In Canada, GILL Interprovincial Lines Limited, a well established trucking business, was acquired in 1970. It has now been consolidated into a national carrier by the acquisition in 1973 of Overland Western Limited and in 1974 of freightlines in Quebec and Ontario. This consolidation added strength to the management of the Canadian operations, which are making substantial contributions to TNT profits.

The acquisition of a 70% interest in Pampa–O.T.T. Group of Brazil in 1973 represented TNT's first investment in South America. Since acquisition, the Brazilian operations have been further developed by the establishment of new terminals in Porto Alegre and Rio de Janeiro and the introduction of a Kwikasair overnight service. TNT's interest in this investment has since been increased to 84.3%.

United Kingdom and European operations commenced in 1973 with an overnight express service between London and Paris. Trading losses exceeded expectations and activities were re-shaped with emphasis on long distance operations and the establishment of an international freight forwarding office in London. TNT's other operations in Singapore, Hong Kong, Korea and Taiwan are all newly established with operations centred around international freight forwarding. In 1976/77 TNT also commenced a Trans Atlantic container shipping service. This is a most exciting and unique start up venture for an Australian corporation.

TNT's progress then as an international company has been very real. Why has an Australian company been very successful in international markets? A lot of the problems that multinational companies receive are not applicable to TNT because of the nature of the business. The managing of TNT operations throughout the world is characterised by a weekly profit reporting system, highly divisionalising operating enterprises within each group or geographic location and a high degree of autonomy making management more practical. The organisational environment is simple and, therefore, able to respond to rapid change. The service that is provided by the company has historically been established within that country and it is only recently that the development of international transport services has extended the product beyond national boundaries.

Constraints on Growth

As an Australian international company TNT faces the same constraints based on growth as other foreign investors. In Australia, New Zealand and Canada further acquisitions are subject to approval by domestic authorities. In other countries a degree of foreign ownership by enterprise is restricted by legislation and in some countries foreign ownership in the industry is totally prohibited. Generally restrictions placed on foreign corporations, where those foreign corporation have genuine contributions to make, are counter-productive for that national economy and this constraint on future growth represents a real fact which must be considered in all future international investments.

There is nothing unique in such restrictions as they are faced by all international corporations. However; because of the structure of our organisation and the general low profile expansion in each country involving a strategy of developing and promoting new services, the presence of TNT in foreign countries has been seen as productive and imaginative and host countries have responded positively to TNT's initiatives.

Apart from Government restrictions placed from time to time on operations in foreign countries there are other restraints placed on growth of an Australian multinational. Expansion overseas depends on the availability of funding and for an Australian corporation this may provide unique problems, for example, borrowing in certain currencies introduces foreign exchange exposure which may be acceptable only to a certain level in the corporation's foreign exchange management programme. This will vary with the size and financial strength of the Australian company. Generally, however, the smaller Australian companies are constrained by the level of exchange exposure they should willingly absorb. Again, restrictions may be placed on the ability of the foreign corporation to gear and on the ability of that corporation to pay dividends. Withholding tax on dividends may be prohibitive beyond certain levels and, indeed, may be controlled completely. Foreign currency borrowing by nationals may be restricted by domestic monetary policy.

All of these factors place substantial pressure on the treasury of a multinational corporation. One of the keys to success for such a corporation is to have the mobility required to deal with such problems. Further constraints on growth of the multinational also includes its ability and willingness to accept political risks.

The Future

An Australian multinational has its own perculiar characteristics and these must be considered in planning and designing activities on an international scale. These would include:

1) **TAXATION**

Australian Tax Law is not designed to cater for development of new services overseas. This means that investment in a start-up operation in a foreign country can be more expensive for an Australian company than, say, for a Canadian corporation who is taxed on a world wide basis. For example, the establishment of an Australian subsidiary or branch to operate a business in the U.S. means that any losses incurred in the formative years will generally not be available for tax relief in Australia. On the other hand, a Canadian corporation may establish a branch in the U.S. and obtain tax relief in Canada under certain circumstances. This clearly reduces the up-front exposure a Canadian corporation has in its international activities and reduces the risk for such a corporation to undertake initial investment. For Australian companies, by contrast, the risk is increased because of the non-availability of tax relief. Naturally, this position is reversed when the new venture reaches profitability.

Australian companies generally with investments overseas have not established international holding companies. This contrasts with European and American corporations who have frequently established international holding companies. The broad network of double tax treaties between the Australian Government and foreign countries has reduced this requirement. These holding companies are, of course, generally formed to reduce the international corporations exposure to potential double tax liabilities.

2) **FINANCING**

Traditionally Australian corporations have financed their expansion through the sale of fixed interest securities, generally secured by means of a charge over the assets of the company or group of companies. This may be done by means of private placement or through the public market with the borrowing corporation seeking to list the securities on local Stock Exchanges. These borrowings are controlled by Trust Deeds which must meet the requirements of the Australian Associated Stock Exchanges.

The Australian Associated Stock Exchanges, in turn, have standards which they require to be included in Trust Deeds for mortgage debentures, debentures and unsecured notes and there is no distinction between standards for the different securities. These requirements include:—
(A) limitations on the amount of borrowing that the borrowing corporation can create from time to time;
(B) the Trust Deed must include a convenant that the borrowing corporation will include in the Trust Deed newly acquired or formed wholly owned subsidiaries as guarantors.

In addition to Stock Exchange requirements the establishment of the Life Offices Association, an Association of the major Life Assurance houses in Australia representing a very significant portion of the Australian capital market, has resulted in the creation of standard borrowing limitation clauses being incorporated into Trust Deeds. These limitations generally restrict borrowings to 60% of total tangible assets. However, certain assets of international companies are not generally available for secured borrowing programmes. This may be because of legal requirements in the country in which the assets are domiciled or indeed, in our case, because of Australia's own legal limitations. For example, in the U.S. and Canada authorities governing the issuing of licences for trucking companies, which includes Interstate Commerce Commissions, may restrict a particular corporation's behaviour including its ability to provide guarantees. These subsidiaries, then, could not join in as guarantors under a Trust Deed. In other countries exchange control consideration which form an integral part of national Government policy may dictate that the national Government place restrictions on commitments made by domestic domiciled corporations in respect of foreign exchange liabilities.

In other cases certain subsidiaries may be restricted by specific legislation which can be of a State, Provincial or Territorial nature. These restrictions may prohibit the pledging of assets or the provision of guarantees to support group activities.

This type of restriction, which is frequently encountered by international corporations, is not generally understood by the Australian capital market simply because of the predominance of corporations which have a domestic base and limited international activities. This has meant that pressure for change in standards established in the capital markets has come from the very few multinationals. It has also resulted in frustrations for those corporations in dealing in the Australian capital market. By contrast, the European or U.S. based international company is not a novelty to local capital markets and, indeed, in certain cases capital markets have evolved in response to the needs of such corporations.

Another aspect which will have to be faced ultimately head-on by Australian based multinational corporations is the security position of Australian Trading Banks. International corporations are frequently financed by the means of unsecured loans supported from time to time with parent company guarantees. However, frequently the Australian Trading Banks have a predominant security position in the assets of the corporation which, of course, relegates other international bankers to a secondary position. It is desirable for Australian based companies to educate the capital market away from security based lending to a more internationally accepted basis of borrowings with lenders ranking pari passu.

3) EXCHANGE CONTROL

Australian based corporations require the approval of the central bank, the Reserve Bank, before transactions can be undertaken in foreign currency. (Under the Banking Act's "Banking (Foreign Exchange) Regulations".) Generally, the Reserve Bank has been most helpful in assisting corporations to develop international activities, however, in the early days traditional restrictions built up over the years by the Bank did place some difficulties in the way of international companies. In particular, the Bank is not prepared to approve in advance the remittance of funds for loan repayments whether in the form of guarantees or actual debt obligations. This was an inhibiting factor until the position became more generally understood by the international capital markets. The central banking system prohibits dealing in foreign currencies and as a result there has not been established in Australia an adequate market for forward exchange commitments. Nevertheless, the Bank does provide a market for corporations to buy forward on trading account and most recently there has developed an unofficial hedging market to provide some assistance on capital account. This latter market is very imperfect and lacks the sophistication required by an international corporation.

191

Another aspect of exchange control which has recently emerged is its use by the Government as a means of pre-screening so called tax haven based transactions. Again, this is an area where both the Tax Department and the Reserve Bank have been constructive and sought to relieve the bureaucratic burden for those international companies which have a genuine motivation for using corporate structures in these tax haven countries. However, it is an additional restriction on the flexibility that Australian companies have in becoming international corporations.

General

In addition to the characteristics mentioned, an Australian multinational corporation faces the same problems as are frequently experienced in multinational corporations domiciled in Europe and the Americas. These include the problems of communication, time differences and distance as well as the increasing problem of managing foreign exchange exposure, the need to have greater flexibility in liquidity management and financing and the need to have a management team that is mobile and well tuned to the unique requirements of each host country.

Australian international companies face a much broader growth horizon than those Australian companies whose activities are purely domestic. Expansion overseas has the positive effect of sharpening management skills at all levels of operation as well as administration and finance. Successful investment overseas is rewarding to shareholders and has a positive benefit on the national economy. TNT is proud of its international activities and the progress they have made. The history of start-up operations in New Zealand now generating attractive profits and dividend streams, operations in Canada showing very positive contributions to our own growth; the expansion of TNT through Bulkships into shipping domestically and internationally, via Union Steam Ship Company, and the development of new ventures in the U.K., coupled with the creation of new concepts in Brazil have been significant achievements for an Australian company. In addition to these investments that have already achieved a level of maturity, TNT's investments in the U.S. in land transport and our entry into North Atlantic shipping services represent areas where future growth will emerge to benefit the shareholders.

Successful international investment is a result of sound pre-planning and good management; it is not something that is the exclusive domain of overseas corporations. TNT is proud to have been an innovator in bringing an international flavour to the Australian capital market, and are anxious to continue to act as a successful Australian innovator.

THE TRANSNATIONAL CORPORATION: A CRITICAL

ANALYSIS OF ITS PROSPECTS

*By Michael T. Skully**

When faced with the problem of prediction, it is often useful to examine the past, and from that determine what factors have caused the present to develop. Such a process is of particular value in predicting the future role that the transnational corporation (TNC) will play in the world's economy.

The transnational corporation, itself, is not at all a new phenomenon, and one can find examples of it operating in a corporate form as early as 1555.[1] If our discussion can use the word "enterprise" rather than corporation, such transnational enterprises were found in operation in world commerce as early as 2500 B.C.[2] These early organizations, however, were quite different from today's transnational firms and it is really only in the post-war period that the TNC's have taken on the position that they occupy today.

The post-war period gave many U.S. firms the incentive for overseas expansion, and Americans soon replaced Europeans as the leaders in foreign investment. The reconstruction of Europe required substantial capital and virtually all types of foreign investment was encouraged. Their investment capital, coupled with technical expertise gained during the war, allowed the U.S. based transnationals to take a strong position in Europe's more growth orientated industries and develop even more rapidly than the rest of the European economy. The regional and international moves to reduce tariffs assisted the post recovery by expanding trade, and encouraged the development of the integrated production structure that characterise many European based transnationals today.

The transnationals' virtually unrestricted, overseas expansion continued throughout the 1950's and indeed it was only in 1960 that the idea of the "multinational" firm came into being.[3] Jean Servan-Schneiber sounded the alarm over the American enterprises' domination of European industry,[4] and from then on transnational corporations have come increasingly under criticism and even investigation by a variety of national and international government organizations.[5] The future of the transnational corporation is of course dependent on an infinite number of variables, but most likely they could be classified into one of three interrelated groups: the future of technological growth, the future relations between national governments, and finally the future relationships that will exist between nation states and the transnational corporations themselves.

Technological Growth

As mentioned previously, much of the transnationals' post-war growth could be traced to the rapid technological improvements that came as a by-product of the war related increase in R and D efforts and not surprisingly, much of these efforts were related to the communication and transportation industry. In communications, the ease in which home-office — affiliate contacts could be made greatly changed the role requirements of local management and the transnationals'

*Lecturer in finance at the University of New South Wales, Sydney, Australia.

This article is a result of papers presented at seminars on the future of the multinational enterprise held at Sydney University, Australia, in conjunction with the Graduate Business School Club in December, 1975, and at the Institute of East and West Studies, Yonsei University, Seoul, South Korea, 1976.

general concept of operations. For until rapid communications existed between the two they were forced to operate on a very much decentralised basis.

When decisions needed to be made the local manager rather than the home office was forced to make them. Now phone and telex communiations put the local manager directly in touch with the home office and, since most places are within a day's flight, home office "re-inforcements", if needed, can soon be on hand. The inability to effectively co-ordinate overseas affiliates meant establishing separate organizations in each country and little hope of running a world wide, integrated production process. Now such co-ordination is feasible and the shortened transportation time between affiliates has allowed many firms to operate on that basis. The improvement in communication and transport, too, has brought the world closer together, and the ease and speed in which foreign trade can now be conducted has assisted in the growth of international commerce and, as a consequence, the transnational corporation. The technological growth of course has not been confined to transport and communication, and throughout the industrial world the production process and product demands have become increasingly complex. At one time capital was just viewed as a labour substitute in the production process, but now product development as well as product manufacture has grown to be an increasingly capital intensive effort. The technical skills are by no means strictly confined to R and D; and marketing, financing, and production techniques have grown to be equally important. The ability of the transnational corporation to combine these skills to their best advantage is probably its most notable achievement. The improvement of our transport and communication system is just beginning and the Concorde's supersonic air transport, satellites, and video phones will undoubtedly work to both bring the world closer together and assist in managing the transnational's world wide affairs.

Products will continue to become increasingly sophisticated and their related marketing, financing, and production requirements more complicated. All of these developments need not mean a bright future for the transnational for it is in the way that governments allow the transnationals to utilise their skills that will determine their future. The transnational is not the only source of technology and governments may even choose to develop their own supply through government run domestic, regional, and international R and D efforts and implement the results through similarly owned corporations.[6] Only the future will tell, but the past experience and lack of success of similarly organized efforts would seem to point that the transnational corporation will remain the principal supplier of commercially applicable technology.

Relations Between National Governments and their Significance on the Future of the Transnational Corporation.

The relations between nation states will be likely to have the most drastic effect on the TNC's future. Obviously such things as a world war or another regional conflict such as Vietnam is going to have a very drastic effect: the Middle East conflict and the resulting oil embargo quickly showed its effects on the international oil companies; Détente in East-West relations, too, has been reflected in substantial TNC's involvement within the Comecon countries, and promoted the growth of East-West trade.

Second in importance only to the potential of military or economic warfare will be the national attitudes that develop on tariff protection and regional integration. In the post war world economy there has been a much greater interdependence between nation states but whether this will continue remains to be seen. The highly technical content of so many industrial goods produced today points increasingly toward the benefit of economies of scale. Many countries are obviously too small to support the production costs and from an economic viewpoint the movement toward lower tariffs and regional integration should continue. The economic factors though while important, are not the most important ones when considering the future of regional integration and free trade movements. Their success is dependent largely on the member countries' willingness to delegate authority and power to the organization to regulate part of the country's otherwise domestic affairs. Most regional and international agencies have suffered due to economic nationalism and the consequential unwillingness of members to relinquish any of their sovereignty. To a large extent such organizations as the EEC, COMECON, CACM, and the Andean Group have succeeded, but most other groups have been very much less successful.[7] The United Nations, itself, provides perhaps the best example of the latter group.

The final area in governmental relations to consider is the future national attitudes towards economic development in both the developed and developing countries. In the past economic growth has been an unquestioned good, but now the idea of growth for growth's sake has come under criticism. Once the basics of life are achieved, people are beginning to question whether the pollution of our land, water, and air are worth a few additional dollars in one's pay check. Ecological and other social welfare considerations are playing an increasingly important part in both our public and private economic decisions. A slowing of economic growth and a move from consumption to a better "life style" will not be without its effects on the transnational. Within the developing countries, too, attitudes are changing toward development, but there the emphasis will still tend to be growth orientated and generally help to increase the size and consumption levels of the world economy — and likewise the market for the transnational company.

The Relations between Nation States and Transnational Corporations

The relationship that develops between the transnational corporation and national governments is by far the most influential factor in the future of the multinational enterprise. While no transnational corporation, national government and their respective relationships would be exactly the same, they can still be classified into three broad interconnected groups: the company's relationship with its home country; its relationship with its host country; and finally its relationship with regional and international government organizations.

Home Country Relations

Up until recent years transnational companies received little trouble from their home countries and often found them very beneficial in mediating or assisting their negotiations with existing or prospective host countries. After all if rational discussion could not solve the problem to the transnational's liking one could always "send in the marines". However now days most home country diplomatic or military assistance is not always so beneficial. In response to foreign meddling the so-called "Calvo doctrine" has been adopted by most South American countries. The doctrine says basically that a foreign company receiving assistance from its home country automatically forfeits by law all of its property and other rights in the host country.[8] The home country's ability under international law to intercede on the behalf of its overseas companies was limited anyway, and the World Bank's International Centre for Settling of Investment Disputes (ICSID) seems a much more impartial conciliator or arbitrator — if the help of some international agency is in fact necessary.[9]

The home country's influence can fall into other areas affecting a transnational's operations. In addition to restrictions on overseas investment another important area is taxation and the potential double taxing that a company may receive from both home and host countries. The argument as to which country has the right to tax may result in both doing so. More important, though, is the home country's ability to directly regulate a company's operations in another country. The U.S., for example, insists that it can use its various regulatory powers, especially in the areas of anti-trust regulation, on the overseas affiliates of U.S. based firms. The German government has recently taken a similar attitude. All of which points to potential conflict between host and home country directives — and troubles for the transnational. Hopefully the moves toward internationalizing taxation and corporate law will assist in solving many of these type problems.

Host Country Regulations

In the 1950's and early 1960's most countries, developed or otherwise, welcomed foreign investment with open arms and offered substantial tax concessions, free lands, extensive tariff protection, and virtually anything else they could give to ensure that a new factory or development project would be established within their borders and not someone else's. The only policy that could be said to exist toward foreign investment, if there was any at all, was to get as much as one could. Those days of a buyer's market for foreign investment have changed and today most countries have developed at least some sort of constructive policy in evaluating the merits of foreign investment. While in some cases it is strictly a dollar and cents cost/benefit analysis, more often the social aspects of the project and its relationship to national development plans are given equal consideration.

Not only have attitudes changed but it is now much more of a supplier's, than a buyer's market. Where small countries before had to offer extensive incentives to offset their smaller market potential, they now have the opportunity of joining regional economic groupings and substantially improve their bargaining position. International supplier organizations, such as OPEC, have also given added bargaining power to countries which previously had been in a rather weak position. Such regional and international organizations can be of further assistance by exchanging information on their respective foreign investment agreements and by providing support staff augmentation to host country's negotiating teams. In addition to these factors there has actually developed some competition within the area of foreign investment. There are a greater potential number of foreign investors especially with the growing importance of the Japanese, European and other non-U.S. based companies. Finally there is always the potential that the host country may decide to raise its own capital, license the technology, hire the management and develop the project either by itself or through the assistance of multigovernment agencies.[10] While Australia has attempted to control foreign investment through exchange control and the Foreign Investment Advisory Committee, other countries have used their sovereign powers to control technology contracts and their resulting royalty agreements. For example, through its government run, Royalties Committee's efforts, Columbia negotiated a reduction in royalty payments by some 40% — a savings of approximately U.S.$8 million in 1970. It has also greatly reduced the significance of tie in purchase clauses, minimum royalty payments, and virtually eliminated the use of restricted export clauses.[11] Just because the host country is willing to consider the proposal no longer automatically means that a foreigner can own it forever and the provision of local majority ownership has now become a frequent requirement. While the speed and percent of local ownership vary from country to country, the Andean Group's "fade out" policy provides one of the more realistic examples. To gain entry to the Andean Common Market, foreign firms must agree to divest at least 51% of their affiliates to local ownership within 15 years from establishment.[12] Realising that the more integrated, worldwide production styled transnationals would object to the condition, foreign ownership is allowed to continue unaffected as long as 80% of production is exported. Mexico goes a step further and allows 100% foreign ownership only if

100% of production is exported. If the restrictions on foreign investment and the local ownership clauses develop to their fullest extent, the transnational corporation of the future will perform a much different role than before. They may become no more than consultants who provide the host country with a package of technology, capital, and management in return for a fee or certain level of export production. Their importance will then switch to the marketing side and the development of improved technology and production skills. Within the Socialist countries transnationals of all sorts and types seem pleased to accept such arrangements.[13] While in other places, such as the Middle East, they have been forced to accept them. Their responses to these incidences should encourage other host countries to at least consider something similar.

International Relations

It is well and good that all host and home countries continued in their efforts to bring the operations of the transnational companies out into the open, and where necessary under government control. These efforts, however, are limited in their effectiveness and not without their costs for one facet of the transnational company is its ability to avoid more stringent regulations by simply moving its operations out of that particular country. While it is doubtful that a firm would suddenly change its home of residence or simply leave thousands of dollars worth of potentially competitive equipment, the substantial difference in the quality and severity of regulations between countries gives the transnational substantial room to manoeuvre. An international harmonization of rules and regulations would help correct the situation, and not surprisingly a number of international organizations such as the Andean Group, EEC, OAS, OECD, ILO, and the UN, have been attempting to accomplish just that. Whilst it would be desirable to discuss all of these the comments here will be directed solely to the more recent efforts of the United Nations.

Ironically through the efforts of the late President Allende's former government in Chile, the United Nations began its involvement in the Transnational Corporation and subsequently appointed a Group of Eminent Persons to consider the matter. With the *Multinational Corporation in World Development* as their base document this group of 20 government, academic and business leaders heard testimony and reviewed evidence from a wide range of sources, and finally prepared a report to the U.N. Secretary General titled, *The Impact of Multinational Corporations on Development and International Relations* containing some 53 separate recommendations concerning the multinational corporation.[14]

As a result of the Group of Eminent Persons' report, the United Nations has since established two organizations within its structure to deal with the question: The U.N. Commission on Transnational Corporations and The Information and Research Centre on Transnational Corporations. The Commission, composed of government experts from 48 member states, is to give in depth consideration to the issues relating to transnational corporations and, as U.N. Council Resolution 1913 (LVII) puts it, "assist the Economic and Social Council in evolving a set of recommendations which, taken together, would represent the basis for a code of conduct dealing with transnational corporations". The Research Centre, in turn, is designed to support these efforts by developing a comprehensive information system to gather, analyze, and disseminate transnational corporation information and to both organize and conduct research on the political, legal, economic, and social aspects of transnational companies.[15] Perhaps the most consistent idea that comes through from the U.N. studies is the desirability of establishing a so-called international "code of conduct". The Group of Eminent Persons seem to realise the problems associated with sets of rules and instead have suggested "consistent set of recommendations which are gradually evolved and which may be revised as experience or circumstances require", and work as "an instrument of moral persuasion, strengthened by the authority of international organizations and the support of public opinion".[16]

Conclusion

The rapid post war growth in technology, the subsequent speed with which the Western economies were able to recover, and transnational corporation's ability to gain from both provides an explanation as to how the transnational corporation developed into the economic power that it is today. Our technological advancements seem likely to continue and, to a lesser extent, so will our economic growth. Even so, the transnational corporation will not be in the same position to capitalize on them. Governments, which once welcomed foreign investment, are taking a much more selective view on the role it will play in their development, and entry into some areas of industry will be totally excluded. Likewise, investment projects will no longer be evaluated strictly on economic terms. Even if projects are justifiable on social grounds, a growing number of countries will no longer allow foreigners to maintain majority ownership or control over local affiliates for more than a certain number of years. If this divesting process continues, the transnational is likely to take on quite a new function. The emphasis will probably remain on its marketing, product development, and other expertise roles, but actual product manufacturing will become less important.

The future also points to progressively more regulation of the transnationals' operation on both the national and international level. Transfer prices, royalty payments, intra-company loans and other potential areas for tax avoidance are certain to come under close investigation and a number of international organizations are working to create a better understanding of the issues involved and the extent to which they can be controlled. An exchange of information between countries and the harmonization of national corporate and tax laws into a more uniform, world wide system would greatly enhance these efforts. The transnational corporation does indeed have an important role to play in the future of the world's economy, but it will be a substantially modified function in comparison to the past.

Footnotes

1. The Russia Company was organized in 1553 and received its charter in 1555 as England's first joint stock company. See T.S. William, *The Early History of the Russia Company*, Manchester; Manchester University Press, 1956 for further details. Paul J. McNulty, "Predecessors of the Multinational Corporation", *Columbia Journal of World Business*, Vol. VII, No. 3, May-June, 1972 provides a good general summary of the early trading companies.
2. Sumerian traders and later the Phoenicians are cited as establishing the first multinational enterprises with their establishment of overseas branch offices to handle the trade. Mira Wilkens, *The Emergence of Multinational Enterprise: American Business Abroad from The Colonial Period to 1914*, Cambridge: Harvard University Press, 1970, p. 3.
3. David E. Lilienthal in his "Management of the Multinational Corporation", M. Anshaw and G.L. Bach (editors), *Management and Corporations, 1985*, New York: McGraw-Hill, 1960, p. 119, has often been cited with coining the phrase in April, 1950. In August of 1974 the term "transnational" corporation officially superseded the use of "multinational" in the United Nations discussions and consequently is so used in this article.
4. See J.J. Servan-Schneiber, *The American Challenge*, New York: Atheneum Publishers, 1968.
5. The Canadian government would probably rate the most respected of various national government investigations, but virtually all of the OECD countries have conducted some research in the area. At the regional and international level the OECD, EEC, Andean Group, ILO, and the UN have produced some of

the more interesting studies.

6. Mexico's Finance Minister, J.L. Portillo, has suggested the establishment of regional multi-government owned companies be established in Latin America and the Caribbean area to compete with and gradually replace the foreign MNC. *Australian Financial Review,* 3 November, 1975, p. 9.

7. The European Economic Community, the Council for Mutual Economic Assistance, The Central American Common Market, the Andean Common Market. More information on a wide range of usually neglected socialist regional and international economic organizations can be found in V. Morozov, *International Economic Organizations of The Socialist States,* Moscow: Novosti Press Agency Publishing House, 1973.

8. The Calvo doctrine dates back to the late 1800's and was named after the Argentine jurist who devised it. For further details see Donald R. Shea, *The Calvo Clause,* Minneapolis: University of Minnesota Press, 1955.

9. As of 12 October, 1975 71 States had signed "Convention on the Settlement of Investment Disputes between States and Nationals of Other States". Australia signed the 1965 agreement only recently on 24 March, 1975 and as of early 1978 had yet to ratify it.

10. The U.N. has attempted to establish a fund to assist in natural resource exploration and development. Likewise the World Bank, its associated agencies, multi-government efforts, and the various development banks all provide some alternative to multinational provided foreign capital.

11. Constantine V. Vaitsos, *Intercountry Income Distribution and Transnational Enterprise,* Oxford: Clarendon Press, 1974, provides a detailed explanation of the Committee's work.

12. Andean Common Market includes Bolivia, Columbia, Equador, Peru and Venezuela.

13. Leon Zurawicki, "The Cooperation of the Socialist State with the MNC", *Columbia World Journal of Business,* Vol. X, No. 1, Spring, 1975, pp. 109-115 examines the advantages and risks from socialist countries viewpoint.

14. Evidence of the more recent U.N. efforts on Multinational companies can be found in the following: the *Multinational Corporation in World Development,* New York: United Nations, 1973; *The Impact of Multinational Corporations on Development and on International Relations,* New York: United Nations, 1974, its associated technical papers on taxation, technology and investment codes, and the transcripts of the evidence presented to the Group and Eminent Persons; Commission on Transnational Corporations: report to the first session (17-28 March, 1975), Economic and Social Council Official Records: Fifty Ninth Session, Supplement No. 12, New York: United Nations, 1975.

15. Sydney University has recently established a recent project within the Faculty of Economics to gather information on the multinational enterprise and its impact on Australia. Its forthcoming annotated bibliography and other data papers should prove of particular value.

16. There is actually a wide variety of opinion as to how the U.N. proposals should be implemented ranging from a GATT type treaty to actually issuing charters to transnational companies.

EUROPE

European Multinationals and Their Future

By R. Abdelsayed*

INTRODUCTION

During the 1960's it was sometimes said that virtually all multinational enterprises were American in origin. However, the historical record shows that multinationality of manufacturing operations is no American monopoly. During the century and a half that has elapsed since Cockerill of Belgium put up its first foreign plant in Prussia in 1815, the majority of today's large Western European companies have come first to sell and then to produce outside their home countries. In 1970, 96% of the continental European companies on the Fortune "200" list were manufacturing outside their home countries. Even "domestic" coal and steel producers such as Charbonnages de France, owned at least 25% of one or more foreign manufacturing ventures in that year. Moreover, 84% of the firms for which information is available derived 25% or more of their total sales from exports and foreign production in 1970. Already in 1960, 42% of the large continental firms owned manufacturing operations in seven or more countries.

The major expansion in the number of European companies with significant multinational operations, to be sure, occurred in the post World War II era. Despite early efforts such as Renault's establishment of two assembly plants in Russia in 1914, Europe's automobile companies were to have significant international manufacturing activities only after 1946. Anglo-Dutch Shell excepted, continental European petroleum companies with important international operations emerged only during the 1950's. In sectors such as electrical and non-electrical machinery, the few firms with lengthy international experience, such as Siemens, A.E.G. and Bosch of Germany were joined by a host of newcomers, including Thomson-Brandt of France and Olivetti of Italy. Nevertheless, neither the state nor the process of multinationality are unusual for European enterprise.

TECHNOLOGICAL INNOVATIONS AND EXPORTS

The kinds of oligopolistic innovations developed by Europe's nascent multinationals tended to be quite unlike those first commercialized in the U.S. market.

As in the case of U.S. exports that later led to multinational production, it was innovation, or first commercial introduction, that mattered, not first invention. European invention, that is to say, discovery, often led neither to home nor export sales. On the contrary, European inventions were often transferred to the U.S. and first applied there. The examples of penicillin, the computer, and the integrated circuit are cases in point. Even within the European context, the same phenomenon could be observed, for example in the invention of margarine in France followed by first commercial introduction in Holland.

The history of synthetic dyestuffs is another case in point. The invention of synthetic dyestuffs in France and England was followed not by French and English exports, but rather by large-scale commercialization and process and product development in Germany and Switzerland. Massive exports, and then industrial implantation back into the countries of invention later emanated from the innovating German and Swiss enterprises.

After World War II much the same sort of sequence seemed again in motion. The distinctive

*An executive with an European based Multinational Company

post 1945 European innovations in autos, pharmaceuticals, plastics, and metalworking processes, led first to exports and only then to production abroad. There were, however, exceptions to the rule, and perhaps the most notable were the petroleum companies started and owned by governments in France and Italy. Western Europe, as it again abruptly came to realise in the 1970's, has never had the indigenous resources of petroleum that allowed U.S. firms to develop innovative advantages in refining − let alone exploration − comparatively quickly. Of the continental countries, only Holland had oil producing colonies during the first half of the 20th century.

After the Russian Revolution eliminated foreign-owned firms from the Caucassus, Western-European governments felt dependent on either Anglo-Saxon companies or the Soviet government for their oil supply. Some were content with neither choice. One result was what the historian of the Compagnie Francaise des Petroles refers to, in jest, as the "immaculate conception" of that firm out of the debris of World War I. The company was formed at the initiative of the French government to administer that part of the Turkish Petroleum Company awarded to France at the San Remo Diplomatic Conference, as part of the spoils of World War I.

After oil was discovered, CFP's British and American partners in IPC built a refinery in Iraq to process the crude. Thus, politics (and a cash contribution) first put the non multinationally active CFP into the business of both foreign manufacturing (i.e. oil refining) and exporting refined petroleum products. With the experience thus gained, and later with a protected home market as well, such a government-instrument firm could subsequently apply lessons learned in its hot-house environment to foreign countries in the manner of a more "spontaneously generated" multinational. Indeed, even if it never processes, such a firm could and often did, offer a differentiated, non Anglo-Saxon "political" product.

THE ROLE OF HOME MARKET CONDITIONING

Early home market conditioning seems to have played a considerable role. It is clear that the economic characteristics of home markets in continental Europe were different from those facing innovators in the U.S.

Distinctive home markets appear to have left their mark on Europe's nascent multinationals primarily in terms of the kinds of product and process innovations they developed. The frequency distribution of European innovations eventually put into foreign production appears to have long been biased toward material sewing processes, ersatz material substitutes, and goods oriented toward low income consumers.

By way of contrast, the U.S. innovations were typically skewed towards goods and processes that had an appeal to the unique high-income, labor short American market.

CONDITIONING BY DIFFERENT INCOME LEVELS

Part of the explanation for differences between European and American patterns of innovation is in the differences in absolute levels of income per capita. The U.S. was highest compared with European countries.

International differences in income levels are important for innovative activity because consumers appear to behave as if they have a hierarchy of needs varying with their income levels. Evidence suggests that the order in which consumers acquire household appliances is primarily a function of income, rather than of broad cultural factors. Setting aside obvious differences due to resource endowments, it also appears that there is an order of acquisition of industrial goods that is followed fairly predictably as a result of economic growth.

The U.S. market long acted as midwife to the development by U.S. companies of the time saving, convenience products that substituted for high income, high cost labor.

A certain amount of product innovation designed to tap rising consumer incomes appears to have occurred in the European continent in spite of the tendency of the U.S. to lead. For instance, the Compagnie de Saint Gobain, a European firm obtained an innovative lead in mirrors and glass in the early 1700s, well before the U.S. existed as a nation.

A number of observers have commented on the seeming tendency of American companies to innovate new products whereas European firms tended to introduce new manufacturing processes (material saving processes and substitutes) and products designed for consumers with lower incomes than those prevailing in the U.S.

INCOME DISTRIBUTION AND COMPARATIVE INNOVATIONS

The pattern of distribution of personal income in most European countries has been notably unlike that prevailing in the U.S.

It has been referred to the U.S. as a middle class society. European countries, particularly the large continental countries, have often been described as societies composed of aristocratic and semi aristocratic elites on the one hand and peasants and workers on the other — without terribly many people in between.

These contrasts in income distribution made the home environment in which European multinationals were born clearly different from that which nurtured U.S. multinational enterprise.

As the history of the auto industry was to show, European companies tended to introduce either luxury products, or near necessities for the masses. U.S. firms were pulled toward satisfying middle and upper middle income needs.

For French auto manufacturers before World War I, the market demand was much the same. One examination of the market for automobiles between 1899 and 1928 in the French Department of Indre-et-Loire led to the conclusion that "the demand for private automobiles comes principally from the group comprising people of independent means, noblemen and large landowners".

A government report in 1917 went even further. It argued that past successes meant that the orientation of the French industry to luxury demands ought to be elevated to the level of doctrine: ' It is the luxury article that has given birth to our worldwide reputation ... we must defend this patrimony ... it is this that has led to the development of our automobile industry ... purity and harmony of form, even more than luxury manufacture, must be one of the primordial elements of the maintenance of our supremacy".

Much later, in 1970, continental European auto production was once again to equal that of the Americans. In addition, Europe's auto exports in the 1950s, 1960s and 1970s were to be vastly greater than those of America.

In 1946, following nationalization, Renault introduced its low price R-4. Then came Citröen's 2-CV. It was not until the late 1960s that the introduction of Citröen's GX and Volkswagen's Audi gave hints that perhaps broad middle class markets were beginning to become significant on the continent.

RELATIVE FACTOR COSTS AND INNOVATION

The distinctive histories of European and American commercial innovation have been most conditioned by persistent international differences in the relationship between labor costs and the costs of other production inputs. European enterpreneurs have faced the cost consequences of a relative scarcity of land and raw materials. U.S. entrepreneurs have been, and remain, faced with an environment in which labor commands a relative premium because of its scarcity.

The result was a concern for substitution, and saving, of raw materials that recurred again and again in European history.

Innovation of synthetic nitrogenous fertilizers, dyestuffs, rubber and artificial silk, or rayon, constituted one sort of response to the stimuli provided in such markets. Products and processes that saved fuel were another. European firms, for example, pioneered in high efficiency auto engines, electric furnaces, and fuel injection apparatus, as well, as in industrial processes such as that of Solvay for soda-ash, and of Pechiney for producing aluminium with high cost electricity.

In France, relative factor cost conditions before World War II appear to have lain somewhere between those in Germany and those in the U.S. France had long had relatively resource rich colonies. Germany had not. Yet French history is replete with complaints concerning the scarcity on the price of coal petroleum and copper. Descriptions of the early twentieth century days of French firms like Renault, show that industrial entrepeneurs felt that the profits obtainable from introducing labor saving innovations were likely to be considerably less than those that could be secured from cheaper material inputs. Government policies in France perhaps underlay the relatively high cost of imported raw materials even more so than they did in Germany.

At a time when the French population and labor supply was notoriously stable, the Meline tariff of 1892 included tariffs for all, including, absurdly, tariffs on raw materials. In the post-World War I era, and then again after World War II, repeated devaluation of the franc compounded yet further the effect of tariffs. With the loss of the colonies in the fifties and sixties, France's materials/labor cost ratio came to be over four times that of the U.S. in 1963.

The innovative response in France to this relative factor cost situation differed from that in Germany. Market differences might explain the divergence of responses. For example, France had long been virtually self sufficient in agriculture and had access to substantial phosphate deposits in its North African colonies. Thus, a race to synthetic nitrogen for fertilizers was unlikely to be as interesting for French firms as for BASF. Nevertheless, historians have agreed that protective and autarkic policies, rather than stimulating French industry, provoked France to turn inward, to allow its markets to be dominated by "Malthusianism", under which coalitions of interests maintained production at relatively low levels and high prices. In making their case they frequently cite the fact that French inventive successes were often merely preludes to Swiss and German innovations in industry such as chemicals. French legal, patent and educational structures are all said to have blocked innovation, regardless of market or factor-price conditions.

"Malthusianism" notwithstanding, innovative responses were often forthcoming. A French enterprise developed rayon in 1892 when a silkworm disease and protective tariffs had raised French prices of natural silk. France, along with the U.S. in the same year, was one of the twin birth places of aluminium in 1886. Because of strategic fears, tariffs, a booming electrical industry, and an auto industry that led the world, there was a major market demand awaiting aluminium, which was a substitute for copper and other imported non ferrous metals.

Before World War I France was second only to Switzerland in European production of aluminium, and much Swiss production went to supply French needs. Germany had copper; France had very little. Production of aluminium in France and Switzerland exceeded that in the U.S. and Canada from the turn of the century to 1913. More recently, French enterprises have innovated in long-lasting radial tyres, high efficiency, fuel saving automobile engines, electricity-saving processes for aluminium smelting, and in the substitution of clays and shale for bauxite in the production of alumina.

Of the 85 continental companies in 1970 with manufactured goods sales exceeded 400 million US Dollars, 21 were French.

On January 1, 1971, national steel and coal producers like Charbonnages de France and Vallourec of France had at least one foreign manufacturing subsidiary.

TABLE 1: Large French Manufacturing enterprises:–
Company names, main industries and Sales, 1970

Name of Firm	Main industry of firms	Interlocking Ownerships	Total Sales, 1970 ($ Billion)
Aérospatiale	Transportation equipment	French Government (92.6%)	0.6
L'Air liquide	Chemicals		0.4
Boussois Souchon Neuvesel (BSN)	Glass		0.6
Charbonnages de France	Coal	French Government (100%)	0.9
Citröen	Transportation equipment	Fiat (27%) Michelin (55%)	1.4
Compagnie Francaises des pétroles	Petroleum	French Government (35%)	1.9
Compagnie Générale d'électricité	Electrical equipment		1.5
Librairie Hachette	Printing		0.5
Michelin	Rubber		1.2
Compagnie Péchiney, S.A.	Metals		1.6
Peugeot, S.A.	Transportation equipment		1.4
Renault	Transportation equipment	French Government (100%)	2.5
Rhône-Poulenc, S.A.	Chemicals		1.9
Saint Gobain-Pont-à Mousson	Glass		1.6
Schneider, S.A.	Metals		0.6
Thompson-Brandt	Electrical equipment		1.0
Ugine Kuhlmann	Chemicals		1.5
Usinor	Metals		0.9
Vallouréc	Metals	Michelin	0.5
De Wendel Sidelor, S.A.	Metals		1.1
Elf-Erap	Petroleum	French Government (100%)	1.5

Source: *The European Multinationals* – by L. Franko (1976)

The major expansion in the numbers of European companies with significant multinational operations has, to be sure, occurred since World War II. The large French enterprises established or acquired foreign manufacturing outposts. In the sectors of the earliest Continental spread, chemicals and electrical machinery, the pioneers were joined by firms like France's Rhône-Poulenc, Air liquide and Compagnie Générale d'Électricité.

Some recent developments for few of the above-mentioned firms are cited below:–

Librairie Hachette:

Librairie Hachette has become interested in the development of audio-visual techniques, with the object of becoming, as a start, a distributor of audio-visual programmes and later a producer of such programmes. The first applications will be in the field of education.

Compagnie Générale D'Électricité:

During 1973, the range of the group's activities in Canada was extended to the manufacture of electrochemical generators as a result of the acquisition by Compagnie Européenne d'Accumulateurs of a lead battery factory in the province of Quebec. In the U.S.A., SAF gained control of its licence, Crelton Battery Corporation, which manufactures nickel-cadmiums batteries. With the acquisition of 90% of the capital of N.S.A., the sixth largest battery manufacturer in Great Britain, with sales around Fr 12 Million a year, Compagnie Européenne gained a foothold in the British market which is equivalent in size to the French market. In collaboration with the subsidiary G.S.I., a new subsidiary G.S.I. Europe was formed in Brussels, which took over Elaborazione Automatica Dati (EAD), now G.S.I. Italy, and acquired Singer's data processing activity in Switzerland, S.I.S.C. now part of G.S.I. Switzerland.

Thompson-Brandt:

In 1971 in arrangement with Compagnie Générale d'Électricité the Group assumed control of Compagnie Continentale Edison and raised its holding in Compagnie des Lampes from 52% to 76%. During 1972 new subsidiaries were set up in Great Britain, Brazil and Mexico, and in April, 1973, Thompson-Brandt and Lucas Aerospace announced the setting up of a new French Company, Thompson-Lucas, to co-ordinate the activities of three French concerns in the aerospace equipment field.

Citröen:

In Yugoslavia, the assembly and distribution of Citröen cars had been undertaken by Tomos. As the import into Yugoslavia of parts for local assembly has to be matched by exports, Citröen has taken a 49% participation in a new company, Cimus, which, in addition to taking over the activities of Tomos, manufactures components for export to Citröen's French factories.

The Company's South African interests were regrouped under the wholly owned Citröen South Africa and in 1973 the estimated figures for the assembly of the 'D' and "GS1220" models were exceeded by 30%. After the financial association between the company and Fiat being terminated in early 1973, with Fiat transferring its 49% holding in Pardevi to Michelin, the two companies collaborated at the beginning of 1974 in the production and marketing of a commercial vehicle.

The vehicle is assembled at the Turin factory with Citröen supplying most of the parts. In continued collaboration with Audi N.S.U. through joint companies, Comobil for development and Comotor for production, a Wankel type rotary engine has been developed and has been put into production in Comotor's factory at Altforweiler. The engine is fitted to the GS rotary model which has been on sale for a number of months. Technical assistance has been supplied by Berliet both to Sonacom, Algeria, in the production of lorries and buses and to Pol-Mot, Poland, in the production of buses.

Citröen is to launch a car in the autumn specifically designed for Third World markets and intended to be produced locally with about 50% local content, but using essential parts such as chassis, motor and gearbox imported from European mass production lines.

The intention is to compete directly with Japanese models in these markets, and, by assembling locally, match Japanese products in price, while Europeans are likely to make best use of their expertise by working with a local labor force.

Citröen is likely to build on the experience of assembly of its Dalat model built in North Vietnam on the basis of the Dayane 6 and is negotiating for a second assembly plant in Vietnam at Hanoi.

Péchiney Ugine Kuhlmann:

An agreement was concluded with Rhone Progil for the pooling and expansion of manufacture of fertilizers within a new company Société Generale des Engrais G.E.S.A.; participation is on a 50% basis.

In 1973 the nuclear division in an agreement with Westinghouse, Creusot-Loire and Framatone formed a new company, Eurofuel, to produce complete fuel systems for light water reactors. The Group acquired Lorilleux Le Franc, prominent in Europe in the manufacture of printing inks.

In 1974 the company signed an agreement with the U.S.S.R. for the construction of an anode plant in Russia. The agreement also calls for technical assistance in the project to be supplied by the company.

Compagnie Francaise des Petroles:

In 1974 production of crude oil in the North Sea Ekofisk field was estimated at 193,000 b/D. In Indonesia, full development of the field of Bekapai is scheduled for 1975. A well drilled in the Panjilatan structure allowed assessement of the natural gas deposit.

In North America, Total Petroleum extended its exploration activities in the U.S.A., until now confined to the States of Michigan and Illinois, with the acquisition of an interest in a prospecting area in the Gulf of Mexico.

In nuclear energy, prospecting for uranium was pursued in various sites in France, Africa, Australia and the U.S.A.

In September, 1973 application was made for a quotation of 13,888,769 'B' shares on the London Stock Exchange.

Usinor:

In the new Dunkirk plant, the fourth blast furnace with a 14 metre crucible, one of the largest in the world, was commissioned in May, 1973, while the No. 2 steelworks, equipped for continuous casting, commenced operation at the end of 1972.

At the Mardyck factory, the new electrolytic tinning plant for tinplate production was started up early in 1973. During 1973, the company acquired a 50% participation in Solmer at Fos-sur-Mer where the first stage of the steelworks under construction has been completed, having an annual capacity of 3.5 million metric tons of steel.

The indicators of concentration presented for German and French industries in Table 2 seem representative enough, and this data suggests a similarity in the pictures of Continental European and American multinational enterprises. The Continental firms with manufacturing in many foreign countries are all found in oligopolistic industries. However, there is clearly no correlation between the degree of concentration in the main industries of Continental firms and their foreign spread.

Technology:

The special skills, proprietary know how and patent advantages of high technology appear to be at least as closely related to the spread of Continental multinational enterprise as to that of American business abroad.

There were several points of similarity between the American and the Continental multinationals: large size, industry distribution, and R. & D. orientation. Nevertheless, there was

TABLE 2   Measures of Oligopolistic Concentration in Germany and France, various industries

Industry	Germany Market share, ten largest enterprises, 1960	France Percentage share of working population employed in eight largest enterprises, 1963
Food and drink	12.0%	18.0%[1]
Tobacco	84.5	N/A
Textiles	7.2	6.6
Wood, paper, printing	41.5	14.6
Chemicals	40.6	42.0[2]
Drugs	N/A	20.8
Oil	91.5	90.5
Rubber	59.7	50.6
Leather and footwear	37.3	10.6
Stone, clay, glass	51.7	46.8[3]
Iron, and Steel	57.8	63.1
Non-ferrous Metals	44.7	66.4
Fabricated metals	9.3	8.3
Non-electrical machinery	13.4	7.8
Electrical machinery	38.4	35.5[4]
Transport	67.0	52.9[5]

NOTES: 1. Dairy products
             2. Organic chemicals
             3. Glass only
             4. Household appliances
             5. Automobiles only.

Source: *The European Multinationals* — by L. Franko (1976)

no comparison between American and Continental firms when it came to exporting from their home countries. While the average of the 187 U.S. multinationals exported 6.9% of its sales, the average Continental firm exported 26% of its sales volume in 1970.

Diversification:

The largest Continental enterprises were more prone to diversify their product lines than were the American firms.

The tendency of these Continental enterprises was more diversification in their foreign production than they were at home.

THE MULTINATIONAL MANAGEMENT

Communication Patterns:

The cultural effects on communication are not measured by themselves, and there is a relationship to the type of organisation and to the type of managerial structure. The difference in the communication behaviour of people between the United States and British organisations on the one hand, and the French organisations on the other, is unmistakable.

So it is useful to discuss the difference in the oral communication between the French organisations and the Anglo-Saxon ones.

A low rate of oral interaction is indicative of the high rate of written communication.

Indeed, the higher the bureau-cratisation of the structure the more the written communication. However, bureaucracies in different cultures such as those of the United States and of France behave differently and have different rates of oral and written communication. The reasons why such cultural differences evolved have probably to do with the fact that French organisational culture has been influenced by and derived from organisations such as the Catholic Church, the army and the government. In the United States, on the other hand, organisation culture has been more affected by the development of business organisations which have influenced the Church, the army and the governmental organisations, rather than the other way round.

Therefore, while the degree of formalisation is an indication of managerial structure, it is also an indication of the cultural effects on management. This is to say that if two identical organisations had been compared as to their scope of decision making and as to their managerial structure, but operating the one in France and the other in the United States, a significantly higher oral communication would have been found in the latter.

These differences in oral versus written cultures appear in other areas related to the manager's work, whether within or without the organisation.

Education and teaching is an example. The learning processes in the United States are much more participative than those in continental European countries. Professors in France or other continental European countries hardly ever see students out of the classroom, and within the classroom hardly ever hear what the students have to say.

National differences in communication patterns would seem to be the basic and probably the most important cultural characteristic to be overcome in the education of multinational managers.

OTHER NATIONAL DIFFERENCES BEARING ON MULTINATIONAL MANAGEMENT

Education:

The suggestion has been made that the availability of higher education in a country determines its economic growth. This theory is hard to verify because of the differences in educational methods between different countries. Some of these differences affect management style more clearly than the general amount of education available. For instance the difference between the French approach and that of the United States can best be described by saying that one is dogmatic and the other is pragmatic. The French approach is Cartesian, and stands for the most systematic and quantitative assault possible on every problem, while taking into consideration all factors which may influence it.

The Americans, on the other hand, are more interested in the usefulness of the result than in the theoretical side of the method used to approach the problem.

Social stratification:

The differences in learning methods in different countries seem to be related to the degree of social stratification existing in the countries. One way to measure social stratification in a country is by considering social mobility in that country.

While in Britain and in the United States the companies are looking for the best graduates to hire. In France those who are recruiting from the grandes ecoles are the previous graduates hired by the same organisations and they usually go all out to hire from the same school as the one from which they themselves graduated. Thus if you meet in a certain organisation with a top executive from, say, the Haute Ecole de Commerce, there is a good chance that most of the graduates in the organisation are from that school.

209

Another difference between university alumni in the United States and British as against French organisations is an extension of this relationship between university and job. In the Anglo-Saxon countries a degree from a "good" university helps to get a first "good" job, but from then on performance is more important for progress; in France, on the other hand, previous performance has a much smaller significance throughout a person's career. Once a person has graduated from a grande ecole he has in the great majority of cases made it for life. He could be a complete failure, but usually the alumni of his own school would make sure that his career progresses as if nothing has happened. Thus in France one's objective chances to succeed throughout life are much more related to one's education than in Britain.

In Britain the custom of many companies of placing in positions like the board of directors only members of the higher social classes has been gradually disappearing, while it is still common in France. There are still in existence French companies who would not hire a top executive into formal positions of "directeur", somewhat parallel to a vice-president who is a member of the board of directors, unless he belonged to one of the so called 200 best families of France.

Organisation structures:

Organisation structures are related to the sociocultural environment and the emerging educational patterns in the different countries. There is a direct connection between the ability of the organisations to grow, to innovate and absorb new technologies and their propensity to change and adapt their managerial structures to the growing need to absorb broader decision-making processes.

In France, there are few of what might be called "decentralised leaders" in the country and therefore few decentralised structures. As a result organisations cannot absorb broader decision-making processes than their functional structures permit. This fact hinders developments in more advanced technologies, more diversified product lines and more international activities.

The search for raw materials:

If the old conflict between continental needs and Anglo-American sea-power had been the only irritant in North Atlantic relations, perhaps the new reliance of the continent on non-European materials would have only been seen as trade. But some saw it as dependence, however for in a number of extractive industries the fact remained that the post-war market was dominated by the same firms headquartered in the U.S. and Great Britain that had been dominant before 1945. This divergence of views was reflected in different responses by Continental European governments to the presence of these Anglo-Saxon oligopolies.

The French government however, viewed the problem of materials supply by foreign oligopolies with very different eyes. And, by the early 1970's the German and Swedish governments were showing signs of sharing this concern. The problem was felt to be most acute in oil, for in the immediate post war period, the tightest Anglo-American oligopoly was in that industry. It was here that French state owned companies were encouraged to seek resources abroad. While the American majors, and B.P. and Shell had multiplied extractive subsidiaries in the post war period in order to defend established market shares, state owned Compagnie Francaise des Petroles, and E.R.A.P. became deliberately international in order to get direct access to crude.

The moves of the French state oil companies to find resources outside Europe after World War II were in the first instance moves to colonies — especially to Algeria, a territory administered as part of the mother country until independence in 1962. C.F.P., in which the state owned a minority position as well as E.R.A.P., the 100% state company founded in 1945, were both urged to seek French oil.

Political reasons underlay much of this effort. French policy makers felt that: "The fact of buying from others, or the need to buy from others, regardless of the terms at which one buys is itself a dependence."

French military needs for freedom from any possible Anglo-Saxon pressures may have oriented her search for oil to the colonies. But the perennial French balance of payments problems may have played an even greater role in launching oil exploration and extraction after the war.

Until 1958, there was a dollar shortage in Europe. Paying fewer dollars for the economic rents accruing to the Anglo-Saxon majors was one way of reducing the problems. Thus, French governments of many a political complexion found it convenient to seek to pay for petroleum in French francs. This aim in turn meant sourcing first in colonies, and then in franc-zone lands. C.F.P. had learned from its post 1924 share in the Iraq Petroleum concession that the majors were in no hurry to develop fields that could help competition.

Thus, although the majors might predictably follow French initiatives in the Sahara and colonial Black Africa, they could hardly be expected to lead cheerfully in efforts to help the French balance of payments.

C.F.P. proceeded to put much, and E.R.A.P. virtually all, of their exploration efforts into the colonies. After independence these activities became foreign, yet continued membership in the franc-zone was the rule rather than the exception for the newly independent African nations.

Guinea withdrew in 1968, but Guinea had no oil. Until Algeria also left the franc-zone in 1968 and took the main source of petrol-franc oil into the dollar-dominated world, the foreign extraction activities of French state oil firms met the goal of paying for much of France's oil francs.

The behavioral metamorphosis of the Italian and French state-owned, international firms was reflected in their relations with governments of the countries in which extraction took place. In the 1950's and early 1960's these state companies were newcomers to the oil business; they were willing to make deals with host countries that were much more generous than those offered by the majors. E.N.I., E.R.A.P. and C.F.P. were all leaders at one time or another in revolutionary arrangements that traded refineries, technical assistance, host country participation, or service contracts. However, these are now done mostly by American independents who were now the newest newcomers to the industry.

This third wave of newcomers eventually began to challenge the established positions of the state owned companies of Continental Europe. It was now the turn of the one-time challengers to defend the sanctity of contracts and to attempt to share up the oligopoly. At the time of Algerian independence, technical assistance and favorable tax deals were seen by the Algerian government as being an adequate quid-pro-quo for continued 100% ownership of concessions by the French companies. But in 1968, Getty Oil, an American firm, entered an arrangement which gave the Algerian state 51% ownership participation, a commitment to invest over $16 Million in exploration, and a much more favorable share of the financial returns. The handwriting was on the wall, and in 1971 51% of the concessions of the French state firms were nationalised. The companies reactions to these nationalisations were quite like the majors' reactions to similar host-country moves If anything, the dispute was made more contentious by the direct involvement of the French government. After two years it was resolved, largely on Algerian terms, but only after the French government and the French companies had threatened to veto World Bank loans to Algeria and to repatriate Algerians working in France.

Despite flare-ups such as these, producing countries long remained more willing to give the benefit of the doubt to the Continental European state instruments than they were to the majors.

The change in behavior of the European state companies was understandable, for their very success in breaching the walls of the old oligopoly had accelerated a movement that by 1971 threatened to bring down the whole vertically integrated international structure of the industry.

Adelman, Penrose, Vernon, and others have described how the increasing diffusion of technology and the increasing number of firms in the industry led both to price declines for crude, and to the beginnings of vertical disintegration in the industry. But perhaps it was precisely because the old oligopoly was losing control over oil supplies and prices, that the very concept of internationally integrated state-owned enterprise was far from having universal support in Europe.

FRANCE AND ITS COLONIES

France was, of course, the Continental European country most thoroughly conditioned by a heritage of colonial expansion, and trade relationships started in colonial times were often followed by the establishment of foreign manufacturing. Still, almost none of the large French firms set up manufacturing in the French Empire prior to the mid 1950's: trade, not investment, was the norm in colonial relationships. In 1955, one year before her independence, Tunisia received 75% of her imports from France; in 1956, 49% of Morocco's imports came from the mother country; and in 1959, 78% of Algeria's foreign purchases also came from France.

The first major move by French enterprises into manufacturing in the colonies came as part of the effort to ward off the threat of Algerian independence between 1959 and 1961. Although no tariffs were placed on imports into Algeria, the French government offered massive subsidies to firms willing to undertake local production. Subsidies were also available to non-French firms willing to manufacture in Algeria but few had had prior business relationships with French Africa.

Therefore, of the 13 subsidiaries set up in French Africa between 1959 and 1961 by large continental enterprises, 12 were established by French parents.

During the three years following Algerian independence in 1962, French establishment of manufacturing subsidiaries in French Africa dropped to nearly nothing. Afterwards, the rate of establishment rose markedly, but many of the new subsidiaries were not set up by French companies.

In 1971 French parent enterprises owned, about half of the 127 manufacturing ventures located in French Africa by all the large Continental, British, American, and Japanese enterprises in the comparative Multinational Enterprise Project.

The increase in manufacturing activity by non-French enterprises in French Africa during the 1960's took place at a time when newly independent governments were deliberately attempting to diversify their trade and investment relationships away from France. A new French enterprise may have become disenchanted with the former French colonies after five of their manufacturing subsidiaries were expropriated in Algeria between 1962-1968.

But French enterprises were also moved to trade, and their manufacture in less developed areas with which they had no colonial ties. Only 15% of their manufacturing subsidiaries in 1971 were in former colonies.

Foreign Investment in Europe:

TABLE 3 Foreign Manufacturing subsidiaries in the E.E.C. owned by the 85 largest Continental and by 187 American Multinational enterprises January 1, 1971-US data as of January 1, 1978

Host Country	Parent Company from:					Total EEC Parents	Switzer-land	Sweden	Total Contin. Parents	Total American Parents
	Germany	France	Italy	Bel. & Lux.	Nether-lands					
Germany	–	42	3	25	42	112	57	15	184	216
France	128	–	11	49	33	221	44	16	281	206
Italy	36	34	–	15	13	98	24	6	128	175
Bel. & Lux.	24	36	10	16		88	10	6	104	81
Netherlands	24	14	4	18	–	60	15	9	84	80
TOTAL IN EEC	212	126	20	117	104	579	150	52	781	758

*Includes data for Royal Dutch-Shell, but not for Unilever
Source: *The European Multinationals* – by L. Franko (1976)

Restrictions on trade imposed by French public policies have perhaps had the greatest effect on foreign location decisions in the E.E.C. For instance, nine of the ten Continental parent firms that have any foreign pharmaceutical production in the E.E.C. have plants in France. A few have several subsidiaries in that country. Indeed, in 1971, almost half of the pharmaceutical manufacturing subsidiaries of Continental parents found in the E.E.C. were French. One obvious stimulus to foreign production in France arises from the fact that the forms of dosage traditionally used in French medical practice — notably the use of suppository rather than capsule forms — often require special packaging. The influence of such traditions on location decisions, however, appears to have been minor compared to that of the French systems of requiring visas for all new varieties and brands of pharmaceuticals. This visa systems, it is said, virtually precludes access to the French market to drugs not undergoing some stage of fabrication in France itself.

In the petroleum refining industry, France has had a system of quotas for crude oil since 1928. This system, still in effect, allocates imports of crude to petroleum companies on the basis of their existing or planned refining capacity in France. By augmenting the pull of the French market, the quota systems has attracted a third of the foreign refinery subsidiaries of the Continental companies within the E.E.C.

Although this legislation has been noted for favoring the development of French-owned oil companies, one of its original aims was to promote the development of refining in France by whatever companies could be induced to enter the country.

EUROPEAN INVESTMENT IN THE U.S.

The direct foreign investment in manufacturing in Europe by American multinational enterprises has considerably exceeded the lesser investment in the U.S. by European firms.

Continental firms investing in the U.S. without strong innovative advantages, faced the competitiveness and unfamiliarity of the American market which led to a very high rate of mortality.

TABLE 4 Direct investment in the U.S. by companies based in Continental European countries in U.S. $ million.

In the U.S. from Continental Countreis	1937	1962	1970	1972	1973
Bel. & Lux.	71	158	338	309	603
France	57	183	286	321	473
Germany	55	152	680	807	768
Italy	N/A	100	100	107	85
Netherlands	179	1,082	2,151	2,357	2,550
Sweden	30	179	208	256	291
Switzerland	74	836	1,545	1,567	1,825
Total Continental investments in the U.S.	436	2,690	5,308	5,724	6,595
In home countries of continental European enterprises by American Companies	785	5,383	16,520	21,206	23,581

Source: *The European Multinationals* — by L. Franko (1976)

For instance, in the aluminium industry which in many ways fits the image of a mature oligopoly par excellence, Continental enterprises ventured into manufacturing in the U.S. only when they were simultaneously confronted by the threat of trade barriers and were convinced that they had a technological advantage.

Pechiney and Alusuisse each set up two smelting subsidiaries in the U.S. during the 1960's. The establishment of these ventures may in part have constituted moves in a series of exchanges of threats with American producers. However, it is arguable that the Europeans were the first to threaten American positions. Throughout the 1960's, the U.S. was a large net importer of aluminium metal. Most U.S. imports came from Canada, but particularly in the early 1960's, significant amounts came from Pechiney's French smelters or from smelters in Norway. American firms responded both by vigorous lobbying for U.S. protection and by marginal cost pricing of exports to continental countries. Pechiney sought a means to stabilize its sales in the U.S.

First it acquired a fabricating company (Alusuisse had fabricated in the U.S. since 1948); shortly thereafter Pechiney was invited by an American firm (which had a market position in competitive non-ferrous metals) to undertake a joint smelting venture to be based on Pechiney's energy-saving technology. The venture enabled Pechiney to hedge against the imposition of U.S. trade barriers and to capitalize on fuel-saving technology more than enabled the firm to overcome the disadvantages of applying relatively labor-intensive European production methods in the U.S. context of high labor cost. As a result of limited hydroelectric sources and American protection of high cost domestic oil sources, Pechiney's U.S. competitors were experiencing higher energy costs relative to their labor costs. It seemed the turn of the U.S. to provide a fertile ground for the application of a European innovation, especially when trade was inhibited.

The tyre and rubber industry is another sector which superficially fit the mature oligopoly category, and Michelin's decision to manufacture in the U.S. in the early 1970's was occasionally interpreted as a response to American activity in Europe. Other factors were also at work, however. First, there was the pull of U.S. market demand on Michelin's innovation.

In 1972, Michelin sold 35% of all radial tyres sold in the U.S., and its sales volume approached 250 million dollars. The tyres came from Spain — Previously, when American raw material costs favored the shorter-lived, belted tyre, there was little demand for radial tyres in the U.S.: Michelin invented (the radial) before the second World War. France was the first country to adopt the radial before being imitiated by other European countries, then the U.S.

In spite of the rapidly growing demand for radials in the U.S., Michelin almost desperately sought to avoid producing in the high-labor cost American market; it saw no special advantage or insurance effect from having the same cost structure as American firms. The company's first North American production site was in Canada. That investment was prompted by fears of U.S. protectionists moves against Spanish production and represented an attempt simultaneously to get a low labor-cost production site, a subsidized plant in a depressed Canadian region, and duty free access to the U.S. market via the U.S.-Canadian free trade agreement on autos and parts. American competitors protested that Canada's subsidization of Michelin's New Brunswick facilities gave Michelin an unfair advantage; the U.S. Government responded to these complaints by putting a 6% surtax on Michelin's imports from its Canadian plant. Only after U.S. demand had created a market, and U.S. government policy had prevented that market from being profitably supplied from abroad, did Michelin become convinced of the practicability of investing in the South Carolina in 1973.

As mentioned earlier Continental firms that established U.S. manufacturing operations without a clear competitive advantage based on technological innovation often ended up making unceremonious exits from the U.S.

During the 1960's it was the turn of France's St. Gobain to experience failure in the U.S. Thinking that its 300 years of experience in polished plate-glass would be sufficient guarantee of viability in U.S. manufacturing, St. Gobain responded to a threat of American import restrictions in 1958 by deciding to build a factory in Kingsport, Tennessee, completed in 1962.

The company did not reckon with the possibility that the float-glass process, innovated at about the same time by Britain's Pilkington, might be made operational by Pilkington's U.S. licensees.

The Pittsburgh Plate Glass had its Pilkington-licensed float plant in operation in 1963, and was followed by nine other U.S. firms in rapid succession.

The result of S.G.'s miscalculation of U.S. competitive behavior followed with all the inevitability of a Greek tragedy. American St. Gobain, the U.S. subsidiary, chalked up losses almost every year.

S.G. finally sold its 57% participation in A.S.G.

BUSINESS-GOVERNMENT RELATIONSHIP IN FRANCE

In France, Pechiney's increasingly frequent statements that it intended to invest less and less, and perhaps cease investing at all in its home country, created an only slightly less explosive reaction there than did AKZO's (Dutch Chemical giant) intention to disinvest in its home country.

During the time when Pechiney appeared to be expanding foreign aluminium smelting primarily in response to host government proddings, trade restriction and investment grants, such statements could have been interpreted as mere negotiating gambits in the never-ending bargaining between electricity-using Pechiney and Electricite de France. But as Pechiney expanded abroad, and particularly as new enterprises (including some in bauxite or electricity-rich countries) threatened to compete on a price basis in order to enter the aluminium industry, low-cost foreign production sites became ever more appealing. For Pechiney managers the importance of electricity as a component element of aluminium costs meant that foreign expansion was an economic necessity.

The French socialist and communist parties, however saw Pechiney's foreign plans as a search for unjustifiable superprofits sought at the expense of French workers. During the 1974 election campaign the French left proposed to nationalize Pechiney-precisely in order to resolve the conflict by blocking the company's plans to act like a global, optimizing enterprise.

Yet, even while the French left was proposing to nationalize Pechiney to bring French state and enterprise goals into harmony, Renault, an enterprise nationalized 28 years earlier was receiving attention both at home and abroad on account of its obscure, but considerable multinational spread.

Although Renault's annual reports said little about them, the French press reported that the firm had both a sophisticated international sourcing systems and a number of holding companies in low-tax countries. As a result some suspicion surrounded the firm's profit reports and transfer pricing practices. Business and labor interests alike harshly criticized Renault's survey concerning its multinational scope, its Swiss holding companies through which probably transit all movements of funds concerning subsidiaries, and its publication of well illustrated annual reports stuffed with production and export statistics, but lacking financial meaning. Attention was called to the danger of financial-base company like Renault-Finance (Switzerland) not only aiding in the financing of foreign operations, but of dipping into the Euro-dollar market to finance the development of the mother company.

Responding to these criticisms an anonymous member of the company's management replied:— People would not permit the Regie (Renault), a multinational enterprise, to manage its finances inefficiently.

European multinational enterprises had shown that they could sometimes come into conflict with a large number of home and host country interest groups simultaneously as a result of changes or aberrations in home government policy. When government policy objectives changed, a company president could wake up to find himself at the head of a multinational company. A shift in French government policy led to such a rude awakening being visited on St. Gobain in 1968 and 1969. For reasons which are still unclear the French government uncharacteristically tolerated a public take-over bid in 1968 by Bussois-Souchon-Neuvesel (BSN) for St. Gobain, one of the continent's enterprises with the lengthiest history of extensive foreign manufacturing operations. Public take-over bids, common enough in Anglo-Saxon countries, had previously been almost unknown in France.

Perhaps the French government was distracted as it picked up the pieces of the May 1968 riots; perhaps it wished to disturb the quiet lives to which some managers had become accustomed in the long-cartelized glass industry. In any event, the structure of the French glass industry was not amicably arranged by private negotiations among enterprises and the Finance and Planning Ministries, as was traditional in France. B.S.N. made its bid in December 1968, and although St. Gobain's defence was successful, St. Gobain was obliged to reveal much more about its finances and operations than it had ever done before.

Previously, few Frenchmen had thought of St. Gobain as a multinational. Suddenly, St. Gobain stood identified in shareholders' and unions' minds as a multinational enterprise, with all the profit and production location options associated with U.S. multinational enterprises. Nevertheless, the company's public relations defense against the B.S.N. gave St. Gobain a reputation of having suddenly and mysteriously conjured up profits out of the nether reaches of a multinational empire. This image was quickly seized upon in the U.S., Germany and Italy by labor unions, which demanded that concessions made to French workers during the May 1968 disturbances be extended on a world wide basis. The suspicion of these unions was that the concessions in France had been made at their expense; they feared that St. Gobain was declaring artificially low profits in America, Germany and Italy in order to pay for labor peace in France.

In the event, the American, German and Italian unions were able to utilize St. Gobain's new multinational image to mobilize their member's support for a three week strike in the U.S., and for protracted negotiations in Germany and Italy.

So St. Gobain was made abruptly aware of unions' perception of the company as a multinational enterprise capable of transfer pricing profits to or from one or another subsidiary as a bargaining weapon.

THE FUTURE OF EUROPEAN MULTINATIONALS

Continental multinational enterprises are increasingly seen as capable of satisfying or blocking fulfilment of the objectives of any number of home and host country interest groups.

In the near future multinational enterprises based on the European Continent, perhaps unlike those based in America, Great Britain or Japan, may face a higher degree of political tension at home than in host countries.

If Europe is to become integrated, enterprises would specialise and relocate production. And with a free trade within Europe, it is likely that Continental enterprises would be obliged to continue the tentative moves they have made in the direction of supranational co-ordination and optimisation of operations.

In 1974 and 1975 Continental enterprises were looking forward to foreign investment, this might have been a reaction for the enormous increase in oil prices and raw materials and the revaluation of most Continental European currencies. Because of these increases in prices, European fuel-saving processes and synthetics seemed to be meeting growing market demand.

If the foreign expansion by the Continental enterprises would not affect domestic

216

unemployment, the move would be indifferent to home-country workers, labor ministries and governments.

Governments have intended to control the behavior of multinational enterprise: developed countries propose to place more controls on outward investment, while underdeveloped countries propose to place more controls on inward multinational enterprise activities.

Therefore when Continental multinationals set up their strategic plannings, they should put more weight on the political, social and economic factors at their home and host countries and compromise all the conflicting interests before making their decisions to achieve their goals and objectives.

But their ability to help or prevent nation's economic and technological development will undoubtedly continue to make them useful for many economic and political ends.

If France has a left-wing Government in 12 months time, its first legislative task upon assuming power will be to nationalise nine major industries that dominate the French private sector.

This would probably have a direct effect on foreign investment in France, people are reported to be quietly shifting funds out of the country, though there is no official confirmation of this.

Inflation is now running at around 10%, however, the Government is naturally concerned to minimise its unemployment problem.

This is running at 5% of the workforce — a high figure in France, where 3% is regarded as being the maximum tolerable level in political terms.

In order to minimise the unemployment figures the Government is directing quite large sums into particular regions and industries such as the steel industry in the east of France.

In the textile industry, for example, there is much headshaking at the way in which funds have been poured into a large cotton textile manufacturer through the device of heavy and premature Government orders.

One does not have to embrace the theories of the doomsayers to see a tough time ahead for France: one where the risks of destablisation will be high.

Combined with the growing ascendancy of the left in Italy, Spain and Portugal, a Government of the left in France, especially one with a tough well-organised communist element, carries profound implications for the future of Europe and the European multinational.

BIBLIOGRAPHY

The European Multinationals by Lawrence G. Franko (1976)
The Multinational Company in Europe by Michael Z. Brooke and H. Lee Remmers (1972)
Jane's Major Companies of Europe 1975
Business History Review, Vol. 48, 1974 — The Origins of Multinational Manufacturing by Continental European Firms — by L.G. Franko
The Financial Review, Wednesday, April 27, 1977 — French politics to-day.

The Future of the Multinational Corporation

from the British Viewpoint

By A.C. Copeman*

To predict the future role of the multinational corporation in the present political and economic climate must appear to be an extremely hazardous exercise.

First of all one must take a view on the future role of the corporation itself. If the corporation is to be debilitated at the rate exhibited at present in the United Kingdom and Australia then there is little point speculating on the future role of the particular form which we call the multinational corporation.

The future role of the corporation will depend very much on our freedom to determine our system of rewards for individual effort, our freedom to invest personal savings as an alternative to present consumption, and our freedom to possess personal property. The corporation is a form of association of people which can be joined by simply buying a share. In Australia we are fortunate that there are almost no onerous restrictions on our buying shares, not only in Australian corporations but in those of most of the countries with which we have close associations — certainly the United Kingdom, the United States, Canada and New Zealand. For a few dollars anyone can own shares in any of the major multinational corporations about which we are concerned. It may be argued that owning a few shares will have no effect on the policies of corporations, but the right to dissent is there, and with sufficient organisation, can be made effective. Certainly the views of a shareholder are in my experience given far more attention than those of a voter in a parliamentary democracy. Most companies are very sensitive to those few shareholders who care to express their views.

The recent intervention of the Australian Workers Union in investment in shares in Winns, the department store chain, is an interesting example of the freedom in our society for individuals or groups to take a significant investment interest in a corporation. There are many companies whose employees could collectively raise sufficient funds to buy control, if not outright ownership, of those companies, but it is a matter of record that such events rarely take place, and employee shareholding schemes and profit-related bonus schemes rarely appeal.

In considering the future role of the multinational corporation in the world economy we must start from an assessment of the present position. There exists in the world an array of forms of association — governments, corporations and the like — which are made up of people who join together in quest of various goals. We have also an array of factories, offices, mines, farms, power stations, systems of transport and communications — material resources — which enable things to be made or transported or messages sent.

We have evolved combinations of the various groups of people with the material resources in order to satisfy man's innate busy-ness, his striving to occupy the day in order to safeguard and improve tomorrow. Our objective is to ensure that these groups of people and these material resources perform the tasks which collectively we most desire. We should adapt what we have if it does not in some way suit what we believe to be the best interests of future generations. In doing so we should examine without emotion what we have and avoid throwing out the baby with the bath water.

Those of us who play significant parts in the day to day workings of multinational corporations have to face frequently the accusation that the multinational corporation possesses

*A director of Consoldiated Goldfields of Australia which is controlled by the UK Goldfields Group.

some extra-territorial power which is an infringement of the sovereignty of each nation within which the multinational corporation operates. Our response to most of the criticism is to ask ourselves first of all what it is we are doing that is so wrong, and then having failed to find anything which clearly sets us apart from locally-owned corporations, we retire in bewilderment until the next attack. The critic usually draws his argument from such matters as the political intervention of ITT in Chile, the subscription terms of an issue of shares in a local subsidiary, or the profits concealed in transfer prices.

There are clearly many occasions when institutions of all types, let alone multinational corporations, require curbing by governments. After all that is what governments are for, and where we are fortunate to have governments which are based on democratic principles, we would expect them to be concerned about undue power in any institution or in any person. What we cannot accept is the assertion that the multinational corporation has power which the government cannot curb if it chooses to do so. In recent years I have read as much as possible of the criticisms levelled at multinational corporations and I regret to say that I have not gained much insight into the basic causes of resentment except insofar as the multinational corporations are largely foreign owned (we do have some of our own!) and may therefore bring a culture which is foreign to that of our own; and they are generally believed to be very profitable (probably because they are large, they are publicly prominent, and they are very businesslike). I am concerned that much of the criticism is a xenophobic luddite-ism which is unconstructive and bent on establishing the multinational corporation as a popular whipping-boy.

The multinational corporation is basically concerned with growth and with maintenance of its opportunities for growth. It sets criteria for profitability which may or may not be met in practice, but it is large and multinational principally because it is an organisation which has certain skills which can be turned to account. It exists, and this at any point in time in some way says it is successful. The unsuccessful companies have fallen by the wayside and are not seen.

During the recent visit of Mr. Herman Kahn, the Director of the Hudson Institute in New York, he was asked on Monday Conference for his view of the future of multinational corporations, and whether they will have a larger or smaller percentage of total world business. I believe his reply worth quoting from the Australian Broadcasting Commission transcript.

"My guess is that they will grow at a rate that is almost twice as fast as gross world product. That means they take a higher and higher percentage. . . . They're not very popular, so you might ask why they grow so fast. The multinational firm probably is the most effective instrument that's ever been devised for rapid modernisation. . . . It's an unbelievably efficient method of transferring technology, of transferring the missing link. If you have anything at all to sell the transnational corporations are willing to come in and supply all the missing links. . . ."

He goes on to say — "You have a good labour force — they'll build the factory, they'll give you the designs, they'll organise it for you, they'll finance it, they'll sell it. You have a good port — they'll bring the labour in . . . ."

If Mr. Kahn is right that the multinational corporation is the most effective means of modernisation, then we *could* look to it for the benefits it can bring to society, provided we have safeguards to restrain or reject those aspects which we do not like. In business life we are very familiar with the speed and yet complexity of decision-making which proper delegation of responsibility can bring, and we have much occasion to contrast this with the inefficiency and slowness of the government bureaucratic process. We believe that the world of business is so complex that to attempt to channel it through a bureaucratic process is extremely inefficient and frustrating of human ingenuity, and unnecessary. State-run industries can compete effectively in the modern world where they *have* to compete, and where they are able to copy standards of organisation and of activity from the free enterprises with which they compete, not because state

219

enterprises as such can be an efficient and continuously competitive form of organisation. We believe that it is better to regulate and encourage competition between free enterprises than to create state monopolies. Moreover, in the world we have a diversity of nations with significant geographical as well as political boundaries. These boundaries tend to harden and soften from time to time depending on political and economic climates. Our belief in a better future for mankind generally carries a preference to see the boundaries softened rather than to be hardened into political and economic nationalism. We suggest that the multinational corporation, properly constrained, properly regulated and encouraged, can play an important part in this softening process, and through its efficiency and flexibility can assist significantly to improve the quality of life. Let us not forget that General Motors brought its car production skills to Australia at the invitation of the Chifley Government.

It is sometimes forgotten that governments, corporations and individuals are all subject to what we call market forces and ultimately to international market forces, which limit and direct our efforts, whether in finance, commodities, manufactured goods or even in migration of people. We are naturally concerned that we should not be unduly and too-rapidly influenced by these international forces. A common criticism voiced against multinational corporations is that they are clearly and immediately influenced by changing international market forces, to the detriment of the host country's economy.

I would question whether it is in fact to a country's long-term detriment that it has within its borders forces which are readily responsive to the international markets. It was said recently by the President of the Bank of America that "the market system remained unique and stronger than any government" including, of course, his own. It is an important question how long any government can ignore the market without destroying the viability of its economy. The market ultimately is the sum of the wishes of people, and unless we coerce people, their wishes will triumph.

I believe that the aspect of the debate about multinational corporations which has been most neglected is that of people. These corporations, like all others, only exist because people — investors, managers, employees, customers and suppliers, are free and willing to contribute their money, their goods or their time. Looking first of all at the investors — very few multinational corporations have any degree of concentration of ownership. There are very few Gettys or Rockefellers who can dominate their firm's policies through their shareholdings. More research needs to be done into the ownership of the major multinational corporations to determine the degree to which ultimate ownership is diffused, through small shareholdings, life insurance policies and superannuation funds, but it is my experience that there is rarely a significant ownership influence on management. In other words management is left to get on with the job of running the corporation as best it can, guided by directors who are rarely substantial shareholders. Its principal incentive is the competition of other corporations.

A number of surveys have been made in the past thirty years of the social and economic origins of the people who manage large corporations. These surveys have shown that a very high proportion of managers have risen to their positions through their own efforts, rather than through some inheritance. There is a strong tendency for those people who inherit a secure economic position to go into the more independent professions such as law or medicine, or to have their own businesses or farms. The man who is attracted to the ladder-climbing exercise of the large corporation is generally striving to achieve a better position in life than he inherited.

The means to advancement in a large corporation is through acquiring a sound foundation in one of the professional skills. The need to acquire and develop these skills leaves little time for the pursuit of power as an end in itself, and advancement in a large corporation must be based on proven professional ability if the corporation is to survive.

The outcome is that the leaders of large corporations are predominantly not the sort of people they are popularly portrayed to be, and this is where so much of the attack on multinational corporations goes wrong. They are usually not wealthy although they are well-paid. They believe that their decisions flow primarily from the dictates of their professional training or from the market place, and only secondarily, if at all, from some head office in a foreign country. Even then they see the situation as a response to world-wide pressures of the market place. In this they see their decisions as being no different from those necessary for the locally-owned corporations with whom they are in competition. Furthermore the man who is prepared to remain with a large corporation in a senior position no doubt has proven ability, but the fact that he has not turned aside to use that ability directly for his own gain in his own business would suggest that he is a cautious co-operative person who is accustomed to the constraints of working as part of a team.

Many of the ablest young people in our community are attracted to organisations which are multinational. In recent times it has not been too difficult for an able person who wanted to make his way in business to get a good basic education, and to further that education by attending other institutions overseas, particularly in the United Kingdom and the U.S.A., and to gain experience in the business and professional world abroad. A very high proportion of our most able people have done just that. It is natural that when they return to Australia they see their future with an organisation which enables them to continue their links with other parts of the world and to keep in touch with the latest developments in their fields abroad. Having lived overseas and enjoyed the hospitality of foreign universities and business houses, they see nothing inherently disloyal or antagonistic towards Australia in working for these businesses back in Australia. They have experienced a wider world which they have found to be very sympathetic towards Australia. Their employment with multinational corporations is not just a matter of being attracted by higher salaries or fringe benefits, it goes deeper into their appreciation of a lively and flexible business world. They are loyal Australians — those who have returned from training and employment overseas have "voted for Australia with their feet" — but they commonly find their most stimulating employment with the multinational corporations. The future strength of multinational corporations as enduring features of the business scene is in their hands, and because these people have ability, these corporations will persist and will continue to move into new fields of activity both commercially and geographically where they can challenge their competitors. Because the world is diverse and geographically-divided there will always be further fields of endeavour which will attract the human and financial resources of the most effective multinational corporations. It is for this reason, I believe, that Herman Kahn says so confidently that the multinational corporations "will grow at a rate that is almost twice as fast as gross world product". They attract people who devise opportunities to create material resources which their financial skills can turn to account. There need be nothing sinister in this, and it is certainly not beyond the power of any sovereign government to regulate.

I believe that this portrait of multinational man should be given serious consideration in looking at the future of the multinational corporation. People of this description, whether they be in New York, London, Melbourne or Sydney, are much more amenable to policy development than they are portrayed, and are not the oppressing ogres of recent journalism. Moreover let us rid ourselves of the notion that there is some sinister influence behind these corporations. This is part of a modern myth which is exploited by people who do not seem to want to look at the facts. Time and again when faced with a difficult decision the managers of multinational companies find that being 'foreign' imposes a greater obligation to consider their responsibility to the host country than if they were locally-owned, and they envy the locals their simpler process of making major decisions which ought to make them more commercially effective.

I believe that practically all people employed by multinational corporations would like to see the degree of local ownership increase, but we have to look at means of attainment which are practicable. We cannot believe in free enterprise and mobility of resources and at the same time contemplate expropriation or nationalisation, particularly if we believe that enterprise itself would suffer in consequence. We must not forget that commerce and industry in the United States of America were once highly dependent on foreign — largely British — capital, and that even today the U.S.A. remains the most liberal country in the world with regard to foreign investment within its borders. Let us also not forget that the world is now waiting rather helplessly for the U.S.A. to lead it out of the current recession! There are occasions when we see the real value to our corporations in having a house of review in London or New York, where others can assess the viability of an investment with the aid of perhaps better information, and a wider view of the risks involved. Or we may be reassured by the thought that behind our activities in Australia, whatever their fortunes, there stands a strong parent to whom we can turn for advice, guidance or finance in times of need. These are real factors in our day to day commercial lives, not matters of sentiment or servitude.

Future of the Multinational Enterprise: the view of a British Academic

By John H Dunning*

The multinational enterprise is approaching a cross roads in its development in the world economy. After an unparalleled and almost unchecked expansion in its activities in the 1950s and 1960s, its future role in economic development is being increasingly questioned. Not so long ago, it was being confidently predicted that, within the foreseeable future, the 300 or 400 largest companies with foreign direct investments would account for 60 to 70 per cent of the world's industrial output outside the centrally-planned economies. In the economic and political environment of the mid-1970s, this prediction seems highly unrealistic. Over the course of the last five years, in particular, quite dramatic changes have occurred which suggest that the international economic order might be substantially reshaped in the years to come.

This article traces the forces making for the growth of the multinational enterprise since 1950, and speculates a little about its prospects. It begins by discussing certain parallels between trade and foreign direct investment as forms of international economic involvement, arguing that they have much in common and provoke similar reactions by governments. It then highlights the main determinants of international production under three broad headings: the general economic and political environment, the attitudes and policies of investing (home) and recipient (host) countries, and the goals, capabilities and strategies of multinational enterprises. Finally, I describe how changes in these conditions have affected the flow and pattern of international production in the last two decades and how changes now taking place, or likely to take place, will affect it in the future.

What is a Multinational Enterprise?

First, however, it is important to be clear what we mean by a multinational enterprise. A multinational enterprise is one which undertakes foreign direct investment, i.e. which owns or controls income-gathering assets in more than one country; and, in so doing, produces goods or services outside its country of origin, that is, engages in international production.[1] Multinational enterprises may be publicly or privately owned. Of the leading 211 manufacturing companies with sales of over $1 billion in 1971 listed in the UN document *Multinational Corporations in World Development,*[2] all save a few engage in international production but at least 12 are state owned. I anticipate that the number of state-owned multinationals may increase in the years to come, particularly as more socialist-inclined and less-developed countries spawn multinationals of their own.

Like animals in a zoo, multinationals (and their affiliates) come in various shapes and sizes, perform distinctive functions, behave differently and make their individual impacts on the environment. The skills and know-how provided by multinationals are different in resource-based industries from those provided in manufacturing industries. The control mechanisms of multinationals which adopt an integrated production or marketing strategy towards their affiliates are not the same as those which treat their affiliates as largely autonomous units. Large

*Professor of Economics at the University of Reading, and was a member of the Group of Eminent Persons appointed by the Secretary-General of the United Nations in 1973 to study the impact of the multinational corporation on world development and international relations.

Reprinted from *Lloyds Bank Review* with permission of the author and publisher.

multinationals from powerful developed countries, operating in small developing countries, in which there is little or no indigenous industry, pose quite different problems from those of their smaller counterparts which compete alongside established producers in advanced markets. Moreover, the extent to which an enterprise engages in international production may be neither its most important characteristic nor the major cause of its impact on the economies in which it operates. Any analysis of multinational enterprises must take account of these structural differences, and any generalizations about their activities should be treated with great caution.

Forms of International Economic Involvement

International production, financed by foreign direct investment, is one of many forms of international economic involvement. A country may be said to be internationally involved wherever at least some decisions over the way its resources are used are taken by institutions (including governments) or individuals in other countries or by regional or international bodies. Such involvement introduces an element of open-ness and interdependence to the participating economies, and produces certain costs and benefits, the balance between which depends both on the form of international involvement and on the conditions under which it takes place. Trade, for example, may bring benefits arising from a more efficient allocation of the world's resources and the opening up of new markets. It may also bring costs, or potential costs, most of which stem from a loss of control of participating countries over their own resources.

Partly because of these costs, completely free trade has not existed for many years; nor are the conditions under which the benefits of free trade were first promulgated often present in the modern world. In retrospect, it is possible to distinguish between a number of phases through which trade has evolved during the last two centuries The years following the industrial revolution were the golden era of free trade, particularly for Britain, its main beneficiary. But, even for Britain, this period was, for a variety of reasons, short lived. Initially, by means of tariffs and other import controls and, later, by the abandonment of the monetary system underpinning free trade, this form of international involvement became regulated by governments.

Until the second world war, attempts to control the volume and terms of trade were undertaken largely unilaterally, with each country seeking to protect its own interests. However, such measures often provoked retaliation and proved to be self-defeating. Efforts were then made to conclude bilateral treaties on trade between countries and/or by groups of countries in respect of particular commodities. It was not until after the second world war, when the IMF formed the basis for the international monetary system and GATT the basis for international trade, that a multinational machinery was created for an orderly system of trade; this, while far from being perfect, avoided the worst features of free trade on the one hand and unilateral import restrictions on the other.

Since countries do not find it in their interests to engage in free trade, it is understandable why they may wish to exert some control over other forms of international economic involvement which have similar effects. Here, we are interested in the open-ness and interdependence introduced by the operation of one country's enterprises in that of another country; sometimes as a substitute for trade, sometimes as a complement to it. Where foreign direct investment provides resources to a host country which enable it to produce goods more cheaply than could have been imported, (exclusive of tariffs or other import duties), then it acts as a superior substitute for trade. This will be the case whenever there are natural barriers to trade, eg transport and marketing costs, or barriers to entry of indigenous producers to necessary knowledge (technological, managerial, marketing) or to the economies of scale and integration possessed by the foreign enterprises.

On the other hand, the terms on which these resources are provided and the control over the way in which they are actually deployed may impose a cost unacceptable to host countries. In such cases, countries will seek either to obtain these resources in other ways or to control the amount, direction and terms of international production. How much and in what form control is exerted depends on the estimated cost/benefit ratio of free international production, compared with that of regulated international production or of obtaining resources provided by multinationals in alternative ways.

It is worth recalling that international production as an important form of international economic involvement is fairly new. Though the multinational enterprise has a long heritage, even at the eve of the second world war the value of international production was only one-third that of international trade in general. In the 'fifties and 'sixties, the growth of foreign production outpaced that of trade, in spite of trade liberalization, and by 1970 had exceeded that of trade in total. In the case of the leading international direct investor, (the US), foreign production is four times as great and, in the case of the second largest, (the UK), it is more than twice as great, as their respective total exports.

A second feature of international production concerns its geographical origins. Even in 1971, two-thirds of the foreign investment stake was of US or UK origin, although these same countries accounted for just over one-fifth of all exports This is an interesting fact in itself. Trade implies economic *interdependence,* as, normally over the long run, a country's exports and imports are fairly evenly balanced. This is not so with international production, where the flow of direct investment may be only one way. The majority of countries in the world are, in fact, substantial net importers of foreign capital; thus the *dependence* effect of foreign investment may be, and usually is much greater than that of trade.

But, over and above these general consequences of open-ness, international production has other effects. These arise mainly because, while trade normally takes place between independent economic agents,[3] international production, financed by foreign direct investment, involves no change in ownership. In trade, buyers and sellers have competing goals; in international production, producing affiliates seek to meet the goals set by their parent companies. These differences are likely to be most pronounced wherever international production gives rise to substantial economies of integration and where its ownership is concentrated in the hands of a few large firms.

Determinants of International Production

There are many factors which influence the level and character of international production. These may be considered under three broad headings: the general international and national economic and political environment; specific policies and attitudes towards foreign direct investment and multinational enterprises by home and host countries; the character and organizational strategy of multinational enterprises.

The general economic and political environment

Given a neutral policy towards foreign direct investment and the multinational enterprise, the general economic and political environment is perhaps the most important influence on international production. Most firms have some choice of what and where to produce, and some influence on their patterns of growth. International production is one option which may be considered as an alternative to production at home, either to supply the domestic or export market. Both domestic and international economic considerations influence this choice, as they do the goods to be produced. In particular, the choice between supplying a foreign market from a domestic or foreign base will be influenced, *inter alia,* by exchange rates, transport costs, tariff and non-tariff barriers, relative input costs, size of markets and the technology of multi-plant operations. On the other hand, the ability of foreign affiliates to compete with local companies will depend on the extent to which their advantages of being part of a larger foreign firm outweigh the additional marketing and other costs of international production.

The determinants of these choices are most often shaped by technological factors and government policies. Advances in communications technology, for example, may make it easier for enterprises to operate geographically separate plants; advances in enterprise-specific knowledge which can be effectively exploited only by large firms give multinationals in research-intensive industries an advantage; tariffs and other import controls induce international production in place of trade, and an overvalued exchange rate of the exporting country does the same thing; policies promoting regional integration may encourage both trade and investment; the discovery of new sources of energy, a changed bargaining position between raw material producers and consumers, and policies towards industrialization may each influence the terms of trade between the developed and less-developed nations. All of these, and other factors, including the role of international trading and monetary organizations, may vitally affect the environment in which foreign direct investment takes place.

Some of these environmental conditions are specific to particular countries: and it is not difficult to establish which countries are attractive to multinational enterprises or which spawn multinationals. Some affect particular industries or forms of investment; others are common to all forms of international economic involvement.

Attitudes and policies towards foreign direct investment

Policies towards international production are, in fact, rarely neutral. Most host and home countries have introduced specific measures to regulate the activities of foreign affiliates in their midst. These include the screening of new investments; controlling the conditions of production by foreign affiliates, or procurement behaviour policies, eg with respect to their pricing practices, their exports, dividend remissions; ensuring the benefits created by foreign direct investment and the share retained by host countries are maximized; and various devices to harmonize the decisions of foreign affiliates with the interests of host countries.

Foreign affiliates may also be treated differently from indigenous firms in respect of more specific issues: access to local capital markets, competition policy, regional incentives and measures taken to improve the balance of payments. Home governments may also use their power to affect the behaviour of their own multinationals: by capital controls, taxation of foreign income, extra-territorial legislation etc.

The character and strategy of multinational enterprises

There are many specific factors which make for more or less international production. These are related essentially to the financial, managerial, marketing and technological capabilities of firms; their size; and their organizational strategies. Not only is it possible to indicate particular industries in which multinational enterprises operate or countries which are net capital exporters; so particular types of firms tend to be pace-setters as international producers. In a manufacturing industry, for example, the single-product firm will be more likely to engage in international production when transport costs are high, scale economies of the plant are low, local customer requirements vary between markets, product differentiation is marked and the natural barriers of entry to indigenous producers are formidable.

For the multi-product or multi-processing producer, there is a choice whether to set up in other countries. In those areas where differences in costs and productivity promote trade, so too will they make for specialization by multinational enterprises and within such enterprises. Since most of the larger multinationals in manufacturing are diversified as regards products or processes, and factor costs do differ more between countries than within countries, there is plenty of scope for this kind of specialization.

Besides technological and size factors, the style of management may differ between companies. As a company's international involvement grows, so its organizational structure changes. Personalities may also play an important part. At the same time, control patterns differ between functions. For example, while decisions on capital expenditure, research and development, and the allocation of export markets may be centralized, those on personnel policy and industrial relations may be localized.

Developments since 1950

It is by analysing the changing conditions for international production that one can best understand what has happened in the last 20 years and what may happen in the next two decades. I believe that, like policies towards trade, those towards international production have followed a fairly distinct evolutionary pattern and that, together with environmental conditions and changes in the organizational structure of the multinational enterprises, they have brought this form of international involvement to a point corresponding to the inter-war years in the development of trade. At the same time, attitudes to international involvement *per se* are themselves undergoing change. Let us consider what has happened in the last quarter of century, since 1950.

The honeymoon period: 1950 to mid-1960s

The precise timing of this phase differs between countries. but it is distinguishable by the especially favourable environment for international production, and particularly that undertaken by US firms. During these years, the US dominated international production as the UK had dominated trade a century and a half earlier. It was the honeymoon period between host countries and multinational enterprises, during which the benefits of foreign direct investment were widely acclaimed. Western Europe, for example, starved of capital, knowledge and human skills and desperately short of foreign currency, had no option but to acquire them from the US which, in 1950, was technologically far and away the most advanced country in the world. American firms were especially welcome for the new resources they provided. In rich developing countries, like Canada and Australia, the need was no less pressing. It was for money and human capital to develop indigenous national resources and to supply products which, because of their small markets, could not be economically produced by their own firms. The poorer developing countries, particularly those with untapped mineral resources, were just beginning to appreciate their own economic potential but, again, were crucially short of the organizational skills and capital by which they could translate this potential into actual wealth. Since the import of goods or technology was not possible because of the shortage of foreign exchange, and as most countries did not have the infrastructure or institutional framework (as did Japan) to rely on licensing, foreign direct investment had a flourishing environment in which to operate. These were the years in which the technological and managerial gap between the US and the rest of the world was at its widest.

Besides these 'pull' factors, there were 'push' factors in the leading capital exporting country: the USA. By the mid-1950s some of the steam had gone out of the domestic economy. Institutional constraints inhibited domestic expansion by merger. Rates of return on capital and growth prospects seemed more promising in other countries. Scale economies and technological developments were favouring the larger firm; the production of knowledge, often financed by government support, was becoming more enterprise-specific and more difficult to assimilate by those who had not produced it; to finance expensive innovatory costs, large markets were necessary; and, towards the end of the period, the dollar became overvalued relative to other currencies.

Within this broad economic environment, international production by American firms flourished. Import protection and the need to exploit new markets also encouraged UK investment in the same period. Because, too, of the need for the package of resources which the multinational could provide, host countries were willing to adopt very generous policies to inward investment. Some attempted to influence the direction of investment or to ensure that it was in conformity with the more pressing national goals — eg improving the balance of payments — but most imposed few constraints. The cost/benefit ratio was rarely calculated, as the benefits were taken for granted. Little attention was paid to obtaining the resources provided by multinationals in other ways.

For the most part, the strategy of multinationals during this period was simple and straightforward. Most affiliates in manufacturing were set up to supply local or other markets in place of imports. The affiliates operated largely independently of each other and were closely identified with the interests of the local economy. Few firms had yet evolved an integrated or global strategy. Though most decisions, especially those taken by newly-established affiliates, were controlled by parent companies, they were usually geared to advance the prosperity and growth of the affiliate. There was comparatively little intragroup trading or product or process specialization within the multinationals. Branch plants were offshoots of parent companies and in only a few countries, eg the UK, did affiliates do much exporting.

Partly for these reasons, partly because so little was known about the effects of foreign affiliates and, partly, because their involvement in local economies was generally small, some of the costs of foreign investment were discounted or not even considered. There was little xenophobia. Free international production seemed to be the order of the day, the equivalent for the multinational enterprise of the free trade era.

Counting the costs: mid-1960s to mid-1970s

In this period, attention switched to the cost of, and alternatives to, international production financed by foreign direct investment. The report of the UN Study Group[4] on multinational corporations identifies these costs. Although it acknowledges the benefits, it recognizes that the multinational enterprise is under criticism. The honeymoon period is over. In spite of impressive research evidence that, on balance, the economic welfare of host countries has been advanced by foreign direct investment, its net benefits are being increasingly questioned. Bad news often makes the headlines more than good news. This certainly has been the case with multinationals, and public opinion about them has been much coloured by incidents in recent years of a disturbing character, as in Chile, for example.

How has this change in attitude come about in such a remarkably short period of time? Will it last? What does it foreshadow for the future? How has it been reflected in government policies towards the multinationals?

On the first question, there are many reasons for the increasing concern about multinationals. Perhaps the most important lies simply in their significance both in domestic economies and in the world economic scene. Currently, more than 20 per cent of the world's industrial output outside centrally-planned economies is supplied by multinationals. In almost every country, affiliates of foreign firms have increased their share of the national product; in more than a score, they now account for over one-third of the output of manufacturing industries. In some sectors, they have acquired a dominating position. Among these are the high-technology industries of the late-20th century: computers, industrial instruments, pharmaceuticals and so on. In less-developed countries, they own or control many vital raw materials: oil, copper, aluminium, zinc; and in service industries, they are, or have been, dominant in insurance, banking and tourism.

Second, with this growing international involvement has come a change in the management style and organizational strategy within multinationals. In the very industries in which international production has grown the fastest, product or process specialization is the most widely practised. In consequence, in these industries, at least, foreign affiliates have become less rather than more like their indigenous competitors, for example, in how they behave and react towards domestic economic policies.

Third, the rapid growth of international production has occurred at a time when most governments have become more aware of the need for centralized economic planning. This was already well in evidence in the 1950s and 1960s but it has accelerated and spread in the last decade. Both in developed and developing countries, the state is participating increasingly in economic affairs. Not only has this been undertaken for the usual Keynesian reasons, but on a much broader front — eg long-term economic planning, urban redevelopment, environmental control, preservation of raw materials — governments now exert much more influence on the way resources are used. It follows, then, that anything which reduces their ability to control the behaviour of foreign firms, without having to resort to special measures, is regarded as a challenge to their economic sovereignty.

From the viewpoint of developing countries, the situation has changed even more dramatically. As countries have become politically independent and are searching for their own identity, they have often tended to reject the ties of the past, including direct investment by foreign companies, which they regard as a form of economic imperialism or colonialism. They have also become more aware of the value of the resources they possess, while, at the same time, their knowledge of how to control the use of these resources has increased. Their contacts with the outside world, particularly through education and contacts with international agencies, especially the United Nations, and the technical aid received from such bodies, have made them conscious both of their economic power and of the wider implications of inward investment. They have become better equipped to evaluate the effects of such investment and of the alternatives to it. As they have formulated development plans, their perception of the contribution of multinationals has widened. Not only are they interested in their impact on technology, employment or the balance of payments, but in how they affect consumption patterns, cultural goals and the distribution of income.

This process of reorientation in outlook has not always been accompanied by the most sensible policies on the part of host countries. All too frequenlty, the multinational has been made the scapegoat for the failure of host governments to manage their economies properly. Though some developing countries will adopt a liberal approach towards inward investment, most have introduced stringent control procedures on types of investment permitted and conditions of production. In some cases, nationalization and expropriation have been resorted to; in others, there has been insistence upon local majority ownership and a gradual disinvestment of assets.

Developed countries, too, have attempted to reduce the costs of and increase the benefits from foreign direct investment. In Europe, the fear has been that American direct investment, particularly in research-intensive industries, would lead to technological dependence on the US. The main weapon used to forestall this has been to encourage 'countervailing power', both by the rationalization of domestic firms and by mergers between European and/or European and US companies. Similarly, there has been concern about the effects of foreign investment on the balance of payments and competition policy, and whether the share of the benefits accruing to the local economy was as much as it should have been.

Home countries have been no less concerned about the impact of foreign investment by their own multinationals on their own balances of payments, employment and competitive positions. In the US, in particular, various efforts are being made by labour and other interests to control the

229

flow of American direct foreign investment.

In part, this reaction against the multinational enterprise has nothing to do with its multinationality as such. Nor is it as widespread as may be thought. Those who are most vocal often represent special interests or have particular political axes to grind. There is much less outcry from the man in the street, to whom the benefits of foreign direct investment are more immediately obvious than its costs. Moreover, the multinational is caught up in a general disquiet about bigness in business, and in the developed countries at least a questioning of economic growth as an end in itself. Greater attention is now being placed on income relativities and on the widening gap between rich and poor countries; on the environment the depletion of natural resources, protecting energy supplies and so on. At every turn, the multinationals seem to be involved and are an easy target for complaint. The present climate of opinion towards them must be interpreted in this broader context.

How have the targets of attack reacted to these views and to the efforts made to regulate their activities? As yet, the statistics would suggest the multinationals' operations have been affected only marginally. The pace of new investment is slowing down, but it is still impressive, at least within the developed world. How long this will continue, if present attitudes to foreign investment persist, is another matter. In recent years, the general environment facing the world's largest companies has been much less favourable to growth. As a result of the realignment of currencies, US companies find foreign investment less attractive than previously. Inflation has produced difficult cash flow situations. Disengagement may be the order of the day, particularly in the uncertain environment of developing countries. The alternative is for companies to adapt their involvement to meet the particular needs of host countries, a course being actively pursued by some of the smaller multinationals, particularly those of Japanese and Continental European origin.

Report of the UN Study Group

It is my belief that we are at the beginning of a fairly fundamental reappraisal, both by countries of the role of multinationals in their development and by multinationals towards the form and direction of their international involvement. The present situation, with few exceptions, ranges from one of uneasy alliance to one of open hostility. Even where the attitudes towards foreign direct investment are still welcoming — eg in much of South East Asia — one wonders how long they will last.

Policies so far adopted towards multinationals have been largely unilateral, and only occasionally bilateral in character. Just as the incentives to investment were originally of this kind, so now are the regulations and constraints. As these constraints multiply, there is a real danger of international production seizing up — as did international trade in the 1930s — to the disadvantage of all nations. Indeed, there is some evidence that such a retrenchment has already begun.

It is at this point that the Report of the UN study group on multinational corporations is particularly pertinent. It rejects both the view put forward from some quarters that the nation state is dead and that the world is moving to economic interdependence and unhampered trade and international production, and also the opposite view that economic nationalism will become the order of the day and international trade and production will be severely constrained.

The group takes as its starting point the need to approach the control of international production from a multilateral viewpoint. It observes that, while at present there are organizations such as GATT and the United Nations Conference on Trade and Development (UNCTAD) which help to create orderly conditions for trade and, to a certain extent, influence the terms of trade, such institutions are necessary to regulate the flow of international production. In its report, the group proposes that consideration should be given to the conclusion of a General Agreement on Multinational Enterprises (GAME) between governments, which would identify and set out the general conditions for international production. These might include, *inter alia,* the harmonization of investment incentives, double taxation agreements, anti-trust legislation, competition policy, controls on capital flows and dividend remissions and questions relating to extra-territoriality. I believe this is on the right lines, although, rather than to focus attention on particular *institutions,* which possess many characteristics other than that of multinationality, I consider that it should be 'issue'- or 'problem'-oriented and that a General Agreement on International Production (**GAIP**) would be a more appropriate nomenclature.

While acknowledging the benefits of international production, the group's report concentrates on the problems which it may cause countries, or may seem to cause. It seeks to identify these and concludes that some are inherent in the nature of multinationality, while many are due to unsatisfactory terms of international production agreed at the point of entry, resulting from inadequate bargaining power of host countries *vis-à-vis* large international investors. It argues that, for the good of all parties, the terms of entry should be fair and seen to be fair; that companies should know exactly what is expected of them by host countries; that, as far as possible, foreign affiliates should identify themselves with the local economies in which they operate; and that countries should not take discriminatory or retroactive measures against multinationals, which have led to so much bitterness and misunderstanding between companies and countries in the past.

Finally, the group argues the need for harmonization of policies of host countries towards international production. Initially, this might be done by the conclusion of voluntary agreements or codes of conduct, in which respect the multinationals themselves can play an important role,[5] or by bilateral treaties on certain aspects of international production. Eventually, over the years, a more comprehensive mechanism is needed to tackle international production, to avoid distortions and to make possible orderly production, while allowing flexibility to countries in particular situations.

As an immediate step to this end, the group proposes the establishment of a permanent Commission on Multinational Enterprises responsible to the Economic and Social Council of the UN, to whom it would make an annual report. This commission would have a variety of functions[6] and it is proposed it should be supported by an information and research centre whose job would be both to collect and to analyse data relating to all aspects of international production. The group also felt that the technical advisory services of the United Nations should be strengthened to assist governments, particularly in developing countries, in their dealings with large multinational enterprises. All these functions are designed to improve the economic environment for direct investment and to get more data about its consequences, including questions relating to income distribution, appropriateness of technology, consumers' welfare and so on.

This approach of the group, directed to creating more harmonious conditions for international production, will most certainly have its critics. To some, it will be felt that the sovereignty of states has been insufficiently protected; that there is nothing proposed which could reduce the dependency of developing countries on foreign capital and entrepreneurship or to improve the balance of economic power between developed and less-developed countries. Here nothing less than a revolution in the whole system and institutional mechansim by which resources are allocated would suffice. On the other hand, those who are looking for a vindication of the existing system of resource allocation can take little comfort either. Though a careful reading of the report will show that the group was cautious not to generalize about the behaviour of all multinationals from its knowledge of a well-publicized few, there was some unease that the economic power of many of the larger multinationals could be used against the interest of countries or particular groups. It felt that, although some conflict is inevitable, because of the differences in goals of companies and countries, unless something is done to create a better understanding, the relationships between multinationals and countries and other interests will deteriorate to the disadvantage of all concerned. One's judgement is, of course, clearly clouded by the way in which one thinks the world economic system ought to be arranged and how in the foreseeable future it is likely to be arranged.

Future Prospects for Multinationals

In all this, I believe that a distinction should be drawn between the future of multinational enterprises in developed and in less-developed countries. Concern is greatest where the countries in which foreign production is undertaken are most different — ideologically, politically and economically — from those making the investment. An investment by a powerful industrial nation, with a belief in the free enterprise economy, made in a small centrally-planned developing economy, where there is little indigenous competition and where cultural and other goals are different, may bring far more tensions than where the same investment is made in a similar environment. For these reasons, I foresee that there may be fewer problems connected with transatlantic investment in the next few years than with that made by advanced countries in less-advanced countries and that, in the future, the development of foreign investment may take two quite separate courses.

So far as direct investment between developed countries is concerned, apart from closer economic integration in Europe, the environment for international production is unlikely to change much. The main problems arising from it will essentially be those normally posed to industrial societies by powerful companies, but in an international context.

A good guide to the approach of the EEC Commission is contained in its document *Multinational Undertakings and Community Regulations,.*[7] Basically, the concern of the Commission is to ensure that the monopolistic power and flexibility of foreign multinationals are not used against the interests of host countries in the Community. There is also some concern lest a lack of harmonization among individual countries on tax, competition and regional incentive policies may induce foreign companies to play one European country off against another. There is, however, less fear than once there was that Europe will be economically dominated by US firms particularly as, in the next decade, European direct investment in the US is likely to grow faster than US investment in Europe and as the technological and managerial gap may narrow further. Nevertheless, the Commission believes that a united European policy towards foreign investment will strengthen the bargaining positions of individual countries. One is less sanguine about their efforts to promote indigenous competition in some of the high technology industries.

So long as there are proper safeguards it would seem that foreign (mainly US) enterprises will continue to be given a qualified welcome to invest in Europe; there seems little pressure among EEC countries to encourage other forms of arrangements with foreign firms. One may expect more public involvement in some industries — eg oil and motor cars, computers and pharmaceuticals — in which foreign companies are actively concerned. A rather more cautious treatment may be accorded to Japanese investment, but as yet this has not created a serious problem.

So far as investment between developed and developing countries is concerned, the situation is very different and there are reasons to suppose that the role of the multinational may undergo substantial change. First, the environment which shapes the economic relationships between the developed and less-developed world is changing. We can illustrate from recent oil developments, where the developing nations are making concerted efforts to improve their bargaining position and terms of trade *vis-à-vis* consuming countries. This is also happening at a regional level, as seen, for example, by the efforts of the Andean Pact countries. When the supply of basic commodities vital to the prosperity of consuming nations is threatened, governments of these nations inevitably become involved; and this could mean that in place of market forces bilateral governmental agreements may determine the conditions and terms of trade. It may well be that international agreements on the supply of a variety of commodities may set the future framework within which multinationals operate. If this is so, the role of multinationals in resource-based industries may be much less decisive than in the past.

With respect to specific attitudes by developing countries to foreign direct investment, even when its advantages are undisputed there is a dislike of foreign ownership. This, then, leads countries to consider alternatives to multinationals. In the belief that they can rid themselves of foreign control over their economies, host countries either encourage divestment or, by 'unwrapping the package' of foreign investment, attempt to buy the individual ingredients from separate sources. In some cases, this may not be difficult to do; capital and many kinds of knowledge can be bought on the open market. But such a policy can be successful only if the local economy has the necessary technological expertise to choose exactly what is needed and, once acquired, is able to assimilate the resources and to use them productively. But, as many countries are finding to their cost, the replacement of international production by production undertaken under foreign licence or management contract is not necessarily less costly; nor does it always lessen economic dependence. Knowledge still has been imported; and, because of imperfections in the diffusion of knowledge and technology, on the one hand, and lack of local capabilities, on the other, the key components of dependence — at least at the firm level — still remain.

At the same time, the sources of the main ingredients of foreign investment are widening. Already, much new capital is flowing from the oil countries; technology is being exported from the centrally-planned economies; and in the 1980s more advanced developing countries may become suppliers. There is some suggestion of a technological convergence among the industrial powers. If this is so, the developing countries will no longer be dependent on the traditional sources of knowledge, nor be bound by the traditional ways of obtaining it.

With political attitudes as they are, with a growing bargaining power of developing countries and with alternatives to such investment becoming available, one might expect the multinational enterprise to invest rather less in developing countries in the future. On the other hand, in some kinds of activity involving centralized decisions they may invest more. The exodus of some firms from high-cost countries to take advantage of lower costs and to concentrate labour-intensive parts of their international operations may well continue and intensify. At the same time, there will be pressure from trade unions and others for a gradual upgrading of the type of work delegated to developing countries.

There are other reasons to suppose direct investment might grow in developing countries. As they become wealthier and their markets grow, developing countries become more attractive to foreign companies. Pressures in the oil-producing countries for more petroleum-processing activities may offer great prospects for foreign petro-chemical and plant equipment companies. As their governments become more stable and expert at managing their economies, the riskiness of foreign investment declines; firms may then be prepared to accept a lower rate of return. As these countries are seen to accord fair treatment to foreign companies, the incentive to invest will increase.

Host countries, undoubtedly, have much to learn about the costs and benefits of direct investment; which is made all the more difficult in developing countries as they struggle to identify their goals of development and the best way to achieve them. In this respect, the advisory services of professional bodies and international agencies can help. So can the multinationals, by a more sensitive understanding of the aspirations of developing countries. The international community can also play its part, by considering whether or not, in the light of the multinationals have made people in rich countries more aware not only of some of the problems existing between rich and poor countries, but of the inadequacies of existing machineries to deal with them.

I would make one final point. I believe that the immense resources of multinationals are not being fully harnessed and that they are able to help governments to reach their goals. They often possess the very capabilities necessary for development but, as yet, they have been used to meet largely commercial demands, mainly in the developed countries. These are not the priorities of developing countries. Since these cannot be satisfied entirely through commercial markets, some co-operation with governments is necessary. In food and agriculture, this has been started with the Industrial Co-operative Programme of the Food and Agriculture Organization of the United Nations, in which many leading multinational companies are involved. Co-operation with governments in social infrastructure, eg for electrification and irrigation schemes, exploration of the sea-bed and similar schemes, is also needed.

Given a world which recognizes the benefits of multilaterally-regulated international economic involvement, and provided that the machinery to accomplish this is adequate, I believe that multinational enterprises still have a vital role to play in world development, but that the nature of this role will change. In general, I believe that direct investment will be a relatively less important channel for the transfer of knowledge; instead, there will be more non-financial investment, eg in knowledge and human skills in developed countries, which will then be supplied to the developing countries on a contract basis. This means that, in place of investment in equity capital — for which the reward is profits — there will be a package of services supplied by one firm to another or to governments — for which the reward will be a management or licensing fee. To the country, for direct investment by ownership will be substituted a contractual relationship of a limited duration, with ownership left in national hands. To the firm, its foreign earnings will take the form of fees for services rendered; and, already, such fees are rising at a faster rate than profits.

The years up to 1914 saw the export of portfolio capital and the migration of labour. Over the last 20 years, the main vehicle of international economic involvement has been direct investment. Perhaps we are now at the beginning of a new period, in which firms will increasingly export a package of services, comprising knowledge, loan capital and human skills, rather than *own* productive facilities. The era of the multinational consultancy firm or agency selling capital services may have begun.

Footnotes

1. Sometimes the term 'trans-national enterprise' is used to describe this phenomenon, To my mind, the important distinction is between multi- or trans-national *producing* enterprises and enterprises which are internationally involved in other ways. See my previous article 'The Multinational Enterprise' in the July 1970 issue of the *Lloyds Bank Review.*
2. United Nations, New York, 1973 ST/ECA/190.
3. Excluding intra-group trade of multinational enterprises.
4. Report of the Group of Eminent Persons on the Role of Multinational Corporations in World Development and International Relations, United Nations, 1974.
5. In this connection, attention is drawn to the *Guidelines for International Investment* prepared by the International Chamber of Commerce.
6. These include providing a forum for the presentation and exchange of views of governments, inter-governmental and non-governmental organizations about the impact of multinationals on world development; undertaking work leading to the adoption of specific agreements in selected areas relating to the activities of multinationals; conducting inquiries, making studies, preparing reports and organizing panels for facilitating a dialogue among the parties concerned; and promoting a programme of technical co-operation, including training and advisory services, aimed, in particular, at strengthening the capacity of developing countries in their relations with multinational corporations. Now Commission on Transnational Corporations.
7. COM 73 1930, Brussels 9 11 73.

The Emergence and Future of German Multinationals.

Dr. Brij Kumar and Prof. Dr. Horst Steinmann *

1. Introduction

The advent and emergence of the multinational corporation as a socio-economic entity which undertakes foreign direct investments, i.e. which owns, controls and manages within a global business policy production facilities abroad[1] has been by and large regionally restricted to within the American and English economies. Indeed US and British firms accounted for more than 75% of all international assets at the end of the sixties[2]. Admittedly renowned continental firms like Royal Dutch Shell, Unilever, Philips, Nestle and a couple of others can be seen as outstanding examples of "truly" multinational corporations. Nonetheless, considered on the whole they are more of an exception than the rule in the array of "multis" of Anglo-saxon origin. The relatively minor role played by continental European firms in shaping the world of multinational corporations and international business applies even more to German enterprise.

Production abroad is by no means an alien phenomenon for many German companies. Siemens for instance had shifted more than 50% of its production to foreign facilities even prior to World War I.[3] And the chemical giant Bayer was running an aniline plant in the United States as early as 1865, just two years after it was established in Germany.[4] However, considering Germany's economic potential as a whole and especially her exporting strength, one would expect more vitality from German enterprise on the multinational scene than manifested by her foreign direct investments in the past. Whereas British and American foreign direct investments in the years 1965 to 1969 averaged around 5% and 7% respectively of their gross national investments in assets, Germany's corresponding figure in this respect was negligible.[5] While countries like Switzerland, Netherlands and Great Britain each derived more than 1% of their gross national product during the sixties from income earned by their multinational corporations abroad, Germany's income earned on foreign direct investments in the whole decade 1961 – 1971 totalled a meagre 1.2 billion DM as against a gross national product of 763 billion DM in the year 1971 alone. Also seen in terms of total percentage of gross national product German direct investments abroad ranged merely 3.1% in 1971 with corresponding figures of the United States and Great Britain hitting as high as 8.2% and 16.7%. Undoubtedly German enterprise in general has been in the past and is even today basically domestic oriented in production as compared to enterprise of other industrialized western nations. On the other hand German enterprise is perhaps more dependent on foreign markets for its sales than enterprises of other origin. This relatively high export orientation of German industry is best manifested by its export coefficient, i.e. in the percentage share of exports in the gross national product: With an (total) average export coefficient of 19.2% for the period 1965 – 1974 Germany ranked first as an exporting nation among all countries of the world (Britain 16.9% and USA 4.4%).[6]

How can one explain this facet of German enterprise as having on the whole the highest export (and total foreign trade) involvement in the world and yet a comparatively low commitment of production abroad? Indeed considering the irrefutable links between trade flows and foreign investment[7], especially in the sense that the former have always been the initial stage in the evolution of the latter[8], and on the other hand the latter play a major part in inducing the

*Management Institute, Friedrich – Alexander University of Erlangen – Nurberg, Erlangen, West Germany

former[9] one would expect a somewhat more balanced relationship between the two than what is to be found among German enterprise.

The explanation of what seems to be a phenomenon unique for German enterprise is to be sought in historical factors extending from the pre war and post war eras.

Pre war era

There is historical evidence that many multinational corporations of British, Dutch, Belgian or French origin emerged directly or indirectly from what we can call the colonial enterprise, which "although primarily concerned with trade and raw materials exploitation in the colonies, also got involved, albeit in a small way, in the manufacture of finished goods required for consumption in the home country or re-export from the home country".[10] Apart from the fact that the evolution of a large number of European multinational corporations can thus be traced back in some way or the other to business and investment in the colonies (e.g. Unilever, Metal Box, Royal Dutch Shell, Dunlop[11]), economic engagement of imperial powers in the colonies led toward a "foreign outlook and orientation" of business in general, thus laying down the path for extensive investment abroad.

Germany on the other hand was one of the few European powers which during the height of colonial epoch in the 19th and early 20th century possessed no colonial empire and therefore neither colonial enterprise nor the general business outlook congenial to foreign investment and production. However, as an advanced industrialized nation, with in fact excess capacities in her factories, Germany had to seek foreign outlets for her products, thus building up a traditionally strong export economy.

The emergence of German based multinational corporation seems furthermore to have been originally deterred by the fact that German industry maintained its basic structure of small and medium scaled enterprise for a long time.[12] As Wilkens has shown, the emergence of multinational corporation, especially the U.S. based is also historically connected with the evolution of the (big) corporation as such, which got under way on quite a large scale in the early part of the century in the United States.[13] This process which generally made companies financially and productwise potent and thus susceptible to foreign engagement, could hardly bear much fruit in an economy like Germany, imbued with traditional structures of family and artisan enterprise. While these enterprises generally lacked resources, especially trained personnel and management know how as well as an open mindedness[14] pertinent for foreign engagement, they had on the otherside often an intricate product knowledge at their disposal, less overheads, were flexible and quick on the trigger, thus possessing qualities favourable for competitive selling abroad and securing export markets.

Post war era

In the period after World War II when multinational corporation and foreign direct investments of major industrialized nations of the western world really picked up momentum, Germany again lagged behind. Several major reasons — basically economic and psychological — can be pinpointed for this post war development:

- In the first place German industry was basically not allowed to conduct foreign direct investment as late as 1952. Even after that investment abroad was restricted to projects with evidence of foreign exchange income. These and other similar restrictions were lifted stagewise; full liberalization of foreign investment for German industry was established only in 1961 with the enactment of the Foreign Trade Act (Außenwirtschaftsgesetz[15] and Außenwirtschaftsverordnung).
- Secondly, German industrial potential and resources were required in the country itself for rebuilding the war torn economy. Enterpreneurs found in the home market enough possibilities for commitment of resources and over and above excellent growth opportunities.

These opportunities were enhanced by the fact that western Europe liberalized foreign trade with the constitution of the Common Market during the fifties, thus making exports the easier and less risky method of serving foreign markets than production abroad.[16]

- Thirdly, German industrial activity abroad in the post war era was hampered greatly by psychological barriers which investors faced. In most cases this activity would have had to take place in former "enemy territory".

And then German investors for quite some time did not quite get over the shock that during the war and the aftermath German assets abroad worth about 20 Million Reichsmark had been expropriated by the allied powers as war reparation.[17] Indeed this was just about the total of German assets and property abroad prior to the war. Connected with these expropriations was also the overseas use of confiscated brand names and trade marks which made German firm names and products more difficult to use abroad.[18]

2. From exports to international production: A short analysis of German direct investments

Overall development of German direct investments

When Germany took up foreign direct investments again in 1952, its total assets abroad after expropriation were estimated at around 2–2.5 billion DM. These assets were mainly located in Switzerland, Portugal, Argentinia, Columbia, India, Pakistan and South Afrika.[19] Even with its over 20 billion RM before the war Germany had never been (for reasons discussed above) real competition for traditional capital exporting countries, now after expropriations it was flung right out of any comparison. Over and above, the assets left over after the war were not included in the new (post war) statistics. So officially and practically Germany began foreign investments in 1952 from scratch. According to the latest figures available total German direct investments abroad as per June 1976 amounted to 44.7 billion DM.[20] This amount is still at quite a distance from the United States and Britain (in 1970 258.9 billion DM and 73.4 billion DM respectively).[21] It is also — as demonstrated earlier — still relatively insignificant in terms of its contribution to Germany's total economic potential. And yet the amount is spectacular in terms of rate of growth, which is the highest in the world. This development can be classified in 3 major phases.[22]

- The first phase between 1952–1961 is characterized by gradual growth (average annual flow of direct investments in the period 1956 to 1961: 570 million DM).
- The second phase 1962–1965 began with an abrupt rise of investments as against the first phase (investment flow 1962: 1113 million DM). Then the flow remained constant until 1965 (average flow in this period: 1119 million DM annually).
- The third phase 1966–1975 is characterized by extremely high investment flows.[23] Especially in the period 1972–1975 annual direct investments averaged 5129.7 million DM. Average annual flow for total period (1966–1975) was 3870 million DM. 77% of all (post war) direct investments have taken place in this phase. Mid 1976 total German direct investments abroad (44.7 billion DM) for the first time exceeded total foreign investments in Germany (44.3 billion DM).[24]

Even though the relationship of direct investments to exports is still rather unbalanced and strongly in favour of the latter, a shift of orientation toward more of the former — although very gradual — cannot be overlooked (Table 1).

Table 1: Economic relevance of German foreign direct investments (and exports)[25]

Year	Ex: GNP (%)	DI: GNP (%)
1970	18.3	3.0
1971	17.9	3.1
1972	18.0	3.2
1973	19.2	3.5
1974	23.1	3.7

Ex = Exports
GNP = Gross national product
DI = Total direct investments abroad

Regional distribution

In terms of regional dispersion, German firms maintain, according to latest figures, operations in over 125 countries of the world. The emphasis there is clearly in western Europe and especially in countries of the EEC (Table 2), with France heading the list.

Table 2: Regional Distribution of German direct investments (mid 1976)[26]

Region	Direct investments Mill. DM	%
Europe	26,153.	58
thereof:		
EEC	15,836.2 (61%)	
Africa	2,733.3	6
Asia	1,759.4	4
America	13,833.4	31
thereof:		
North America	7,959.3 (58%)	
Latin America	5,874.3 (42%)	
Australia and Oceania	264.3	1
Developed Nations	31,399.0 (70%)	
Less Developed Nations	13,313.4 (30%)	

An interesting trend is the increasing importance of North America especially the United States for German direct investments. Since 1971 assets of German firms in this region have almost doubled and according to latest analyses this trend is here to stay.[27]

A further aspect is the distribution in developed and less developed regions of the world. Figures show that German firms, like their counterparts in the the US and Britain, prefer operations in the developed areas.

The proportion of investment among these two regions has remained constant for more than a decade.

Distribution by branch of industry

Out of the total of 44.7 billion DM German direct investments recorded mid 1976, 78% were located in industry, 21% in the tertiary sector (Commerce, banking and transportation) and the rest in agricultural business. Table 3 shows the split up of German foreign investments by branch of industry.

Table 3: Distribution of German direct investments by branch of industry (mid 1976)[28]

Branch of industry	Direct investments Mill. DM	%
Industry total	34,451.7 (78%)	
Thereof:		
Petroleum	2,789.9	8
Chemical	8,445.3	24
Electrical	4,670.8	13
Iron and Steel	3,661.0	11
Automobile	2,811.9	9
Mech. engineering	3,527.1	10
Others	8,545.7	25

By in large of Germany's direct investments abroad have been transacted by and in the chemical-pharmaceutical industry. The structure shown in the table has by and large remained unchanged ever since Germany took up direct investments abroad on a mentionable scale.

3. The multinationalization process

The preceding sections highlighted some major aspects of Germany's involvement abroad via direct investments. Obviously this involvement is nothing else but a reflection of total activity of German multinational enterprise. In order to understand this development as shown in the previous chapters as well as to be able to make some predictions about future trends it is therefore necessary to trace out some pertinent issues crucial to German multinational corporation. The issues to be discussed in this context are:

- Multinationalism of German (multinational) corporations;
- Some major factors behind the trend toward rapid expansion of German multinational corporations;
- Prefered patterns of multinational management among German enterprise.

1. Multinationalism of German Corporations

The question raised in this issue is simply: "how multinational" are German (multinational) corporations? We have attempted to tackle this question on the basis of quantitative criteria depicting the average foreign business commitment and involvement of seven well known German multinational corporations belonging to those three branches of industry which top the list in direct investments (Table 3): Bayer, Hoechst and BASF (Chemical-pharmaceutical), Siemens and AEG-Telefunken (Electrical) and Mannesmann and Krupp (Iron and Steel). The criteria we have chosen to illustrate multinationalism are as suggested by Hederer et al:[29]

- percentage share of total corporate resources involved in foreign subsidiaries (e.g. share of investment, manpower);
- relative contribution of subsidiaries' activities toward achievement of overall corporate goals (e.g. contribution toward corporate sales and income);
- number of countries in which production facilities are located.

We have summarized the results pertaining to the mentioned companies in the following table. In order to lay further ground for judgement of German based multinational corporations we have added a comparison of similar figures based on some selected multinational enterprise of American and British origin.[30]

Table 4: Multinationalism of Selected German Enterprise[31]

Criteria of multinationalism	German enterprises 1975	American British enterprises 1971/72
Share of total corporate *capital stock* employed in foreign subsidiaries	16%	42%
Share of total corporate *manpower* employed in foreign subsidiaries	22%	54%
Share of total corporate *sales* accrued from activities of foreign subsidiaries	18%	52%
Share of total corporate *income* accrued from activities of foreign subsidiaries	26%	44%
Number of *countries*	17	28

The figures show that even the largest and most economically substantial German corporations are behind in their multinationalism as compared to some important American and British Corporations. Nevertheless the importance of subsidiaries' activities in terms of resource commitment and goal achievement is quite evident. The considerable high average number of host countries can furthermore be seen as an evidence of a fair amount of "international orientation" pervasive in management of these German enterprises.

Of further interest in table 4 are also the figures relating to manpower and capital productivity: 16% of total corporate manpower generate 26% of total corporate income. For *one* the productivity of studied German multinational corporations abroad seems to be higher than that of their American and British counterparts (in our sample). Admittedly productivity comparisons strictly speaking may not vouch for objectivity without taking into account factors such as branch of industry and/or location. Nevertheless the figures are not completely void of a certain tendency assignable probably also to the fact that German multinational enterprise is relatively young of age and therefore more modern in production facilities. In spite of lesser experience in international business they are perhaps even managed a little more efficiently. *Secondly,* these figures denote that productivity, especially capital productivity in German multinational enterprise, is higher abroad than at home. The result as a matter of fact coincides with findings related to incomes of American and British multinational corporations.

Multinationalism of German enterprise on these lines is highest amongst those of the chemical-pharmaceutical industry followed by the firms belonging to the electrical and iron and steel industries. These observations tally with data regarding the flow of direct investments according to branch of industry (Table 3).

Taken by themselves the chemical giants BASF, Bayer and Hoechst compare quite

Table 5: Multinationalism of BASF, Bayer and Hoechst (1975)

Criteria of multinationalism	Average figures
Share of total corporate capital stock employed in foreign subsidiaries	26%
Share of total corporate manpower employed in foreign subsidiaries	41%
Share of total corporate sales accrued from foreign subsidiaries	35%
Share of total corporate income accrued from foreign subsidiaries	31%
Number of countries	35

favourably with the above mentioned American and British multinational corporations. On the other hand even leading firms of the iron and steel industry such as Krupp and Mannesmann show a fairly underdeveloped state of multinationalism. For instance the share of total sales accruable to their foreign operations in 1975 averaged just about 10% and the share of manpower employed to 15% on the average subsidiaries with production facilities were maintained in "only" 10 countries.[32]

2) Some major factors behind German direct investment outflows

The specific questions posed in the context of German direct investments are:

- what were/are the forces responsible for such a rapid pace of expansion of German multinational corporations?
- why is the German chemical-pharmaceutical industry on the whole and on the corporate level the leader in the multinationalization process?
- why does German multinational enterprise prefer investments in the EEC zone?

While we can put forth arguments out of economic theory which more or less answer all three questions alike e.g. the general growth motive,[33] there are other factors which, although also applicable to all of the issues posed, have relatively more specification for one or the other.

Rapid pace of expansion abroad

A major factor responsible for the tremendous rate of growth of German direct investments has been undoubtedly the fear of losing traditional export markets. By the time German economy got up on its feet again in the fifties, the traditional scene of the world market as being dominated by the exports of a couple of industrialized nations was changing. The developing nations were building up and protecting indigenous industries, and multinational corporations of British and American origin were on the march, in fact not only in the developing countries but world wide. Manufacturing and marketing on the spot were proving to be far more superior than exporting. The main advantage thereby being that the former was an aggressive strategy, which, in accordance with the findings of Brooke and Remmers, allowed the firms "more effective ways of using any technical superiority they have, and for spreading the cost of research".[34] There was sudden realization that (indispensible) export markets would be lost to indigenous business and multinational enterprise if the "multinational lag" was not overcome soon. This was the factor that triggered off the surgence of German foreign investments that followed in the early sixties. This factor continued and continues to the present day to determine decisively the rapid growth of German entrepreneurial activity abroad.[35]

Another key factor requiring attention as having been specifically influential to the influx of German direct investment abroad seems to lie in the development of the foreign exchange rates of the Deutsche Mark. The consolidation of domestic economy and perpetual balance of payment surplus led to a constant upward drift of the foreign value of the currency since the midsixties.[36] Thus German firms could benefit by falling costs of capital and assets in different countries.[37] Germany, which in the post war years itself had attracted large Pound and Dollar investments because of favourable exchange rates over the DM, now turned the tables by increasing its investments in the Sterling and Dollar areas on a considerable scale. As a matter of fact fifty percent of total German direct investments registered in North-America in 1975 were made after 1970.[38]

Leadership of the chemical-pharmaceutical industry in foreign investments

Even though there is no strict empirical evidence, it is reasonably clear that the leadership of the German chemical industry in foreign investment is best explained by the oligopolistic advantages it could gather in the past century or so. Historical conditions have thereby favoured the accumulation of innovative potential and know how in this industry more than anywhere else. For instance the continental blockade of Germany by Napoleon as well as the two world wars highly enhanced the necessity of substituting imported raw materials by developing synthetics indigenously; Bismarck's widely propagated and acknowledged social and health schemes provided tremendous impetus and incentive to the development of drugs and the drug industry.

As suggested by Fröhlich[39] it seems very reasonable to assume that from this point onward the development of foreign investment of the German chemical industry, more than any other branch, followed in adherence to Vernon's product life cycle concept.[40]

Know how thus accumulated, accelerated to a relatively high degree of product innovation in this branch of industry, thereby shortening the product life cycle. This determined the point when the German innovator's original lead began to be appropriated and imitated by others. Hence innovator's considerations whether average production costs abroad might be lower than the marginal costs of output delivered from Germany became more urgent in chemical enterprise than in firms of other branches.[41]

Preference for EEC zone

The answer to the question posed here is basically to be seen in context with the arguments delivered in the preceding cases. Over and above it is naturally the rich and growing market in the EEC countries which attracts German multinational enterprise.[42] Further reasons worthwhile considering are:

- Liberal investment and trade policies within EEC countries;
- Liberal monetary and transfer policies within EEC countries;
- Multinational enterprise can select location within the European Community in such a way as to benefit simultaneously from common liberal policies and national differentials in economic affairs, e.g. national taxation, fiscal policy etc.;
- The well developed infrastructure throughout the European community allows multinational enterprise a good deal of mobility and flexibility in case of felt national restrictious, e.g. labour laws and labour unrest.[43]
- Geographical nearness of location and cultural empathy of business environment.

3) Multinational Management

Due to limitations of space we shall restrict our discussion to the core question of multinational management: What are the general management pattern and outlook in German multinational enterprise in handling the conflict between fragmentation and unification of world wide operations?

As suggested by Fayerweather the determinants of this basic issue are diversity of environments on one hand and parent-company capabilities as well as global structure on the other.[44] Considering this, the situation in the German multinational enterprise at the moment seems in general to be characterized by a greater degree of fragmentation than their US and even British counterparts which generally favour a more unified pattern of operations abroad.[45]

Now this situation does not necessarily mean that German multinational enterprise is basically more openminded toward its foreign subsidiaries in terms of autonomy than U.S. or British. Indeed considering that German management has often been alleged as being authoritarian,[46] one would expect to find a more unified pattern. The fact is, however, that the choice is by pure necessity. On one hand we can identify quite strong unifying influences in German multinational enterprise. So for instance the parent companies capabilities like technology, productive and product know-how are in the leading German multinational industries viz chemical-pharmaceutical and electrical and electronics very sophisticated and based on extensive research and development concentrated in headquarters. Thus subsidiaries are often part of a company that is much influenced by technological development, and hence impelled to a closer i.e. unified relationship.[47]

Apart from these company characteristics there are also others which exert a considerable pressure toward unification of foreign operations. The most important is the corporate attitude and philosophy regarding multinational activity. German multinational enterprise has been in the past and to some extent still is very much disinclined and reluctant to see and call itself as such although economic criteria by all measures leave no doubt about its status. It is symptomatic of this attitude that for instance the chairman of the board of managing directors of Siemens,[48] Dr. Bernhard Plettner denied in an interview quite categorically that the firm be perceived as a multinational corporation. And Dr. Zahn, chairman of the board of managing directors of Daimler-Benz[49] stated on the occasion of listing the company shares on the Zurich stock exchange in January 1977: "We do not apprehend ourselves as a multinational corporation. We are essentially a national (German) enterprise. . . ."[50]

This attitude is probably attributable partly to historical circumstances and partly to the fact that the emergence of German multinational enterprise coincided with the phase when the multinational corporation in general was being critisized worldwide. This attitude seems then a reaction to immunize the company's image. What ever the reason behind this corporate outlook, it is a strong pressure toward drawing and keeping close of foreign subsidiaries to parent company policies and strategies.

Nevertheless fragmentation influences (at least at present) seem to be quite at par with the above mentioned unifying influences in German multinational enterprise. Above all one must keep in mind that German multinational corporation is young of age. Lack of experience and experienced personnel in headquarters as well as in subsidiaries to handle and manage foreign operations is therefore common. At this stage it seems to be rather an appeasement to manage and organize operations abroad without close control from headquarters or coordination among subsidiaries.[51] As a matter of fact many German multinational firms at this stage do not possess an adequate organizational setting to materialize a greater integration and unification of foreign activities even if they wished.[52] At this stage of maturity and multinationalism most German firms organize their foreign activities on the basis of the International Division. The product group organization or the global organization, which allows far more unification of activities abroad,[53] is suitable presently only for a handful of the largest of the German multinational corporations.[54]

4.   Some aspects of future development

In the preceding we have identified some basic characteristics of German multinational enterprise; in the following discussion we shall now attempt to outline their future development. The emphasis of the analysis shall thereby lie on some new dimensions which in our opinion will be predominant in shaping the future of these basic characteristics of German multinational enterprise.

1)   Economic conditions at home

The role of social legislation

A recent bulletin published in almost all important newspapers in Germany confirmed a development which industrialists all over the country had suspected for a long time: total labour costs in German industry were reported as being the highest among the six largest industrial nations of the world. With 17 DM total labour costs per hour German industry topped the list beating the USA.[55] It is not the hourly wages as such that have rocketed total labour costs so much (wages per hour are still the highest in the USA) but labour social and complementary costs, e.g. furlough gratuity or wages during (partial) lay-offs which have to be incurred by German industry in accordance with social legislation of the country.

These figures are but a mere indication of a development toward a more social setting of economy which German industry faces today and with which it will have to live within the future. As a matter of fact social legislation in Germany today is perhaps the most progressive in the western world next to Sweden. The above mentioned labour complementary costs or worker co-determination are only but a few of the measures which either have been already enacted or earmarked in the country's industrial policy.[56]

However, not all industry (at least for some time) is sympathetic toward the necessity of such measures in society, nor is all industry flexible enough to adjust to changes brought about by them. On the contrary, we have evidence that much of private enterprise in Germany today perceives prevailing and planned social measures as a burden for entrepreneurial activity. It is our impression that on these grounds many German firms will go in for foreign investments in the future mainly in order to avoid such burdens at home. Especially the small and medium sized enterprise, which is in most cases a family business, is likely to resort more and more to foreign investment because it sees its sovereignty jeopardized at home. It seems that in the future this motive for German firms to move abroad will supplement and in some cases even substitute the afore mentioned traditional reasons based on theory of direct investment.

The role of environment and ecology

The future structure of German direct investments abroad is yet likely to be influenced by another factor not foreseen in traditional economic theory, viz. prevention of pollution of environment. Germany can no longer handle new industrial activity in many sectors due to the overstraining of infrastructural amenities and danger of environmental pollution. Not only laws for prevention of pollution limit establishment and expansion of certain industries in many regions, but also mobilized public opinion.

Industries which are first and foremost affected are those which have a relatively high degree of emission of dangerous substances: gaseous, fluid or solid. Especially the chemical and iron and steel industries fall under this category which can only materialize their future expansion plans in foreign locations without such limitations. Subsequently two major implications arise from this development: Firstly foreign investments of the German iron and steel industry are likely to pick up momentum faster than they have before. Investments solely on these grounds have increased in the past and we can safely assume that foreign production of the German iron and steel industry together with the chemical industry is likely to lead the list of German foreign investments in the not too distant future.

The second implication of this development is that the future regional distribution of German foreign investments, especially of the chemical and iron and steel industry, is likely to experience a shift towards countries and regions of the world which are still free of pollution problems. Since most of these regions are located in the developing countries, German foreign investments especially of the iron and steel industry are apt to increase in this part of the world.[58] What is more many of these countries, e.g. Brazil, India, possess the essential raw materials so that together with new steel technologies that are available today the German steel industry will be in a position to compete on world steel markets with its overseas production. The start has already been made. Thyseen, Mannesmann and Krupp have already made first attempts to shift steel production from Germany or other European regions to developing countries like Brazil.[59]

2) Labour Unions and Industrial Relations' Policy

The emergence and growing activity of the German multinational enterprise is now gradually beginning to catch the interest of German labour unions. Thereby two outstanding problems determine the present scene. Firstly, there is the problem of exporting jobs. It was during the 1975 recession and the aftermath, that labour unions for the first time began critisizing German multinational corporations for investing abroad. However, the position of the unions in this question is ambivalent. On one hand they do fear that German firms maintaining operations abroad not only export jobs, but also allow them to avoid social legislation at home. On the other hand union economists also see the necessity of foreign investments especially because they also lie in their own interests: for instance German foreign investments ascertainably enhance exports from home and thus secure jobs at home.[60] German production abroad can also evidently contribute to reduction of the contingent of foreign workers in the domestic industry and thus not only make jobs free, but also help to reduce social conflict in the country.

Secondly there is the problem of control of workers' interests in the multinational corporations. As seen by the German unions, multinational corporations possess the possibility of manipulating workers in the sense that they can threaten to shift production from one country to another. In fact this strategy is suitable to play workers off in different countries against each other.[61]

In the face of these problems and the potential dangers that German unions see in the concentration of capital, which is evident in the multinational movement, the top association of German labour unions (Deutscher Gewerkschaftsbund) chalked out at its 9th congress in 1972 a series of demands aimed at curbing the scope of control of multinational enterprise.[62] Some of these demands were the right to strike and to arrange strikes for all entities of German multinational corporations (i.e. for the parent company *and* the subsidiaries abroad), introduction of democratic control and worker participation in management on a global basis, stronger influence of workers in all subsidiaries in shaping their job environment, etc.[63]

Naturally the difficulty in practical implementation of such demands lies in the very fundamental fact that multinational enterprise derives its power from unified operations in diverse environments. In other words the situation is characterized by a single block of corporate interests facing disunited national — and what is more — dissipated worker interests. Nevertheless such demands reflect the beginning of change in management and control structures of German multinational enterprise. As a matter of fact, the chances of realizing such social innovations have increased ever since the European Federation of Labour Unions became involved in the matter. It is hoped that with the support of this organization some consensus among member national unions can be achieved thus paving the way for the incorporation of effective worker control at least in multinational enterprise based and operating in the European Community.

Admittedly progress in the implementation of worker control in multinational enterprise is slow inspite of the fact that various models have been developed[64] and the question has gained priority in international organizations like the ILO. However, we can safely assume that in the not too distant future decision making in multinational enterprise in terms of unification and fragmentation will not only be guided by corporate interests but by worker interests as well. Perhaps this causes the balance to sway toward more fragmentation of corporate policy since incorporation of worker interests can mean at least more allowance for local working conditions in strategic decision making.

3) Most country interests

A shift toward fragmentation of multinational corporate policy is also to be expected in the future on grounds of host country pressures. It is quite clear that one cannot automatically equate profit maximization for stockholders in one country with the welfare of consumers and workers in another. Therefore, multinational enterprise has to make more allowances for incorporation of host country interests in decision making. Although there has been a lot of discussion over this subject in the last couple of years, an effective solution has still to be found. As a matter of fact even the Guidelines for Multinational Enterprises recommended by the OECD in June 1976 were not according to expectations. The Guidelines recommend in a very vague fashion that multinational enterprise take into account in their decision making national laws and economic objectives of the host countries. This indeed is a minimal demand which does not need any explication. What is missing, however, is an organizational solution for the accomplishment of the demand.

What is rather needed in the long run then is an institutionalized incorporation of economic, social and political objectives of the host country into stragegic decision making of multinational enterprise. Obviously, this implies adequate representation of host country officials in the highest decision making bodies of multinational enterprise and, of course, an international legislation to enforce this practice. Admittedly this process will mean an increasingly politicalization of multinational business. But then, it is not already politicalized when parent-country governments and multinational corporations collaborate to achieve their objectives, e.g. Ford in Brazil, United Fruit Company in Guatemale and ITT in Chile? The only difference is that in our case politicalization is from the host country side as well.

We think that it is quite realistic to assume that in the near future host countries will be compelled to seek institutionalized participation in strategic decision making of multinational enterprise and, that the latter will be obliged to allow for such modus vivendi. And our impression is that generally speaking German based multinational corporations are ideologically and psychologically more prepared to deal realistically with this situation than perhaps Americans or even other Europeans. After all German industry has had 25 years to get accustomed to industrial democracy at home on the basis of worker co-determination; an extension of such a model to its multinational corporations where participation of host country interests is similarly institutionalized could therefore be considered as a future development quite within the realm of feasibility.

Footnotes

1. In order to avoid lengthy and unappropriate discussions in this paper on what is to be understood under multinational corporation, we have simply presented what we think is the essence of various definitions and conceptions found in literature on the subject, e.g. M. Brooke and H. Remmers, *The Strategy of Multinational Enterprise,* London 1970, p. 5, R. Vernon, *Sovereignty at Bay,* New York 1971, p. 4.
2. J. Dunning, "The Multinational Enterprise: The Background", in: J. Dunning (Ed), *The Multinational Enterprise,* London 1971, p. 19.
3. E.H. Sieber, "Die multinationale Unternehmung, der Unternehmenstyp der Zukunft", in: *Zeitschrift für betriebswirtschaftliche Forschung,* 22 (1970), p. 414.
4. M. Holthus, R. Jungnickel, G . Koopmann, K. Matties und R. Sutter, *Die deutschen multinationalen Unternehmen.* Frankfurt 1974, S. 1.
5. H. Krägenau, "Entwicklung und Forderung der deutschen Direktinvestitionen", in: H. Scharrer (Ed), *Förderung privater Direktinvestitionen,* Hamburg 1972, p. 479.
6. Based on data in: Statistisches Jahrbuch, *op. cit.,* p. 649 and p. 696 and M. Holthus et al., *op. cit.,* p. 18.
7. D. Robertson, "The Multinational Enterprise: Trade Flows and Trade Policy", in: J. Dunning (Ed), *op. cit.,* p. 18.
8. J. Behrman, *Some Patterns in the Rise of the Multinational Enterprise,* Chapel Hill N.C., 1969 p. 42; W. Dymsza, *Multinational Business Strategy,* New York 1972, p. 7.
9. For a theoretical treatise on this relationship see e.g. D. Robertson, *op. cit.,* p. 186. Empirical evidence is demonstrated e.g. in a recent study of 116 American multinational companies which shows that the sample's exports rose faster than did those of the average U.S. manufacturer during 1970 – 1973. *A Business International Special Research Study,* New York 1976, p. 5.

10. A. Phatak, *Evolution of World Enterprises,* New York 1971, pp. 4-5.
11. A. Phatak, *op. cit.,* p. 111 and following pages. For the evolution of many French multinational enterprises in this sense see C.A. Michalet and M. Delapierre, *The Multinationalization of French Firms* (Academy of International Business), Chicago 1975, p. 9.
12. It is interesting to note that even today in times of industrial concentration through mergers and amalgamations only 1% of all registered German companies (about 2 million in total) belong to the category of big enterprise. The other 99% is classified as small and medium sized business. Although admittedly the importance of big corporations like Siemens, Bayer, Krupp, Volkswagen etc. in terms of economic potential and power, by far exceeds their number in proportion, small and medium sized business represent an important factor in the German economy. They employ 56% of the working population and product 2/3 of the gross national product. *Nürnberger Nachrichten* 29.12.1976.
13. M. Wilkens, *The Emergence of Multinational Enterprise,* Cambridge Mass. 1970, p. 72.
14. We have used this term rather in Brysons's sense, that opportunities abroad are often lost because of blocks that are not recognized and that lie deep in our socialization process. These blocks ("hidden resistances") condition risk attitude, prejudice and other values in a way, which is detrimental to foreign engagement. G. Bryson, *Profits from Abroad,* New York 1964, p. 37.
15. *Deutsche Direktinvestitionen im Ausland.* (Eine Untersuchung der Handelskammer Hamburg) Hamburg 1969, p. 24.
16. G. Hederer, C.D. Hofmann and B. Kumar, "The Internationalization of German Business", in: *Columbia Journal of World Business,* Sept-Oct 1972, p. 39.
17. H. Krägenau, *op. cit,* p. 477. The estimate of 20 Billion RM quoted from H.-G. Meissner, Betriebswirtschaftliche Probleme von Auslandsinvestitionen, in: *Zeitschrift für Betriebswirtschaft,* 35, (1965), p. 714.
18. Bayer for instance can still neither use its firm's name nor its trade mark (Bayer cross) in the United States. M. Holthus, et. al., *op. cit.,* p. 10.
19. Deutsche Direktinvestitionen *op. cit.,* p. 24.
20. Runderlaß Außenwirtschaft Nr. 28/1976 (14.10.1976), Bundesministerium für Wirtschaft, Bonn 1976.
21. A word of caution is at point when comparing German direct investments with those of USA and Great Britain. The former represent the sum of investment flows to foreign countries only, where as the latter represent the total book value of all foreign operations, i.e. they include capital raised in the most countries as well as reinvested profits from operations. On this basis (and including the sum of 2–2.5 billion DM remaining after expropriation) the stock of German foreign investments would be higher than actually registered in official German statistics. However, even on this basis German investments abroad could hardly exceed those of USA and Britain. First of all the difference as such is extremely wide and secondly German (post war) industrial operations are relatively young, thus leaving them with lesser scope for capital raising locally and also reinvesting profits from foreign operations.
22. H. Krägenau, *op. cit.* p. 478.
23. The high nominal value of investments flows is of course partly also to be accounted for by inflation rates e.g. prices of German industrial goods between 1970–1975 rose by almost 35%. Statistisches Jahrbuch, *op. cit.,* p. 444.
24. Based on data in Runderlaß, *op. cit.*
25. Based on data in: Statistisches Jahrbuch *op. cit.,* p. 649 and 693, Runderlaß, *op. cit.*
26. Runderlaß, *op. cit.*
27. H. Giesecke, Ansturm auf den U.S. Markt, in: *Manager Magazin,* Dec. 1973, p. 115; H. Schlichtung and H. Krüger, *Deutsche Niederlassungen in den USA,* Frankfurt 1975, p. 14 and following pages.
28. Runderlaß, *op. cit.*
29. G. Hederer, B., Kumar und G. Müller-Heumann, Begriff und Wesensinhalt der internationalen Unternehmung, in: *Betriebswirtschaftliche Forschung und Praxis,* 22 (1970), p. 517.
30. These enterprises are: Ford, ITT, Standard Oil, Union Carbide, International Harvester, Eastman Kodak and British Tobacco.
31. Sources: Annual Reports of the mentioned Companies (1975), and *Multinational Corporation in World Development,* United Nations, New York 1973, p. 130.
32. Source: Annual Reports of Krupp and Mannesmann 1975.
33. M. Holthus et. al., *op. cit.,* p. 155.
34. M. Brooke and H. Remmers (1970) *op. cit.,* p. 234.
35. This can be seen in accordance with the traditional theory of direct investment, which suggests firms expand abroad to exploit their monopolistic advantage. S. Haygmer, *The International Operation of National Firms, A Study of Foreign Investment.* Ph. D. Dissertation (M.I.T.) Boston 1960; C. Kindleberger, *American Business Abroad,* New Haven 1969.

36. In the period 1965-75 the Deutsche Mark gained 53% percent in value over the British pound and 35 percent over the US-Dollar. *Statistisches Jahrbuch der Bundesrepublik* 1966 and 1976, Wiesbaden 1966 and 1976, p. 407 resp. p. 681.

37. Although the implied theoretical relationship between exchange rates and foreign investment is not totally compatible with Alibers "currency area phenomenon" for explaining direct investment, it does have it's roots therein. R. Aliber, "A Theory of Direct Foreign Investment", in: C. Kindleberger (Ed.), *The International Corporation,* Cambridge, Mass., 1970, p. 21.

38. Although these figures may not be, strictly speaking, empirical evidence of the implied relationship between the DM revalorization and German foreign investment, they do discern a certain tendency toward the validation of the argument.

39. F. Fröhlich, Multinationale Unternehmen. *Entstehung, Organisation, Management,* Baden-Baden 1974, p. 32.

40. R. Vernon, International Investment and International Trade in the Product Cycle, in: *Quarterly Journal of Economics,* 80, (1966), p. 190.

41. For similar considerations, see R. Vernon, "Future of Multinational Enterprise", in: C. Kindlesberger (Ed.) *op. cit.,* (1970), p. 375.

42. M. Holthus and G. Koopmann, Multinationale Unternehmen in der EWG, in: *Wirtschaftsdienst,* 55 (1975), p. 12.

43. We are using the terms "fragmentation" and "unification" in accordance with Fayerweather. Although it is difficult to define the terms exactly, one could say that the basic issue involved here is that of autonomy of foreign subsidiaries. J. Fayerweather, *International Business Management: A Conceptual Framework,* New York 1969, p. 133. Brooke and Remmers use the terms "open" and "close" to depict the some phenomenon (1970), *op. cit.,* p. 68.

44. J. Fayerweather, *op. cit.,* pp. 133-134.

45. M. Brooke and H. Remmers. *The Multinational Company in Europe,* London 1972, pp. 77-79.

46. So for instance the findings of Hartmann: "Time and again, the (German) 'Unternehmer' has proven to be uncompromising and insistent on undivided authority". H. Hartmann, *Authority and Organization in German Management,* Princeton, N.J. 1959, p. 105. See also R. Lewis and R. Stewart, *The Managers – A New Examination of the English, German and American Executive,* New York 1961, p. 171.

47. This tallys with the general findings of M. Brooke and H. Remmers (1970), *op. cit.,* p. 69.

48. Siemens was ranked no. 24 on the list of the 200 world largest multinational corporations. Multinational corporations, *op. cit.,* p. 130.

49. Daimler-Benz was ranked no. 31 on the same list.

50. See the article: "Daimler-Benz: Wir sind keine Multis", in: *Frankfurter Allgemeine Zeitung* (20.1.1977), p. 11.

51. For similar conclusions see G. Hederer, C.D. Hoffmann and B. Kumar, *op. cit.,* p. 40; B. Kumar, *Führungsprobleme internationaler Gemeinschaftsunternehmen in den Entwicklungsländern,* Meisenheim 1975, p. 188.

52. M. Holthus et al., *op. cit.,* p. 165.

53. M. Holthus et al., *op. cit.,* p. 165. This type of organization in German multinational enterprise corresponds with the patterns US and British multinational firms followed in their early stages. L. Wells, The Multinational Business Enterprise: What kind of International Organization, in: *International Organization,* 25 (Summer 1971), p. 451; R. Vernon, *A Decade of Studying Multinational Enterprise* (10th Annual Progress Report, Multinational Enterprise Project 1975, Harvard Business School), Boston 1976, p. 10.

54. M. Brooke and H. Remmers (1970), *op. cit.* pp. 31-34.

55. Industrielle Arbeitskosten im internationalen Vergleich 1970–1976. A Study of Institut der Deutschen Wirtschaft, Frankfurt 1977 (For comparison according to the same source: U.S. 16 DM per hour, Great Britain 7.50 per hour).

56. For a discussion for instance on worker co-determination in German industry see e.g. G. Schwerdtfeger, Mitbestimmung in privaten Unternehmen, Berlin 1973.

57. In a questionnaire survey of the medium sized industry conducted by the Chamb ers of Commerce and Industry Koblenz and Trier in 1975 most of the firms indicated their willingness to start production abroad mainly because they expected social burdens to increase in Germany. Auslandsinvestitionen und Mittelstand. *Eine Untersuchung der Industrie- und Handelskammer Koblenz und Trier,* Koblenz 1975, pp. 17-18. For further details on this issue see H. Steinmann, B. Kumar and A. Wasner, *Die Internationalisierung von Mittelbetrieben. Eine empirische Untersuchung in Mittelfranken,* Schriften zur Zeitschrift für Betriebswirtschaftslehre, Wiesbaden 1977, p. 56.

58. This tendency is likely to be pertinent also to multinational corporations of other origin. Last but not least plans to boost up production of iron and steel in the developing countries have been propagated by the United Nations; their materialization to a large extent will depend on greater multinationalization of iron and steel producers of the industrialized nations (UNIDO conference on problems of Iron and Steel Production in Developing Countries, Vienna Feb. 1977).

59. "Stahl von Rio"' *op. cit.*

60. The decision of Volkswagen to put up an assembly plant in the United States was accepted by the unions and worker representatives on the Advisory Board of the company only after the Chairman of the Management Board could show evidence that not only jobs were not endangered in Wolfsburg but in fact new jobs would be created because of increased exports.

61. E. Piehl, Thesen zu einer betriebsnahen Strategie der Gewerkschaften gegenüber den Multinationalen Konzernen, in: *Gewerkschaftliche Monatshefte,* 22 (1972), p. 42.

62. W. Spieker, Möglichkeiten des Arbeitnehmereinflusses in Multinationalen Unternehmen, in: *Gewerkschaftliche Monatshefte,* 24 (1973), p. 108.

63. W. Spieker, *op. cit.,* p. 108.

64. See for instance E. Piehl, *op. cit.,* and W. Spieker, *op. cit.,* p. 110.

THE FUTURE OF PUBLIC AND CO-OPERATIVE ECONOMY IN THE

ERA OF MULTINATIONAL CORPORATIONS

by Ferdinand LACINA and Eduard MÄRZ*

The history of public and co-operative economy is hardly less old than the history of European capitalism. It is true that Western Europe, especially France and England, was comparatively slow in the introduction of economic nuclei of a non-capitalist or anti-capitalist nature, if one disregards the early, mostly unsuccessful, experiments of the socialist utopians. The experience of Central Europe is, however, strikingly different. It will be remembered that public-economy enclaves are found in the Austria of Maria Theresa and Joseph II and in the contemporary Prussian kingdom. Their origin may be traced back in the main to three causes: public interest in new sources of revenue (tobacco and salt monopolies, etc.), considerations of industrial policy (manufacturing industries of Linz and Vienna) and considerations of State policy (postal administration).

In the 19th century, the State, the *Länder* and the municipalities took over a large number of services. The most spectacular example is provided by the railways, which were taken over by the authorities for a variety of reasons: military and strategic interests, a tariff policy taking the needs of the entire economy into account and, lastly, the promotion of regional interests. It was realized even at that time that the expansion and administration of certain branches of the economy, including particularly the railways, could not be governed purely by the principles of the market economy. A deficit in a particular enterprise was accepted if the resulting social benefits were valued more highly than the losses sustained by the enterprise. The same principles were later applied also to the health and educational services.

Another important motive behind the nationalization (or communalization) of certain economic functions was the desire of the State (and of its most prominent social classes) to prevent the formation of private monopolies. This applies particularly to the large utility companies (power, urban transport, telephone, water) which sooner or later became public property in all Western and Central European countries. Similar considerations are today also being applied to mining, metallurgy and the petroleum industry, because here, too, the danger of concentrations of economic power is particularly great.

During the world economic crisis industrial enterprises and banks in difficulties were taken over by the State, particularly in Italy, France and Austria. At that time the well-known national institute for reconstruction (I.R.I.) was created in Italy, while in France the railways and in Austria the most important bank were nationalized. The French State acquired supervisory powers over the petroleum industry. The wave of nationalizations after the Second World War was above all marked by the idea of planning. This is expressly referred to in the first Austrian nationalization law. The nationalized sector is also regarded as the backbone of planning in France. Similar economic and social considerations govern nationalization in the United Kingdom. On the other hand, planning in Sweden and the Netherlands is not accompanied by any noteworthy nationalization measures.

It may be noted in passing that a public monopoly is not automatically protected against the temptation of an abuse of economic power. Experience has shown that State monopoly enterprises have sometimes used their power over the market ruthlessly. They have also

*Scientific Consultants, The Credit Institute – Banking Association, Vienna, Austria.

occasionally shown a lack of interest in innovation and have given little attention to customer service. It was therefore recognized at a relatively early stage that the maintenance of traditional forms of legal organization for enterprises does not provide a suitable basis for the management of public enterprises. However, experiments with new institutional forms have been made only in the United Kingdom, and they have not entirely removed the shortcomings.

The American Challenge and the Oil Crisis.

In the past two decades, the industrial development in Western Europe has been governed mainly by two factors: the rapid expansion of the so-called multinational corporations and the massive transfer of income to the petroleum-producing countries as a result of the oil crisis. Let us first deal with the phenomenon of the multinational corporations, which has been the subject of much comment.

Even before the First World War, the concentration of American capital affected areas beyond the confines of the United States. By direct investments (i.e. founding subsidiaries and taking over existing enterprises), United States corporations were able to expand their power and influence step by step in Canada and in the advanced industrial countries of Europe. At the end of the Second World War and particularly after the establishment of the European Economic Community, the "American challenge" to use Jean-Jacques Servan-Schreiber's term, unmistakably gained strength. Towards the end of 1975, American investments totalled $133,200 million, $49,600 of which were placed in Europe. The bulk of these investments was concentrated in the capital-intensive growth sectors of the European community. It should be added that the net capital balance of the United States with Western Europe has been adverse for some time owing to the chronically adverse United States balance of payments. (Since 1973, when the US capital balance with Western Europe peaked at $-45,600 million, it has improved somewhat to $-41,000 million in 1975.) Nevertheless, the net increase of American investments in Western Europe in 1975 was $4,839 million compared with a net increase of direct West European investments in the United States of $1,906 million. However, the gap between American investments in Europe and European investments in the USA has continuously narrowed. In 1974 US investments in Europe were roughly three times as much as European investments in the USA, while a year later the difference was noticeably smaller. (Earlier figures are unfortunately not strictly comparable.)

The superior size of American corporations and their dominant position in many industries are such that American investments in Europe are likely to remain substantially larger in the foreseeable future. It is interesting to note that the spectacular depreciation of the American dollar has not reversed the trend, because United States subsidiaries in Western Europe are today financing expansion mainly with the aid of profits and bank credits. At the present stage, the export of American capital to Western Europe plays only a secondary part as an instrument of the "American challenge". As time progresses, West European as well as Japanese capital exports to the United States may well outstrip capital export in the reverse direction, for the two first named regions at present expand economically at a faster pace than the USA. (To give just one indication of future developments: according to an estimate of the US Department of Commerce the 200 biggest "non-US-corporations" had a turnover in 1964 which amounted to 45 percent of the 200 biggest US corporations; in 1974 their turnover measured up to 80 percent of the 200 biggest US corporations.)

The consequences of the oil crisis of 1973/74 cannot be fully gauged even today. The precarious trade and payments balances of many Western industrial countries were dealt a further heavy blow by the steep rise in the price of oil and some other raw materials. The weakened position of some countries has been reflected in declining production and in unemployment. There are signs, however, that almost all of the industrial countries are gradually adjusting to the new situation. (Especially noteworthy is the case of the United Kingdom which may well succeed to remedy its difficult balance of payments position in the space of two or three years.) The situation seems far more difficult in the non-oil developing countries which so far have been able to balance their accounts by borrowing from the oil-rich nations and even more from American banks. Since the latter have been heavy recipients of short term funds from some of the OPEC nations, their lending operations to the non-oil developing countries is an interesting aspect of the complex recycling mechanism set in motion by the events of 1973/74.

The sudden boon of increased oil prices faced the oil exporting countries with the problem of what rational use they were to make of the millions daily flowing into their coffers. As far as we can make out today, the income from oil exports is spent on larger imports of goods, short-term loans to foreign debtors and not least on portfolio investments in some of the large Western corporations. Direct investments have so far been made only in a few cases, because neither the Arab countries nor Venezuela nor Iran possess the managerial and technical knowledge to enter that field on a large scale. The well-known cases of Iran, Libya and Kuwait buying substantial minority interests in such great concerns as Krupp, Fiat and Mercedes-Benz were motivated to no small extend by the desire not to exercise managerial functions, but to learn how managerial functions are being exercised.

The rapid expansion of the multinational corporations, their dominant position in some European key industries and the new dangers of foreign control by the capital of the oil-exporting countries have induced the industrial countries of Western Europe to devise a number of direct and indirect methods of economic intervention. Certain strategies have been developed to maintain and expand independent economic positions: the merger and concentration of national enterprises under the guidance of public authorities, the promotion of new products and production methods by State credits and State participation, and the prevention of the sale of enterprises which are of key importance for industrial development. Two further aspects should be mentioned in this connection; some of the above measures have their origin in the desire of the public authorities to prevent crises and protect jobs; in addition, there is a tendency, particularly evident in Sweden and the United Kingdom, to combine measures of industrial policy with social aims, in other words to match greater industrial growth by a greater measure of industrial democracy. The following examples of State intervention in the economy of six Western European countries will illustrate these various motives and measures.

France.

It has been the declared aim of French economic policy for years to improve the industrial structure by direct and indirect State intervention and to strengthen the competitiveness of French enterprises by promoting amalgamation. The French authorities not only reorganize State participation in industry, including for example, the petroleum and chemical sectors and the aircraft industry, but they also promote concentration in many economic branches by massive State support. The most outstanding example for this is the French steel industry, in which not only amalgamations, but also major projects for co-operation have been initiated and endowed with considerable financial means. In 1966 the French government provided 2,800 million Francs for the reorganization of this industry, in 1973 the industrial complex in Fos received public moneys in the amount of 2,650 million Francs. In 1976 the French State came to the aid of the crisis-ridden steel industry with a subsidy in the amount of 1,400 million Francs. For the year 1977 3,000 million Francs are to be provided for the double purpose of maintaining employment and modernizing plant and equipment.

In recent times the reorganization of the telephone industry was carried out under the pressure of the French government. This is to provide the basis for a long-range concept of modernization of the hitherto underdeveloped telephone and communication system of France. The French Thomas-Brandt-CSF Company acquired subsidiaries of the Swedish corporation L.M. Ericsson and of the American ITT, and was thus capable to strengthen considerably its position in this branch, not at least through the conclusion of licensing contracts with the former owners.

The creation of a new legal form of association, the *groupement d'intérêt économique*, was an attempt to make it easier for medium-size and small enterprises to co-operate and to offer large enterprises a suitable method of organizing themselves for the joint operation of certain specialized production lines.

In 1970, the *Institut de développement industriel* (IDI) was founded with a share capital of FF 333 million by the State and by banks, most of them State-owned. The law requires the IDI "to strengthen, by temporary intervention, the capital base of those enterprises which suffer from a lack of capital of their own and thus to contribute to the more rapid growth of French industry". The capital has so far been increased to more than FF 500 million, the French State's share being 48 per cent, while the remaining 52 per cent is in the hands of 14 credit institutes. Up to the autumn of 1974, 70 enterprises received funds totalling FF 434 million, partly through direct participation of IDI in their capital and partly in the form of credits. The annual turnovers of slightly more than half of the enterprise supported in this manner are in the range of up to S 150 million, while those of 21 are up to S 600 million and 12 enterprises have still higher turnovers. The main beneficiaries are the metal-working and mechanical engineering sectors, and the building, food and electrical industries. In 1972 a subsidiary of IDI was founded to finance branches of French industrial enterprises abroad.

Towards the end of 1976 the IDI was promised to receive a yearly capital endowment of 120 million Francs by the French authorities. The capital stock of this holding company is supposed to reach 1,200 million Francs in 1980. The future primary activites of the IDI will be as follows: to secure the steady flow of capital to medium sized companies by acquiring property rights; to transfer foreign dominated enterprises into French ownership; and to reorganize individual branches of industry. Activities of the latter type are to be carried out on the basis of sectoral plans which are being drawn up by the IDI in close cooperation with the government or regional development agencies. The IDI has already acquired property rights in some important industries, such as agricultural machinery, auxiliary equipment for automobile and computers, and printing machinery.

The structural crisis in French coal mining, which caused the State-owned French Collieries to suffer ever greater losses, led to the attempt to widen the range of production by adding coal-based chemicals to it. The subsidiary founded for this purpose, the *Société Chimique des Charbonnages* (CdF-Chimie) which, with a turnover of nearly S 9,000 million is today the fourth largest chemical group of France, has recently succeeded in penetrating the petrochemical sector. The giants of the French chemical industry, Rhône-Poulenc, Pechiney-Ugine-Kuhlmann and CdF-Chimie, were reorganized and Ugilor, a manufacturer of acrylic fibres was associated with the chemical offspring of the French Collieries. The nationalized coalmining industry has succeeded in advancing into the production of construction material, synthetics and into the construction trade by setting up another subsidiary, the Société Industrielle et Commerciale de Charbonnages (SICCA).

Towards the end of 1974 a complete reorganization of the French automobile industry was initiated which was supported by the State with a loan of 1,400 million Francs. The State-owned Renault Company took over the well known lorry producer Berliot, hitherto connected with the Citroen concern, and combined it with its own lorry producer Saviem. The privately owned Peugeot Company acquired, in 1974, a minority share of the Citroen SA which produces light motor vehicles. In 1976 there was finally a complete amalgamation of the two automobile producers Peugeot and Citroen. Peugeot-Citroen have now a share of 37.5 percent of the French automobile market. Moreover, Peugeot has strong ties to the State-owned Renault Company through its cooperation agreement concluded in 1966. The lorry producers Berliot and Saviem dominate the French lorry market wtih a share of more than 50 percent.

Federal Republic of Germany

The total industrial property of the Federal Republic of Germany is estimated at 3,200 million DM in the year 1974. More than 400.000 employees are employed by State-owned subsidiaries in the industrial sector.

Through the merger of VEBA, in which the German State has a major share (43 per cent — the remainder of the capital is held by a large number of investors) with Gelsenberg AG, the efforts to establish a German petroleum corporation under public control were at least provisionally brought to a conclusion. The commentator in the Swiss *Weltwoche* summarizes the motives for this merger, for which the State made more than S 5,000 million available, as follows: "The Government in Bonn had always been the matchmaker, because it did not like the idea of a few multinational oil companies sharing 75 per cent of the German mineral oil market, while many small German companies had to be content with the remaining 25 per cent. There was always the unspoken fear that in an emergency the multinational corporations might give priority to the American or British over their German interests on the principle that charity begins at home, even if the subsidiaries of Esso, Shell or BP were joint stock companies constituted under German law. After the merger, VEBA-Gelsenberg became the largest concern in the Federal Republic, dealing not only in oil but having considerable interests in the electric power, inland shipping, chemical and fuel industries.

Furthermore, the State owns substantial property in the sectors of bituminous coal (9.7 percent of total production), steel (9.6 percent of total production) and aluminium (48.3 percent of total production). Through its minority holdings in the Volkswagen works (the Federal Republic and the Province of Niedersachsen own 20 percent each) the State has a share in the German production of automobiles of 27.3 percent. Moreover, by providing substantial financial aid, the Western German State supports private industrial enterprises primarily in the sectors of atomic energy, aircraft, shipbuilding and computers.

Sweden.

Sweden's State enterprises were amalgamated in 1970 in a holding company of *Statsföretag AB*. The largest member of this group, numbering about 35,000 employees, is the LKAB ore mining company. The holding company has interests in the most varied branches of industry, such as tobacco, cellulose, paper and steel, but also in the service industries (restaurants and hotels). In 1970, the pharmacies were nationalized and in 1971 a State corporation was established by the amalgamation of several pharmaceutical firms; this new entity manufactures roughly a quarter of all Swedish pharmaceutical products. Without the public paying much attention, the Swedish State acquired interests in the most varied sectors. It obtained participation in two oil prospecting companies, and has since 1973 controlled 50 per cent of AB Eiser, the textile firm. It has also amalgamated the State-owned *Sveriges Kreditbank* with the Credit Institute of the Postal Administration, thus turning it into the country's largest bank. In 1974 the State took over the majority of shares of the biggest Swedish brewery and assumed, in 1975, control over two shipyards (Götawerken and Eriksberg) which had encountered considerable financial difficulties.

Since 1973, the Pension Fund, which has hitherto contented itself with subscriptions to loans and the financing of credits for large projects, has been authorized to participate directly in Swedish enterprises. The most important step in this direction was the subscription to 5 per cent of shares newly issued by the Volvo motor vehicle company, making the Pension Fund the largest shareholder of that firm.

Great Britain.

The Conservative Heath Government took office in 1970 with the firm intention of reducing State influence on industry which had been greatly extended in six years of Labour administration. The Industrial Reorganization Corporation (IRC), formed for the purpose of State capital participation, was dissolved. Denationalization, however, was kept within fairly modest limits (the most important example is the sale of Thomas Cook and Sons, the travel agency, to a private capital group). The nationalization of the British steel industry was not reversed, and in 1971 the Conservative Government found itself compelled to nationalize yet another company. Rolls Royce, which had got into difficulty, could be saved from bankruptcy only by a State take-over.

Of even greater importance on grounds of principle is the Industry Act introduced by the Conservative Government in 1972, which provided for the financial support of private enterprises by the State up to a maximum of £550 million in each case, *inter alia,* also by the acquisition of shares. The Labour Government later summarized the principles of State intervention in industry in a White Paper, which was submitted to Parliament by the Ministry of Industry in August 1974. Central features of this programme are the establishment of the National Enterprise Board (NEB) and the ordering of the relationships between large enterprises and government authorities under "planning agreements".

One of the functions of the National Enterprise Board which was founded in 1975 is to act as a trustee of State-owned industrial holdings. At present, the most important of these corporations are the automobile producers British Leyland (with a public share of 95 percent) and Rolls Royce (100 percent), the tool producer Herberts (100 percent) and the electronic firm Ferranti (62.5 percent). The NEB holds a minority share in a number of companies, some of the better known of which are ICL (with a public share of 24 percent) and two important enterprises of the electrical equipment industry, Cambridge Instruments (28 percent) and Brown-Boveri-Kent (17.7 percent).

Through the acquisition of share capital the NEB is to facilitate the reorganization of industries and the creation of jobs in regions which have been affected by special economic difficulties. The NEB is permitted to acquire shares only to the extend of 30 percent. Should the management of a firm in question object to State participation at such a level, only 10 percent can be acquired by the NEB. Transactions which go beyond the above mentioned limits require a special consent of the government.

Thus a majority position was acquired, in 1976, in the important electronic firm Data Recording Instruments and minority positions in Twinlock, an office equipment producer, Child & Beney, a container producer and Reed & Smith, a paper manufacturer. Another interesting project in which the NEB participates is the "Anglo Venezuelan Railway Corporation" which was founded for the purpose of constructing a railroad in Venezuela and of providing the required railroad equipment.

In order to promote national interests in the realm of mineral oil production another State agency, the "British National Oil Corporation" (BNOC), was founded in 1975. The British government, with the aid of this corporation, seeks to obtain control over the companies exploring oil in the North Sea which are in their great majority in private and foreign hands. As a matter of principle, the BNOC is to be given the right to sell 51 percent of oil production. A first agreement was concluded with the Conoco-Gulf group in the beginning of 1976. It ensures that the BNOC take part in the decision making of the consortium as well as the right to purchase 51 percent, at a later date even up to 57 percent of oil production at market prices. A similar agreement was concluded with the British Petroleum Corporation of which a minority of shares is now owned by the British State and with the Murmak Oil Corporation. In the beginning of 1977, after long preliminary negotiations, an agreement was signed with the Shell-Esso group too which controls the biggest North Sea oil field of Brent.

Italy

The public sector has made a great contribution to the expansion of the Italian economy. In 1972, its share in the total investment was around 39 per cent, while its share in total employment was only about 13 per cent. Starting with the control of certain raw material industries, the Italian State holding corporations have for some time conducted a policy of penetration into the consumer goods and service sectors. Among very recent initiatives, mention should be made particularly of the work of GEPI, which was assigned the task of reorganizing and restructuring private enterprises by acquiring participations in them. Up to the year 1976 the GEPI has made investments of a structural nature in a total of 97 enterprises with more than 40,000 employees, concentrating mainly on the clothing industry, electronics, shipyards and agricultural machines.

For the reorganization of these enterprises a sum of 10,000 million DM were provided, three quarters of which were directly contributed by the State. In the mean time 16 of the reorganized companies have been returned to private ownership. One of the most important cases of this kind was the well known automobile firm Innocenti which once was part of the British Leyland concern.

In the recent past the strategy of the Italian State enterprises has been subjected to sharp criticism, especially by that part of the Italian left which has up to now been a steady supporter of the public sector. The criticism focused on what was believed to be a process of bureaucratization and serious shortcoming in economic management, above all on the charge of the pursuit of specific interests unrelated to the problems of the development of society as a whole.

In order to meet this criticisms, a law for the reorganization of industry was prepared and has been subject of parliamentary discussion in the beginning of 1977. It provides for the merger of all existing public financial agencies within the next four years which then will have access to financial means to the extend of 7,500,000 million Lira, 4,500,000 of which are to be set aside for state enterprises.

Moreover, public participation in the various holding companies is to be reorganized. These measures have become necessary as a result of difficulties with which the EGAM holding company has been confronted. In this way the 18,200 employees working in enterprises in which the EGAM has a share are to retain their jobs. A new government body whose creation was demanded by the parties of the left will be responsible for the allocation of financial means on the basis of sectoral investment plans.

The Austrian Situation.

The importance of public enterprise in the Austrian economy may be described with the aid of a recently published study.

In the 466 public enterprises investigated, around 404,000 persons were employed, i.e., about 18 per cent of all workers and employees. The main spheres of activity by these enterprises were utilities and transport (86 per cent of all those employed in those sectors work in public enterprises), credit and insurance (43 per cent) and industry and trade (20.5 per cent). Within industry, for which we will now give further particulars, public enterprises operate mainly in mining (quarries and underground mines) (57.5 per cent of all those employed work in public enterprises), metal production and working (34 per cent) and chemical industry (25 per cent).

Through the amalgamation of State participation in industry in the Austrian Holding Company ÖIAG and the reorganization of nationalized enterprises by sectors, the preconditions were created for a more active role of the nationalized industry.

The organizational form of the nationalized iron and steel industry was decisively changed in several stages: in 1973, a large enterprise of international rank was created by a merger of the mass steel manufacturers VÖEST and Alpine, with which the two nationalized high-grade steel manufacturers Gebrüder Böhler and Schoeller-Bleckmann were associated as subsidiaries. The two State-owned shipyards were amalgamated and joined to the VÖEST-Alpine concern. During the current year, the three hitherto independent nationalized high-grade steel makers were amalgamated to form the Vereinigte Edelstahlwerke AG. In order to avoid a lack of co-ordination in the petrochemical sector, the State enterprises ÖMV AG and the Chemie-Linz were associated to form a joint venture. Since 1974, the main State enterprises in the non-ferrous metal sector have also been concentrated in the Vereinigte Metallwerke AG.

The advantages of a mixed economic system have become particularly evident at a time of recession, where countries with a clear dominance of private capital (such as, for example, the Federal Republic of Germany) have seen mass dismissals, while Austria has been maintaining its policy of full employment even during this period. Long-term development plans enable the nationalized industry to maintain a high level of investment and to influence thus the entire investment climate favourably. The greater stability of the nationalized industry is not only a consequence of the above-mentioned measures of reorganization, but also of the offensive strategy pursued by some enterprises in this sector. In recent years, the State has penetrated new branches of the manufacturing industry, such as plastics processing, heating technology, carpets, engineering, construction of large industrial installations, etc. Despite these attempts at a well-planned investment policy in the State sector, the weak point of Austrian industrial policy must be sought in the fact that most of the measures are aimed at a higher level of investment, while the structure of investments has been more or less neglected. Fortunately there have been signs in recent years that this defect is to be made good by greater emphasis on qualitative targets whenever use is made of industrial promotion policy tools. When public resources are made available for investments, such as have been announced by the Government, subsidies will be granted particularly for large-scale industrial projects which are to be selected on the basis of their value for the labour market and for industrial growth.

In the long run, however, industrial policy will hardly be able, with such improvised measures, to achieve its aims of increased economic independence, radical structural improvement and curbs on excessive foreign control. The following steps appear to us today to be particularly urgent: the establishment of a corporation for capital participation, such as has long been asked for (on the model of the French IDI) by the amalgamation and expansion of existing industrial promotion institutes; the co-ordination of the nationalized industry with the large State banking concerns, which would *inter alia* have to be supported by a central investment planning authority;

public participation in enterprises whose continued existence and economic viability is to be assured by the massive use of State resources.

Development Prospects for European Public Economy.

What has been said will make it clear that European public economy has entered a period of rapid expansion in recent years. The reasons are fairly obvious: in the first place, most countries apparently desire to counter the massive penetration of foreign capital (by multinational corporations or oil-producing States buying up existing firms) through a more active role of the State in the economy. Hardly less important is the increasing pressure to pay greater attention than hitherto to collective needs. Certain crises, such as environmental pollution, the collapse of urban transport in the large towns, and also the bottlenecks in the supply of raw materials and energy have thrown doubt on the rationality of private economy in many sectors and led to increased efforts to solve these problems within the framework of public economy. Lastly, mention must be made of the stabilizing function of the public sector, which is of particular importance during the current world economic recession, the worst since the Second World War. The maintenance of a large volume of investment and employment in the public sector, which is less subject than the private sector to the compulsion of short-term profitability, represents, next to the labour policy tools, one of the main methods available to the State to combat the unfavourable effects of market fluctuations. The take-over by the State of enterprises requiring reorganization, a measure often adopted as a result of public pressure, may at first sight appear to be merely a "socialization of losses" sustained in the private sector. As the development since the world economic crisis of the 1930s has shown, however, such take-over may be the beginning of far-reaching structural changes in the national economy. One example of this is the Italian IRI, which was originally founded to reorganize private enterprises and has demonstrated considerable dynamic force since the War.

For these reasons, a further expansion of the public sector, which will *inter alia* penetrate new branches of the economy, may be expected. The trend is reinforced by the ever more frequent demand for a remodelled work process and the participation of workers and employees in management, a demand for the satisfaction of which, we believe, public enterprisees are better able to develop suitable forms of organization than private corporations.

THE FUTURE ROLE OF THE WESTERN AND

COMECON COUNTRIES' MULTINATIONALS IN

WEST-EAST-WEST TRANSFER OF TECHNOLOGY.

Jozef Wilczynski*

The disparity of technological levels between the East and the West[1] has been one of the generally accepted facts of East-West relations.[2] The Eastern technological lag can, of course, be partly explained on historical grounds. Whilst industrial revolutions began in the leading Western countries (England, France, Germany, the USA, Sweden, Japan) during 1780–1880, the real leap in the USSR did not occur before the late 1920s and in Eastern Europe (Czechoslovakia and the German DR excepted) till the late 1940s.

The other explanation is more fundamental, inherent in the Socialist economic system of the traditional type, as conceded by a Polish economist:

> . . . the Socialist economy was not able to develop effective methods for the stimulation of technological progress and a further utilization of technology in the interest of a more dynamic growth.[3]

The absence of private enterprise, the limited scope for the acquisition of private property bureaucratic controls and the rewards to the management incommensurate with the risk involved are not conducive to innovations. These inhibitions existed in their extreme under the old centralized, directive system of planning and management prevalent up to the early 1960s (early 1950s in Yugoslavia).

Thus to give evidence of the "gap" derived from Western as well as Socialist sources. In Hungary in the mid-1960s 39 per cent of the products of the machine-building industry was officially classed as partly obsolete, 47 per cent as completely out of date and only 14 per cent measured up to world technological standards.[4] The replacement production cycle of new products in the electronic industry in Poland as of the early 1970s was 13.5 years, compared with 1-3 years in the USA;[5] as reported in 1971, the average price per kilogram of Polish lathes exported to capitalist countries was $1.20, but for the imported lathes on the average Poland paid $5.30.[6] In the USSR in 1962, the lag in civilian technology in different branches of the economy ranged from 5 to 40 years behind the USA, and the lag was in fact greater in that year than in 1940;[7] in 1965 the proportion of the products of the machine-building industry which was below world quality standards was at least 31 per cent.[8]

But even Czechoslovakia and the German DR — industrially the most advanced Socialist countries, with a long technological tradition — have been lagging behind the West. In Czechoslovakia in the late 1960s, 61 per cent of Czechoslovak engineering exports was officially rated below the quality levels demanded in world markets;[9] at the same time, the production of building materials with regard to quality range and *per capita* figures was 5-15 years behind the levels in advanced capitalist countries.[10] The average production replacement cycle of technologically new products in industry in Western countries is about six years, but in the German DR in the early 1970s about one-half of the industrial products had been introduced six or more years before.[11]

*Associate Professor of Economics at the Royal Military College of Australia, University of New South Wales, Duntroon, Canberra. This paper was originally presented to the 47th Congress of the Australian and New Zealand Association for the Advancement of Science, Hobart, Australia, May, 1976, and has since been published in *Acta Oeconomica*, Vol. 15, Nos. 3-4.

Technological levels can also be indicated by the extent of computerization and the production of advanced chemicals. Although in 1970 Comecon claimed 33 per cent of the world's industrial output,[12] it had only 6 per cent of the world's stock of computers (mostly of first and second generations at that). In that year the number of computers per one million of population in the European Comecon countries ranged from 2 in Romania and 5 in Bulgaria to 21 in the German DR and 23 in the USSR; at the same time, the world average stood at 31 and the figures for Japan, Great Britain, Switzerland and the USA were 56, 91, 145 and 344 respectively.[13] The *per capita* output of synthetic fibers in 1972 (in kilograms) was 1.0 in the USSR, 2.2 in Poland, 3.2 in Czechoslovakia and 4.1 in the German DR — compared with 5.9 in Italy, 6.7 in the United Kingdom, 10.7 in the FR of (West) Germany and 11.6 in the USA.[14] Similarly the output of plastics and synthetic resins in 1973 (also in kilograms) was only 6 in Yugoslavia, 9 in the USSR, 11 in Hungary, 15 in Romania, 24 in Czechoslovakia and 29 in the German DR, whilst in France it was 32, in Japan 42, in the USA 56, in the FR of Germany 81 and in the Netherlands 138.[15]

Further evidence of the technological gap is provided by the "Eastward" transfer of Western technology. At first (up to the early 1960s) the Socialist countries in some cases engaged in illicit industrial espionage and imitated Western products without proper compensation. In trade with the West, they have largely been importers of sophisticated manufactures, including complete industrial plants, whilst mostly exporting primary products. Thus in the early 1970s, the proportion represented by manufactures was more than three-quarters in total Socialist imports from the West, but less than one-half in total Socialist exports to the West.[16] Eastern imports include such technologically advanced items as scientific instruments, control apparatus, communications equipment, third-generation computers, ships, helicopters, aircraft, nuclear equipment and complete metallurgical, petrochemical power and other industrial plants.

The Socialist countries have also been most anxious to enter into industrial co-operation with Western firms as an avenue for the assimilation of technology. By the mid-1970s, these countries (including Yugoslavia) had entered into about 1,600 industrial co-operation agreements. Furthermore, Hungary, Romania and Yugoslavia have also entered into joint ventures with Western firms. The number of these ventures in 1975 exceeded 100 and more were in the process of negotiation. Another important form of the transfer of Western technology is through licenses. By the mid-1970s their total number purchased by the Eastern countries reached the figure of about 2,000. It is significant that in their relations with Western partners, the Socialist countries are most anxious to deal with large companies noted for their technological reputation.[17]

So much about the Eastern technological lag behind the West. However, contrary to what one would expect, there is now also a "Westward" flow of technology from the Socialist countries. The main purpose of this article is to discuss the nature of this flow and indicate some implications for the Western countries and their multinationals.

Socialist Industrialization and Technological Progress

In the Socialist development strategy, industrialization has been accorded top priority. In addition to ideological and social considerations, rapid industrial development has been embraced as the most effective avenue for overcoming backwardness and for accelerating technological progress. Industry has benefited from the priority allocation of investment, transfers of superior labor from other branches of the economy and from foreign trade practices designed to protect and speed up industrial development. These policies have produced remarkable results.

The rate of growth of industrial production in the Comecon region has been rising nearly twice as fast as in the West, and Comecon's share in the world's industrial output increased from less than 18 per cent in 1950 to 33 per cent in 1972. In the latter year Comecon's industrial output was twice as large as that of its Western European rival, the European Economic Community.[18] In a relatively short span of time and with practically no economic aid from the capitalist camp, the East has been transformed from backward and stagnant agricultural nations into dynamic and progressive economies. The Comecon countries now satisfy 95 per cent of their needs of machinery and equipment from domestic production and from other member nations, so that only 5 per cent (25 per cent of their *import* requirements) has to be obtained from the West.[19]

In order to create more favorable conditions for technological progress, since the early 1960s the Socialist countries have embarked on some far-reaching reforms.[20] These have included decentralization and a greater freedom of initiative accorded to enterprises, the adoption of profit as the main criterion of enterprise performance, the strengthening of material incentives, a flexible use of financial instruments and a substantial commercialization of research and development.

Central planning has been essentially retained and in fact, from the technological standpoint, strengthened. Central planners have been relieved of routine microeconomic details and so they are now in a better position to concentrate on technological developments of macroeconomic, long-run significance. The five-year plans are now supplemented with "scientific and technical plans" which are co-ordinated on the Comecon scale by the Committee for Scientific and Technical Co-operation. Central planning together with the social ownership of the means of production and the selective use of market instruments under the new economic system provide several advantages for the acceleration of technological progress.

Up to about the early 1960s the Socialist countries were preoccupied with basic industrialization, with lesser concern with the most up-to-date technology. But since that time their strategy has been revised in favor of the accelerated development of the technologically most progressive branches of industry. This policy, known as "structural policy", "selective development" or "leading development programs", assigns priority to such branches of production as machine-building, electrical engineering, electronics, scientific and technical apparatus, chemicals (especially advanced petrochemicals, synthetics, pharmaceuticals), light metals and vehicle building.[21]

It is not generally realized in the West that in a number of specific fields the Socialist countries have reached impressive levels of technology equal to or ahead of the most advanced capitalist nations. These fields include metallurgy, metal-working machinery, power-generating equipment, textile machines, food-processing installations, laboratory and medical apparatus, communications equipment, shipbuilding and aviation.

Thus the USSR, the Socialist rival of the USA, is a recognized world leader in the technology of automatic and semi-automatic welding, the blast-furnace smelting of iron ore, the electrolytic extraction of zinc, magnetohydrodynamic and turbo generators, fast-breeder reactors, thermonuclear fusion, the high-voltage long-distance transmission of power, stereoscopic color television as well as in the production of some of the most complex weapons and military equipment. The Soviets built the world's first nuclear power station (1954) and the first nuclear-powered surface vessel (1959), put the first satellite into orbit (1957) and the first man into space (1961), and they detonated the most powerful weapon in history (a 58-megaton hydrogen bomb, in 1961). The Soviets make the world's most powerful forging presses (of 75,000 tons) and turbines (of 1,200 MW), the fastest hydrofoil ("Burevestnik") and the largest helicopter ("V-12"). The USSR also has the largest hydroelectric power station (at Krasnoyarsk) in the world, the largest airline ("Aeroflot") and the largest telescope (at Mount Zblenchukskaya, in the Urals) and has overtaken her leading capitalist rival (the USA) in the total production of such items of steel, metal cutting machines, diesel and steam locomotives, buses, tractors and books and in the number of engineers and scientists.

The Westward Flow of Embodied Technology

The Socialist countries have become important exporters of technologically advanced items. Thus the share of machinery and transport equipment in their total exports to other Socialist nations rose from 30 per cent in 1960 to 44 per cent in 1972 (in their exports to the Third World, the proportion remained at 36 per cent).[22] But what may appear more surprising is the fact that the West has also been finding Socialist industrial equipment of increasing interest. Over the 1960-72 period, the annual value of the Western imports of machinery and transport equipment from the East rose from $205m. to $950m. This class of imports from the East has been rising faster than the total imports from the East so that its proportion during the 12 years increased from 8 to more than 10 per cent.[23]

Some of the Socialist exports in question obviously contain technology previously acquired from the West. But not as much as some Western critics are inclined to believe. First, the technology acquired by the Socialist countries before 1960 in the more or less illicit ways is now outdated and Socialist exports based on it have little chance of competing with Western products. Second, the licenses purchased more recently normally include clauses restricting the Socialist export of the items involved to Western and other countries. Third, the technology obtained from the West is often further adapted and improved by the Socialist licensees, so that the items exported embody indigenous technological contributions, too.

Table 1 shows examples of machinery, equipment and means of transport containing advanced technology exported to the leading industrialized countries of the West. Amongst the Western customers are large multinational corporations whose technological leadership in the capitalist world is well known.

For a long time the Socialist countries were heavy importers of metal-working machinery from the West (to the extent the Western strategic embargo allowed them). But in the last decade most of these countries have developed impressive production capacities for the most up-to-date varieties, including automatic, semi-automatic, numerically-steered, laser-equipped and special purpose types.[24] Czechoslovak, Hungarian, Polish, Soviet and Yugoslav metal-working machines and tools have been in use for years in the plants of such companies as ASEA (*Swe*), British Leyland (*UK*), British Steel (*UK*), Fiat (*It*), Ford Motor (*US*), General Electric (*US*), General Motors (*US*), Gutehoffnungshutte (*FRG*), Hitachi (*Ja*), Krupp (*FRG*), Mitsubishi (*Ja*), Montedison (*It*), Renault (*Fr*), Rheinstahl (*FRG*), Siemens (*FRG*), Toyota Motor (*Ja*), VÖEST-Alpine (*Au*), Volkswagen (*FRG*) and Volvo (*Swe*).[25]

General Electric (*US*) and General Motors have purchased Soviet electronic and computer components, and Hungarian software and telecommunication equipment have been acquired by AEG Telefunken (*FRG*), Compagnie Internationale pour l'Informatique (*Fr*), Philips (*Ne*) and Siemens.[26] Amongst the customers for the Czechoslovak unique spindleless spinning machines are such entities as Courtaulds (*UK*) and Frotierweberei Vossen (*FRG*)[27] and for the Polish textile dyeing machines — Kleinwefers Krefeld (*FRG*).[28] A wide range of technologically advanced machinery and equipment has been imported from the USSR: electric motors (including turbo-generators) — by Innocenti (*It*), Rauma-Repola (*Fi*), Technip (*Fr*) and J.M. Voith (*Au*);[29] metallurgical presses — by ASEA (*Swe*), Creusot-Loire (*Fr*), Pechiney-Ugine-Kuhlmann (*Fr*) and Wartsila (*Fi*);[30] mining equipment — by Gutehoffnungshutte (*FRG*) and Rheinstahl (*FRG*);[31] and welding machinery (including electro-slag welders) by Cockerill (*Be*), Hitachi (*Ja*), Ishikawajima-Harima (*Ja*), Mitsubishi (*Ja*), Mitsui & Co (*Ja*) and Svenska Kullagerfabriken (*Swe*).[32]

The Socialist countries have also been modernizing or constructing industrial plants in the West. Thus Poland has delivered a complete automatic foundry to Elin-Union in Austria.[33] The USSR has modernized and expanded oil refineries for the ELF group in France and has delivered a

Table 1 Examples of the Scoialist Exports of Embodied Technology to the West

Exporting Socialist and Importing Western Country			Description
Bulgaria	–	FR of Germany	Communications equipment
Bulgaria	–	United Kingdom	Hoisting equipment
Czechoslovakia	–	France	Electrical machinery
Czechoslovakia	–	FR of Germany	Metallurgical equipment
Czechoslovakia	–	United Kingdom	Spindleless spinning machines
German DR	–	FR of Germany	Measurement apparatus
German DR	–	Sweden	Photographic equipment
German DR	–	United Kingdom	Optical goods
Hungary	–	France	Computer software
Hungary	–	FR of Germany	Telecommunications equipment
Hungary	–	Sweden	Special containers
Poland	–	Belgium	Textile machinery
Poland	–	FR of Germany	Railway equipment
Poland	–	Norway	Cargo ships for liquid gas
Poland	–	Sweden	Floating repair dock
Romania	–	Norway	Container ships
USSR	–	Belgium	Welding equipment
USSR	–	Canada	Turbine generators
USSR	–	FR of Germany	Jet aircraft
USSR	–	Japan	Heavy forging equipment
USSR	–	Sweden	Radio navigation equipment
USSR	–	United Kingdom	Printing Machinery
USSR	–	USA	Automatic transformers
Yugoslavia	–	FR of Germany	Cargo ships
Yugoslavia	–	USA	Heavy electrical equipment

Sources Based on literature published in the Socialist and Western countries

rolling mill for Hoesch Werke in the FR of Germany and cold-rolling tube mills to Japan (for such companies as Kobe Steel, Mitsubishi Metal, Sumitomo Metal Mining, and Tokyo Shibaura Electric), France, the FR of Germany, Sweden and the USA.[34] Bulgaria has supplied ultra-modern complete tobacco-processing plants to Italy and at present Soviet enterprises are participating in the construction of a huge metallurgical complex at Fos-sur-Mer (near Marseilles) in France. The Soviets have also constructed a complete electric smelting plant in Sweden (for Svenska Kullagerfabriken) and a nuclear power station (and another is under construction) in Finland. It may also be mentioned here that the USSR has signed contracts for the supply of enriched uranium or other materials for the development of nuclear power to Austria, Belgium, Canada, Finland, France, the FR of Germany, Japan, Spain, Sweden and the United Kingdom.[35]

Other technologically sophisticated items exported to the West include automatic communications equipment (by Czechoslovakia, Hungary, Poland, the USSR, Yugoslavia), control, measuring and precision instruments (Czechoslovakia, the German DR, Hungary, Poland, the USSR, Yugoslavia), diesel locomotives (Bulgaria, Czechoslovakia, the German DR, Poland), food processing plants (Bulgaria, Czechoslovakia, Poland, the USSR), helicopters and hydrofoils (the USSR), medical and hospital equipment (Czechoslovakia, the German DR, Hungary, Poland, the

USSR), oil exploration and drilling equipment (Romania, the USSR) and thyristors (Czechoslovakia, the USSR).

It is rather ironical that most of the items cited in this section were at one stage or another on the Western strategic lists, barred from being exported to the Socialist countries.[36]

For some time in the past the Socialist exporters of machinery and equipment were noted for inadequate after-sale engineering services. But great strides have been made in recent years to improve such services and in this drive Socialist multinational enterprises have played an important role. Many of these enterprises, which have been establishing subsidiaries all over the world in the best bourgeois tradition, now have impressive networks of servicing, repair and even research centers to cater to local requirements.

Thus "Avtoexport" of the USSR, which is concerned with exporting 50 types of motor vehicles and 450 related types of items, has established a network of 2,700 servicing stations, spare parts depots, and workshops outside the USSR; one-third of these is located in the West, mostly in North-Western Europe, and some of them are joint ventures with local capitalist firms.[37] "Iskra-Commerc" of Yugoslavia, exporting a large variety of electrical and electronic goods and equipment, has some 600 subsidiaries and agencies throughout the world.[38] "Skoda" is a Czechoslovak multinational with a long tradition of exporting automobiles, buses, trucks, tractors, electric locomotives, industrial equipment, and chemical, food processing, metallurgical and power-generating plants; it operates subsidiaries and agencies (including service stations, workshops and spare parts depots) in 100 foreign countries.[39]

Other Socialist multinational enterprises which provide scientific or technical services, and some of which engage in local production in the West, include "Aviaexport" (aircraft) of the USSR, "Balkancar" (vehicles and hoisting equipment) of Bulgaria, "Energomashexport" (power equipment) of the USSR, "Medicor" (medical supplies and equipment) of Hungary, "Polimex-Cekop" (industrial plants) of Poland and "Traktorexport" (tractors) of the USSR.

The Sale of Licenses to the West

The most convincing form of the transfer of the advanced Socialist technology to the West is the sale of licenses. Many readers may be surprised to know that this channel of the "Westward" flow of technology has now assumed substantial proportions. By the mid-1970s the total number of Socialist licenses purchased by Western countries reached the figure of about 700. Admittedly, most of the inventions sold to the West are minor, of a limited impact. Nevertheless these inventions are obviously technologically sophisticated and economically worthwhile if they have been bought by Western firms operating, as they are, in a highly competitive technological environment.

To the total figure of 700 licenses sold, Czechoslovakia contributed more than one half, followed by the USSR, Hungary, the German DR, Poland, Yugoslavia, Bulgaria and Romania (in that order). The USSR, compared with Czechoslovakia and Hungary, is a recent entrant to the Western license market. Western visitors to the Trade Fair in Frankfurt/M in June 1970 were startled to see the USSR's offer of 400 licenses for sale; so far the Soviets have sold licenses to firms in at least 35 countries.[40] There are now several firms in Western countries handling the sale of Soviet licenses, such as Finsilta in Italy, Heine Bros. in Australia, Patent Management in the USA and Sofracop in France. But even Bulgaria, which is generally regarded as about the least developed Socialist country (disregarding Albania), patented 40 inventions in 1974; at the recent International Salon of Inventions and Novelties in Geneva, Bulgaria emerged in the top class with regard to the prizes won in relation to the number of exhibits displayed.[41]

The sophistication and magnitude of the inventions made in the Socialist countries have been increasing rapidly. Taking the seven European Comecon countries (i.e. without Albania and Yugoslavia), their average receipts per license sold to the capitalist world in the 1960s was only one-eleventh of what they paid per purchased license, but by the early 1970s this ratio had improved to one-quarter.[42] The annual earnings from the sale of Socialist licenses to the West in the mid-1970s amounted to $40m. (compared with some $500m. spent on Western licenses).

The fields in which the Socialist countries have technology for sale of interest to Western firms include above all the following:

(i) *Metallurgical processes* — Bulgaria, Czechoslovakia, Hungary, Poland, Romania, the USSR and Yugoslavia.

(ii) *Electrical engineering* — Bulgaria, Czechoslovakia, Hungary, Poland, the USSR and Yugoslavia.

(iii) *Metal-working machinery* — Czechoslovakia, the German DR, Hungary, the USSR and Yugoslavia.

(iv) *Textile machinery* — Bulgaria, Czechoslovakia, the German DR and Hungary.

(v) *Pharmaceuticals* — Czechoslovakia, the German DR, Hungary and the USSR.

(vi) *Petrochemicals and other chemicals* — the German DR, Romania, the USSR and Yugoslavia.

(vii) *Food and feed processing* — Bulgaria, Hungary, Poland and the USSR.

(viii) *Medical apparatus* — Czechoslovakia, Hungary, Poland and the USSR.

(ix) *Soldering and welding* — Hungary and the USSR.

(x) *Coal mining and processing* — the German DR, Hungary and the USSR.

A sample list of the Socialist licenses purchased by the well-known Western firms is given in Table 2. Some of these licenses, as well as others not included in the table, represent inventions of major consequence which have been acquired by more than one firm. Thus the Bulgarian license for the electrolytic refining of copper at high current densities has been purchased by firms in Italy, Japan, Spain, Sweden and the USA (not to mention such less developed countries as Brazil, Chile, India, Peru and Zambia). The highly successful Czechoslovak invention of a spindleless spinning machine has also been acquired by (in addition to San Giorgio) Toyoda (*Ja*) and by firms in 20 other countries. The Hungarian process for the extraction of protein from grasses for animal feeding has also been bought by Alfa-Laval (*Swe*), Anhydro (*De*), Scholler-Bleckmann (*Au*) and others. The Polish method for forging crankshafts, purchased by Sulzer, has also been in use in other firms in the FR of Germany, Japan and the United Kingdom.

The Soviet technology for liquid self-hardening mixtures, used in the production of casting rods and moulds, has been adopted by Kobe Steel (*Ja*) and companies in Denmark, France, the FR of Germany, Italy, Sweden, the United Kingdom, the United States and elsewhere. Another major Soviet invention, for the evaporation cooling of blast furnaces, has been most successfully applied not only by Nippon Steel but also by Broken Hill Pty (*Australia*), Gutehoffnungshutte Sterkrade (*FRG*) and in such countries as Belgium, Canada, France, Italy, Luxemburg, the United Kingdom and the United States. The metal used in the construction of steel frames for the Anglo-French Concorde supersonic airliner is produced on the basis of a Soviet license for electroslag refining used by Cie Electro-Mecanique (*Fr*), Crueusot-Loire (*Fr*), Svenska Kullagerfabriken (*Swe*) and others.

The Socialist countries attach a good deal of importance to the sale of their technology to the West. They are prompted not only by their desire to earn hard currency but also by broader considerations of a psychological and political nature. They are anxious to correct the view prevalent in the West that the Socialist countries are technologically stagnant. In fact the ambitions of Socialist leaders go further, in their determination to demonstrate that socialism is not only a superior social system but it also has the capacity — now that high priority is assigned to technology — to catch up and surpass capitalism technologically.

These considerations largely explain the fact that the number of patents registered by the

Table 2. Socialist Licenses Purchased by Leading Western Firms

Western Licensee*	Socialist Licensor Country	Industrial Application
American Home Products (*US*)	USSR	Pharmaceutical drug "pyroxam"
Ataka & Co (*Ja*)	German DR	Steel bar fagotting machine
Bausch & Lomb (*US*)	Czechoslovakia	Soft contact lenses
Bignier-Schmidt-Laurent (*Fr*)	German DR	Contact plates for oil processing
British Steel (*UK*)	Bulgaria	Protective coating for graphite electrodes
Brown, Boveri (*Swi*)	Romania	"Vulcan" type of pumps
Chemetron (*US*)	USSR	Continuous welding electrodes
Chesterfield Tubes (*UK*)	Hungary	Large steel cylinders
Continental Engineering (*Ne*)	Hungary	Sorbitol (for vitamin C)
Creusot-Loire (*Fr*)	Poland	Carousel furnaces
Demag (*FRG*)	USSR	Metal-cutting machines
Innocenti (*It*)	USSR	Tube cold rolling mills
Mannesmann (*FRG*)	Czechoslovakia	Automatic mandrel rod changers
Mitsubishi (*Ja*)	Hungary	Extracting proteins from grasses
Montedison (*It*)	USSR	Polycarbonates
Nippon Steel (*Ja*)	USSR	Cooling of blast furnaces
Reynolds Metals (*US*)	USSR	Casting of aluminium ignots
Rhone-Poulenc (*Fr*)	USSR	Gas permeating membrance
Salzgitter (*FRG*)	USSR	High-pressure polyethylene
San Giorgio (*It*)	Czechoslovakia	Spindleless spinning machines
Sulzer (*Swi*)	Poland	Forging of crankshafts
Sumitomo (*Ja*)	USSR	Pneumatic transport pipeline
Texas Utilities Services (*US*)	USSR	Underground gasification of lignite
Toyo Engineering (*Ja*)	USSR	Chemical disposal of waste
Universal Oil Products (*US*)	USSR	Tube reducers

*For country abbreviation, see footnote 25 p. 21

Source. Based on literature published in the Socialist and Western countries.

Socialist countries in the capitalist world has more than doubled since the early 1960s. In the mid-1970s their annual applications exceeded 20,000, of which one-half was actually granted. These figures are about twice as high as those representing patents applied for by capitalist countries and granted in the East.[43]

Conclusions and Prospects

The well-established Western conviction of the East-West technological gap, although well-founded in the past and to some extent still justified, may very well become pointless in the future. In some fields of technology the Socialist countries are already equal to or ahead of the West. It is not unreasonable to assume that — owing to the now accepted priorities — rapid technological progress in the East will continue, and central economic planning can be effectively utilized to facilitate such developments. It is likely that in the future there will be no clear-cut gap. It can be expected that in a number of spheres the West will be technologically superior but in some (fewer) the East will be in the lead, whilst in others both the West and the East will be more or less equally advanced.

The rising technological levels in the Socialist countries are certain to lead to the intensification of their export of industrial products to the West. In this export drive Socialist multinational enterprises will be playing an important role. Although they are likely to concentrate on marketing, they will also tend to expand local assembling and production in Western countries, partly on the basis of joint ventures with capitalist firms.

In addition to the Eastern nationally-owned multinational enterprises (as discussed in this article above), a new type of large entrant to Western markets is feasible — viz. multinationally-owned organizations under the auspices of Comecon. So far about 50 of such entities have been established, but they are still in their infancy and their activities have so far been limited to the Comecon countries. However, some of them — especially those concerned with the co-ordination and development of production and services in the fields of advanced technology — are likely to extend their operations to the West. The entities in question may include (the name is followed in brackets by the location of the head office, the year of foundation and the field of operation):

(i)   "Interatomenergo" (Moscow, 1973; nuclear power equipment).
(ii)   "Interatominstrument" (Warsaw, 1972; atomic apparatus and appliances).
(iii)   "Interchim" (Halle, GDR, 1969; light chemicals).
(iv)   "Interchimvolokno" (Bucharest, 1974; chemical fibers).
(v)   "Interelektro" (Moscow, 1973; electrical equipment).
(vi)   "Interpodshypnik" (Warsaw, 1964; bearings).
(vii)   "Intersputnik" (Mowcow, 1972; satellite telecommunications).
(viii) "Intertextilmash" (Moscow, 1973; textile machinery).

The two types of the Socialist international enterprises may become a factor to reckon with in capitalist markets. Their export drive may include price-undercutting and other forms of competition. As protective measures in Western (as in other) countries are directed more against manufactures than primary products, the Socialist exporters will probably encounter new waves of discrimination against their industrial products in Western markets. But it may be assumed on the basis of experience in the recent past that once the Socialist enterprises establish their foothold in the market, they will want to co-operate and avoid market disruption. Economic commonsense will dictate specialization in accordance with the principle of comparative advantage, and the sooner it prevails the better for the parties concerned. The West may very well find the East as a highly desirable trading area, with a greater capacity for the export as well as import of highly sophisticated manufactures than the Third World. Historical experience suggests that with rising *per capita* income industrial products assume an increasing role in foreign trade and the best customers for a country's industrial exports are in fact other industrially developed countries.

Footnotes

1. The "East" in this article includes the nine European Socialist countries, viz. Albania, Bulgaria, Czechoslovakia, the German Democratic Republic, Hungary, Poland, Romania, the USSR and Yugoslavia; seven of these countries (i.e. Albania and Yugoslavia excepted) plus Cuba and Mongolia are full members of Comecon (Council for Mutual Economic Assistance, originally established in 1949). The "West" embraces what is designated in United Nations publications as "Developed Market Economies", viz. the rest of Europe, North America, Japan, Australia, New Zealand and South Africa.
2. For major Western studies available in English, see A. Bergson, *Planning and Productivity under Soviet Socialism* (New York: Columbia U.P. 1968); M. Boretsky, "Comparative Progress in Technology,

Productivity and Economic Efficiency: USSR versus USA", US Congress, Joint Economic Committee, *New Directions in the Soviet Economy,* Part IIA (Washington: GPO 1966); P. Sager, *The Technological Gap between the Superpowers* (Bern: Swiss Eastern Institute 1971); A. Silberton and F. Seton (eds), *Industrial Management: East and West* (London: Pall Mall 1973); S. Wasowski (ed.), *East-West Trade and the Technology Gap* (New York: Praeger 1970); E. Zaleski *et al., Science Policy in the USSR* (Paris: OECD 1969).

3.   J. Meisner, *Kapitalizm a socjalizm* [Capitalism and Socialism] (Warsaw: PWE 1973), p. 129.

4.   I. Oleinik, ["Material and Technical Base of the Socialist Camp"], *Voprosy ekonomiki* [Problems of Economics] no. 9, 1967; 128.

5.   Lidia Bialon, ["Technical Standards and Technological Progress in the Electrical Engineering Industry in Poland"], *Gospodarka planowa* [Planned Economy], Warsaw, no. 3, 1974: 163.

6.   *Gospodarka i administracja terenowa* [Regional Administration and Management], Warsaw, no. 9, 1971: 4.

7.   M. Boretsky, pp. 149-59.

8.   B.A. Dubovikov, *Osnovy nauchnoi organizatsii upravleniya kachestvom* [Foundations of Scientific Quality Management] (Moscow: Ekonomika, 1966), pp. 272-73.

9.   *Ekonomicka revue* [Economic Review], Prague, no. 6, 1968: 310.

10.   *Hospodarske noviny* [Economic News], Prague, March 19, 1970: 8.

11.   Lidia Bialon, p. 163.

12.   *Rynki zagraniczne* [Foreign Markets], Warsaw, XVI, no. 103 (1972): 1.

13.   J. Wilczynski, *Technology in Comecon* (London: Macmillan 1974), pp. 114-16.

14.   *Statistisches Jahrbuch der Deutschen Demokratischen Republik 1974* [Statistical Yearbook of the German DR for 1974] (East Berlin: Staatsverlag 1974), p. 52*.

15.   *Statisticka rocenka CSSR 1974* [Statistical Yearbook of Czechoslovakia for 1974], Prague: SNTL 1974), p. 581.

16.   United Nations *Monthly Bulletin of Statistics* XXVIII (September 1974); xviii-xxxv.

17.   For further details, the interested reader is referred to the author's forthcoming book, *The Multinationals and East-West Relations* (London: Macmillan 1976).

18.   *Zycie gospodarcze* [Economic Life], Warsaw, XXIX, no. 20 (1974): 13.

19.   W. Iskra and H. Kisiel, *RWPG Integracja gospodarczas,* [Economic Integration in Comecon] (Warsaw: KiW, 1971), p. 48. *Vanshna targoviya* [Foreign Trade], Sofia, no. 3, 1971: 21.

20.   The reforms in Yugoslavia began in 1950 whilst Albania is still essentially adhering to the traditional centralized and directive system.

21.   To illustrate by reference to Czechoslovakia. The 1971-75 plan embodied 43 "leading development programs" – 19 in the machine-building, 14 in the chemical, 6 in the light and 4 in the metallurgical industries. Amongst the types of products specified were numerically-steered lathes, electronic data processing equipment, synthetic fibers, plastics, motor vehicles and nuclear equipment. K. Kovar, ["Leading Development Programs"], *Planovane hospodarstvi* [Planned Economy], Prague, no. 3, 1972: 49-54.

22.   United Nations *Monthly Bulletin of Statistics* XVIII, no. 3 (March 1964): xii-xxxii and XXXIII, no. 9 (September 1974): xiii-xxxv.

23.   Ibid.

24.   There are three unique types of metal-working machines developed in the USSR which have aroused special interest in the West. One type is equipped with a laser beam, which can raise the temperature to several thousand degrees (centigrade) in a thousandth of a second, being capable of making holes in diamonds. Another model recently developed is a unique milling machine weighing 180 tons; it is designed for milling non-ferrous ingots of up to 5 tons, it embodies several automatic and semi-automatic devices (including semi-automatic suction of shavings and metal dust) and it can be operated by one man. There is also a giant metal-working machine adapted for handling objects of up to 20 meters in diameter and weighing up to 56 tons. It can work with a precision of up to 40 microns.

25.   The abbreviations for Western countries used in this article are:

Au	=	Austria	*Fr*	=	France	*No*	=	Norway
Be	=	Belgium	*FRG*	=	FR of (West) Germany)	*Swe*	=	Sweden
Ca	=	Canada	*It*	=	Italy	*Swi*	=	Switzerland
De	=	Denmark	*Ja*	=	Japan	*UK*	=	United Kingdom
Fi	=	Finland	*Ne*	=	Netherlands	*US*	=	United States

26.   *Die Wirtschaft des Ostblocks* [Economies of the East], Bonn, May 21 1974: 10; *Hungarian Exporter,* Budapest, no. 5, 1974: 5; *Soviet News,* London, July 16, 1974: 266.

27. *Czechoslovak Foreign Trade*, Prague, no. 3, 1972: 21.
28. *Polish Foreign Trade*, Warsaw, no. 7, 1973: 20.
29. *Foreign Trade*, Moscow, no. 4, 1972: 36-37 and no. 6, 1972: 16.
30. *East-West Commerce*, London, no. 5, 1973: 8; *Ekonomicheskaya gazeta* [Economic Gazette], Moscow, no. 29, 1974: 22.
31. *Die Wirtschaft des Ostblocks*, October 9, 1973: 4; *Ekonomicheskaya gazeta*, no. 7, 1974: 21.
32. *Ekonomicheskaya gazeta*, no. 7, 1974: 21; *Foreign Trade*, no. 5, 1972: 48.
33. *Polish Foreign Trade*, no. 8, 1973: 20.
34. *Foreign Trade*, no. 7, 1972: 10; no. 6, 1973: 32-34; no. 12, 1973: 51.
35. *Die Wirtschaft des Ostblocks*, March 19, 1974: 8; *Eastern Europe Report*, Geneva, 2, no. 12 (1973): 167; *Planovoe khoziaistvo* [Planned Economy], Moscow, no. 5, 1974: 85.
36. For example of strategic lists as administered in the mid-1960s see, *Board of Trade Journal*, London, June 12, 1964, Annex; US Senate, *East-West Trade*, Hearings before the Committee on Foreign Relations, Part I (Washington: GPO, 1964), pp. 221-25.
37. *Ekonomicheskaya gazeta*, no. 47, 1973: 21; *Foreign Trade*, no. 9, 1973: 30.
38. *Delo* [Work], Ljubljana, August 8, 1973: 4; *Privredni pregled* [Economic Review], Belgrade, August 16, 1974: 4; *Yugoslav Survey* Belgrade, no. 3, 1973: 169-72.
39. *Czechoslovak Foreign Trade*, no. 4, 1974: 14-19.
40. *East-West*, Brussels, no. 16, 1970: 5; *Sotsialisticheskaya industriya* [Socialist Industry], Moscow, March 15, 1974: 2.
41. *Zycie gospodarcze*, XXX, No. 8 (1975): 14.
42. R. Osterland, ["More Intensive Exchange of Scientific and Technical Achievements through Integration"], *Die Wirtschaft* [The Economy], East Berlin, no. 37, 1972: 27.
43. Author's estimates based partly on K. Jankowski, *Polityka patentowa w krajach RWPG* [Patent Policy in the Comecon Countries] (Warsaw: CIINTE 1970), pp. 12, 14.

The Prospects for the Cooperation between the

Socialist Countries and the MNCs.

By: Dr. Leon Zurawicki*

As the level of East-West foreign trade and economic cooperation gains in significance, the need for Socialist countries and enterprises to chose their Western partners carefully will become of even greater importance. This refers particularly to the choice of the Western states which are to become the main trade and economic partners of the Socialist countries. Indeed the gravitation toward certain Western countries, if it is to be binding in the longer run, is somewhat risky from the point of view of the Socialist economies.

In such a context the reliance on state to state negotiations is of importance for under formally ratified agreements the terms and conditions can be directly enforced. Apart from their goodwill aspects, such treaties also provide concrete obligations on both parties and allow the general framework of this trade to fit within socialist economic planning. In addition they frequently include special credits or barter agreements which can help ease the problems such trade — if not carefully disciplined — may cause for the socialist partner's balance of payments.

Although interstate agreements offer substantial attractions to the Socialist countries, most trade is still eventually conducted at the enterprise level; a socialist state or enterprise on one side and a capitalist enterprise on the other. While it might be desirable to chose an enterprise which operates solely within one country and therefore have the full agreement backed at both the government and corporate level, the choice of enterprises will undoubtably include firms whose scale and scope of activities surpass the frontiers of one country. It is here then that the multinational corporation must enter our analysis as the highest percentage of East-West foreign trade and economic cooperation is accomplished through MNC's.

A simple explanation for this phenomenon would be that these enterprises dominate the world market and therefore East-West business relations. This would be a superfical interpretation though for there are many reasons why multinationals have proven popular business partners with the socialist countries.

Perhaps the foremost consideration is that the advanced R & D efforts conducted by most MNC's allow them to offer the most modern of products and technology. Similarly the scale of production of most MNC's mean that they are in a position to easily undertake large contracts and due to their greater economies of scale offer more moderate prices than smaller capitalistic enterprises. Due to their larger scale operations, the MNC's, too, generally offer a complete product line or package so that the socialist buyers need to deal with only one rather than a group of suppliers; a situation better fitted to the general framework of socialist planning and management. Since MNC's pursue global activities, they are more adapt at dealing with new products and conditions in different parts of the world. This is an important factor if the socialist partner wishes to have better access for its products in the West. It similarly means that as a result of their long experience in international business, MNC's are surely better qualified to handle specific transactions with the Socialist countries. The fact that so many large MNC's have set up specialised departments or affiliates to develop contacts with the East, proves that this market attracts more and more firms and further aids to a better understanding between partners.

*Associate Professor, University of Warsaw, Warsaw, Poland

Before we pass to more detailed comments on different types of East-West economic co-operation and the prospects for MNCs, let me present a general hypothesis, which if holds true, will certainly influence the evolution of mutual relations. In my opinion the market of the developed capitalist countries will in future, that is at least during the next 10-15 years, become more and more oligopolistic. This phenomenon will be marked by the growing market concentration and the strengthening of the position of MNCs. One possible consequence thereof is that for the potential newcomers, i.e. from the socialist states, it will be much more difficult to enter the Western markets.

On the other hand the saturated Western markets will not necessarily absorb its own production, whereas the structure of industrial output of economically advanced capitalist countries may not correspond to the changes in demand in this area. It may be also justifiably assumed that following the growth of welfare the consumption of material goods in the West will increase less dynamically than before.

In contrast the socialist and developing countries for years to come will constitute expanding markets, whose specific feature will be strong demand for investment goods. Inadequate as it is, I nevertheless think that in economic and welfare terms the analogy may be drawn between the actual situation of the European socialist countries and the EEC at the moment of establishing the Common Market. Hence the potential of Eastern Europe has attracted many globally oriented Western enterprises.

The economic contacts between the socialist countries and MNCs take various forms. In the following I shall try to present the classification and characteristics of the most typical business relationships:

Imports

Classical foreign trade plays still the most important role in the mutual contacts. As far as imports are concerned, MNCs compete according to the same principles as any other enterprise. However, because MNCs' activities are geographically dispersed they are more attractive partners to the socialist countries. Dealing with MNCs means for the Eastern countries the possibility of reducing their balance-of-payment deficits. Since MNCs have the flexibility to export from different currency areas, the payments may be made either by clearing agreements that favors socialist exports (mostly developing countries) or in the currency of the market most receptive to socialist goods. Also because of the scope and variety of their activities MNCs themselves may likely be interested in barter transactions, especially with fuels and raw materials.

The question of the bargaining power of contracting parties is a very important problem in this as well as other types of transactions. I would not like to prejudge whose position is stronger. But only point out that in comparison to the early sixties when the capitalist firm realized inflated profits from supplies to the socialist markets, the socialist countries have become increasingly aware of the competition among MNCs and are making efforts to take advantage thereof, particularly when the capitalist firms quote excessive prices.

One can imagine that Western economies will for a long time to come supply the socialist with specific goods, and thereby maintain the structure of the international division of production. It is more likely, however, that the socialist countries after having mastered and applied new product technology will make strenous efforts to reduce their dependency on the foreign suppliers by substituting these goods with home production. This does not mean of course, that the socialist countries will tend to autarky within their own system, but in some industries of consumer durable goods it is pretty possible. Nonetheless, the fact that many of articles now imported by the East will eventually be manufactured at home should not discourage Western producers from supplying the socialist countries. Rather the capitalist manufacturers should be advised to accelerate the pace of technological progress and in any case to increase exports of their most technologically advanced products.

Exports

Somewhat different cooperation problems appear when the exports of the socialist countries are considered. Eastern countries are interested in promoting the sales of their products in Western markets. One way of achieving this aim is through their direct presence in these markets. Exports alone usually do not create closer links with MNCs. They are, however, quite often channeled through the specialised companies owned by the socialist states and Western capital. These mixed capital companies enable the socialist manufacturers to enter Western markets on equal terms with local competitors for the price of sharing profits with capitalist partners. Can such a form of activity sufficiently attract the MNCs? There are three reasons, which deny it:

- MNCs are obviously not interested in engaging themselves in the activities which will encourage more competitors to enter "their" market.
- Until now the scale of the above mentioned operations is rather small.
- The influence of the MNCs in such partnerships would be limited because socialist countries insist on owning a controlling interest in order to maintain full freedom of the most important decisions.

As it was mentioned before, the simple foreign trade transactions do not relate the MNCs too closely with the socialist countries. However, they are of course profitable for both sides and for that reason this form of economic co-operation not only deserves continuing but can also be referred to as a yardstick for evaluation of relative profitability of alternative and more elaborated types of business relationships.

Licensing Agreements

Licensing agreements often involve complex considerations for both East and West. They have numerous advantages for the socialist states. The license permits the introduction to socialist countries of technical and organizational expertise relating to the production of a specific product. Apart from the direct influence upon the execution of present contracts this factor is of long-term value to the socialist countries. As socialist workers and technicians become acquainted with modern technology, they are able to develop a future capability to produce not only the licensed but also similar products based on adaptation of Western technology in their own country. Furthermore, the improved qualifications of the workers will make it possible to acquire new licenses, also from other than up to now Western enterprises, and thus enable the transfer of technology on more competitive terms. The use of licenses undeniably helps to satisfy growing home demand for modern products while substituting for potential and actual imports. On the other hand the purchase of licenses is often considered by the socialist countries to be one of the stimuli to expand their exports to the West. The more so that at least in the short run their balance of payments may be seriously affected as the costs of licenses have to be re-imbursed.

However, it should be stressed that the marketing possibilities for the products manufactured under licensing agreements are not promising in the West. The oligopolistic markets of Western countries are dominated by MNCs, after all, the same which sign the licensing agreements with socialist countries. The MNCs put heavy emphasis on product diversification, trademarks, publicity and sales promotion, with relatively little emphasis on price itself. In such a situation entry into Western markets is effectively blocked by those firms already there and it is impossible for the licensed product to compete against the original article. Only a very sharp price competition à la japonaise might bring results. However putting into jeopardy the economic rationale of such an undertaking, does not always bring satisfying results. On the other hand the possibility of price competition is often precluded by the terms of the license agreement which set the exact price for the licensed product at home and abroad. Faced with a set price, the only way for the socialist licensees to compete with the original licensors is to refuse to follow the price increases of the latter. Since this strategy, either, may not always be successful, it is important that the possibility of exporting to capitalist countries not be a deciding factor in the acquisition of a license.

It should be mentioned that also many MNCs are quite aware that their exports of consumer goods to the socialist countries will shrink as modern technology develops in these countries. As a result they will naturally tend to offer the obsolete, incomplete or too costly. The general sparing attitude of the socialist countries with respect to the Western currency expenses will make it even easier.

The financial results of any licensing agreement depend ultimately upon often complex payment mechanisms. When a license agreement is entered into and paid for in cash, this amount represents the total cost of the license. By increasing production over the licensor's expectations, the licensee can achieve greater economies of scale. Similar results may also be achieved in applying elements of the license to the production of other articles. This is of course only a possibility — in fact it may happen that the actual output remains below the anticipated figure — but the mechanisms and the organization of the socialist economy help to accomplish it.

When a more flexible payment method is used, e.g., when royalties are paid on a per unit of production basis, the licensor's income becomes directly related to the scope of the licensee's production. In such a case the licensor's interests are more effectively protected even if the license is resold. Nevertheless, neither the amount of the licensor's income nor the dates of its collection can be determined in advance. This uncertainty significantly affects the licensor's risk. Though the problem of pricing uncertainty will not be examined in detail here, it should be noted that MNCs can bear such risk more easily than smaller enterprises oriented towards their home markets. Thus a licensing agreement with the flexible system of pricing may be convenient for MNCs and the socialist countries. Finally, it is significant that closer coordination of the COMECON countries (in general terms anticipated in their Complex Program) with respect to the acquisition of Western licenses may bring additional advantages. For example, often two or more socialist countries contract simultaneously for similar transfers of technology with various MNCs instead of contracting for one and sharing it within the framework of COMECON, thereby reducing the overall costs.

Industrial Cooperation

Generally speaking, from the socialist countries' viewpoint, industrial cooperation acts as a substitute for direct exports of final products to the same extent that licenses substitute for imports. It may involve subcontracting component manufacture or technical consulting. Industrial cooperation is often connected with the purchase of licenses and technology. Its advantages for the socialist countries are following:

- It permits close commercial contacts with a Western partner, thereby promoting long range stability in productivity. Orders can be accepted and produced in advance to the advantage of the planned economic systems of the socialist countries.
- It facilitates access to modern technology without additional costs.

273

- Once the cooperation links with MNCs are established the socialist countries can try more easily to develop commercial relations with the other countries in which the Western partner's subsidiaries operate.
- It may give rise to more elaborated forms of economic cooperation, e.g. joint ventures in the future.

However, this type of cooperation has some disadvantages for the socialist countries. First of all although East-West industrial cooperation makes it easier for the socialist producers to enter the highly monopolized capitalist markets, the impact of these socialist producers on Western markets is not noticeable.

The consumer purchases goods bearing the trademarks of Western manufacturers but remains unaware of the identity of the socialist producers. The socialist supplier therefore participates in the commercial success of the final product only through the mediation of the Western partner. In such circumstances the expansion possibilities of the socialist exporters are seriously limited.

In many cases the industrial cooperation takes the form of one-way subcontracting. The degree of profitability of multi-component product is greatest at the end product stage. Hence the profit in a subcontract will relatively be inferior to the profit of the final product. Industrial cooperation involving subcontracting can only prove to be beneficial to the socialist countries when they might gain valuable technological expertise. In turn this expertise would permit industrial cooperation on a more advanced level in the future.

Another consequence of industrial cooperation is that socialist countries become dependent upon the business cycle of the Western economies. The more the socialist countries are tied to the West, the greater the risk that business cycles in the latter will provoke economic fluctuations in the former and thereby jeopardize the continuity of cooperation. The risk is increased by the fact that the highly specialized components manufactured in socialist countries fit only the final products of a particular firm (e.g. the case in automotive industry). To minimize the effects of Western business cycles on the local economy the socialist enterprises seek the most stable, large and diversified Western partners. MNCs clearly belong to this group, the more so that their activity is just oriented towards becoming immune to business cycles.

Still another difficulty arises when technological and organizational adjustments are required of socialist producers. Often agreements require the socialist manufacturer to improve quality, technical control and to deliver more promptly. In practice these demands produce problems and tensions that hamper further cooperation. Management systems in the MNCs differ from the multilevel planning management systems of the socialist countries. The limits imposed on the freedom of individual enterprises by the socialist countries can be inconvenient for the Western partners. Furthermore, cooperation agreements are often signed on behalf of the socialist countries by intermediary foreign trade enterprises who may not be competent concerning capabilities of potential partners. This fact could lead to the wrong choice of partners on both sides. Of course, these difficulties can be overcome, but for the moment they remain quite troublesome.

However, it is the transfer pricing which presents the most important problem in industrial cooperation. Generally speaking as far as transfer pricing is concerned, socialist partners are exposed to double risk. First, the prices of licenses, technology, acquisition or lease of equipment may be high. Secondly, the prices paid by the Western partner for intermediate products supplied by the socialist countries may be too low. These low prices reflect not only the bargaining power of the Western partner but also, in some cases, inaccurate calculating systems and exchange rates applied in the socialist countries. In order to remedy these inequities and to take full advantage of the industrial cooperation, it is logical that socialist suppliers should quote similar prices as that paid in analogous transactions in Western markets. This appears to be necessary when the accelerating growth of labour costs in the West is taken into account. If the cooperation agreement is based upon fixed labor costs, the Western enterprise will realize extra profits at the expense of the socialist countries whose actual wage rates will increase independently of the agreement rate. For this reason a pricing system with provision for steady cost increases should be negotiated for goods produced through mutual cooperation.

The scope and profitability of industrial cooperation with the West depends, in great part, on a revised system of tariff protection and the elimination of other trade barriers to mutual commerce. Currently, component products delivered by socialist producers to the Western partners are subject to the ordinary customs duties for finished products, even though some parts and materials (e.g. plastics, synthetic fibres) comprising the component were originally supplied to the socialist partner by the Western partner. Consequently the final price of the product is raised artificially. Thus, it would be in the best interest of both Eastern and Western business partners to put pressure on the governments of the capitalist countries to change their actual custom policy and elaborate a more refined one.

Joint Ventures

Joint ventures are, theoretically, commonly owned mixed enterprises located in both East and West. As a practical matter, at least when industrial undertakings are considered, they exist only in the socialist and, to a small extent, developing countries. These enterprises can be highly competitive. They combine the advantages of both partners: modern technology and marketing skills on one side and a relatively cheap labor force in a stable economic environment with dumped inflationary or deflationary pressures, on the other. Joint ventures are delicate undertakings requiring careful identification of both socialist and capitalist interests and generally involve the common desire to expand sales and profits. MNCs offer strong positions in many Western markets backed by sound technology, patents and trademarks. The socialist partners guarantee accessibility to Eastern markets and the possibility of planned sales. This should be particularly attractive for MNCs because of the fact that the socialist countries for the reason of economies of scale will not engage themselves in joint ventures with too many partners at once. As a consequence at the moment a given MNC starts operation in the socialist market, it will find itself in a less competitive environment than in the West.

Many practical problems must be solved, however, before harmonious collaborations can be achieved.

One problem involves the percentage of shares to be owned by each of the partners in the mixed enterprise. The difficulty is not necessarily how the profits will be divided but who will have effective control of management and, thus, the power to make major decisions. Practice confirms that the socialist countries must not lose this control. Thus, in all joint ventures with capitalist firms the socialist states must control over 50% of the equity.

Another problem even more important is the question of the total scope of joint ventures with the West in the socialist economies. Although it may be premature to examine the overall effects of joint ventures on socialist economies, careful analysis of this subject suggests two factors which will be useful in formulating general policies for joint venture participation by socialist countries. The first is the possibility that the socialist partner will be able to continue production independently and, more importantly, to develop sales not only at home but in foreign markets. The second is the degree to which socialist economies will be subject to Western economic fluctuations as a result of the increased participation of Western capital. Balance-of-payment difficulties for the socialist countries may arise should the Western partner decide to transfer tis profits abroad, or, more importantly, decide to withdraw capital invested in the joint venture with the Eastern partner. This risk of developing a balance of payments burden will increase in proportion to the share of foreign capital invested in mixed enterprises in the socialist economies. In a simple credit transaction the debt is repaid after a definite period of time. In joint ventures Western partners collect profits on a continual basis which then might be transfered abroad, either in whole or in part

Thus, it is worth considering not only the optimum ratio of East-West capital investment in joint ventures, but also whether or not the joint ventures should have limited lifetimes. If one believes that in the future socialist countries will be able to compete in the most difficult markets, then each joint venture should have a limited existence. One method of providing for this limitation is for both parties to agree that after a certain number of years the socialist partner would have the right to buy shares held by the Western partner. Another method would provide for the gradual phase out of the Western partner over a number of years, with the socialist partner buying 2% to 3% of the Western shares each year until the enterprise is totally owned by the socialist state. The policy to limit the life of a specific joint venture would not preclude the establishment of new mixed capital enterprises at any time in the same or other industries. Without the continual creation of new joint ventures, Western capital, forced to withdraw from existing joint ventures, would be transferred abroad, thereby requiring socialist states to develop a more active balance-of-payments policy.

Another problem involves the re-investment by the capitalist firms of profits earned from the joint ventures. The short-term policies of the socialist states regarding joint ventures would aim toward encouraging local re-investment by the Western partner until a "safety threshold" is reached. In this regard it should not be forgotten that once there-investment opportunities for the Western enterprise are blocked, the rate of economic growth for the counry will slow down. The reduced growth rate may in turn, provide other disturbances, including balance of payments difficulties.

A very important issue for the socialist countries is how to incorporate the specific activities of joint ventures into general economic planning. Also the degree of autonomy allowed the joint ventures should be considered. The fact that more than 50% of each of these mixed enterprises is controlled by the socialist partners ensures that the firm will conform to the general policy of the host state. Nevertheless, when it comes to structuring the exact production schedules and sales programs, conflicting interests may arise. For example, a Western partner may wish to expand the home production despite a policy of the host country directed towards expanding exports. Since conflicting interests may touch on fundamental differences between the operations of socialist and capitalist enterprise, it will not be easy to satisfy both partners. The capitalist firms, especially the MNCs, have wide economic independence, whereas the socialist enterprises follow directly the policy of the socialist state whose goals are not always expressed in terms of profits, prices and turnover. Thus, it is clear that some compromise between the two systems must be reached. Nevertheless, since the concept of joint ventures between East and West is relatively new, only experience will show which mechanisms for compromise will be most effective. For the socialist countries it would be very profitable to take advantage of the strong competitive position of Western partners in their home markets and orient the strategy of the joint ventures towards exports, provided that such strategy complies with the economic goals of the socialist countries. One goal to consider is satisfying the needs of the socialist countries home markets. Attention should be drawn to still another point. In the calculus made by MNCs the relatively cheap labor force plays often the dominant role in decisions concerning industrial cooperation and joint ventures with the socialist countries. However, this relative cheapness of the labor force in the socialist countries may be of temporary character, when the dynamic rate of economic growth and welfare and the aspirations of their societies are taken into account and fully realized. Thus it should be rather other factors which are given greater weight when the long term decisions concerning the joint ventures are to be taken by MNCs.

Scientific and Technical Cooperation

One of the positive results of increased scientific and technical cooperation between East and West is the introduction of modern products into the markets of the socialist countries. Also, this type of cooperation gives both partners the opportunity to pursue different applications of shared research. Depending on the circumstances and the cost-benefit calculation, R and D cooperation may either result in common production, sale of technical expertise and patent rights or individual manufacturing by each partner. Although East-West cooperation in the area of R and D may be the direct result of the contacts originally established by state and governmental agencies, as a practical matter socialist countries deal directly with the largest capitalist firms, with the emphasis on applied research.

Notwithstanding the advances of Western technology, the socialist countries are attractive partners for R and D cooperation in view of their large source of qualified scientists and technicians. Moreover the organization of research in the socialist countries which, no matter the industry concerned, is concentrated in the state institutions, makes it possible to draw on the results achieved at various centres. By utilizing this resource, scientific cooperation may lead to the realization of significant projects in the Western countries as well, e.g. the construction of nuclear power supply stations. Finally, R and D cooperation need not be limited by or subordinated to the aims of industrial cooperation as is generally the case for other forms of East-West cooperation. For example R and D might be used to develop and improve the infrastructure of the socialist countries e.g. urban transportation systems etc.

The Appearance of the Socialist Multinational Enterprise

The preceding considerations relied upon the assumption that the bilateral East-West economic relations engage on one side the socialist state or the state enterprises, and the MNCs on the other. It is, however, worthwhile to examine the eventual changes, which the establishment of the socialist multinational enterprises (SME) might cause. At the moment this form is still in the embryonic stage and the activities of the few SME are limited to the area of two COMECON countries in each case, but pro futuro their role will gain in significance. One of the effects of creation of the SME as the instrument of deepening the socialist integration will be the more effective utilization of productive capacities in the COMECON countries, greater concentration and scale of undertakings. Similarly the strength and competences of these operating units will increase. The question arises then: will SME be better partners or stronger rivals to the MNCs? The second question may certainly be answered positively. The first, however, is more complex. Though one can hardly mention the examples of the closer cooperation between the MNCs themselves, it is by no means precluded in the contacts with SME. On the contrary, the incentives to cooperation result from the general technical-economic situation, described above, and not from the organizational form of the economic units. It should also be taken into account that with broader authority concerning more complex productive tasks and at the same time disposing greater economic potential SME in many cases will reach the size of capitalist MNCs, which may facilitate understanding and mutual agreements.

Besides, the possible effects of the SME activities on the markets of developing countries and on the Western markets ought to be considered. Owing to the particular form of links with the scientific centres contributing to the technological progress SME may successfully apply for the turn-key contracts for the plants requiring diversified and complex equipment. In this particular case because of the scale of their interests and the flexibility of manoeuvring within their large organizations SME may even surpass MNCs.

277

Conclusions

No matter what the form of East-West cooperation, the final benefits to the socialist states will depend on the conditions negotiated in specific agreements. In this regard, the bargaining strength of the socialist countries should be considered. Contrary to some views, the desire for East-West cooperation is not limited to the East alone. There are many factors which will motivate Western enterprise, in particular MNCs, to seek the advantages of cooperation with the East.